MW01628166

WOMEN IN ART

Women in Art

Artists, Models and Those Who Made It Happen

NINA HEYN

Solari Inc.

First printing June 2024

Published by:
Solari, Inc.
P.O. Box 157
Hickory Valley, TN 38042 USA
solari.com

ISBN 978-1-956682-04-5

Picture research: Lorraine Beck
Copyeditor: Claire Viadro
Design and layout: Paul Howson
Author's photo: © Joanna Braszczewska-Groszek

Printed in China

Typeset in Neue Haas Unica 9.25/14pt

Cover image:
Olga Boznańska. *Japanese Self-Portrait*, 1892. Oil on cardboard.
Collection of the National Museum, Wrocław.
Photo: Arkadiusz Podstawka/National Museum Wrocław.

CONTENTS

FOREWORD

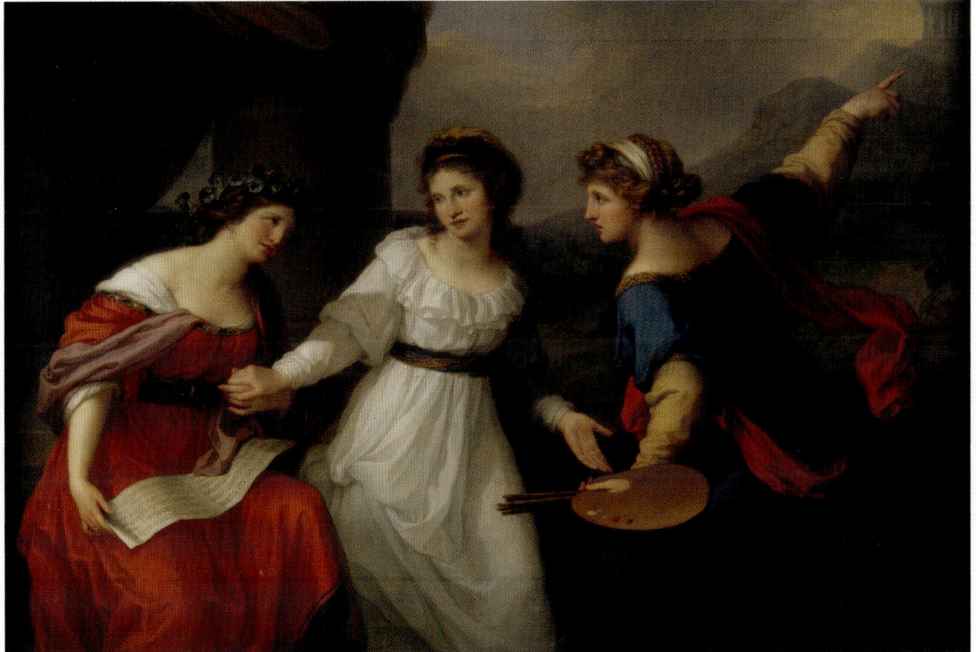

Angelica Kauffmann. Self-portrait in *The Artist Hesitating Between Painting and Music*, 1794. Oil on canvas.
Nostell Priory, West Yorkshire.
Photo: National Trust Photographic Library/John Hammond/Bridgeman Images

Out of 1001 paintings presented in the compendium *1001 Paintings You Must See Before You Die* (Ed. Stephen Farthing, revised edition 2018), a paltry 48 entries are works by women artists. Even without any statistics, art lovers have long been aware that there should be more female art images included in any major review of art history, but it seems it may take a while for books to improve on the 5% included in *1001 Paintings*. Things are changing much faster in museums—for a good decade now, art galleries and museums everywhere in the world have been mounting big and small exhibitions devoted either to women artists or cultural movements in which female contributions are highlighted.

This book was born out of both opportunity and dissatisfaction. An opportunity provided by my publisher, Catherine Austin Fitts, who offered me a chance to write about art... with no demands as to content. "Write what you want," she said. Since I wanted to write about various female artists, I was happy... until I discovered how little information is available. Even in compendia of "female artists," some artists are practically never covered; for example, Hilma af Klint, Olga Boznańska, and Magdalena Abakanowicz are not well-known outside their native countries or the somewhat rarified world of art historians. Others, like Artemisia Gentileschi, have been covered in numerous books but in her case with her artistic legacy muddled by a narrow focus on a "wronged woman" story, even though this only partially explains Artemisia's achievements. So, another part of the reason I have written my take on women artists is my dissatisfaction with how little I could find about some of them and their art. This is also a reason why I have chosen to include artists spanning disparate eras and styles. It is less about *when* any particular female artist can be placed in history and more about *what* they had to say or *how* they said it. This does not mean that the historical and anthropological context of their creativity is not meaningful—in fact, just the opposite.

For women, much more so than for men, the society and times in which they lived determined their art—what, how, and when they could paint, draw, or sculpt. In Europe, for many centuries—let's say the Renaissance through the late 19th century—women were not allowed to study male nudes and consequently unable or discouraged from doing historical paintings where an accurate knowledge of human anatomy was needed. While society approved of recreational painting by young unmarried ladies (not an option for women who had to work for a living, such as factory workers, peasants, or servants), professional painting required membership in a guild. As late as 1770, Elisabeth Vigée Le Brun had her paints confiscated for practicing her craft without a license, and only after she was allowed to join Académie Saint-Luc, to which her late father belonged, was the young artist permitted to paint professionally. Edma Morisot, the sister of Berthe Morisot—one of the founders of Impressionism—had as much talent as her sister, as evidenced by Edma's portrait of Berthe from 1865. However, Edma followed the accepted social protocol of 19th-century French society; as soon as she married at age 30, she stopped painting. We did not lose Edma the artist to war or poverty—we lost her to a social convention.

Another example of an obstacle solely affecting women was that of Rosa Bonheur, who had to obtain police permission to wear trousers in public. She wanted the freedom of movement (and she was also openly gay, so pants were perhaps what she preferred to wear anyway), but she had to use the justification that her paintings of horses and domestic animals at farms necessitated a man's attire. She did get a permit but imagine how absurd this was—male painters did not have get permission to wear painter's smocks, or trousers for that matter. So, until the 20th century, when a lot of the social barriers finally fell down, women artists faced obstacles that had nothing to do with their skill at painting. And yet these women prevailed, at least in creating art—even if not necessarily achieving success during their lifetimes. I'm fascinated by their stories and by the ways in which they coped with ceilings that were not even the proverbial glass ones—the barriers were visible, formalized, and unbreakable.

I entitled this book *Women in Art* because I'm interested not only in "women who do art" but also "women who are the subject of art." This is why Part I is devoted to women as models and subjects of paintings, and particularly those who were portrayed at work. Throughout art history, painters produced countless society portraits, nudes, and allegorical, religious, or mythological images of women, painted for clients seeking spiritual or aesthetic comfort. However, in some paintings, it is more interesting to look at what these women do than what they are or what they symbolize.

This book does not aim for an academic review, replete with research footnotes. It is meant to be a collection of stories about art and women who created it. I'm interested in their personal vicissitudes, the context in which they lived and created, the obstacles and opportunities they encountered, and finally, what their works can still tell us—an audience removed by decades or hundreds of years from the time of the works' creation. In art, there is the point of view of the artist and her or his contemporaries, but there is also the point of view of the viewer, who is usually in a completely different time and place. As Mary Beard once asked, *"[I]s it the looking that determines what we actually see?"* In every era and every country and every society, we see things differently.

Regardless of *when* we are looking at art, it is *what* we are looking at that should be considered before we judge the work by who its author is. These works of art are good not because they were created by women. Art knows no gender or time—it is either perceived as good or bad, it either moves somebody's soul or it doesn't, it either shows us something interesting, profound, shocking, or beautiful or it doesn't. It is, of course, also "in the eye of the beholder." This is where I part company with so many feminist-leaning authors of art books and essays. I realize that a big part of Artemisia Gentileschi's life was determined by the injustice that was done to her, that Frida Kahlo's stormy relationship with Diego Rivera influenced her paintings, and that perhaps Hilma af Klint was robbed of her title as a pioneering abstractionist. When I talk about their life stories, it is with the aim of giving their paintings a context and facilitating deeper understanding. At the end of the day, however, it is the art itself—and not their gender or biography—that makes me admire some of these artists. There are many female artists, especially in modern times, who are famous, included in anthologies, and praised with exhibitions and art criticism. They are not in this selection because their art leaves me cold and their biographies do not tell any interesting stories. This is my highly subjective anthology, my effort to spotlight some artists who happen to be female and perhaps are less appreciated for their art than they should be.

All of these art stories originally appeared as postings in my ongoing website entitled *Food for the Soul* (https://food4thesoul.solari.com/). Some of them I originally wrote as reportages from exhibitions all over Europe and the U.S.

PART I

Women At Work

CHAPTER 1

MASTERPIECES

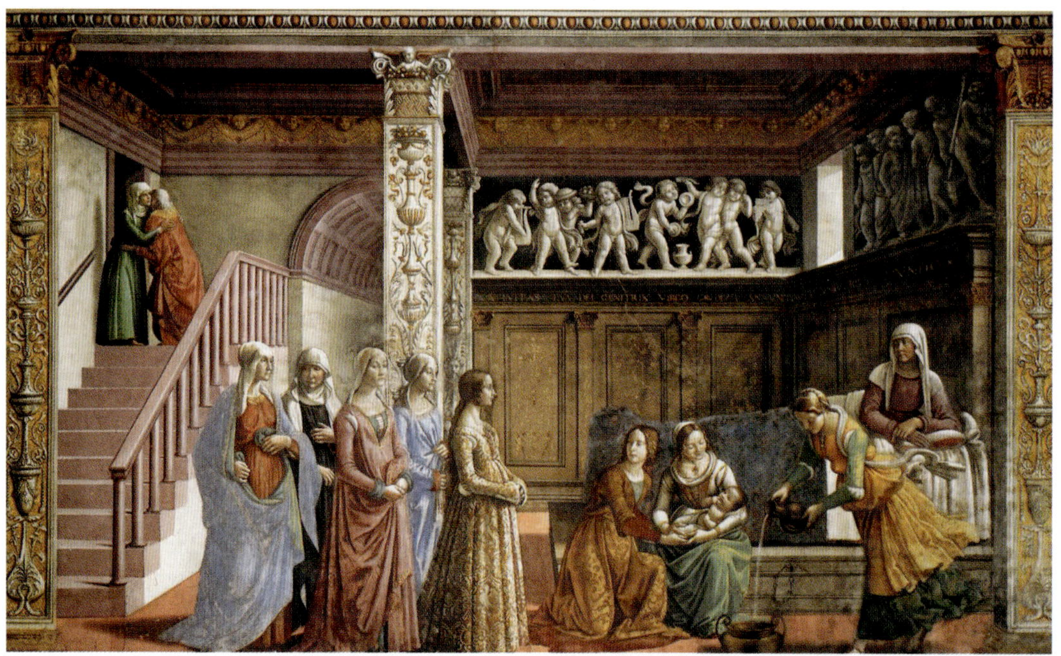

Domenico Ghirlandaio. *Birth of the Virgin*, 1479–85. Fresco.
Santa Maria Novella, Florence.
Photo: Public domain via Wikimedia Commons

The majority of figures in paintings, especially those created before the 20th century, are male. The paintings show men heroically fighting or representing religious or mythological figures, men hunting, or men suffering the toil of existence. Women appear mostly as Madonnas or saints, sometimes as mythological figures, in formal portraits for sitters' salons, or as nudes for private viewing. However, this section is a series on women doing something else —what the majority of them would have been doing all those centuries: working.

Some mythological and religious scenes are famous for what is presented in the main part of the picture (for example, Titian's *Venus of Urbino* and Ghirlandaio's *Birth of the Virgin*), but in this section on women at work, we can sometimes ignore the main image in favor of what is happening on the periphery. This can be an apt metaphor for women's work in general, because often women's housework or even their professional achievements remain unsung—if not downright taken for granted.

Domenico Ghirlandaio's fresco, *Birth of the Virgin*, is one of the masterpieces of the Florentine Renaissance. Ghirlandaio had already decorated the most prestigious buildings of the Sistine Chapel in the Vatican and Palazzo Vecchio in Florence when, in 1486, he was commissioned to paint a fresco cycle, including the *Birth of the Virgin*, for a family chapel of Giovanni Tornabuoni inside the church of Santa Maria Novella.

At the very center of this composition, the artist placed the patron's child—Tornabuoni's daughter Ludovica—dressed in a golden brocade gown and surrounded by her equally sumptuously dressed companions, one of whom is looking at us rather than at baby Mary. Ludovica is standing stiffly in her formal dress, looking at Mary's young mother Anne, who is resting after the birth. As beautiful as St. Anne is, however, the viewer's eye is more drawn toward a figure below—a young servant who is graciously leaning to pour bath water. Ghirlandaio's sketch of this servant figure has survived to the present day, so we know how carefully he planned the folds of the yellow garment and the bent-forward pose. Because women gave birth at home and typically would have been attended by their female friends, relatives, and servants, such a domestic scene would not have been unusual. Ghirlandaio takes this domestic setting but decorates the room in a most ornate frame of carved columns and a frieze of cherubs, populating the tableau with his patron's family. However, the most gracious figure in the fresco is not the noble Ludovica; it is the lowly but graceful servant.

Baroque artist Francisco de Zurbarán also undertook the popular theme of Mary's birth. Zurbarán was nicknamed the "Spanish Caravaggio" due to his mastery of light and shadow as well as a large body of religious paintings. He had many commissions from monasteries for painted altarpieces, and he was a favorite painter of King Philip IV. Though famous for his mastery in painting folds of white fabrics (resulting in many commissions from Capuchin monks), he was also a master of color. His *Birth of the Virgin* is a canvas where strong primary reds, yellows, and blues are arranged in an oval around the red center. Like Ghirlandaio, Zurbarán featured the commissioning donor prominently—an aristocratic lady dressed in the latest fashion who looks at us on the right. Unlike Ghirlandaio, Zurbarán was much more realistic about the birth process (he married three times and had several daughters); his St. Anne looks exhausted and definitely in need of the restorative broth proffered by attentive servants. I particularly like the image of an old midwife—a woman without whose assistance many a birth could have ended in tragedy. This working woman would not have been much acknowledged by aristocratic clients like the lady in the yellow gown, yet the artist placed her in the center of his canvas. She is the one who helped bring baby Mary into the world.

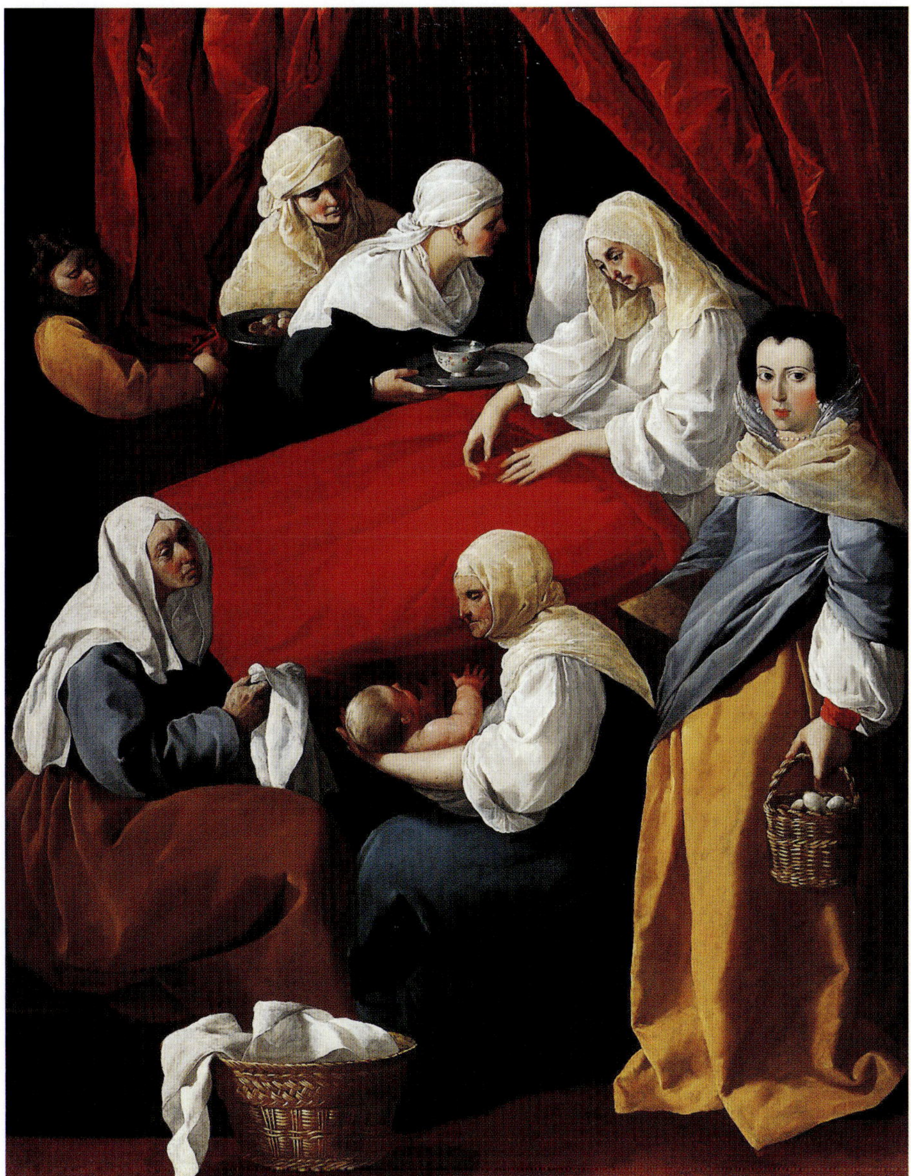

Francisco de Zurbarán. *The Birth of the Virgin*, 1629. Oil on canvas.
Norton Simon Museum, Pasadena.
Photo: Public domain via Wikimedia Commons

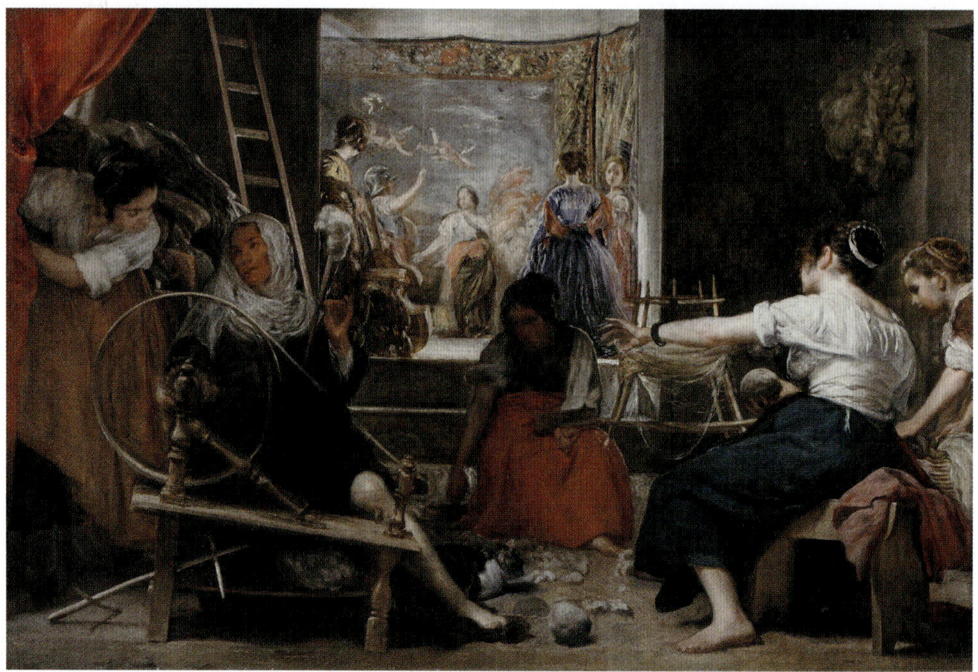

Diego Velázquez. *The Spinners* or *The Fable of Arachne/Las Hilanderas*, c. 1655–60.
Oil on canvas.
Museo del Prado, Madrid.
Photo: Public domain via Wikimedia Commons

Together with *Las Meninas* (page 49), *The Spinners* belongs to the canon of Velázquez's greatest masterpieces; it is impossible to do it justice in barely a few sentences. The painting is a retelling of the myth of Ariadne, the young and talented weaver who dares to create a tapestry showing the loves of gods, thereby incurring the wrath of Athena (Minerva). When the proud weaver realizes her mistake, she hangs herself in anguish, but Athena transforms her into a spider, a creature condemned to incessant weaving. Velázquez presents both moments from the story; in the foreground, Athena is disguised as an old woman spinning alongside Ariadne, while in the next room, the goddess of war is revealed as Pallas Athena who berates the hapless spinner. In the 18th and 19th centuries, this canvas was often thought to be just a scene depicting the manufacture of tapestries (possibly based on the Royal Tapestry Factory of St. Elizabeth in Madrid), and this is why it is entitled *The Spinners*. Mythological interpretations became popular later and although they are now firmly established, for the purpose of our working women theme, let's look at the women simply as weavers.

By Velázquez's time, tapestry had had centuries of recognition as a form of artistic expression just as noble and precious as painting. The tapestry in the back room of *The Spinners* is actually based on Titian's *Rape of Europa* (page 204) because Velázquez is contrasting here the high art of tapestry in the back room with the simple craft of spinning wool that takes place in the front. However, we can also look at the front room's scene as a portrait of real weavers at work. The hard-working spinners are working barefoot—even the goddess who is disguised as an old woman. You feel the warmth of the room, and you watch the wheel spinning and the kitty playing with a ball of yarn. For all its mythological and sophisticated theme, this is an intimate scene of women busy at a task that requires skill, speed, and concentration.

Despite occasional lustful glances by contemporary tourists visiting L'Uffizi museum in Florence, Titian's *Venus of Urbino* was not meant to simply titillate but to portray marital love. The small spaniel and the myrtle and roses are symbols of faithfulness and constant love. The painting was commissioned in 1538 by Guidobaldo II della Rovere (who soon afterward became the Duke of Urbino) for his bridal chamber. Since then, it has become one of the most popular canvases in all of Italy and art history.

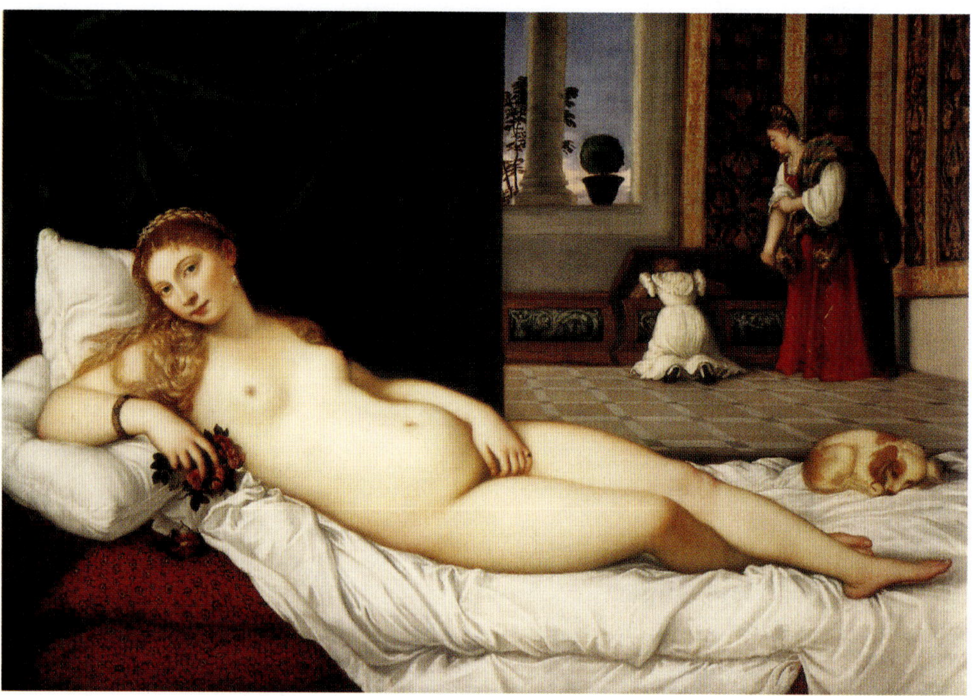

Titian. *Venus of Urbino*, 1538. Oil on canvas.
Galleria degli Uffizi, Florence.
Photo: Public domain via Wikimedia Commons

The painting, itself inspired by Giorgione's *Sleeping Venus*, was famously referenced three centuries later in Manet's *Olympia*. It has been studied for its compositional mastery for ages. However, if we ignore the heroine of this picture for the moment, we notice two other women—perhaps a maid and a lady-in-waiting, who are searching for their mistress's gown. The maid, who is rummaging in a chest (no walk-in-closets with racks in those times), is supervised by a woman in red who is already holding a gold and green gown as perhaps the first choice. Even if Venus herself is preoccupied with just looking gorgeous, the household is busy keeping her in style —clothes have to be prepared for the mistress of the house. With the clean floor and a plant that presumably has been watered, it is clear that this beautiful palace (an actual view of Urbino's residence) was well taken care of by women such as the two figures in the background.

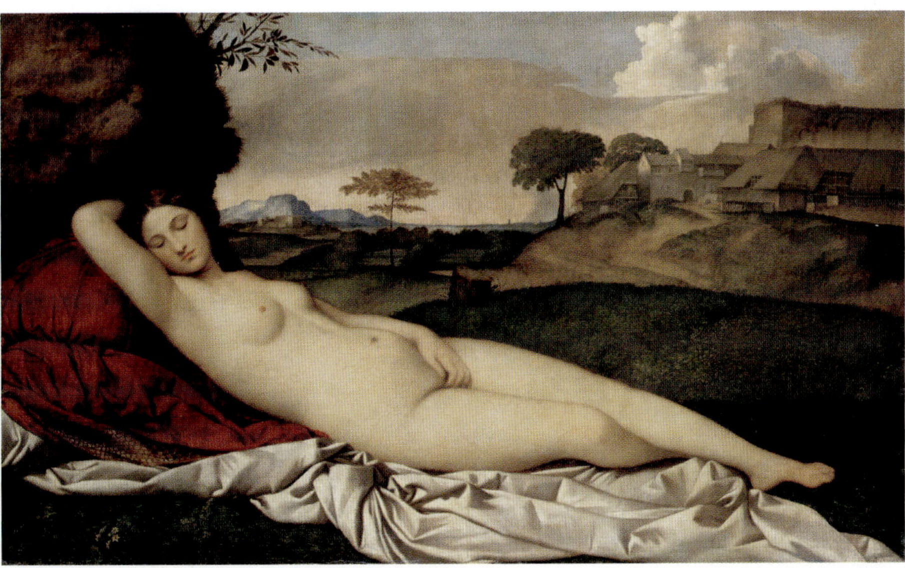

Giorgione. *The Sleeping Venus*, 1508–10. Oil on canvas.
Staatliche Kunstsammlungen Dresden.
Photo: Public domain via Wikimedia Commons

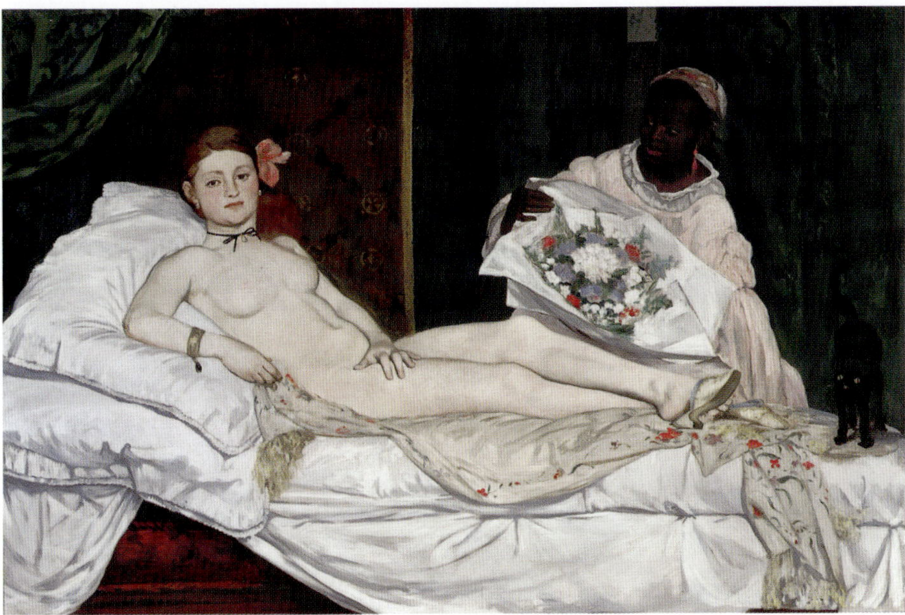

Édouard Manet. *Olympia*, 1863. Oil on canvas.
Musée d'Orsay, Paris.
Photo: Public domain via Wikimedia Commons

Tintoretto, born in the year of da Vinci's death, represented a new era of European culture. The calm and elegant style of the High Renaissance gave way to mannerism and the religious fervor of the Church opposing the Reformation. Intimate religious pictures gave way to monumental canvases. Tintoretto, who by age 20 was already so accomplished that apparently a jealous Titian released him from apprenticeship, lived long enough to participate in this artistic and intellectual shift. Over the last 20 years of his life, his painting style changed from lighter and more colorful works to darker pictures enlivened by just a few points of light and splashes of color.

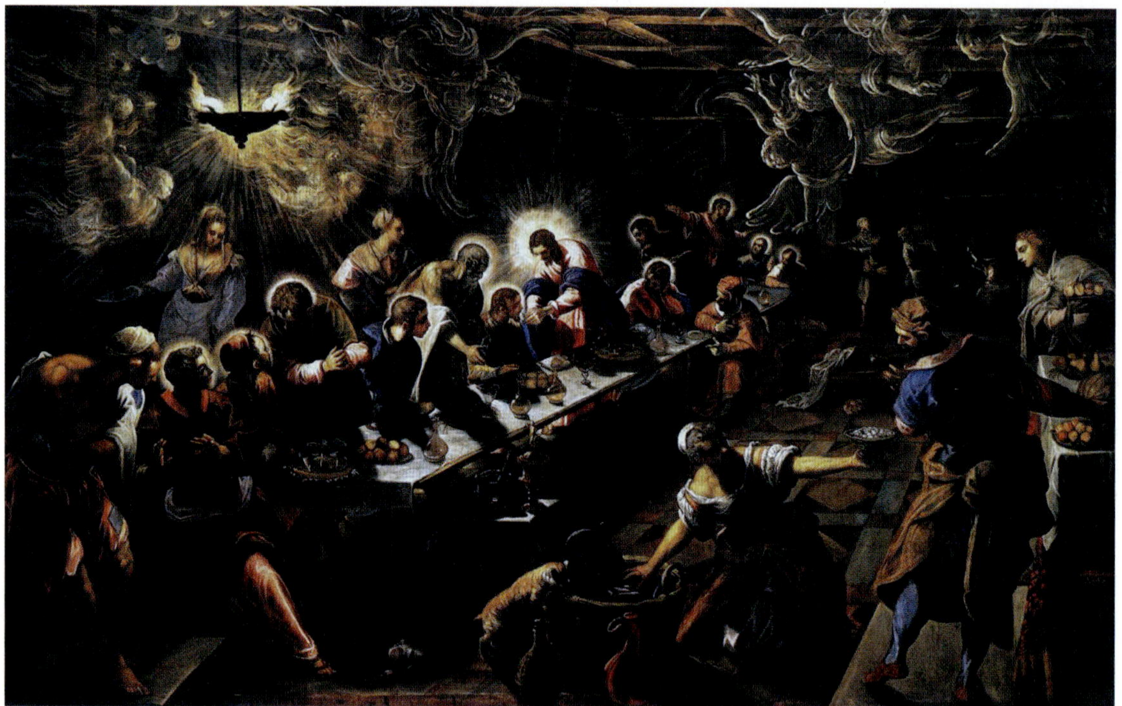

Tintoretto. *The Last Supper*, 1594. Oil on canvas.
Church of San Giorgio Maggiore, Venice.
Photo: Public domain, via Wikimedia Commons

He painted *The Last Supper* in the last year of his life—the culmination of his skill and style. This Last Supper is so different from da Vinci's orderly, symmetrical composition. Here, the table is placed at a rising diagonal, while the ceiling is populated by ghostly swirls of angels. There are only two sharp light sources: a lamp that symbolizes divine spirit and a shining halo over Christ's head. The light shines over the stretched-out arms of a servant who is reaching toward the basket. In this painting, the supernatural elements of divine and angelic presence mix with the mundane activity of a group's mealtime. Women are serving food, a cat is trying to climb into a basket, and the apostles look like typical Venetian youths of the 16th century. No matter how exalted and spiritual an event this is, life has to go on—and women are working hard to feed the diners.

Even old masters did not create their paintings in an artistic vacuum. They looked at people around them to capture their faces, gestures, and tasks. This is how we get these little glimpses of hard-working women, tucked somewhere in dramatic tableaux and telling us real-life stories.

CHAPTER 2

AT HOME

This chapter deals with women captured by painters in their most accessible milieu—working at home. The tasks depicted may be some of the most mundane, but the artists who painted their work found in these humble scenes an opportunity to play with color, texture, and light, creating gems of fine art that now grace the most prestigious museums.

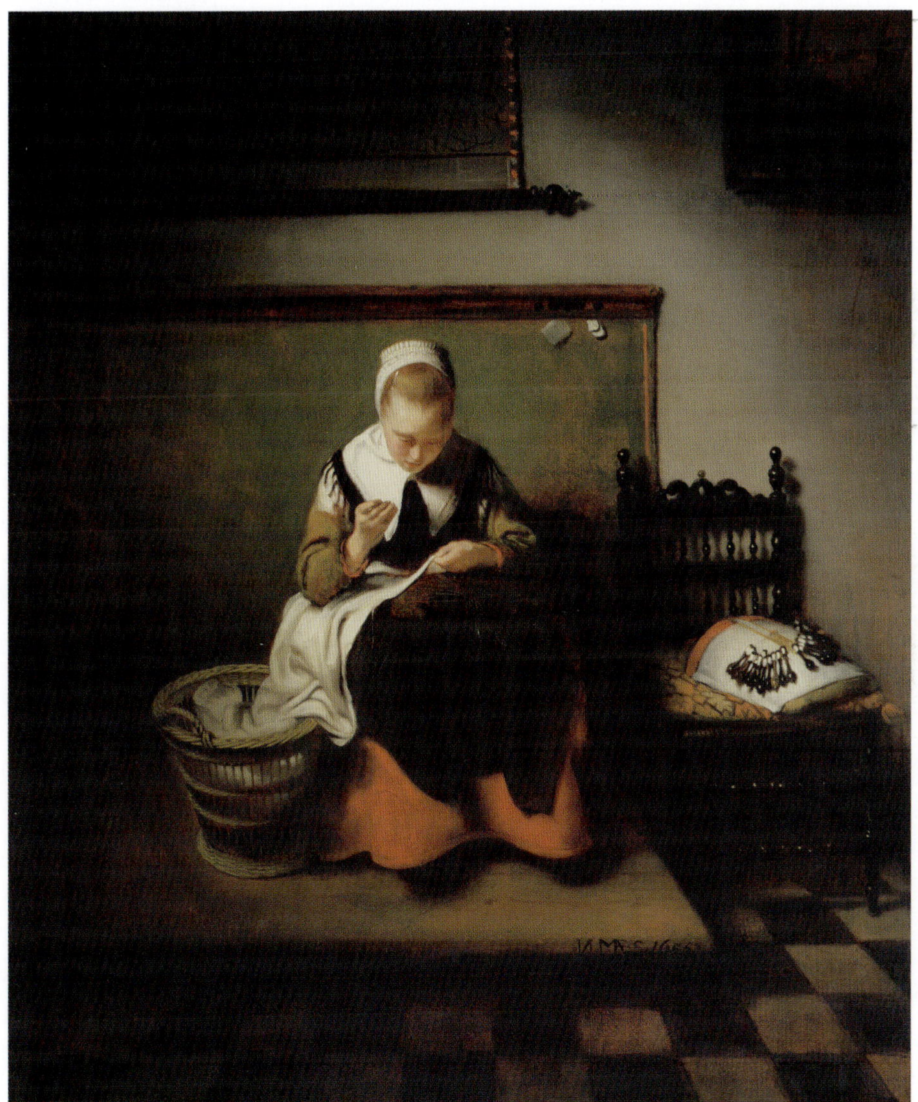

Nicolaes Maes. *A Young Woman Sewing*, 1655. Oil on canvas.
Harold Samuel Collection, Guildhall Art Gallery, City of London.
Photo: Guildhall Art Gallery/Harold Samuel Collection/Bridgeman Images

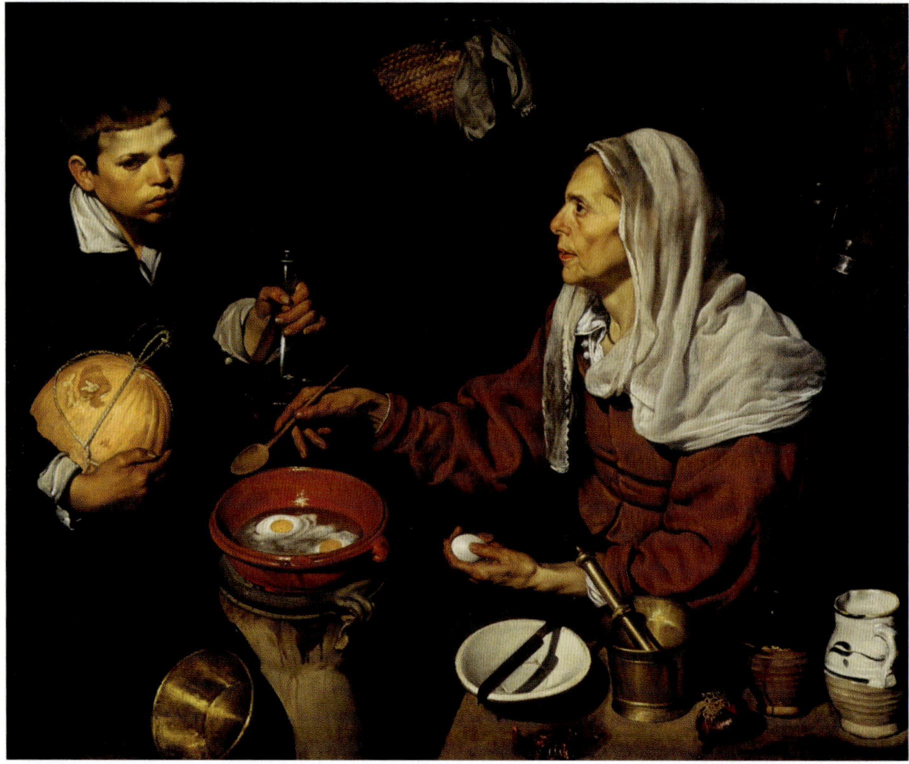

Diego Velázquez. *Old Woman Cooking Eggs*, 1618. Oil on canvas.
Scottish National Gallery, Edinburgh.
Photo: Public domain via Wikimedia Commons

Velázquez was just 18 or 19 when, around 1618, he painted *Old Woman Cooking Eggs*. He was living in Seville at the time, and in the same year he married the daughter of his teacher. The model for the cook in this painting was most probably his future mother-in-law (her face also appears in the famous *Christ in the House of Martha and Mary*).

At the time, collectors and critics considered the genre of kitchen scenes—called bodegones—the lowest kind of a commissioned job because the art portrayed "workmen of scant knowledge or reflection" and featured ordinary people cooking and drinking. Sometimes, bodegones would simply be still-life arrangements of foodstuffs. These paintings were popular, but they were not very respected. It took the young Velázquez to raise this humble genre of home decoration to the level of fine art.

Our modern eye is accustomed to the intense colors of synthetic dyes and the clarity of lines offered by even most amateur photos. *Old Woman Cooking Eggs* was painted in the early 17th century by a teenager, without these modern shortcuts, yet all of the details are so vivid and precise that you can feel the texture of the smooth, shiny surface of a mortar with pestle, so different from the rough clay of a water jug. Anybody who has ever cooked eggs-over-easy would recognize this mouth-watering moment when the eggs are almost done. Velázquez uses *chiaroscuro* to bring out of the shadows the two figures: a sullen boy who clutches a bottle and a melon (cleverly enveloped with string for easy carrying) and a woman cooking the eggs on a brazier. The two figures have the gravitas—the serious looks and poses —suitable for a religious scene, except that we are looking at domestic cooking rather than a supper at Emmaus. This painting amounted to a Velázquez calling card: "I have just completed my apprenticeship, and this is what I can do with the most ordinary of themes and the few pigments at hand." Five years later, he was working at the court of King Philip IV of Spain.

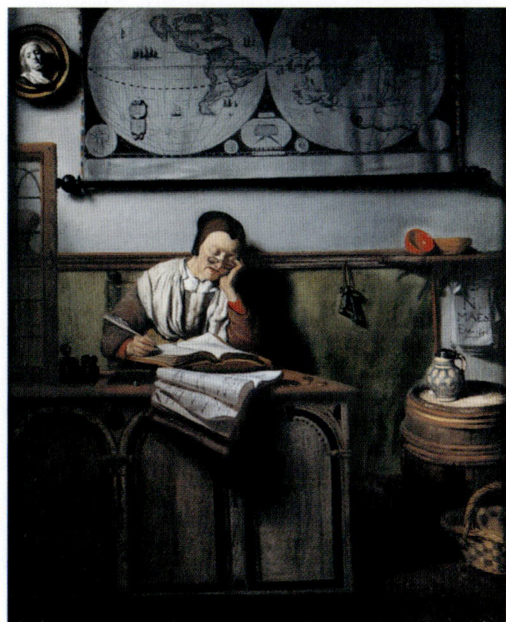

Nicolaes Maes. *The Account Keeper*, 1656. Oil on canvas.
Saint Louis Art Museum.
Photo: Public domain via Wikimedia Commons

Nicolaes Maes spent several years at Rembrandt's studio before becoming one of the most prominent genre painters of the Dutch Golden Age. He lived most of his life in Amsterdam, painting portraits, religious themes, and sometimes, intimate scenes of domestic life. Although Maes painted some moralizing pictures of eavesdropping maids, most of his genre pictures were of hardworking housewives or servants. These genre scenes were less valued in his time, but today, ironically, we appreciate them more than traditional lofty subjects.

The Dutch Republic was a society that was Protestant and industrious, valuing austere, organized, and moral life. Women were expected to excel at the domestic crafts of sewing and lacemaking, servants or farm tenants were required to be hard-working and respectful toward their masters, and men were supposed to devote themselves to responsible management of finances and trade. This was the theory, but there were, of course, many exceptions to these prescribed roles. For example, some women managed to advance in the professional world by forming their own textile manufacturing guilds or, especially if they became prosperous widows, managing family businesses. *The Account Keeper* is a portrait of just such a woman. Her reading glasses and some wrinkles indicate that she is middle-aged and perhaps a widow, left to keep the family estate going. Or perhaps she is just checking household expenses, but in any case, this is an educated person. There is a map of the world on the wall (as a nation of shipbuilders and merchants, the Dutch were very aware of the world outside local polders), and this kitchen corner with a carved desk has obviously been used as an office for a while.

Women bent over sewing or lacemaking late into the night were also a frequent subject of many Dutch artists, and Maes painted his own version in *A Young Woman Sewing* (page 13). Between her sewing in a basket and half-started lace on her left, we can see that this young woman has no chance to be idle. Maes is very sympathetic to his subject, placing her on a sort of a dais, dressed in starched and brilliant whites that attest to her laundering skills. A Rembrandt-style soft light bathes her studiously bent head. She could be a goddess of domestic work if such a thing existed.

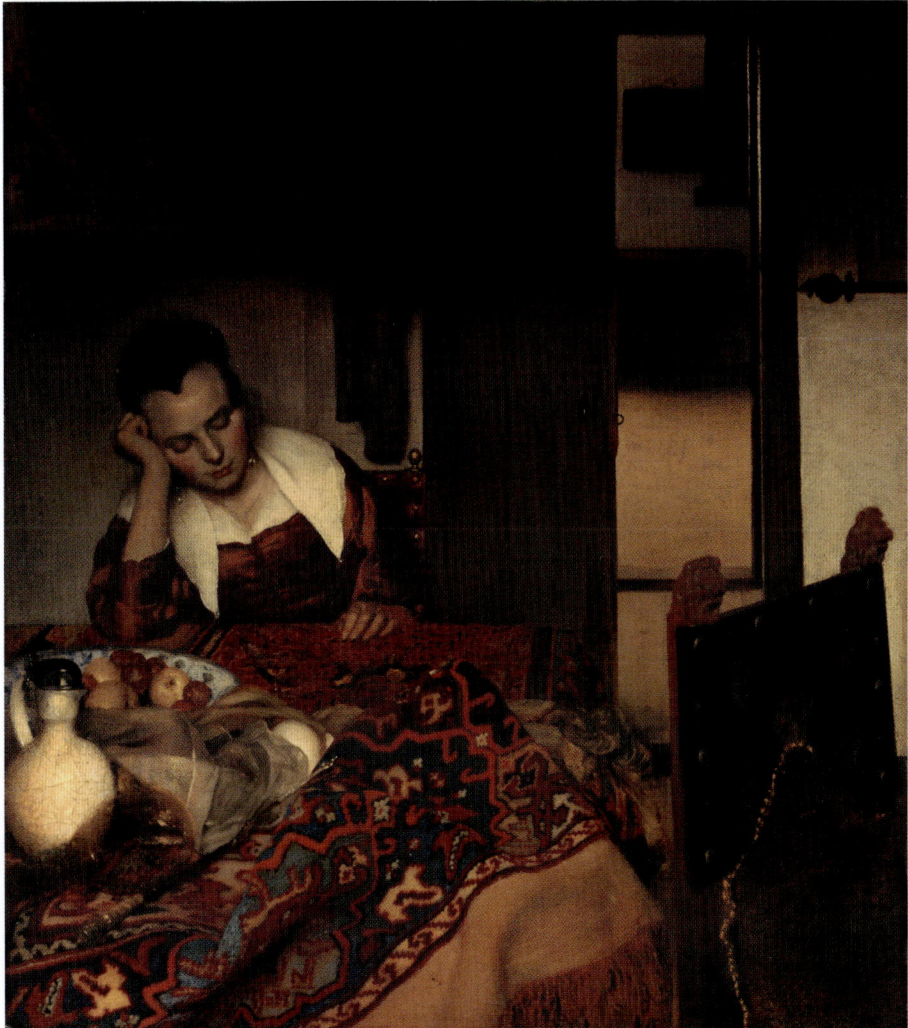

Johannes Vermeer. *A Maid Asleep*, 1656–57. Oil on canvas.
Metropolitan Museum of Art, New York.
Photo: Public domain via Wikimedia Commons

Idleness was a sin in Protestant homes. Sunday sermons—but also literature and art—put pressure on all the female members of a household, servants and mistresses alike, not to waste a minute of their time. One of the artistic means of communicating this message were moralizing pictures that criticized idleness. One of Maes' paintings, explicitly entitled *The Idle Servant*, is of a mistress turning to us, the viewers, to point out her maid asleep among unwashed dishes.

In Vermeer's case, it's hard to tell if he was sympathetic to idle servants, but looking at *A Maid Asleep*, I'd like to believe that he was far from moralizing. Certainly, he created a more complex composition than just a snapshot of domestic life. His maid sits at a table decorated with a sumptuous Anatolian kilim rug (check out the brilliant art documentary, *Tim's Vermeer*, to realize how tedious it was to paint every knot in this rug). Some light is creeping over the white Italian wine jug. Perhaps this maid got up before dawn to light fireplaces, and now she has perched herself at a table for a catnap before the household wakes. This was Vermeer's first attempt at genre painting. He emulates Maes (who also created a canvas called *Old Woman Dozing*), but at the same time, he is far from criticizing his subject for slacking off at her job. Originally, *A Maid Asleep* also had a small dog (now covered by the Spanish chair) and a man standing in the doorway. Perhaps this was to be a scene of the type of social interaction that appears in many Vermeer paintings; however, those elements are absent from the final version. Interestingly, art historians have produced a vast literature interpreting the meaning of this and other Vermeer paintings of women in domestic settings (including one supposition that the maid is only pretending to sleep but is really avoiding a lover). I prefer the simpler explanation that this is a sympathetic portrait of a very tired young woman who is trying to catch a few minutes of rest before the beginning of a busy day.

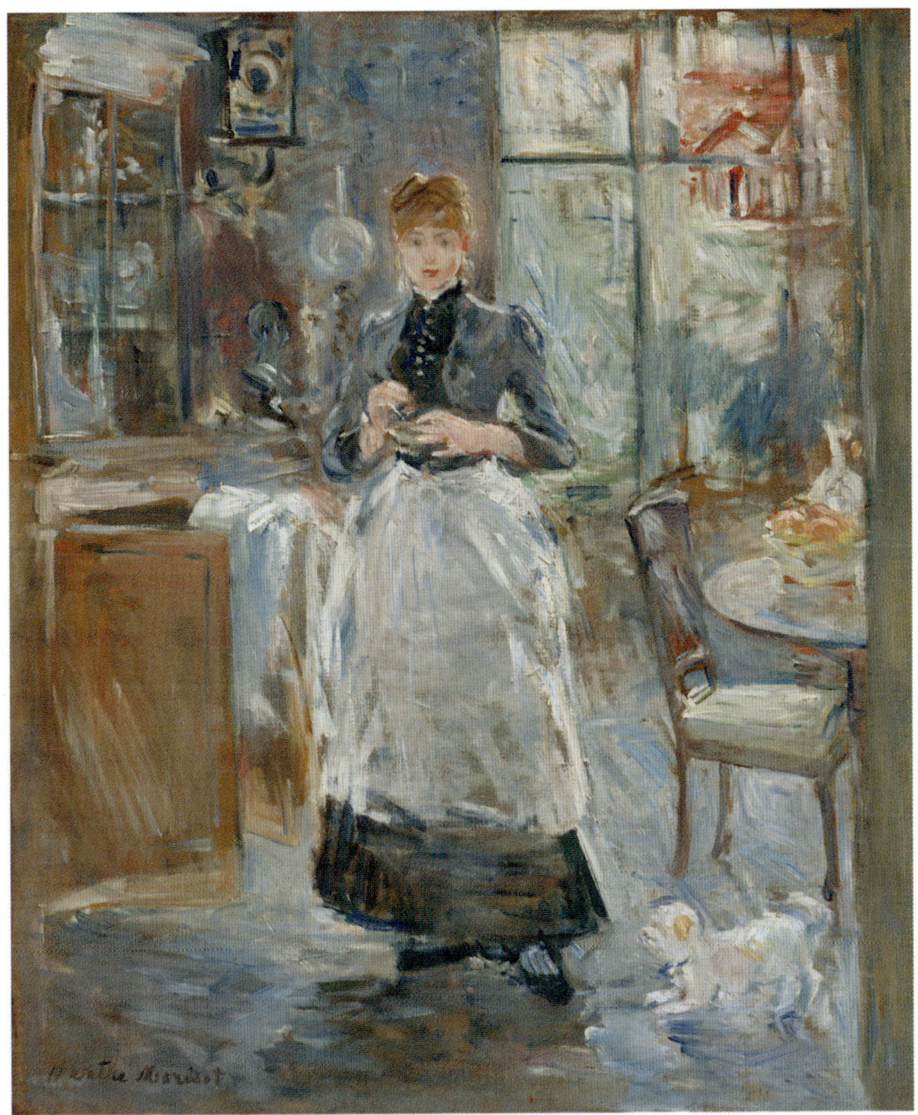

Berthe Morisot. *In the Dining Room*, 1886. Oil on canvas.
Chester Dale Collection, National Gallery of Art, Washington D.C.
Photo: Courtesy National Gallery of Art, Washington D.C.

Berthe Morisot exhibited in the Impressionists' first group exhibition in 1874, and she was one of the "founding members" of the movement, but at the same time she remains the least known of them all. As an upper-middle-class woman, wife, and mother, she had less time and opportunity to practice her profession (such as painting male nudes in studio settings to learn anatomy for historic scenes). From the start of her career, she focused on her family and friends as subjects and used domestic settings for her scenes. Examples include paintings of her sister taking care of her newborn, her husband playing with her own daughter Julie, and her domestic help as models for *The Cherry Tree* and *Young Woman Picking Oranges*. It's not that the male Impressionists did not paint women; it's just that they were different images of women. Degas painted ballet dancers, while Renoir painted soubrettes at city dance halls or carefully posed nudes and Manet painted waitresses and prostitutes at wine bars. It took women artists like Morisot and Mary Cassatt to really capture unguarded and unposed moments of domestic life—children playing, mothers tending to them, and servant girls going about their chores.

Morisot's *In the Dining Room* is a scene that can only be observed coming down to the dining room in the morning for breakfast. Bright sun is streaking into the room where a maid is about to turn from the breakfast table toward a half-open sideboard. A little dog is at her feet, perhaps happy to have human company when most of the household has not yet stirred after the night's rest. Everything is blurred, the way things sometimes are in the morning sun. We are so used to Impressionist art now that we accept these loose brushstrokes as part of the style, but in the 1880s, this was a novel (and much criticized) way of showing people and interiors. The white apron is barely marked in a few energetic slashes, to accentuate the half turn and create one white streak starting from the dog and going all the way to a cloth on the sideboard. While the style is intentionally sketchy and unfocused, Morisot still manages to convey the woman's poise and relaxed manner. This maid is well-dressed and looks confident and purposeful. Working in Morisot's employ must have been a happier job than in many other Parisian homes.

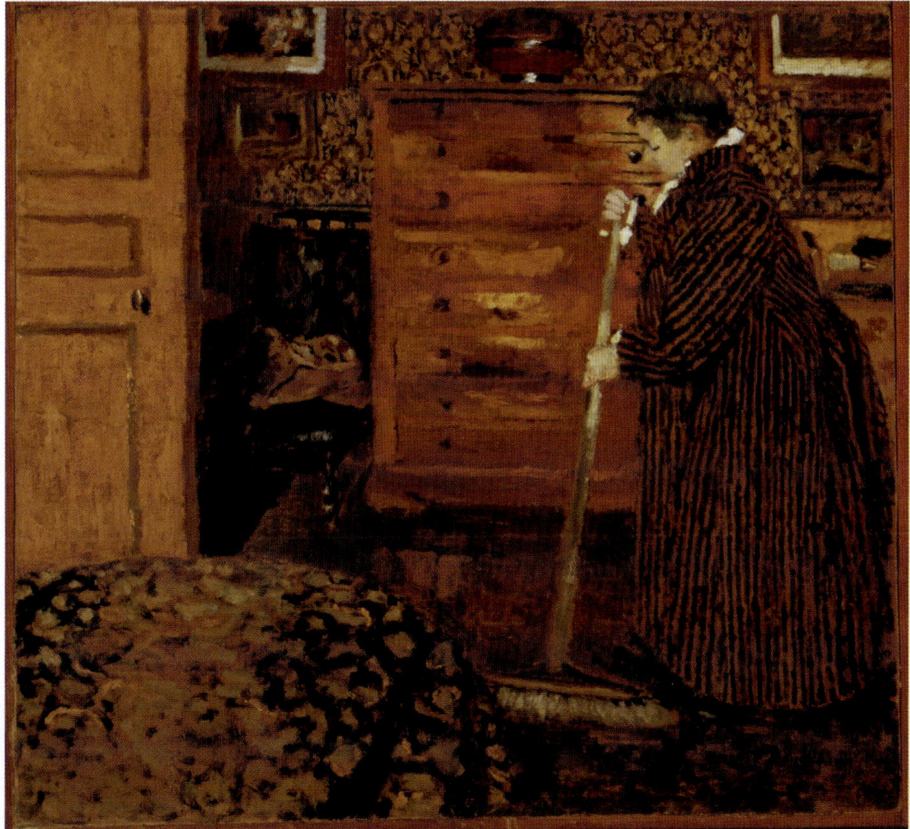

Édouard Vuillard. *A Woman Sweeping*, 1899–1900.
Oil on cardboard mounted on cradled panel.
The Phillips Collection, Washington D.C.
Photo: The Phillips Collection, Washington D.C./Acquired 1939/Bridgeman Images

Not all the women working at home were servants, of course, especially if the work involved just some light tidying up. Édouard Vuillard never married, living happily with his mother and his sister who were dressmakers. His house was always full of fabrics and designs that feature prominently in his numerous canvases. Vuillard's life and art spanned both the 19th and the 20th centuries. Before 1900, the artist belonged to the Nabis movement, which emphasized patterns and colors and cleared the way for upcoming abstract art. The Nabis were strongly influenced by Japanese art and a belief that decorative arts were of equal importance to traditional fine arts. These ideas were a perfect fit for Vuillard who, surrounded in his family residence by all kinds of patterns and colors, created unique compositions that almost blend the colorful designs with the occupants of the cluttered Victorian interiors.

In *A Woman Sweeping*, the central figure (Vuillard's mother) forms a part of this uniformly brown composition. Light-brown furniture blends with brown wallpaper and a carpet, and even the woman's house dress is striped brown like some large beetle. This is a totally domestic scene. Madame Vuillard surely would not have received guests or clients in this brown dress, and she would perhaps not have even agreed to be painted in this way if not for the fact that the portraitist was her son (who actually painted her hundreds of times). This deliberate "symphony in brown" was unusual for the Nabis, who tended to use strong color contrasts. It must have been an artistic challenge to paint a tender and loving portrait of a woman at work, using almost exclusively the brown-black palette and the most mundane subject of sweeping the floor.

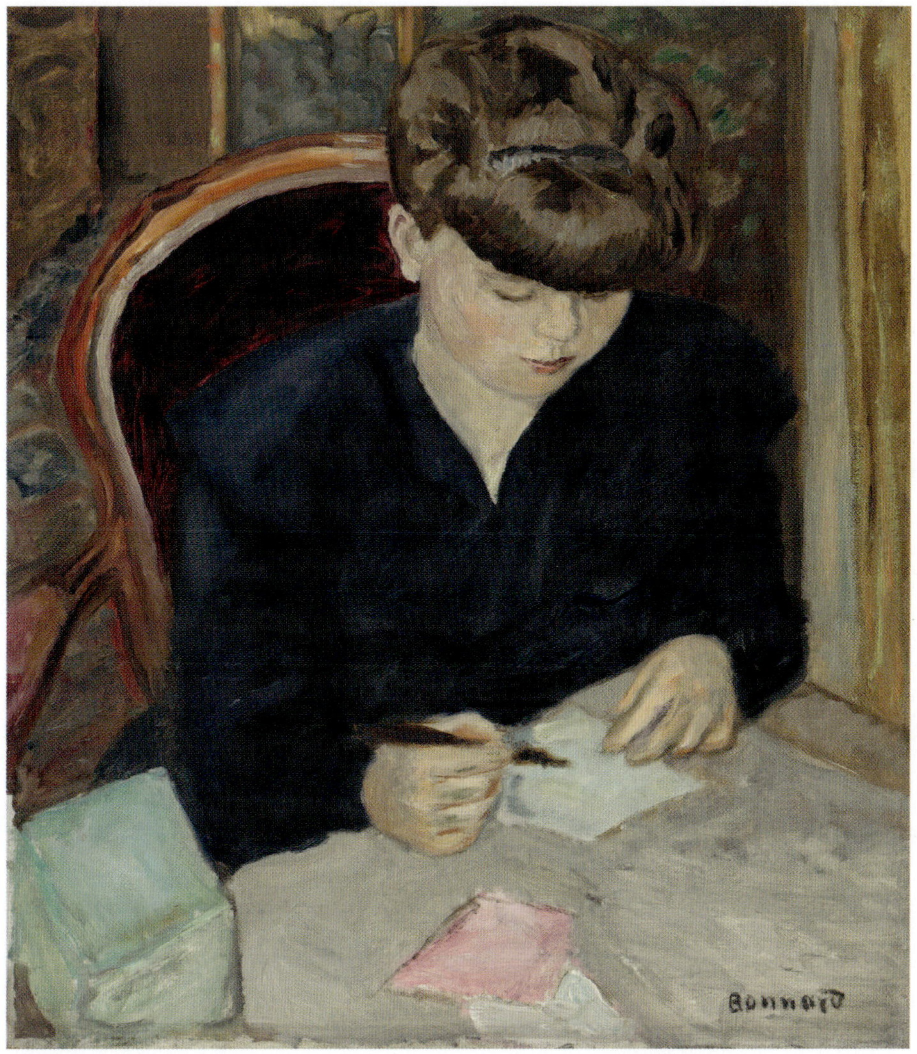

Pierre Bonnard. *The Letter*, c. 1906. Oil on canvas. Chester Dale Collection.
National Gallery of Art, Washington, DC.
Photo: Wikimedia Commons

CHAPTER 3

OUT IN THE WORLD

Women have not always been stuck at home just sewing and running households. They have also been out in the fields as farmers or trading in the markets as merchants. Industrialization brought women into cities, sometimes to work in shops and factories, but sometimes into new and more specialized professions—actresses, ballerinas, nurses, teachers, typists, telephone operators, and scientists. In the 20th century, the two massive World Wars brought about further changes in traditional work roles, forcing men to accept women as administrators, operators of heavy machinery, car mechanics, or journalists. Meanwhile, painters recorded these moments of cultural and economic transition in their art.

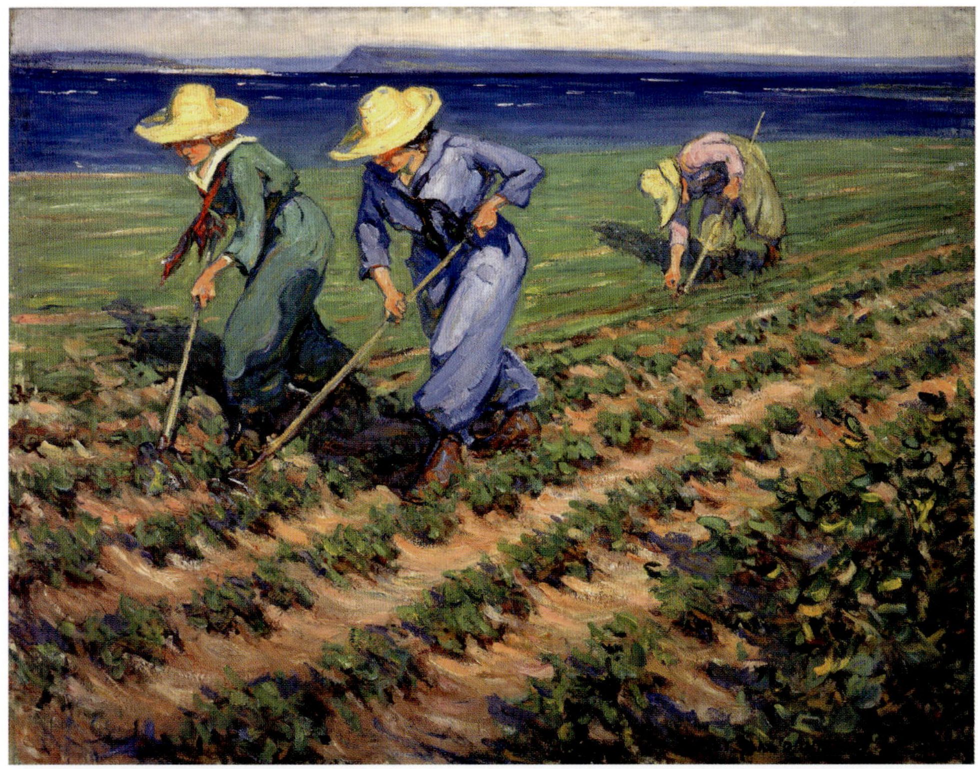

Manly Edward MacDonald. *Land Girls Hoeing*, 1918–19. Oil on canvas.
Canadian War Museum, Ottawa.
Photo: Public domain via Wikimedia Commons

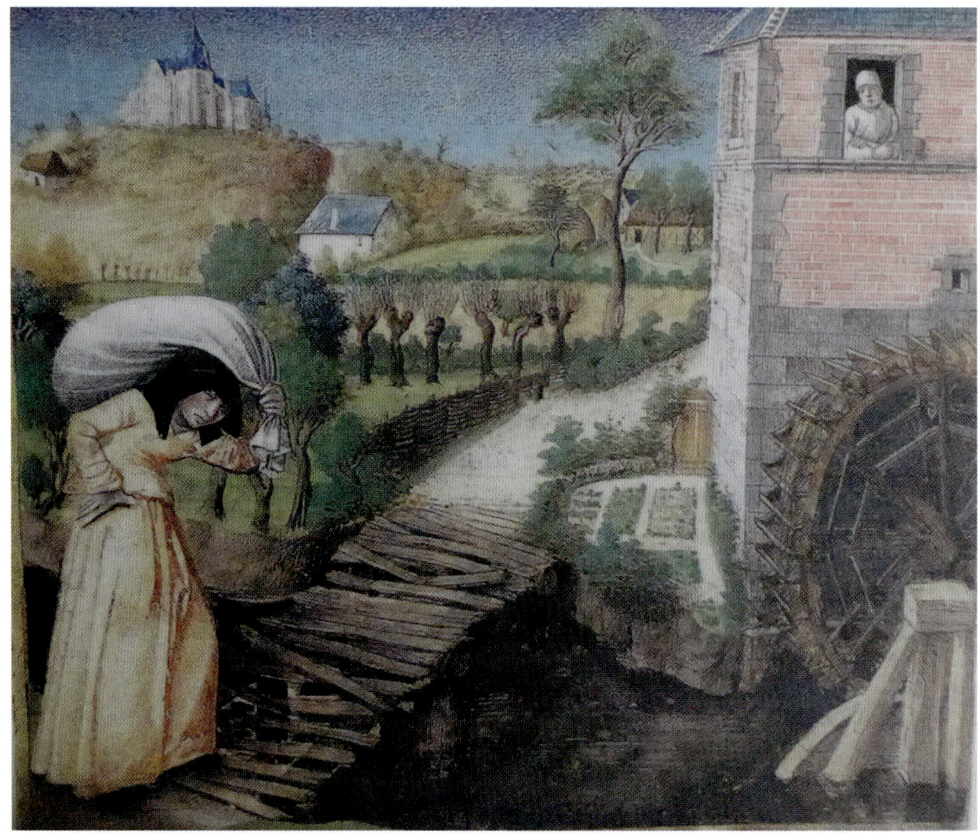

Copy of Barthélemy d'Eyck miniature (attrib). *Mortification of the Vain Pleasure/Le mortifiement de vaine plaisance*, c. 1455. Illumination on parchment.
Bibliothèque municipale de Metz.
Photo: Public domain via Wikimedia Commons

There is a saying that a picture is worth a thousand words. The image from this manuscript, a copy of a miniature, attributed to Barthélemy d'Eyck, is a perfect illustration of the division of labor between the sexes. It shows us a woman carrying grain to a water mill, nearly bent in half under the burden of her sack. The man in the window, the miller, is relaxedly waiting for the peasant woman to cross the rickety bridge to his mill. Though this illustration was probably drawn from real life, it can also serve as a metaphor for life in the Middle Ages for many women.

The image comes from a devotional book, *Mortification of the Vain Pleasure*, by the French aristocrat René d'Anjou. The "Good King René," as he is known in France, employed the eminent illustrator Barthélemy d'Eyck, whose miniatures are among the finest examples of medieval art. D'Anjou was a Duke of Anjou and, briefly, a King of Naples, but he had a life full of ups and downs. Although he inherited many titles and honors, he also experienced the deaths of his two sons—murdered by poison—as well as constant conflicts over succession and land rights. His most enduring legacy, however, is in the domain of the arts. The duke was a talented writer and a lifelong patron of artists. He is credited with creating, or at least commissioning, several richly illustrated manuscripts that are a testament to late Gothic culture, further inspiring centuries of Romantic literature and art later on.

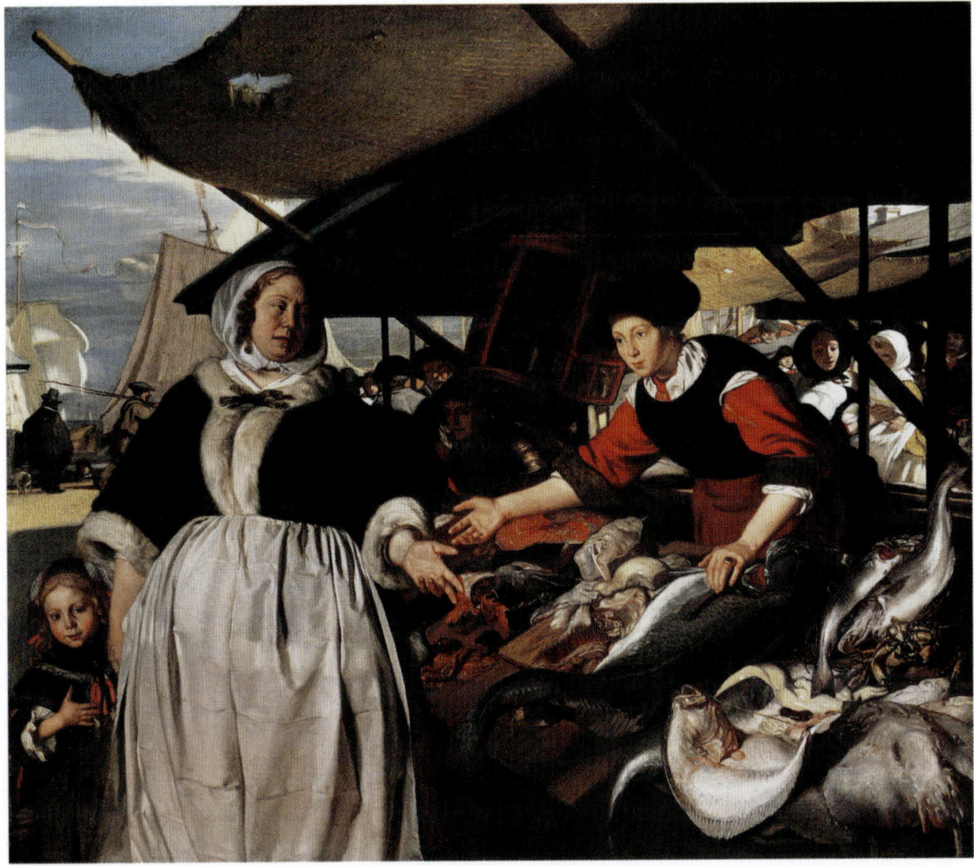

Emanuel de Witte. *Adriana van Heusden and Daughter at the Fishmarket*, c. 1662.
Oil on canvas.
National Gallery, London.
Photo: © NPL - DeA Picture Library/Bridgeman Images

If we advance 300 years further along art history's timeline, traveling from a French wheat field to a prosperous Dutch town, we see the much more complex world of the Dutch Republic during its mid-17th-century heyday. Emanuel de Witte's painting of a fishmonger offering her wares to a housewife is an interesting way to accomplish what originally must have been a simple commission to paint his landlord's wife. De Witte specialized in painting churches and building interiors, having studied architecture. This is possibly the reason we see here a complex structure of intersecting lines—created by poles of an awning, ship sails, the position of the fishmonger's body and hands, the slanted display board, and even the twisting fish. They all crisscross, adding energy and interest to the composition.

Adriana van Heusden, the wife of de Witte's landlord and patron, is presented here in her full glory as a prosperous housewife and successful mother. Her coat is lined with mink, and her daughter is healthy and smart—throwing curious, intelligent glances from behind her mother's fresh apron. What is perhaps even more interesting for us several centuries later are the pieces of information we can deduce from other elements of the painting. For example, there are seaworthy ships in the busy harbor—a sign of bustling international commerce. There is a throng of shoppers and traders, indicating that the country is prosperous. And then there is the display of all kinds of fish, vividly painted in the best tradition of Dutch still life. The wares are being presented by a seller who, despite being a secondary figure in the commissioned portrait, draws the viewer's attention in equal measure. She is a working woman whose work clearly keeps her prosperous and happily busy. She is wearing jewelry and nice clothes, and she spends her days interacting with customers and other merchants.

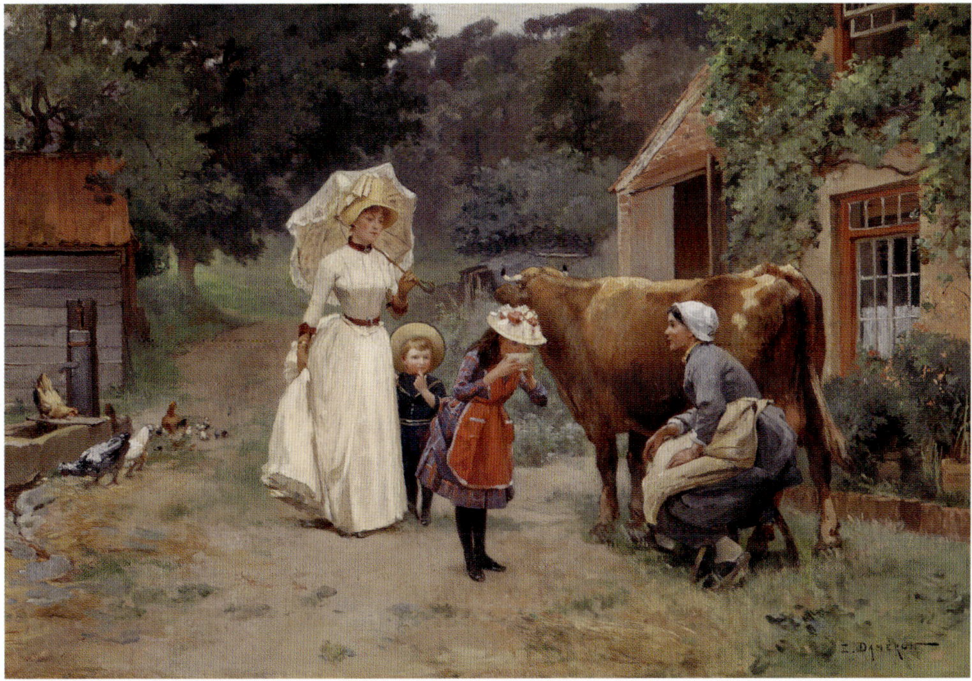

Émile Charles Dameron. *Visiting the Farm*, 1908. Oil on canvas.
Private Collection.
Photo: Public domain via Wikimedia Commons

The minor French landscape artist, Émile Charles Dameron, painted *Visiting the Farm* in 1908. Perhaps the painting was meant just as a pleasant genre scene extolling the virtues of a healthy life in the countryside. At the time, drinking milk "fresh from the cow," as is being done in the center of this picture, was recommended as protection against tuberculosis and other diseases. What we also have in this "cute" country scene, though, is a juxtaposition of the fates of two different women. They are the same age, but their lives are not the same. One was born affluent, and her only responsibility is to be a good mother and wife. The other was born a peasant, and her fate is to be a milkmaid. Their momentary encounter will end as soon as the child has finished tasting the milk and her mother has paid with a coin for the treat. One of the women will probably work hard all her life, while the other one will probably remain a society lady, not doing any work. Many novelists and painters of the time considered it their duty to make society aware of the toils of the poor. Perhaps this was Dameron's intention in this painting—but if so, he expressed it in a subtle way in a pleasing picture.

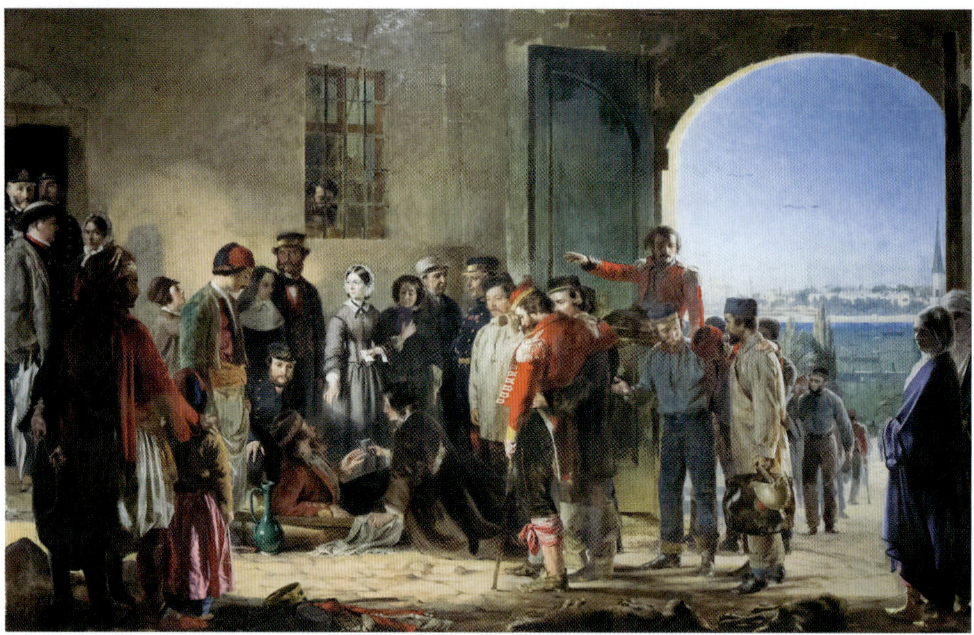

Jerry Barrett. *The Mission of Mercy: Florence Nightingale Receiving the Wounded at Scutari*, 1857. Oil on canvas.
National Portrait Gallery, London.
Photo: © Stefano Baldini/Bridgeman Images

Florence Nightingale was a very educated, upper-class Englishwoman who rejected traditional expectations of marriage and a life of leisure. Instead, she found her calling when she went to aid the British war effort during the Crimean War in 1854. There, she launched the modern profession of a nurse (as opposed to the amateur care provided in battlefields by untrained servants or wives of soldiers). With a public plea to English society back home, she raised funds for a proper field hospital, and she used common sense and rules of hygiene to decrease the number of infections and bacterial diseases. A few years later, she founded the first school of nursing in London.

The Mission of Mercy: Florence Nightingale Receiving the Wounded at Scutari was painted by Jerry Barrett, who traveled all the way to the front to portray this famous pioneer. Although she rejected his multiple requests to pose, he managed while there to make a sketch, complaining that his model considered posing a waste of time. Had the nurse been consulted on the painting, she might have corrected an inaccurate portrayal of nursing. The real Nightingale would most likely not have allowed a wounded soldier to lie down in the dirty straw on the ground. With barely 38 nurses tending to thousands of sick and wounded, Nightingale was dealing with staggering numbers of patients—over 4,000 soldiers died within the first winter. Nightingale used her skills of organization and statistical analysis to decrease the ravages brought about by dysentery, blood infections, and typhus. *"Every nurse ought to be careful to wash her hands very frequently during the day"*; this was Nightingale's directive, surely a novelty given the mid-19th-century state of medicine.

In the end, Barrett was right—posing for the picture was as important as nursing. The painting, for all its compositional artifice and grandstanding, is a vivid portrayal of an exceptional person who overcame the barriers of her social class, sex, and social customs to create a new profession. Thanks to the artist, we have at least an imaginary commemoration of Nightingale's pioneering work.

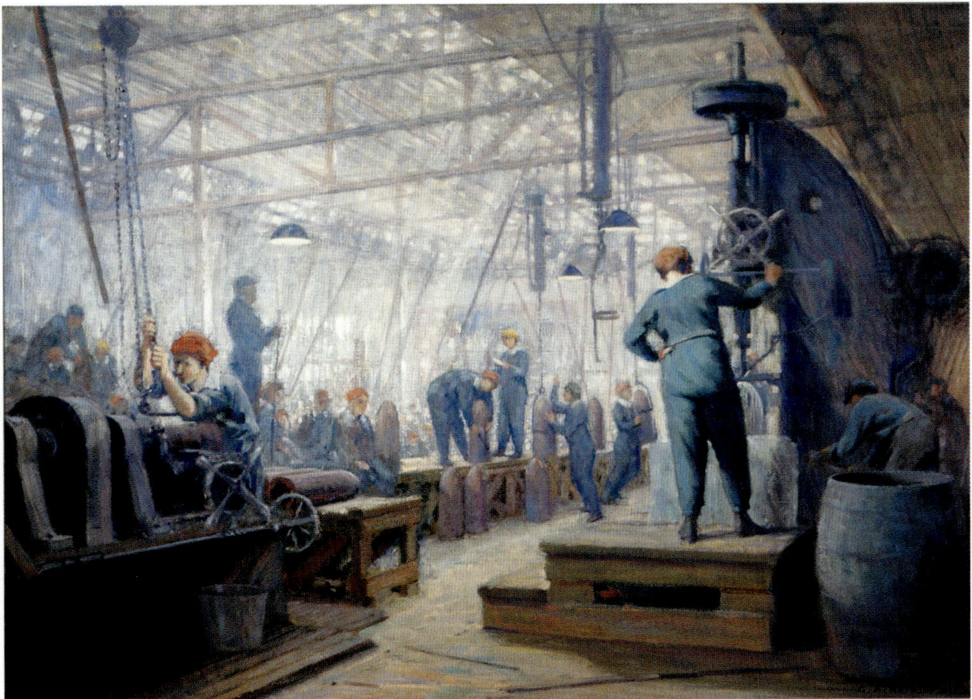

George Agnew Reid. *Women Operators*, 1919. Oil on canvas.
Canadian War Museum, Ottawa.
Photo: Public domain via Wikimedia Commons

Canada's War Museum has in its collection some artworks that portray women pushed into the workplace by World War I. One of the artists, Manly E. MacDonald, was an Ontario artist of the early 20th century who often painted farming activities from his surrounding countryside. His painting titled *Land Girls Hoeing* (page 25) draws on this farming theme, with one exception—the farmers are young women who volunteered to keep Canada's food production going. These women, who would get nicknamed "farmettes," would often wear loose, improvised overalls and broad-brimmed hats to protect their city-dweller complexions. The diagonal slashes of the produce rows and the girls' movements going the other way give this picture an alluring energy of accomplishment. These young women are also doing more than hoeing soil. They have a purpose that is driving them forward: to help with the war effort and "do their part" while their men are at the front. In 1918, there were 2,400 such women working the land in the Canadian region of Niagara.

Another painting from the same collection portrays factory workers at a car factory in Toronto. Here are women doing, for the first time, jobs that were the exclusive domain of men until the war came on. By 1917, about 25,000 Canadian women were working in factories, some of them in the production of weapons. George Agnew Reid, who studied in Paris toward the end of the 19th century, had become an eminent Canadian artist by the early 20th century. Reid participated in a commemoration of the Canadian WWI effort with *Women Operators*, a great painting that does more than just document factory work. The central space is lit with sun streaks coming through the roof onto women in blue overalls. Their orange headscarves stand out against the blue-gray lumps of the machines. There is a chilling contrast between the figures of these women and the objects they are handling—which are mortar shells.

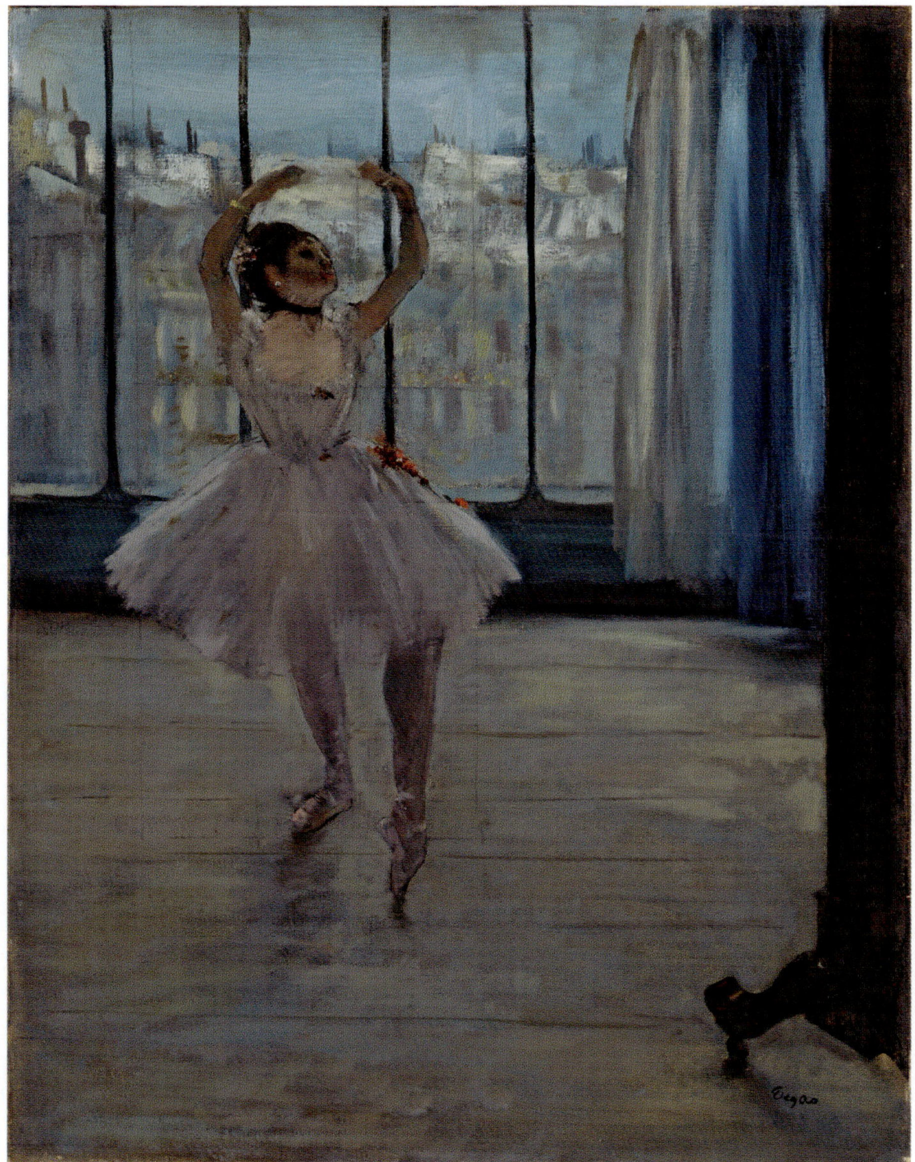

Edgar Degas. *Dancer in Front of a Window*, 1875. Oil on canvas.
The Shchukin Collection, The Pushkin State Museum of Fine Arts, Moscow.
Photo: Public domain via Wikimedia Commons

Let's not end this panorama of working women with a war picture, however. Let's go instead to one of the perennial favorites of the 19th century. Although *Dancer in Front of a Window* is by Degas—the ultimate eulogist of everything "ballet"—it also documents a technological change, hinted at by the painting's alternate title: *Dancer Posing for a Photographer*. This ballerina, a woman who works very hard every day to perfect her difficult skill, is not only posing for a painting but she is shivering in the morning light, striving to stand still for an unseen camera. While many of Degas' paintings of ballerinas are bathed in the pinkish light of a busy studio or the warm tones of a theater stage, this is a winter scene with snow on the roofs and a cold blue light that underscores the chill in which the dancer is holding still for both photographer and painter. In this case, it was probably the same person, because Degas was an accomplished photographer himself. He was fascinated by the new medium and used it a lot in his work and private life.

Technological and societal changes would soon bring about new roles for working women. While Degas' dancer would not have become a doctor, pilot, or politician, a few decades later, others soon would.

CHAPTER 4

THE TOIL

There is nothing attractive about toil—the mind-numbing effort of farming or doing some menial, repetitive tasks—to the person who is doing it. It can, however, be appealing to artists as a subject, especially if such hard-grinding toil is experienced by the "weaker sex." Artists could show hard work in a sympathetic light, often with an express purpose of tugging at the gallery public's heartstrings.

Jewish Woman with Oranges is one of the most famous canvases in Poland. Alexander Gierymski was born in Warsaw, and his early paintings from the last quarter of the 19th century portrayed the city's working class and the poorest inhabitants of the riverbank quarter. This portrait of a street-seller was painted in three versions. One of them is believed to be completely lost; one (*Jewish Woman with Lemons*) is at the provincial museum in Katowice; and this one, the most famous, went missing for decades. It was stolen in 1944 from the National Museum in Warsaw—just after the Warsaw Uprising against the German forces occupying the capital—eventually resurfacing in 2010 at an auction in Hamburg. It had to undergo an extensive restoration before being hung again (with great ceremony) at the National Museum in Warsaw. It belongs to the canon of Polish masterpieces, and even during the decades when it was missing, it was still included in Polish school textbooks.

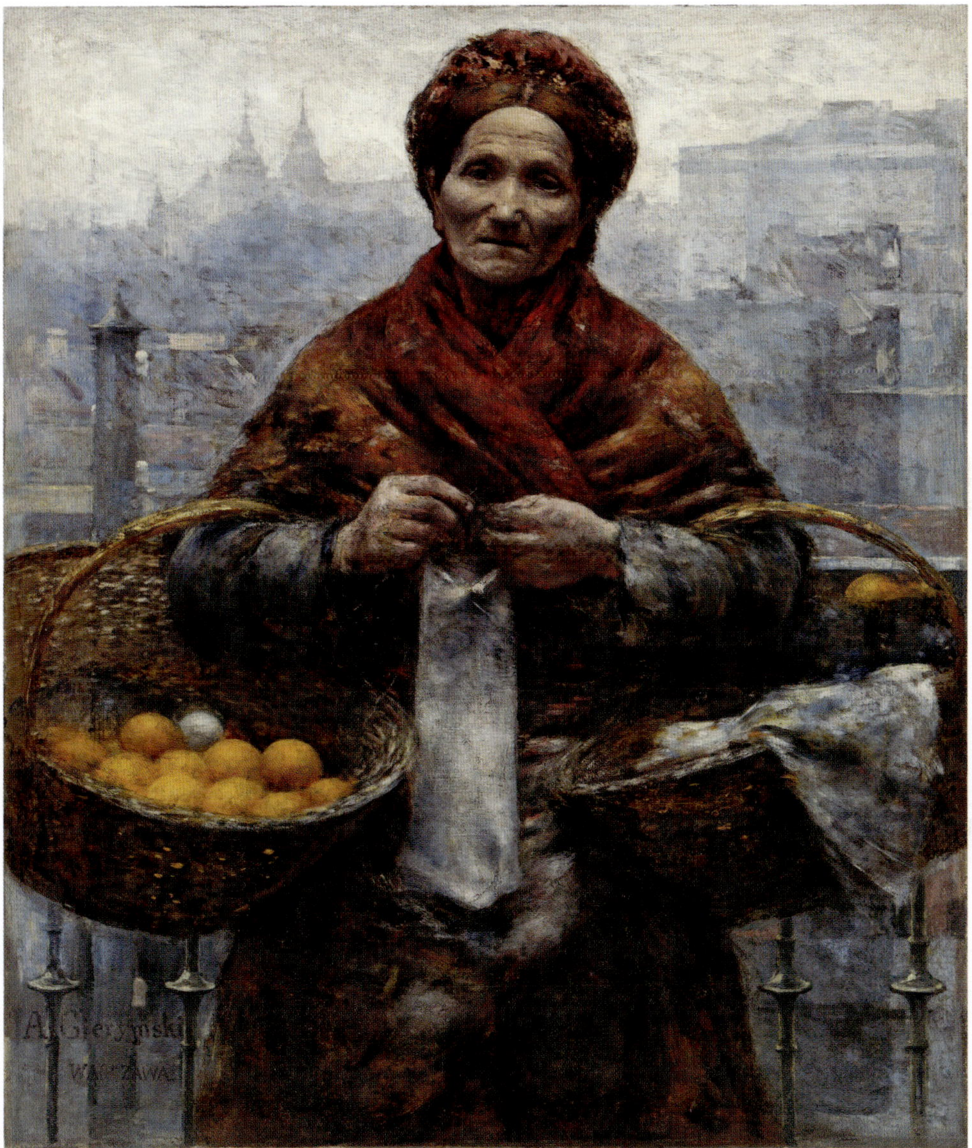

Alexander Gierymski. *Jewish Woman with Oranges*, 1881. Oil on canvas.
National Museum, Warsaw.
Photo: Public domain via Wikimedia Commons

Gierymski was a realist painter (at least until he got exposed to Impressionism when he emigrated to Paris) and to create this painting, he actually used a photograph. However, a fuzzy black-and-white photograph would have only furnished a rough guide for a painting in which the brightly hued oranges of the woman's rusty-colored shawl and red hair contrast with the blues of the city panorama and the gray sock the woman is knitting. Although Gierymski was famed for his deft use of color as well as his nuanced nightscapes, this is not why this painting is so remarkable. The old woman's expression of hopelessness is what stops the viewer's gaze. She has clearly spent a long time in poverty and misery. She is peddling luxurious, imported objects, but her own life is barely a subsistence. She does not even have a stall to sell her wares, and she is trying to make a few more coins by knitting. This old woman belongs to the poorest class of people who have to work regardless of age and for very little reward. Sad as this image is, however, it is a magnificent piece of fine art.

In 19th-century Paris, apparently as many as one quarter of all women working there were employed in laundries. Because laundry services were often open to the sidewalk, it would have been easy for an artist to watch the women's activity all day long. Degas was as fascinated by the women working in these steamy rooms as he was by ballet dancers, jockeys, and orchestra musicians. He painted laundresses for about 25 years, starting in 1869. The portrayals of the labor of Parisian workers by Degas and fellow French painter Honoré Daumier went in tandem with literary descriptions of the laborers' ceaseless work found in novels by Emile Zola and the Goncourt brothers.

This particular composition, called *Women Ironing*, is actually one of four versions by Degas (the other, very famous version is displayed at the Norton Simon Museum in Pasadena). While Degas was one of the Impressionists in terms of his loose-brushstrokes style, his use of light, and his focus on themes of daily life, he was a realist at heart, striving to capture every nuance of people's behavior. This is what he is doing in this painting, which registers a point in time in the young woman's long day. Hot, thirsty, and exhausted, she is taking a moment to stretch and to take a sip straight from the bottle, even while yawning uncontrollably. The other laundress does not even react—she is pressing the hot iron into the fabric as quickly as she can. Irons at the time had inserts (slabs that in some places were called the iron's "soul") that were periodically heated in the oven; they had to be used quickly before the heat of the insert dissipated. Laundering and ironing were hot, relentless toil.

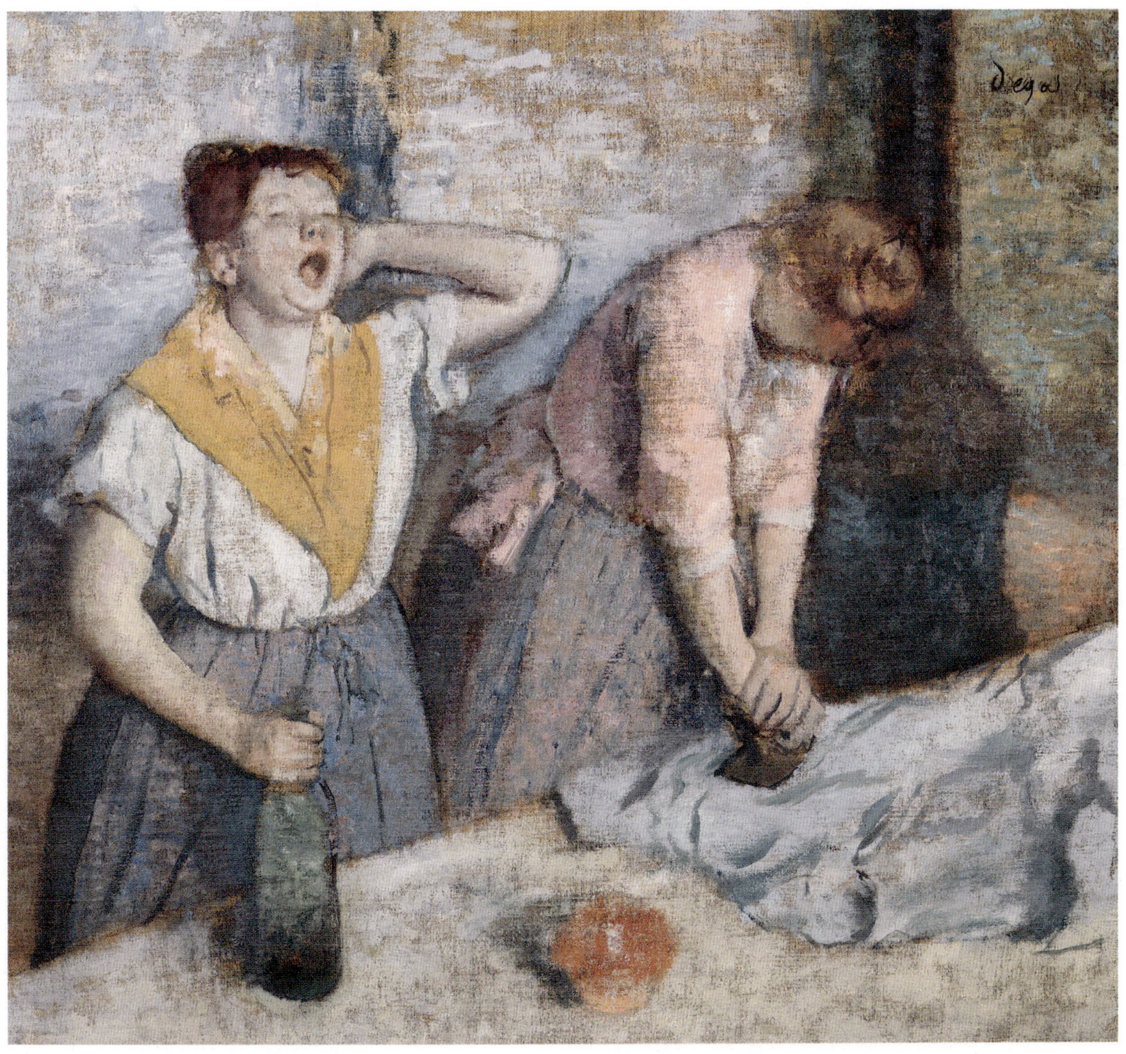

Edgar Degas. *Women Ironing/Les Repasseuses*, 1884–90. Oil on canvas.
Musée d'Orsay, Paris.
Photo: Bridgeman Images

Painted in more or less the same period but thousands of miles to the east, *The Washerwomen* by Abram Efimovich Arkhipov, a Russian realist painter who lived and worked both in Tsarist Russia and later in the Soviet Union, shows us the same theme of women laboring all day long in a hot room handling soaked fabrics.

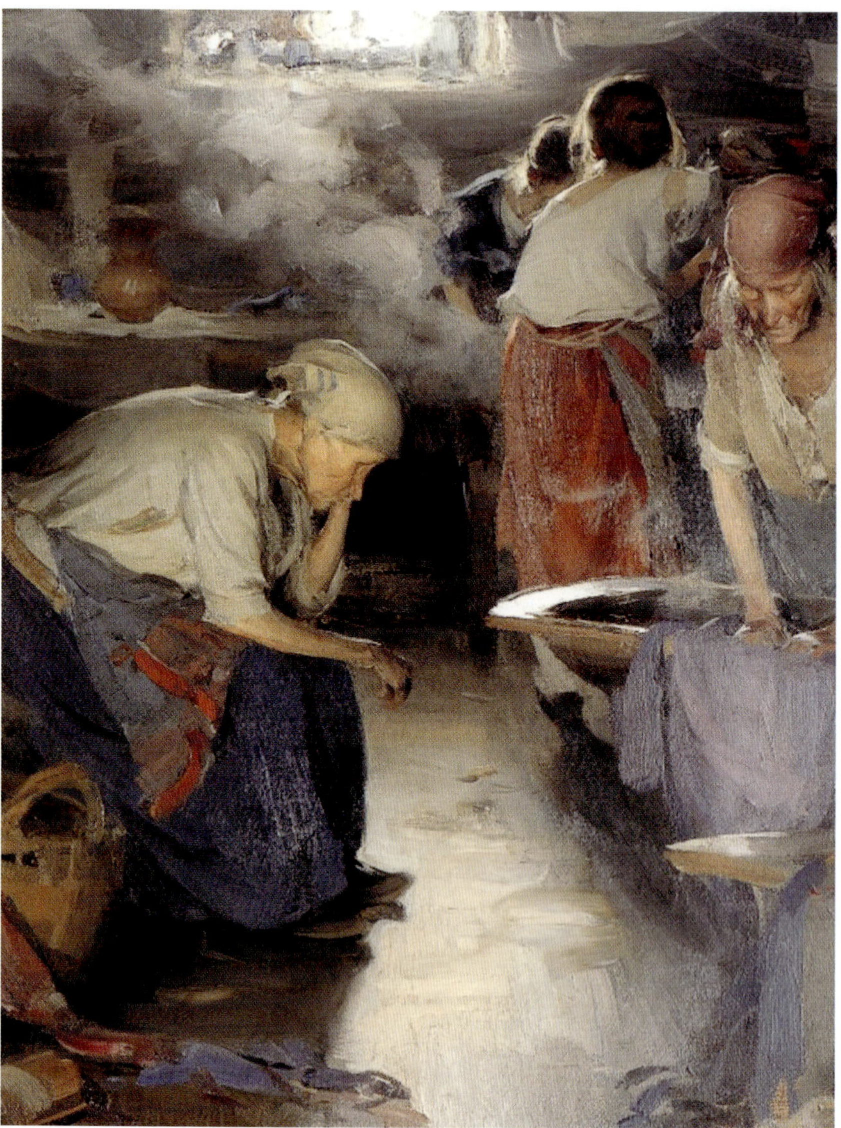

Abram Efimovich Arkhipov. *The Washerwomen*, 1901. Oil on canvas.
State Tretyakov Gallery, Moscow.
Photo: History and Art Collection/Alamy Stock Photo

Arkhipov was born in a village, and even though he spent most of his adult life in Moscow, he never forgot his country roots. He specialized in realistic portrayals of the life of the common people—both in villages and in cities. He painted many scenes from the lives of working women. For *The Washerwomen*—one of his more celebrated works—he went looking for models among the public laundries in the city. Like Degas with his ballerinas, Arkhipov would spend hours sketching these laundry workers. Unlike Degas, he painted en plein air, seeking realistic scenes of work in cities and villages; these days, he might be a photojournalist, such was his fascination with capturing life as it happened. This is why this painting has such realistic clouds of steam and smears of water on the floor—he painted what he saw in the most dramatic way possible. The heroines of this canvas are the two women in front, their bodies gaunt from physical exertion, their faces prematurely aged. One of them is intent on keeping up with the younger ones, while the other one, utterly exhausted, is just dully sitting. There is nothing left in her—no physical strength, no hope for a change, and no spiritual spark. She is completely spent. While the Degas painting is colorful and might even bring out a smile at the laundress who is yawning so unabashedly, Arkhipov's portrait of the same activity, painted in dark colors, is hopeless and accusatory. This is a portrait of people reduced to animal stupor—they will work like horses until they collapse.

For Gustave Courbet, protesting against the monarchy and the privileged classes was a life mission. In fact, he got into major trouble during the 1871 Paris Commune revolt, when he was a leader of the Communards group that toppled the column in the Place Vendôme. Courbet objected to this symbol of war and Napoleon's imperialism with a "damn the consequences" attitude. The consequences were severe for him, however; he was found responsible and ordered to pay for the new column—an enormous sum of 323,000 francs (about $1.3 million today). He was forced to go into exile to Switzerland where he eventually died, never seeing his city again.

From the very start of his career, Courbet aimed to scandalize his fellow artists, critics, and the gallery public alike. His early canvas, *The Burial at Ornans*, depicted ordinary village people instead of historical or religious figures; his self-portrait, *The Desperate Man*, was that of a wild man; and his *Young Ladies on the Banks of the Seine* was universally panned by critics as being too shocking for an exhibition display.

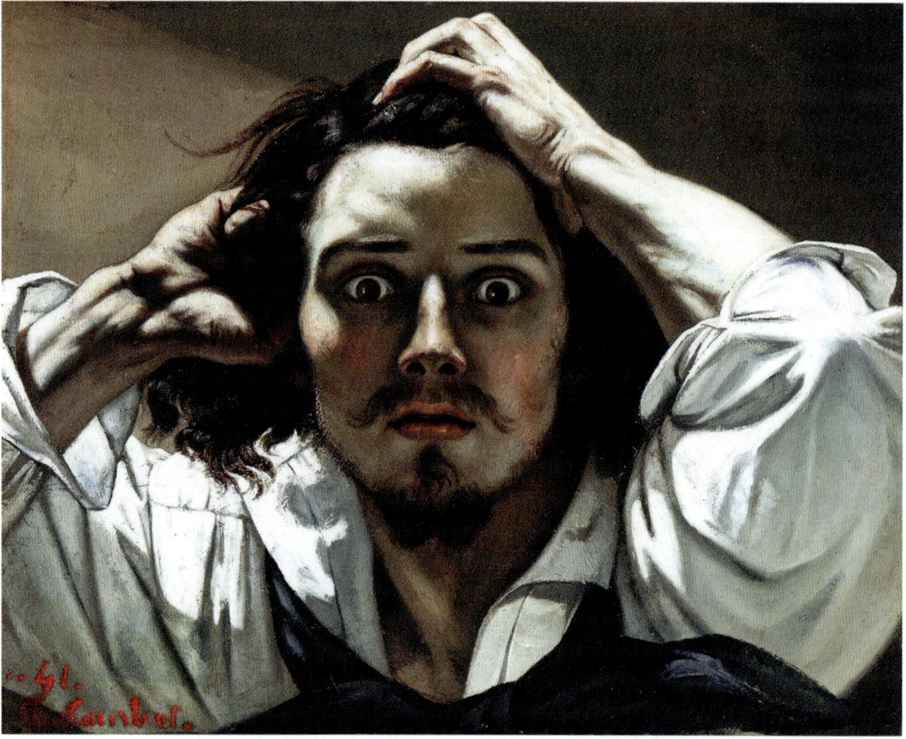

Gustave Courbet. *Self-Portrait (The Desperate Man)*, c. 1843–45. Oil on canvas.
Private collection.
Photo: Public domain via Wikimedia Commons

In 1866, when he painted his most scandalizing nude act, *The Origin of the World* (as recently as 2018, I witnessed a teenage boy gasp in shock when he stumbled on this painting at the Musée D'Orsay), he also painted *The Poor Woman in the Village*.

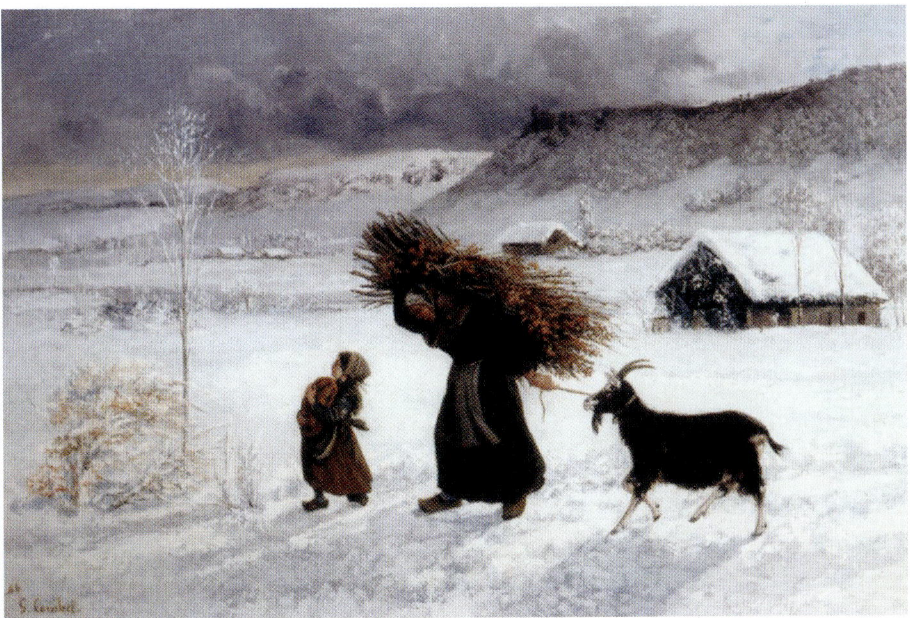

Gustave Courbet. *The Poor Woman in the Village*, 1866. Oil on canvas.
Private collection.
Photo: Public domain via Wikimedia Commons

It's not his best canvas, tottering dangerously close to the Victorian cuteness of genre pictures—what with a snowy landscape, a cute goat, and an even cuter little girl leading the small group—but there is no mistaking the burden that the woman is carrying. The wood bundle is almost bending her in half; her only treasure is that milk-giving goat, and she obviously has no choice but to labor hard to provide for her child. Cute or not, Courbet says, this is how poor people struggled, far away from the salons of Paris.

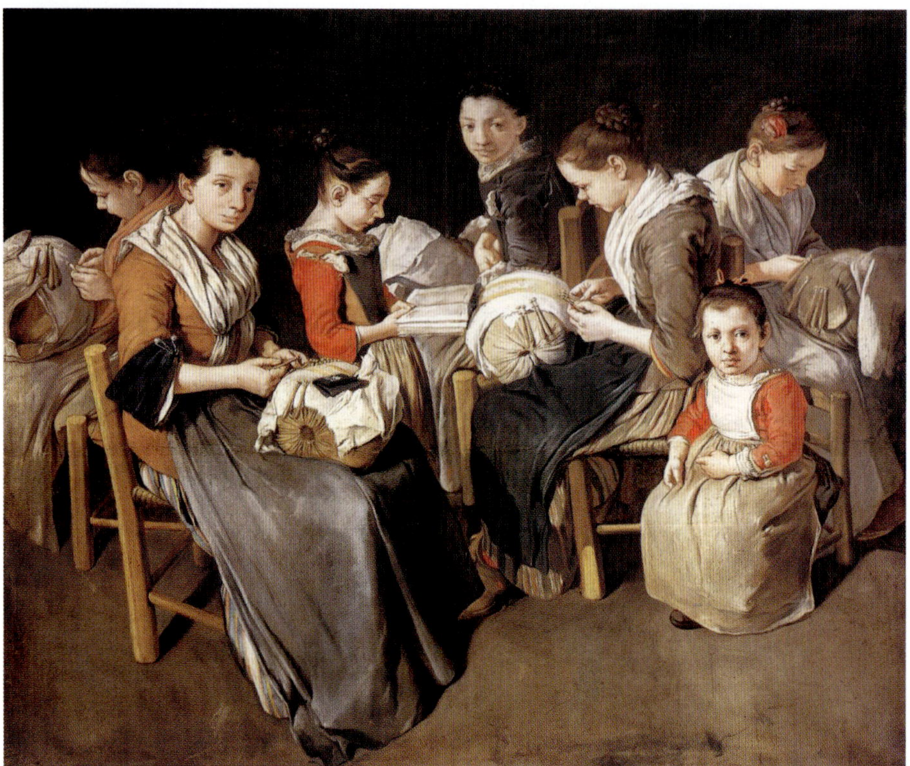

Giacomo Ceruti. *Women Working on Pillow Lace (The Sewing School)*, 1720s. Oil on canvas. Private collection.
Photo: Public domain via Wikimedia Commons

Eighteenth-century art is that of Rococo tapestries, frescoes, and paintings full of mythological allegories and religious scenes rendered in an excessive style of twisted lines and bulging fabrics. François Boucher (in tapestry) or Giovanni Battista Tiepolo (on ceilings) created decorations well suited to all the multitiered wigs, satin ribbons, puffy silk gowns, masque balls, and elaborate etiquette that would eventually end with the French Revolution, Napoleonic wars, and technological changes of the 19th century. While the music of the period reached heights of clarity and precise construction, especially once Mozart and Handel appeared on the scene, Rococo paintings went in the other direction—toward an opulence that outdid the Baroque to the extreme. Not surprisingly, art eventually swung toward Neoclassicism when the excesses became... well, too much.

In this context, it is even more remarkable to look at *Women Working on Pillow Lace*, painted around 1720 by Italian artist Giacomo Ceruti. His art was far removed from the mythological extravaganzas of his contemporaries. Like Jean-Baptiste-Siméon Chardin, Ceruti painted the other side of society, the one that was shown in satires and genre paintings but less often observed with a realistic eye. Here, he portrays work at an orphanage in Brescia, the city in northern Italy where he lived and a place known for its Dutch-style industriousness. Orphanages often were glorified workhouses. Girls and young women with no families and no dowries were put to work at the earliest age possible. There is one girl here who is reading the Bible to all the other girls, who are bending over their boring and exacting work of lace-making. Their faces are curiously similar, as if Ceruti wanted to say that this mind-numbing work deprived them of individuality. These girls are staring at us expressionlessly as if their life had ended even before it began.

Realist paintings of the 18th and 19th centuries were probably some of the last direct expressions of artists' empathy toward the toil of the poor. With the advent of photo reportage, the burden of portraying women at work, and especially excessively hard work, largely shifted from fine art to photography. By the 20th century, most fine artists had moved on to abstract or surrealist paintings, pop art, or performance and installation art.

CHAPTER 5

PRINCESSES AND SERVANTS

We do not know who illustrated the *Book of the City of Ladies*, but we know the author: Christine de Pizan (or de Pisan). This miniature portrays her as the woman in a blue dress who is placing a hand on her book and receiving the Lady of Reason (with a mirror), Lady Rectitude (with a ruler), and Lady Justice (with a measuring cup). This is also an allegory of de Pizan setting out to write her book, which is metaphorically imagined as the construction of a wall, using a "spade of intelligence" and a "mortar of ink" in a "field of letters." Real princesses would not have been doing masonry, but this symbolic portrayal of the creative process and writing remains as relevant today as it was then—we still refer to "building sentences" and "constructing a story." What is more unusual, of course, is the fact that de Pizan was a woman writing at the end of the Middle Ages; at the time, educated women might have written letters or personal poems, but not actual books—and they certainly would not have written books as a way to earn a living.

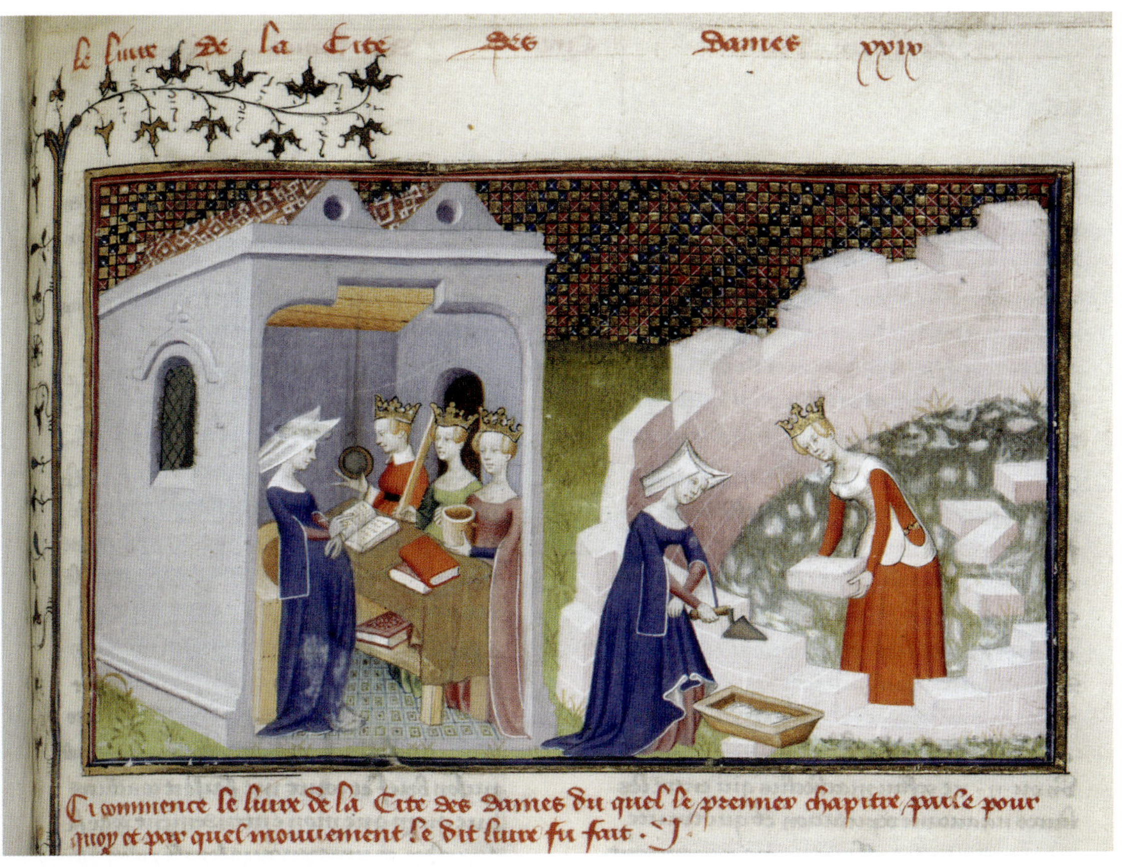

Christine de Pizan. Miniature from *Book of the City of Ladies*, c. 1405.
Illumination on vellum. British Library, London.
Photo: © British Library Board. All Rights Reserved/Bridgeman Images

De Pizan came from Italy with her father, an astrologer, to the Parisian court of King Charles V called "the Wise." There, she had a happy marriage and three children, but by age 25, she found herself widowed. Having lost all three of her protectors —her husband, her father, and her royal patron—she then spent decades trying to survive by writing and copying, all the while taking care of her children and relatives. All of this took place during the Hundred Years' War—not the easiest time for anyone to survive.

De Pizan never remarried, and her single status actually became her professional weapon—as master of her own time and decisions, she could devote herself to intellectual pursuits. She could also retreat to her own room (a rarity in those times) to study and compose her writings, eventually becoming not only an accomplished poet but also a commissioned writer of the king's biography. Having experienced first-hand what it was like to live without the usual (in her time) safety net of men providing income and protection, de Pizan wrote this book in defense of women's value in society. In it, she lists numerous famous women—from mythological Amazons to the Empress Theodora, and from all the saints to all the queens (165 women altogether)—whose achievements and virtues rivaled those of men.

Her book was also a response to a very popular allegory, the *Romance of the Rose*; the medieval love story had been started as a typical romantic poem, but it was completed by a different author, a misogynist who criticized women as wanton, false, and useless creatures. *City of Ladies* was copied and illustrated in Paris under de Pizan's supervision. The fact that such manuscripts were precious enabled the author to make a living from their production. Toward the end of her life, de Pizan retreated to a convent, a rare safe place during the raging conflicts of the never-ending war. Her last poem was written in 1429 in praise of Joan of Arc—another brave woman who proved her worth against male warriors.

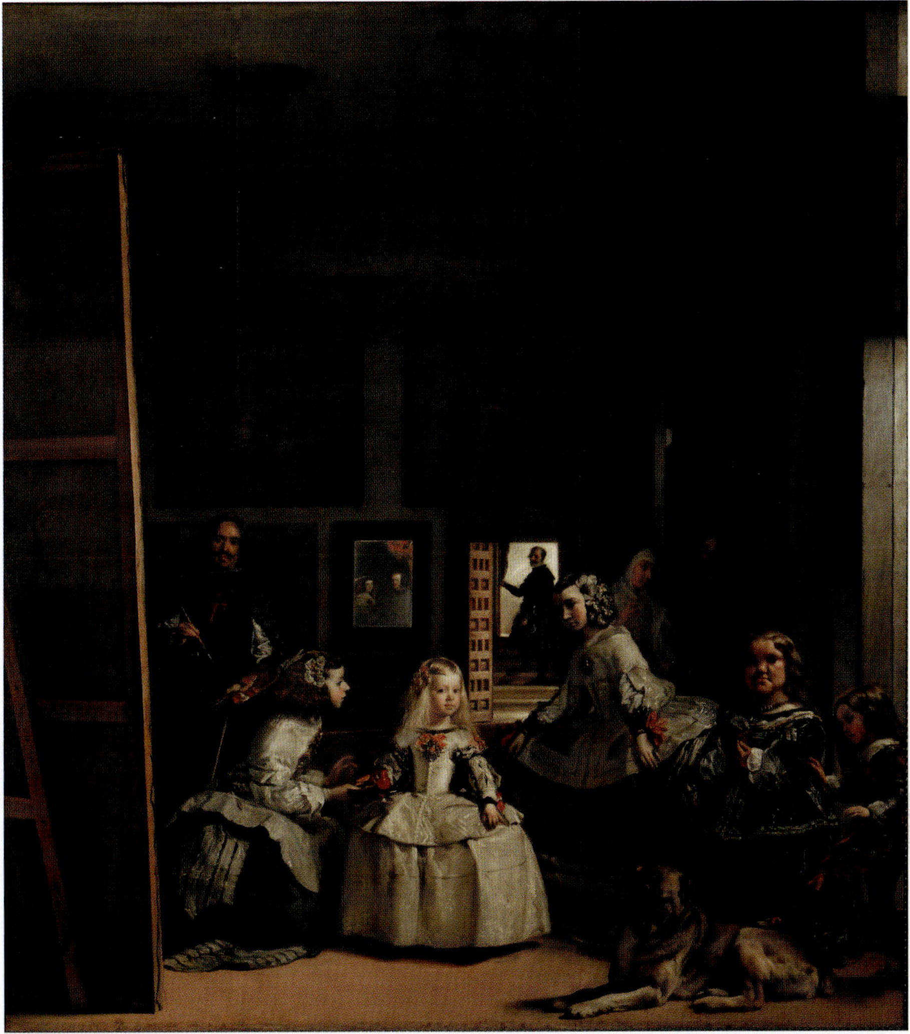

Diego Velázquez. *Las Meninas*, c. 1656. Oil on canvas.
Museo del Prado, Madrid.
Photo: Public domain via Wikimedia Commons

Las Meninas (The Maids of Honor) was a celebrated canvas from its very beginning. The centerpiece is a portrait of the Infanta Margarita Teresa, who was a royal princess and a daughter of King Philip IV, so the painting immediately entered the Spanish royal collection. It is one of the most complex compositions in the history of art, showing a group of people in the center, a figure in the back, and—reflected in the mirror—the royal couple of Philip IV and Queen Mariana. The mirror either reflects them as they enter the room, or perhaps it just reflects their portrait that the artist is creating on a big easel. This is also a commentary on the art of painting, as well as an optical illusion (which every painting is, by its very nature) and a discourse on Velázquez's position as an artist-creator rather than just an artisan.

There have been countless books and dissertations written about this painting all over the world, and Picasso painted about 40 variations on the theme of this painting. However, we can also just examine this quite familiar masterpiece from the point of view of the people who appear in it. Here, we have both princesses and servants; the royals; courtiers; and a special royal servant in the person of Velázquez. The little crown princess is standing stiffly, turning her head away from a kneeling maid and a jug that is being offered to her. This is not really an ordinary five-year-old child; this is someone trained from toddlerhood to command, to keep straight and immobile when the occasion demands, and to treat her entourage as servants. She knows not to smile in public, and she would never attempt any carefree holding of hands. She may have amusing companions—a massive but docile dog and a pair of little people (the Spanish court was famous for its precious dwarves)—but her dress and posture are regal and formal. We only see Infanta's parents indistinctly in the mirror (what a brave way to portray a royal patron), and we can infer that Velázquez is painting them in the huge canvas in front of him. Thanks to this "picture-within-a-picture" structure, we have three royals in one room (the royal couple are reflected in the mirror) and a retinue of the titular meninas and various courtiers.

However, the most important royal servant here is Velázquez himself. This was 17th-century Spain, ruled over by an absolute monarch whose wealth came from military conquests and whose right to rule—viewed as ordained by God—meant that everyone in his kingdom was his servant. Unlike a free-spirited artist of the 21st century (who might take on a commission but otherwise be a respected and famous person), a 17th-century painter like Velázquez would have been considered a craftsman—perhaps admired for his skill but with a position at the royal court that amounted to little more than being a wall decorator, with no military power, no noble title, and no independence. As a result, Velázquez was quite obsessed with social advancement and always in pursuit of ennoblement; toward the end of his life, he spent more time being the marshal of the royal household than as an artist. In this virtuoso painting, ostensibly just a portrait of a little princess, he positions himself as different from the royal servants—he is in the process of creating an artwork that will outlast all the royals in the picture. And so it did.

St. Elizabeth was a 13th-century royal princess who became venerated for her devotion in serving the needs of the poor. Daughter of the king of Hungary, she married a German duke at age fourteen, bore him three children, and, after a few years of happy marriage, was widowed at the age of 20. Left in a castle with her disapproving mother-in-law, she sought refuge in her piety.

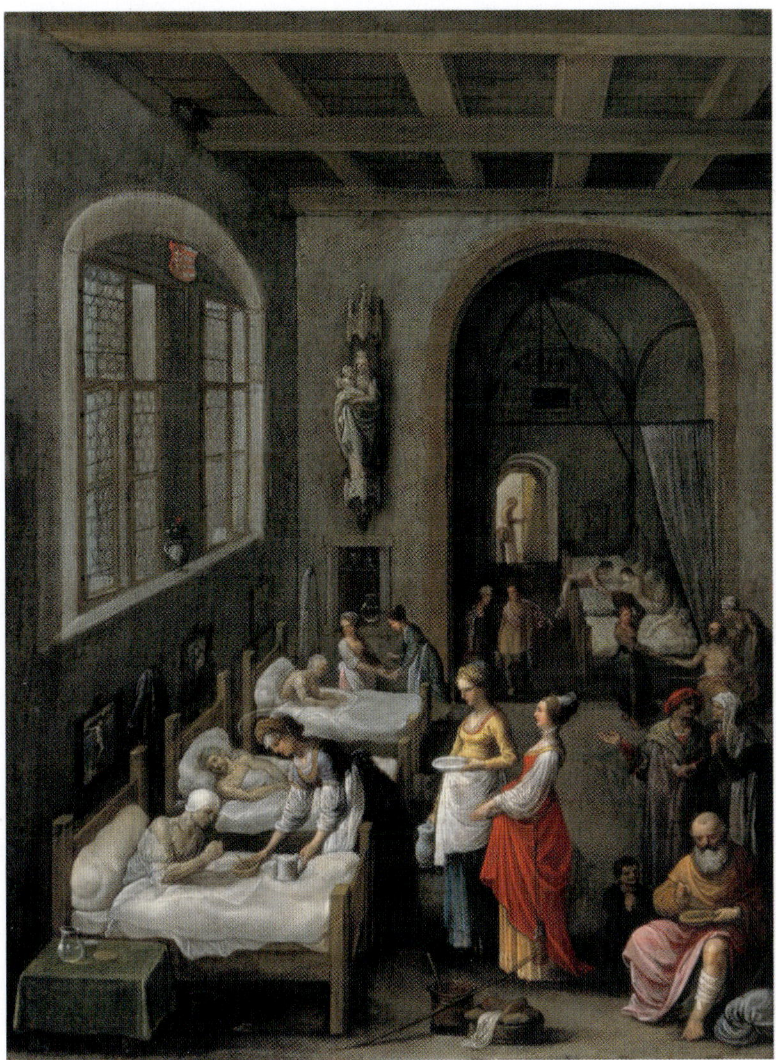

Adam Elsheimer. *Saint Elizabeth of Hungary Bringing Food for the Inmates of a Hospital*, c. 1598. Oil on copper.
Wellcome Collection, London.

From a young age, Elizabeth was heavily influenced by the order of the Franciscans and the idea of service to the poor and the sick. An apocryphal story of her sainthood tells of her meeting her husband when she is carrying some bread for the poor. Knowing that her husband disapproves of her excessive engagement with the affairs of the lower classes, she lies to him, saying that she is just carrying roses. When he makes her disclose what she is hiding underneath her cloak, lo and behold, she is found to be holding a bouquet. This is the so-called "miracle of roses of St. Elizabeth." Apocryphal stories aside, Elizabeth was famous for renouncing her royal birth and princely status in favor of humble service to the poor. Her charitable work culminated in her founding and running a hospital and a shelter. Unfortunately, she did not last long; after exposure to leprosy and other diseases, she died at age 24.

A 16th-century painting by Adam Elsheimer immortalized this role of St. Elizabeth as a tireless caregiver. Elsheimer was a very "international" artist (born German, worked in Italy, passionately collected in England, influenced Rubens and other Dutch artists). The full title of this small painting is *Saint Elizabeth Offers a Bowl of Food and a Tankard of Drink to a Male Patient in the Hospital in Marburg, Germany*. St. Elizabeth, identified with a halo, bends over a sick patient while two of her assistants wait behind her with some bowls. Elsheimer paints a lot of realistic details—a pisspot under the bed, a rope to pull down a chandelier for changing candles, bandages on a patient's leg. Despite their avowed humility in service to the poor, the three ladies are dressed in the full splendor of colorful gowns, and there are other beautiful splashes of color, such as the green velvet of a tablecloth and the pink-orange robes of a man sitting in the front. Elsheimer made full use of the copperplate on which this oil was painted. Copper backing was not often used in paintings, but here it allowed for vivid colors and the picture's glossy sheen.

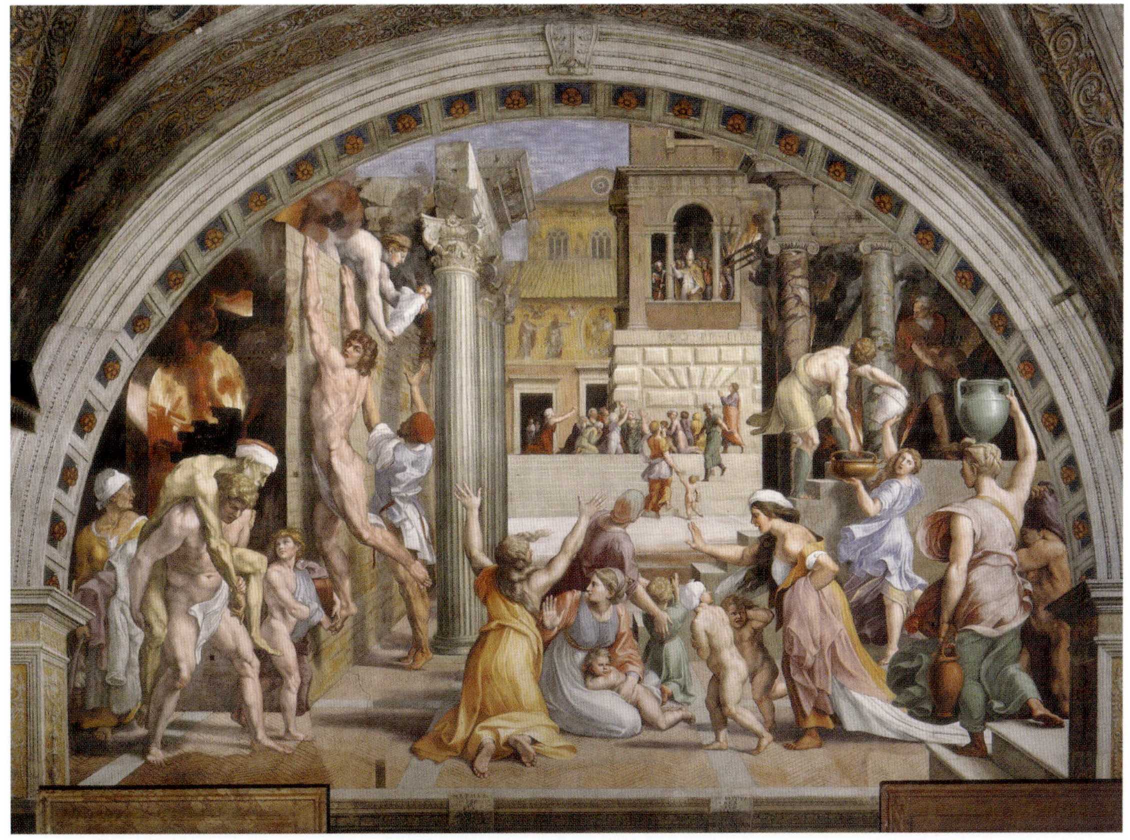

Raphael. *The Fire in the Borgo*, 1516. Fresco.
Stanza dell'Incendio di Borgo, Apostolic Palace, Vatican Museums and Galleries, Vatican City.
Photo: Public domain via Wikimedia Commons

This is the last painting in these chapters about "women at work," following the principle that you leave the best for last. Raphael does not need much introduction, since any art lover is familiar with his exquisite Madonnas, portraits, and religious scenes. He spent decades decorating the Vatican walls, first for Pope Julius II and then for his successor, Pope Leo X, who was installed in 1513.

A year later, Raphael, who already had under his belt the decorations for three other rooms, including *The School of Athens*, created illustrations of great deeds by previous popes for the private dining room—a retreat where the pope would listen to readings and songs and entertain friends. The frescoes in this room include the crowning of Charlemagne, a naval battle at Ostia, and a miracle by the 9th-century Pope Leo IV, who extinguished "by the sign of the Cross a great fire, which had burn'd down the quarter where Saracens and Lombards liv'd." It is from this fresco, entitled *The Fire in the Borgo*, that this Vatican room derives its name, Stanza dell'Incendio.

Frescoes, which demanded the very fast work of applying paint onto wet plaster, were completed by a team of painters. Raphael would design the painting and execute some parts, while the rest would be completed by his assistants. Giulio Romano, a pupil at Raphael's workshop and later a famed court painter and architect for Federico Gonzaga of Mantua, received partial credit for creating this fresco, but the design of the artwork and key parts of the painting are credited to Raphael.

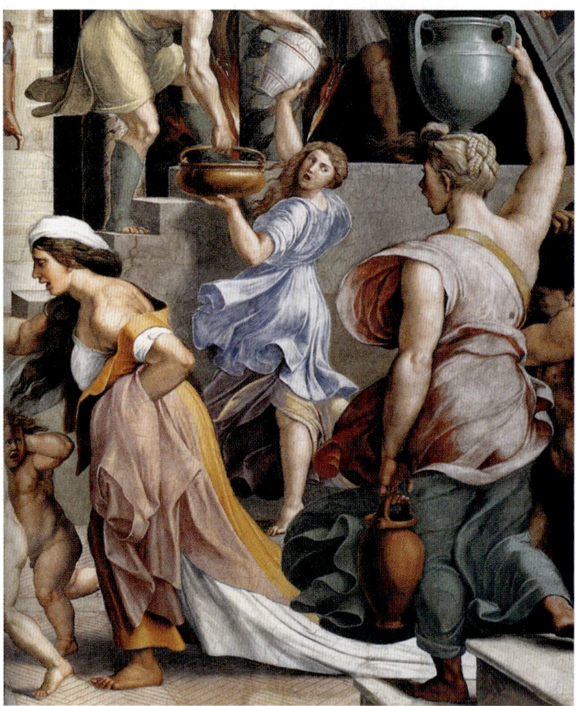

Raphael. Detail from *The Fire in the Borgo*, 1516. Fresco.
Stanza dell'Incendio di Borgo, Apostolic Palace, Vatican Museums and Galleries, Vatican City.
Photo: Public domain via Wikimedia Commons

Raphael placed the fire-suppressing pope in the center but far away, in a loggia. To the left, we see people saving themselves from the fire—a woman is handing over her baby, while a terrified man is climbing down the wall, and an old man is being carried out. In the center, a group of women and children display mixed reactions; some are clearly still gripped by the panic of the disaster, but others have already noticed the miracle of fire abatement. However, the most outstanding part of this fresco is the portrait of two women carrying water. The one in the back—in the water line with two men—is calling out for more jugs and is intent on dousing the fire. However, the other woman, who has dutifully carried in more water, is already aware of the fire's disappearance. She is not even looking at the water line. Mouth agape, she is observing the fire's sudden disappearance. She is the closest to us, the viewers, and it is through her astonishment that we are intended to perceive this miracle.

These two water-carrying women are some of the most gracious human figures in the history of art. Raphael borrowed constantly from all the masters he could—Perugino (who was his teacher), da Vinci (who he met around 1506), Michelangelo (Bramante secretly let him in to study the Sistine Chapel being painted), Botticelli (whose art he could study at the Medici court in Florence), and many others. These two servant women perhaps borrow some of their statuesque figures from Michelangelo or antiquity, but they are really Raphael's own creation. His serving girls are more regal than princesses by other artists.

PART II

Exhibitions

All the stories in this part were originally written as coverage of exhibitions, real ones that I attended in person and virtual ones that were organized by museums, but due to the pandemic in 2020–2021 they were only open to press coverage via online access. An exhibition of Artemisia Gentileschi in London and a Frida Kahlo exhibition in San Francisco are examples of such virtual exhibitions.

CHAPTER 6

SOFONISBA ANGUISSOLA (c. 1535–1625) LAVINIA FONTANA (1552–1614)

"Her paintings were celebrated for their calm and gentle style, and for the particularity that she was a woman, and had risen above the usual course of those of her sex, for whom wool and linen are some materials appropriate for their fingers and hands."

~ Father Andrés Ximenez writing about Lavinia Fontana in 1764

Sofonisba Anguissola and Lavinia Fontana were two talented 16th-century portraitists who are almost completely unknown outside art history books. Why? Mainly because they were women. The trend is changing with more museums mounting exhibitions that specifically celebrate art created by women. This time, a major reappraisal of female contributions to art was a gift of the Prado National Museum. In 2020, the Prado was in the midst of celebrating its 200th anniversary, with the exhibition *A Tale of Two Women Painters* as the icing on the cake in one of the most venerated art collections in Europe. The exhibition presented over 60 works meticulously gathered from collections and museums from around Europe and the U.S. It is encouraging that the home of Goya, El Greco, and Velázquez created such a delightful showcase of two female artists who are finally receiving their due recognition in the Old Masters' club.

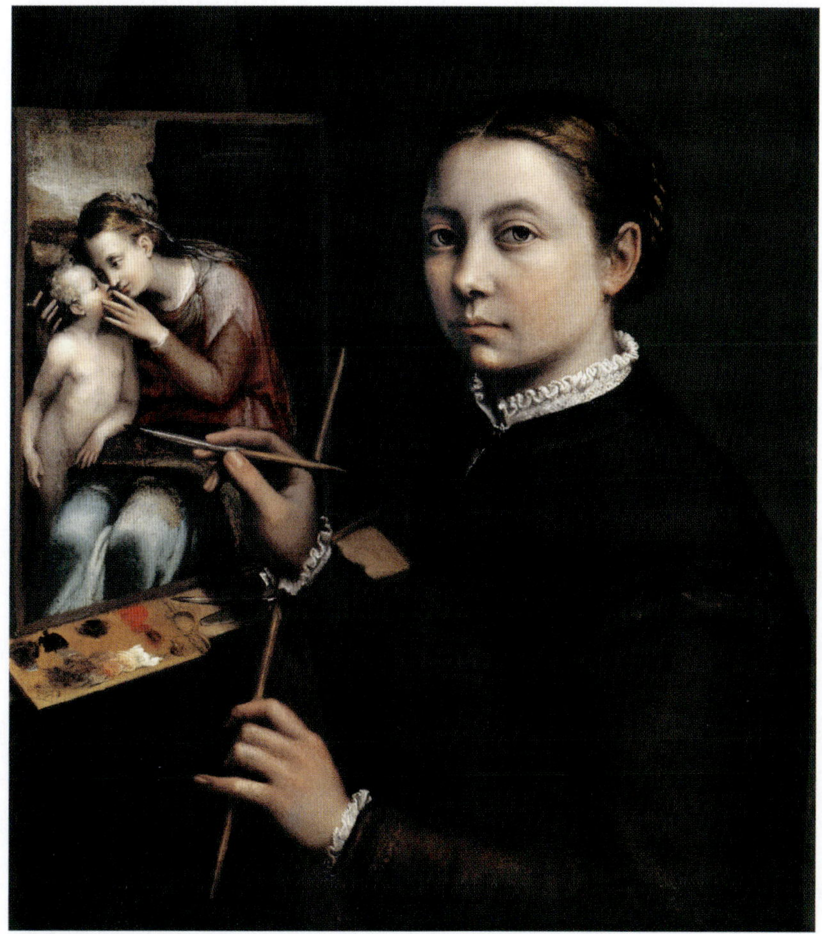

Sofonisba Anguissola. *Self-Portrait at the Easel*, 1556–57. Oil on canvas.
Muzeum Zamek, Łańcut.
Photo: Public domain via Wikimedia Commons

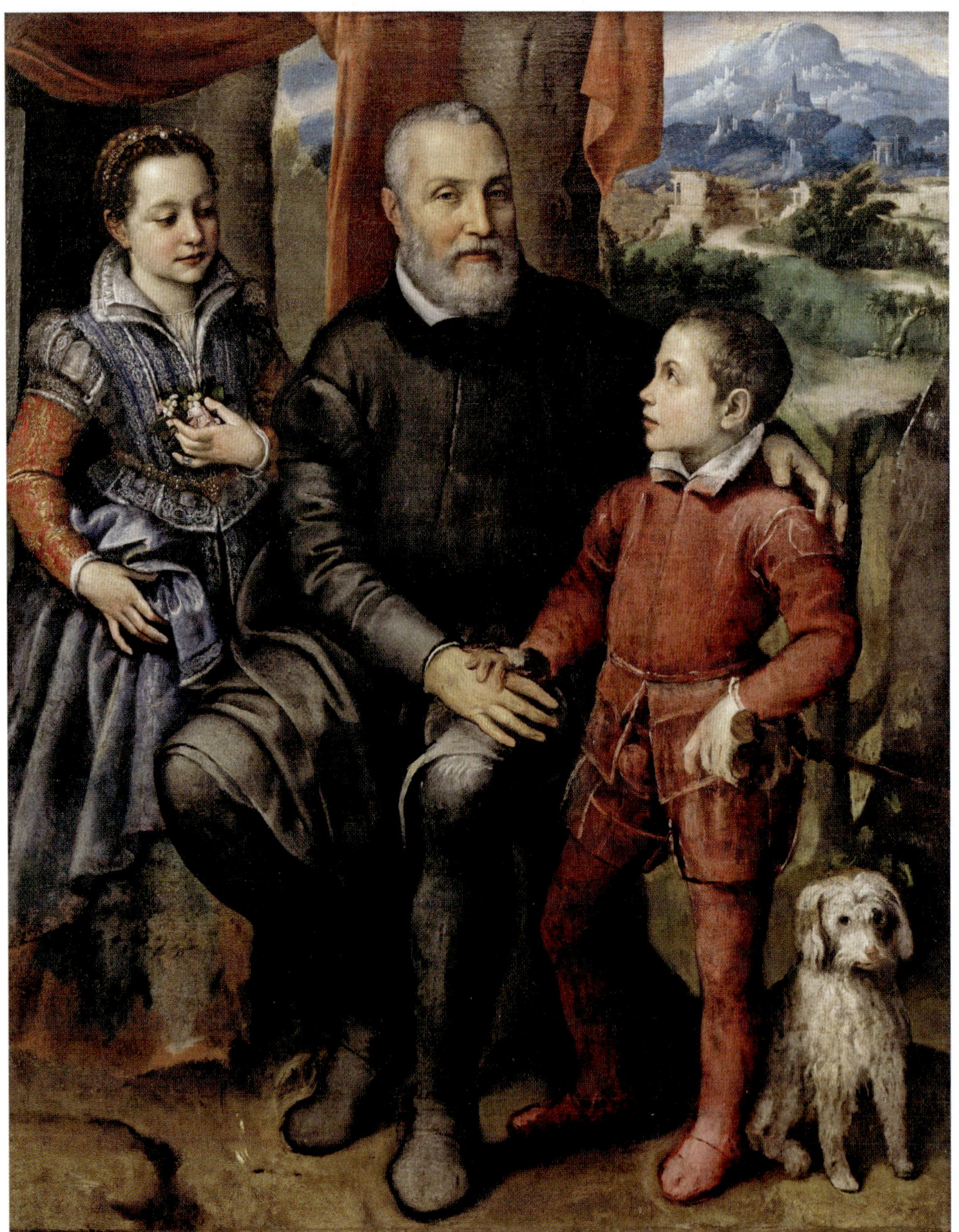

Sofonisba Anguissola. *Portrait Group with the Artist's Father Amilcare Anguissola and Her Siblings Minerva and Astrubale*, c. 1559. Oil on canvas.

Nivaagards Malerisamling, Niva.

Photo: Public domain CC0 via Wikimedia Commons

During her lifetime, Sofonisba Anguissola was famous and much praised. Her father was a socially ambitious but perennially cash-strapped minor noble in 16th-century Italy. He recognized early on that Sofonisba's and their family's ticket to prosperity was through her gift of art. He first provided his daughter with art teachers, then sent her drawings to Michelangelo, and when she attained a solid reputation as a portraitist, he helped her to secure a position as a lady-in-waiting at the court of the Spanish king Philip II. Anguissola's art training was appropriate for a lady's education of the time, but as she surpassed any amateur efforts, she became a pioneer—a professional female artist getting formal commissions. She is the only woman painter mentioned by Vasari in his famous *The Lives of the Most Excellent Painters, Sculptors and Architects*—the first biographical art book that, to this day, is the ultimate source of information on Italian Renaissance painters.

During her youth in Italy, Anguissola painted herself and her family—the subjects most accessible for a lady at home—but in a way that was far from conventional. One of the highlights of the Prado exhibition was a picture called *The Chess Game,* loaned from a castle in Poland. This is one of the most original family portraits ever done. We see three Anguissola sisters (Lucia, Europa, and Minerva) playing and laughing at a game while supervised by a nanny. Even though such young girls would surely have spent a lot of time playing games and talking, this is not a realistic documentation of family life. Anguissola dressed her sitters in elaborate silks, pearls, and gold thread, painted a classic if fictitious landscape suitable for a formal court portrait, and put the chessboard on a priceless Persian carpet. She created a carefully imagined and constructed narrative told in splendid visuals. This picture as well as her other family portraits display an imagination and color that stand out from the stiff conventions of Renaissance portraits.

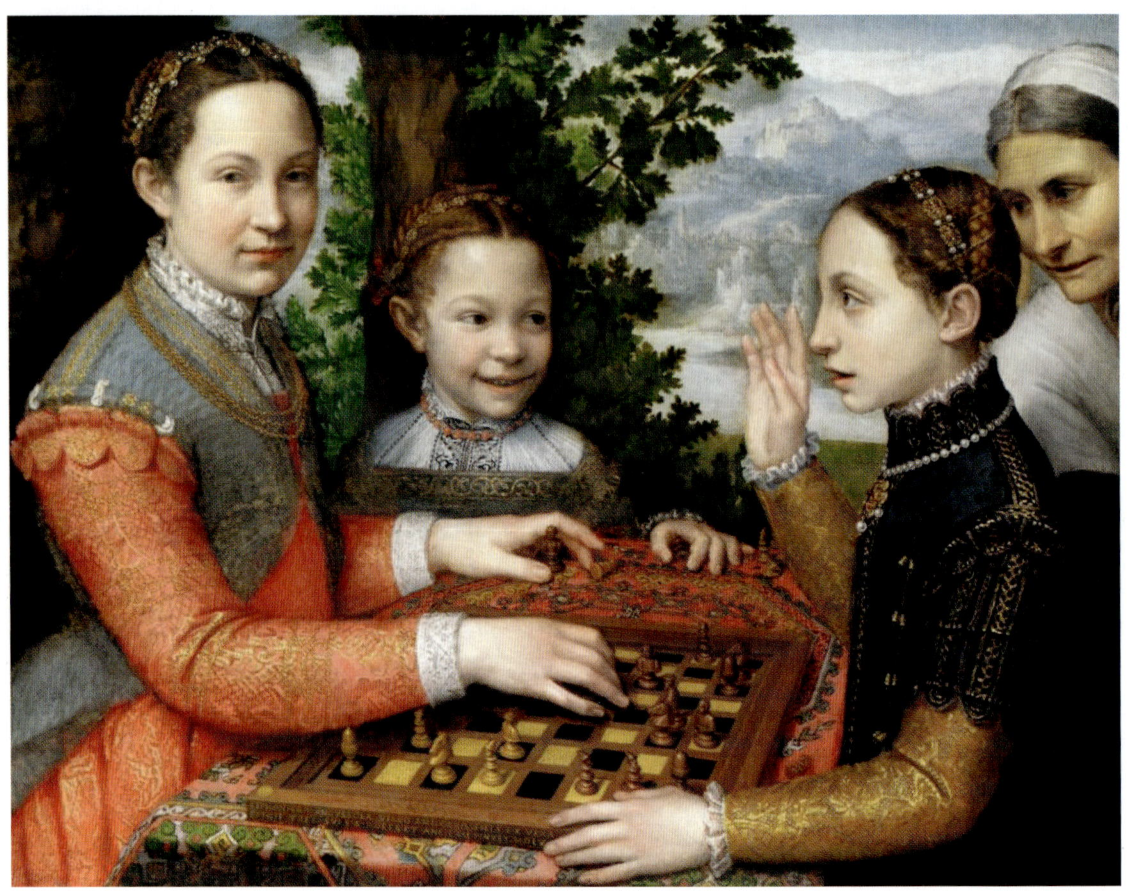

Sofonisba Anguissola. *The Chess Game*, 1555. Oil on canvas.
The Raczyński Foundation at the National Museum, Poznań.
Photo: Public domain via Wikimedia Commons

Being a painter, even one as accomplished and famed as young Sofonisba, was not a socially acceptable life goal for a lady, so the next "career step" was to secure her a post at the royal court of Spain. There, she became a painting teacher for Queen Isabel de Valois, and as a member of the royal entourage she was rewarded in jewelry and costly fabrics. However, she was not considered a court painter, despite numerous royal family portraits she executed during that time, and her pictures from that period are not signed. This is probably one of the reasons why her contributions to world art and Spanish portraiture have been so neglected for centuries. As soon as Anguissola passed away in Italy, at the impressive age of 94, her fame and respect started to fade away all the way to obscurity for a good 300 years.

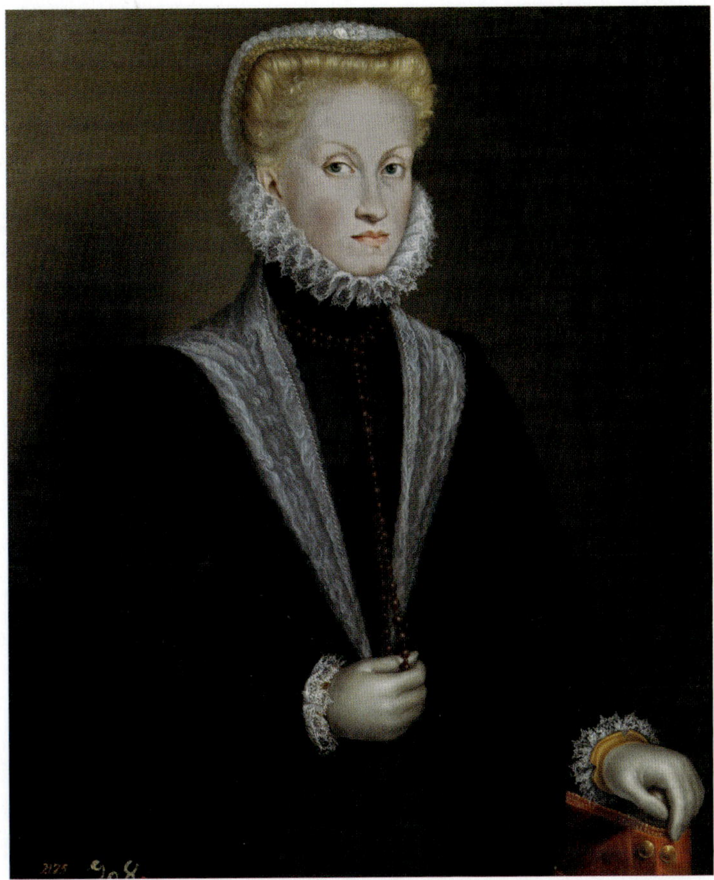

Sofonisba Anguissola. *Queen Anne of Austria*, c. 1573. Oil on canvas.
Museo del Prado, Madrid.
Photo: Public domain via Wikimedia Commons

Her oblivion as an artist became even more pronounced when her Spanish court paintings became ascribed to other artists, all male of course. As late as 1948, the official portraits of Spanish royalty—Philip II and two of his wives, Anne of Austria and Isabel de Valois—were still attributed to the Spanish painter Juan Pantoja de la Cruz (1533–1608). There was even a debate that they might be copies of paintings by the official court portraitist of the time, Alonso Sánchez Coello (1531–1588). Anguissola's name did not even enter into critical consideration for these paintings for several centuries. It took a female art historian, Maria Kusche, to reevaluate accepted attributions in the second part of the 20th century. In fact, the Prado exhibition presented several important court paintings for possible attribution as Anguissola's.

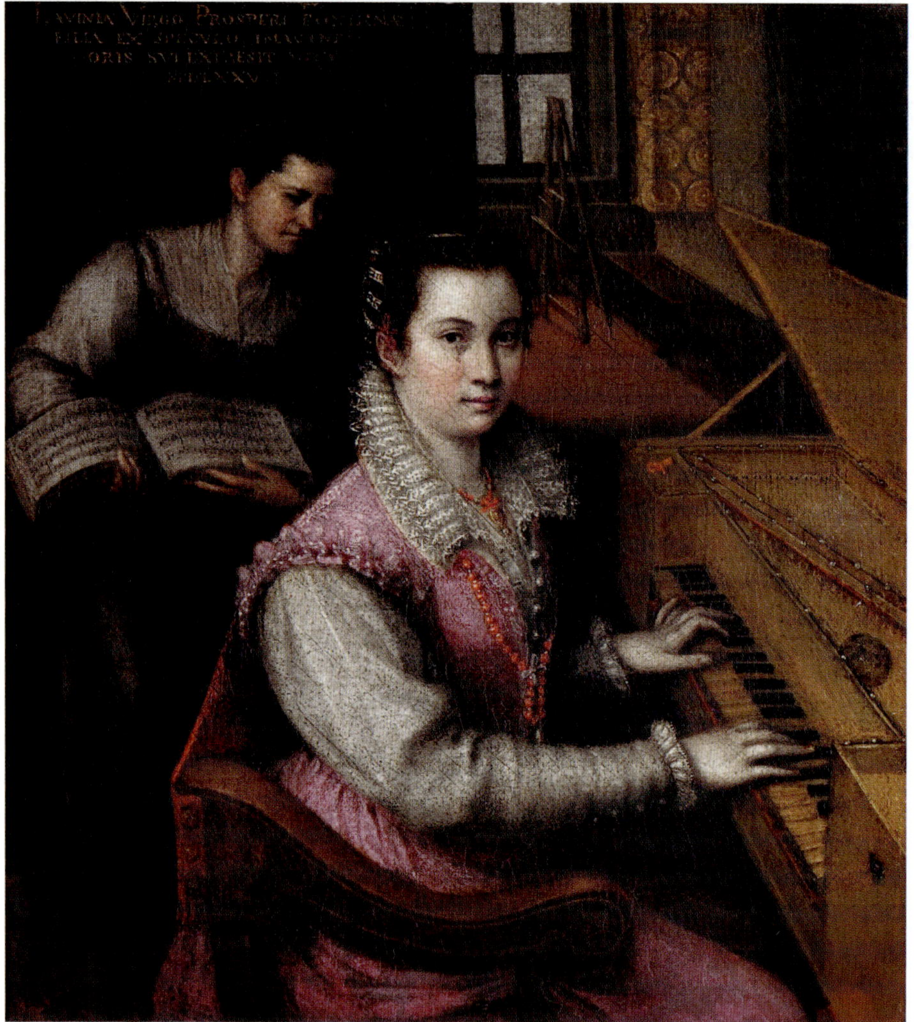

Lavinia Fontana. *Self-Portrait at the Spinet*, 1577. Oil on canvas.
Accademia Nazionale di San Luca, Rome.
Photo: © Fine Art Images/Bridgeman Images

The exhibition also juxtaposed Anguissola's lifetime output with that of her artistic follower Lavinia Fontana, another Italian woman whose sheer talent allowed her the position of a professional artist and whose works were sought after by nobles, kings, and popes. One of her earliest paintings from 1577, *Self-Portrait at the Spinet*, is a direct reference to Anguissola's very similar self-portrait. Some of its elements follow the intellectual conventions of the time—showing a lady at a musical instrument was a way to signal the refinement of the sitter, in this case Fontana herself. Since the musical notation is held by the servant away from her eyes, this gives a further clue that the sitter is able to read the musical notation but does not even need it since she knows it by heart. While these were prevailing artistic conventions, Fontana's skill was anything but conventional. The skin tones are delicate and glowing while her sumptuous dress displays all the shades of mauve.

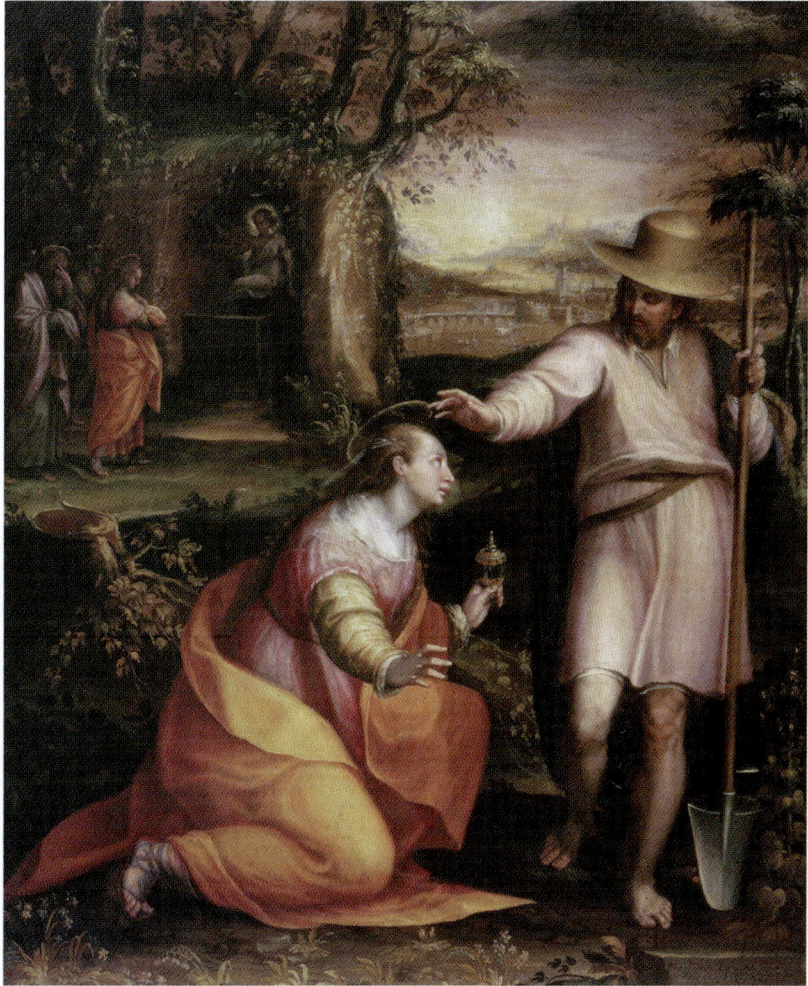

Lavinia Fontana. *Noli Me Tangere*, 1581. Oil on canvas.
Galleria degli Uffizi, Florence.
Photo: Bridgeman Images

In fact, the artist must have loved this in-between combination of purple and pink because she painted several major paintings with women dressed in this hue, most notably her masterpiece of *Judith and Holofernes*, as well as her painting *Noli Me Tangere*, where both Mary Magdalene and Jesus are wearing clothes with a hint of that color.

Unlike Anguissola, a noblewoman whose service at the Spanish court was a socially appropriate career, Fontana was the child of a painter with a modest social position, and she did not travel outside her native Bologna. Instead, she married and then had 11 (sic!) children. In between her family duties she managed to complete altarpieces, beautiful commissioned portraits, and religious scenes for churches and aristocratic collections. She even excelled at a genre that was basically closed to women artists of her time—the nudes. Because women were not allowed to sketch nude models at art classes (too indecent) or conduct autopsies (ditto!), they were not hired to provide this kind of art for home decorations. A cheeky *Mars and Venus* painting from 1595 is proof that Fontana, a stately wife and mother, fearlessly broke this convention, too.

It is quite amazing that artists as unique and interesting as Anguissola and Fontana could practically disappear into obscurity for several hundred years. Anguissola, who in her 90s gave painting tips to Anthony van Dyck when he visited her in Italy, has been forgotten to such an extent that some of her art is still being reattributed.

The exhibition *A Tale of Two Women Painters* took place at the Prado National Museum in Madrid between October 22, 2019 and February 2, 2020.

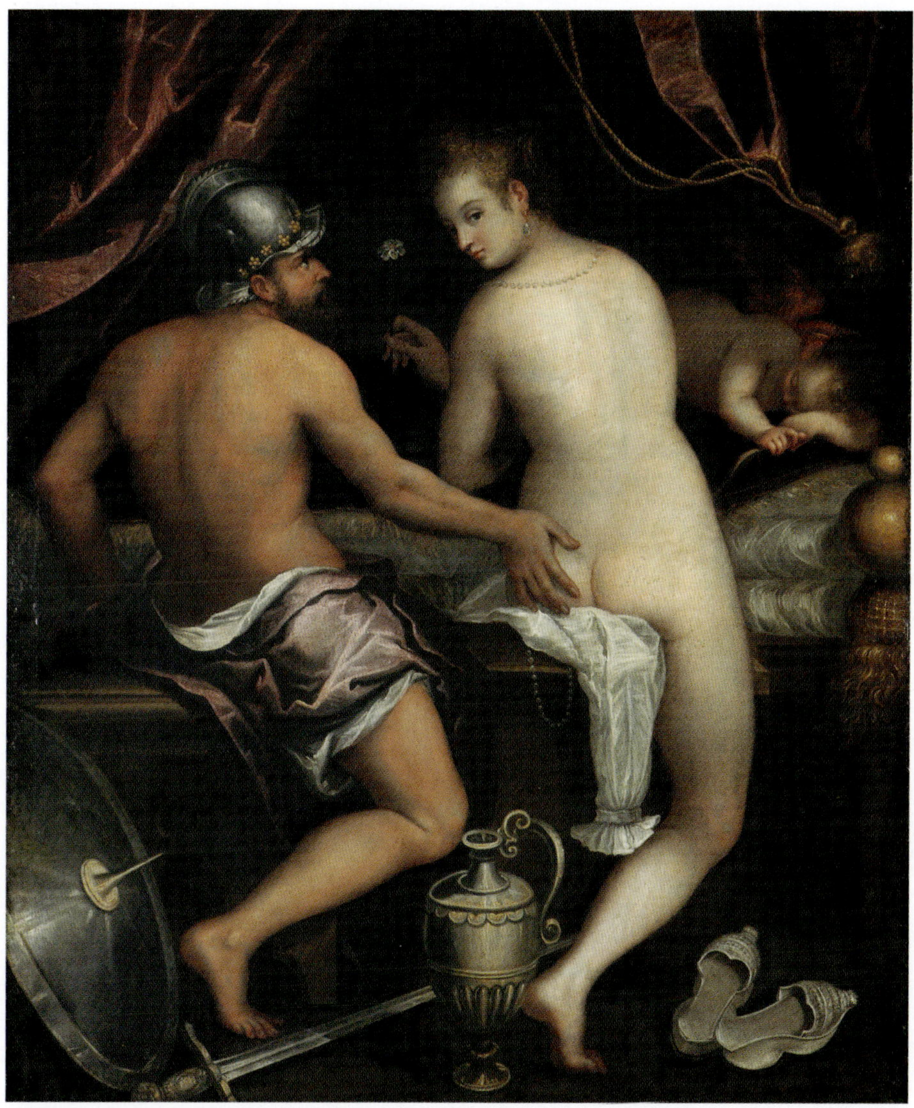

Lavinia Fontana. *Mars and Venus*, c. 1595. Oil on canvas.
Fundación Casa de Alba, Madrid.
Photo: Heritage Images/Fine Art Images/akg-images

CHAPTER 7

ARTEMISIA GENTILESCHI (1593–1653)

"...[W]ith me Your Illustrious Lordship will not lose and you will find the spirit of Caesar in the soul of a woman."

~ Artemisia Gentileschi

(Letter to her patron Antonio Ruffo in 1649, defending a price she quoted for painting "eight figures, two dogs, a landscape and water")

London's National Gallery was about to open the UK's first-ever exhibition of paintings by Artemisia Gentileschi when the global quarantine put an end to it for a while. This is a virtual tour of this ambitious overview of the life and art of the Baroque's most famous female artist.

For the last few decades, Artemisia Gentileschi has been a poster child in feminist-skewed art criticism. In modern times, this 17th-century painter is sometimes more celebrated for what happened to her than for her art.

Artemisia started to learn painting as the only daughter of Orazio Gentileschi, an established painter in Rome. Her three brothers did not have artistic talent, but Artemisia exhibited gifts from an early age as evidenced by her first version of *Susanna and the Elders*, painted when she was barely 17. A year later, her life was thrown off its orderly course. She was raped by Agostino Tassi, a painter working with her father on some frescoes, and who was hired to teach her perspective drawing. Instead of trying to "bury her shame" in silence, as would have been expected in those times, Artemisia and her father sued the painter in court. At the trial, the wheels of justice rolled unevenly. Artemisia was tortured by having her fingers crushed, and she underwent a humiliating medical examination. Tassi was found guilty but, protected by the Pope, he was punished with just a short exile into the

Roman suburbs. Eventually, Artemisia moved on. She became an established artist, married, and bore four children. The trauma of her assault got channeled through her pictures. However, in art history Artemisia's drama has become more prominent than her artistic achievements, at least as far as the general public goes.

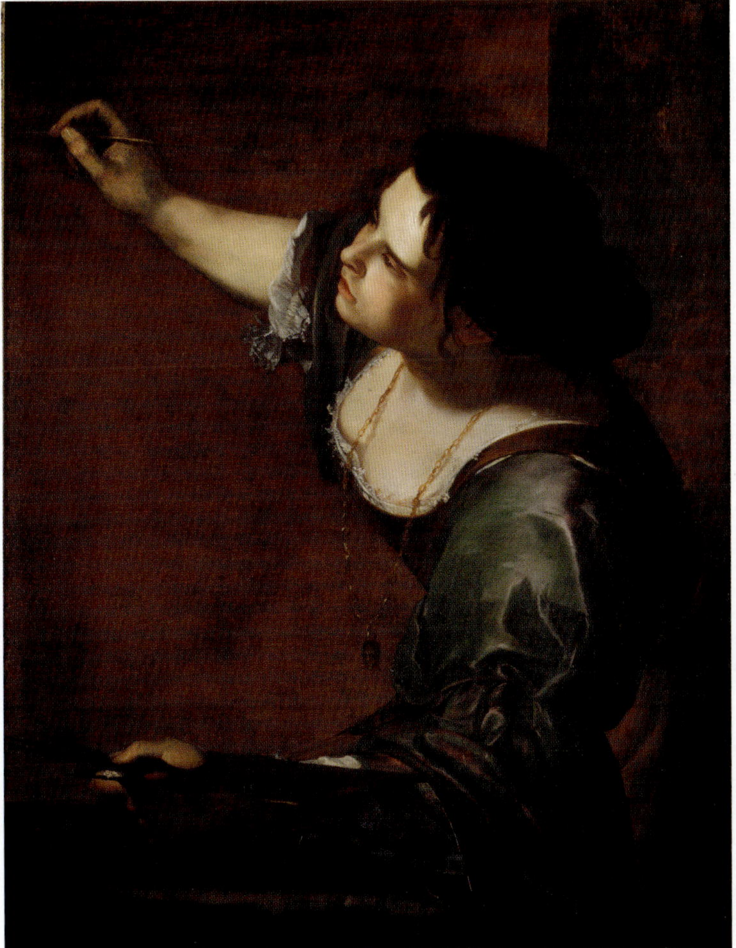

Artemisia Gentileschi. *Self-Portrait as the Allegory of Painting (La Pittura)*, c. 1638–39. Oil on canvas.
The National Gallery, London.
Photo: Royal Collection Trust/© His Majesty King Charles III, 2022/Bridgeman Images

This is slowly starting to change, and Artemisia is getting her professional due as one of the most interesting artists of her time. In fact, in November 2019, one of her paintings of Lucretia sold in Paris for about $5 million. In terms of artistic recognition, Artemisia's paintings are also getting star treatment. In December 2019, when the Seattle Art Museum displayed one of her most famous paintings, the 1612 version of *Judith Beheading Holofernes*, during an exhibition of Italian masterpieces loaned from Neapolitan Museo di Capodimonte, this canvas was the highlight of the show.

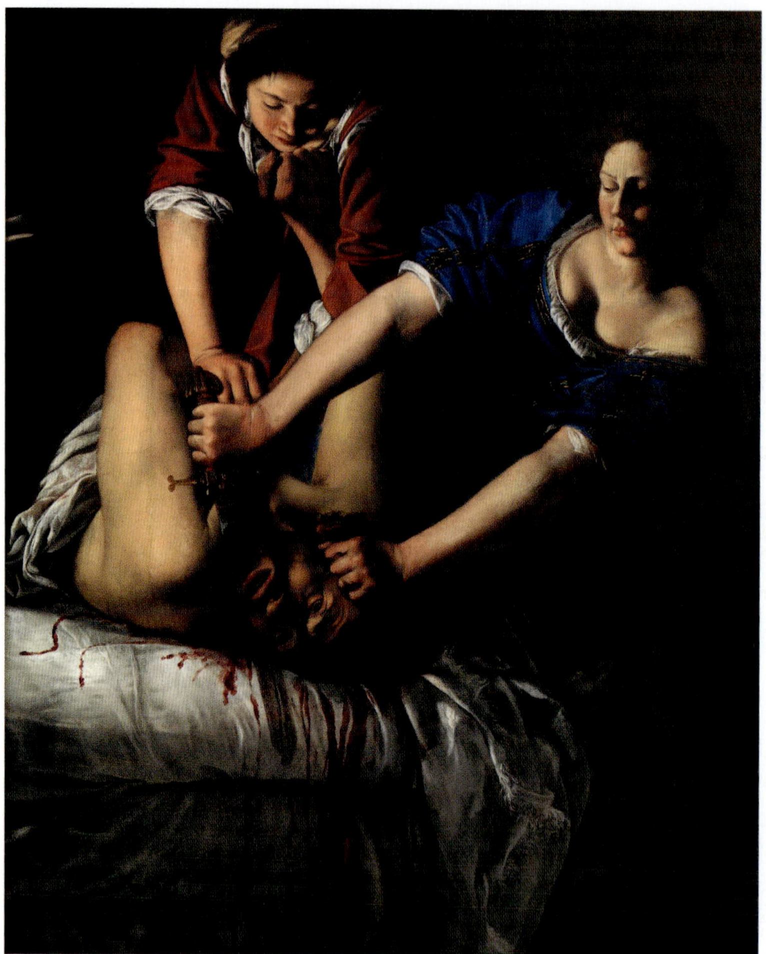

Artemisia Gentileschi. *Judith Beheading Holofernes*, 1612–13. Oil on canvas.
Museo di Capodimonte, Naples.
Photo: Public domain via Wikimedia Commons

Strong female subjects have been popular as part of a "power women" theme in literature and art since the Middle Ages. The story of the brave Jewish woman Judith who, assisted by a faithful servant, cuts off the head of Assyrian warlord

Holofernes, has inspired numerous paintings, including the one by the Roman master Caravaggio, whose *chiaroscuro* style and dramatic compositions strongly influenced first Orazio and then Artemisia. Orazio was not only an early follower of Caravaggio's style but also his personal friend. When Artemisia was just six years old, the two artists went to prison together for criticizing another painter's altarpiece.

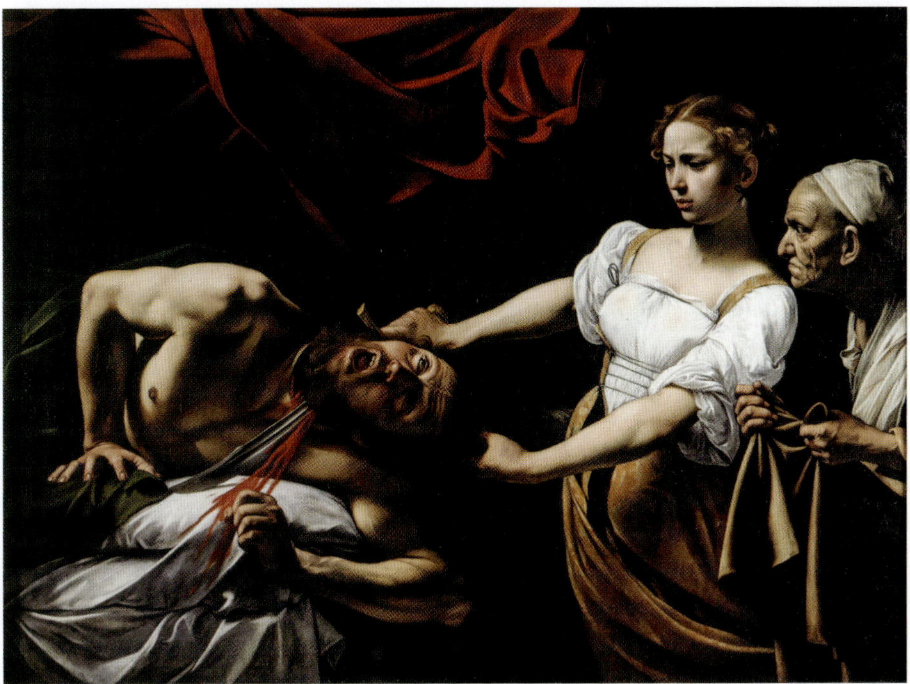

Caravaggio. *Judith Beheading Holofernes*, c. 1598–99. Oil on canvas.
Palazzo Barberini, Rome.
Photo: incamerastock/Alamy Stock Photo

Judith, as painted by Artemisia, does indeed reference the earlier, famous Caravaggio painting. Her composition captures the same gruesome moment of actual beheading and a similar position of Judith's hands, but the artist has made this subject her own. Caravaggio portrays a woman unsure of herself, sad, and regretful for having murdered a man she's just had in her bed. She leans stiffly away from the man she is slaying, baby-faced and virginal in her spotless white dress. Artemisia's Judith purses her lips in business-like concentration as if she is a cook slicing a duck's throat for dinner. There is no doubt or regret—she is doing a job that needs to be done. She does not gloat, but she does not flinch, holding

Holofernes's neck in the strong grip of her wide hands. To add to the realism of the scene, the maid does not stand idly by her side but holds the writhing Holofernes down. Here is another, later version of the theme—with the same strong hands that pin the man down.

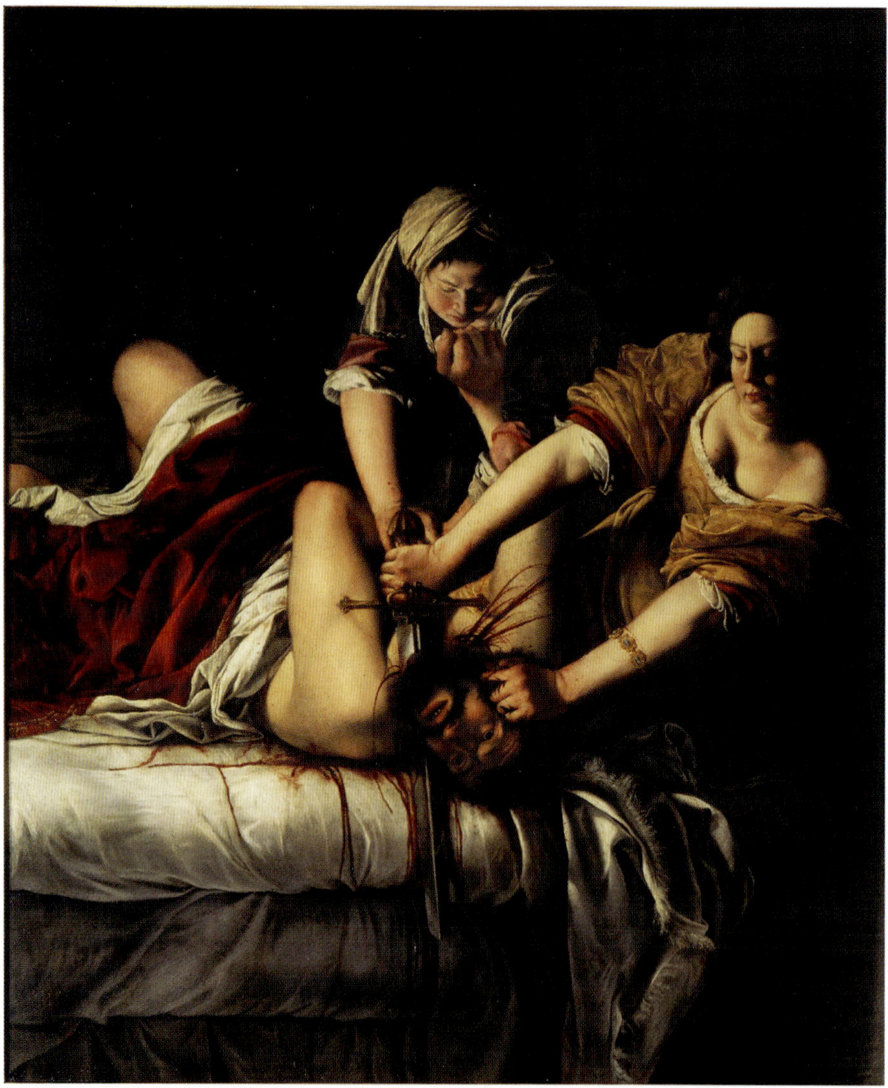

Artemisia Gentileschi. *Judith Beheading Holofernes*, c. 1620. Oil on canvas.
Galleria degli Uffizi, Florence.
Photo: Public domain via Wikimedia Commons

Artemisia painted several versions of Judith, so you could say that this was her "art therapy," or at least that the theme important to Artemisia was that of a woman wrestling for control with a man who coveted her. But as much as these paintings convey the rage and frustration of the young woman overpowered, humiliated, and deceived by Tassi and his accomplices, she also took up other "female" themes in her art.

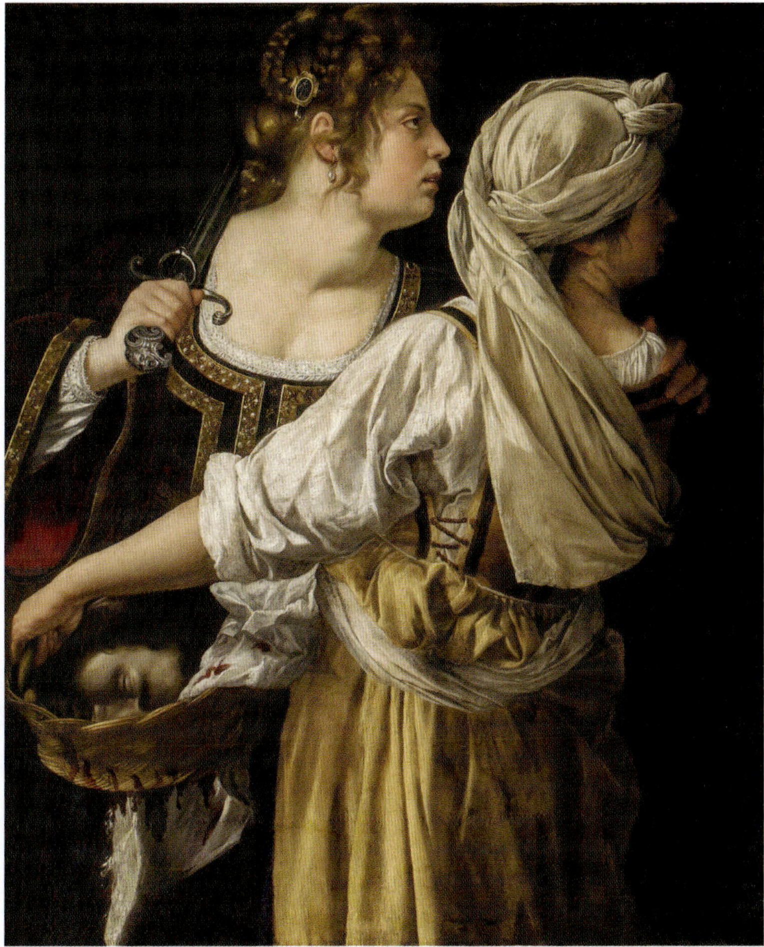

Artemisia Gentileschi. *Judith and Her Maidservant*, 1614–20. Oil on canvas.
Galleria Palatina, Palazzo Pitti, Florence.
Photo: Public domain via Wikimedia Commons

The London exhibition curators brought over one of the most famous versions of Judith, from the artist's Florentine period. Right after the trial that exposed

Artemisia's "loss of respectability," she was hastily married off to Pierantonio Stiattesi (a minor painter who squandered her money), and she moved away from her native Rome to the Medici court in Florence. This Florentine version from about 1615 shows Judith after the deed is done, but she holds her servant's arm, her sword raised in readiness, listening anxiously for sounds of guards running in. This is a portrait of vulnerability and anxiety, much different from the relaxed, classicized way that other male painters have painted this scene. For Artemisia, this is a psychological portrait of hunted women, not just a picturesque biblical scene.

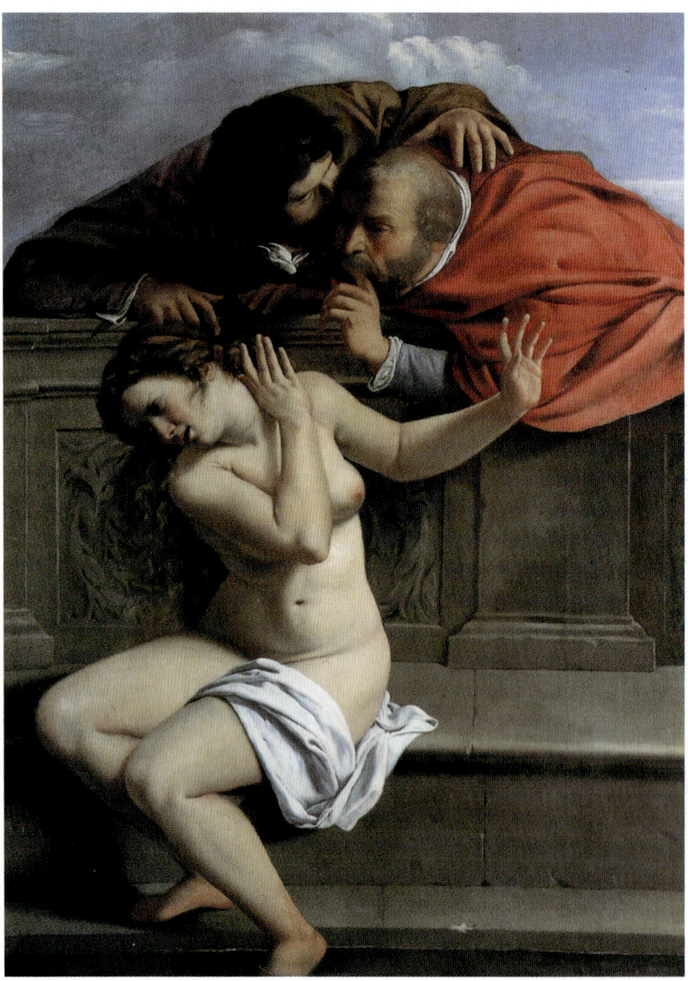

Artemisia Gentileschi. *Susanna and the Elders*, 1610. Oil on canvas.
Schönborn Collection, Pommersfelden.
Photo: Public domain via Wikimedia Commons

Even before her assault, a teenage Artemisia painted her version of the popular biblical story of Susanna and the Elders—a young woman being harassed by two men who surprise her at a bath (i.e., naked), ogle her, and threaten to sully her reputation if she does not succumb to their advances. In art, this story was often an opportunity to paint nudes for a socially acceptable display. Artemisia's version is very much her own composition—Susanna is twisting her body away from the ogling men who lean close to her, barely fenced off by a retaining wall. The artist kept going back to this theme for years.

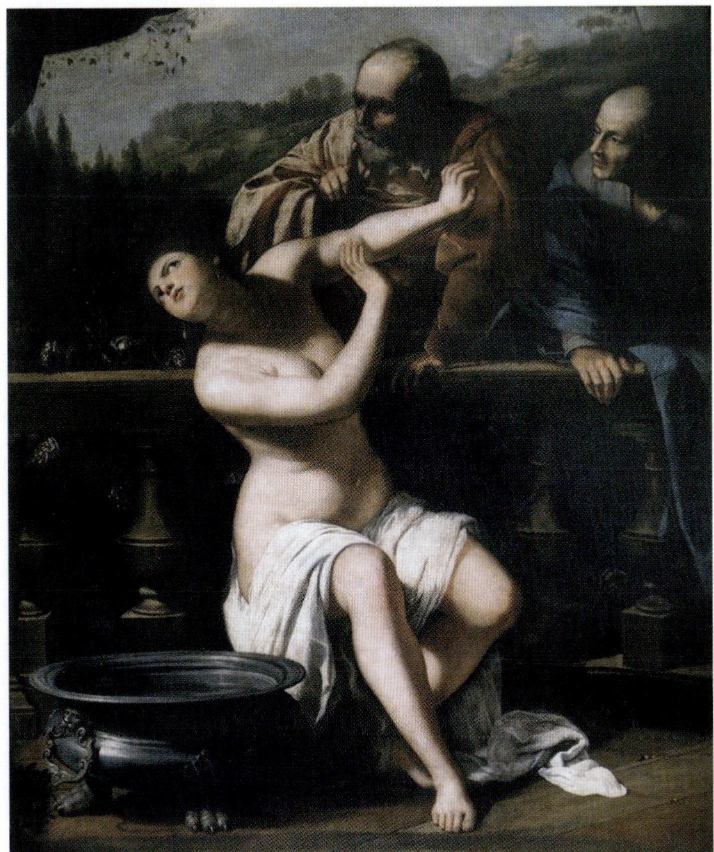

Artemisia Gentileschi. *Susanna and the Elders*, 1649. Oil on canvas.

Moravian Gallery, Brno.

Photo: Domenico Gargiulo, CC BY-SA 4.0 <https://creativecommons.org/licenses/by-sa/4.0>, via Wikimedia Commons

More dramatic versions were painted after her rape: one in 1622, another in 1649, and yet another in 1652.

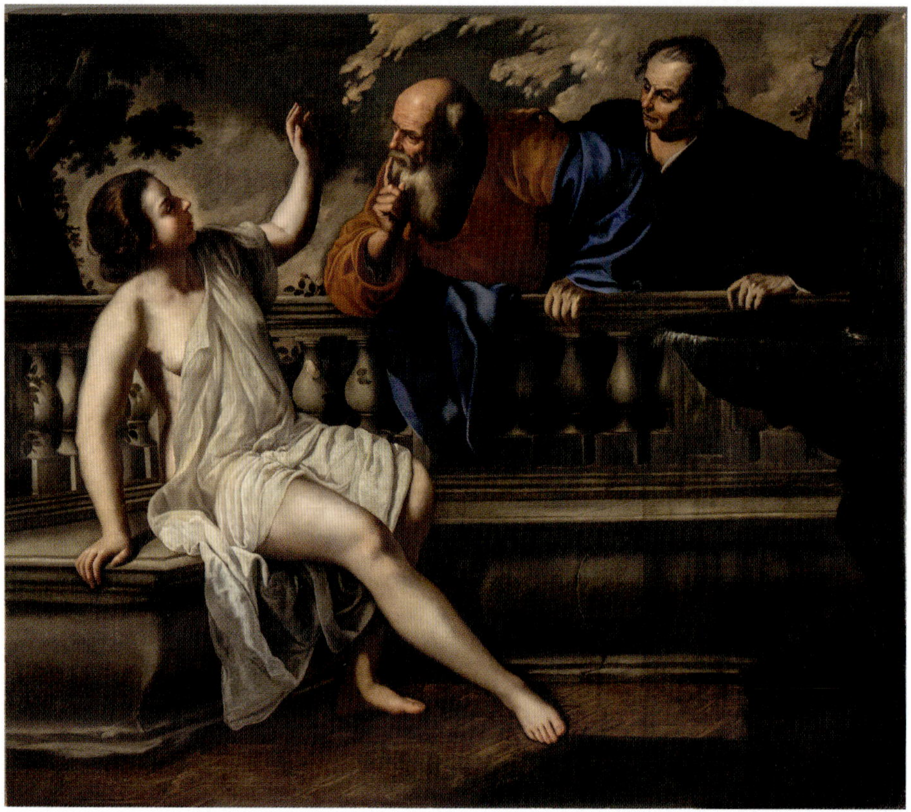

Artemisia Gentileschi. *Susanna and the Elders*, 1652. Oil on canvas.
Private collection.
Photo: Public domain via Wikimedia Commons

Most of her surviving paintings feature women—such as biblical Bathsheba, Cleopatra, and St. Magdalene—and many of them can be read in the context of her trauma. However, 400 years later, what really remains is the art itself.

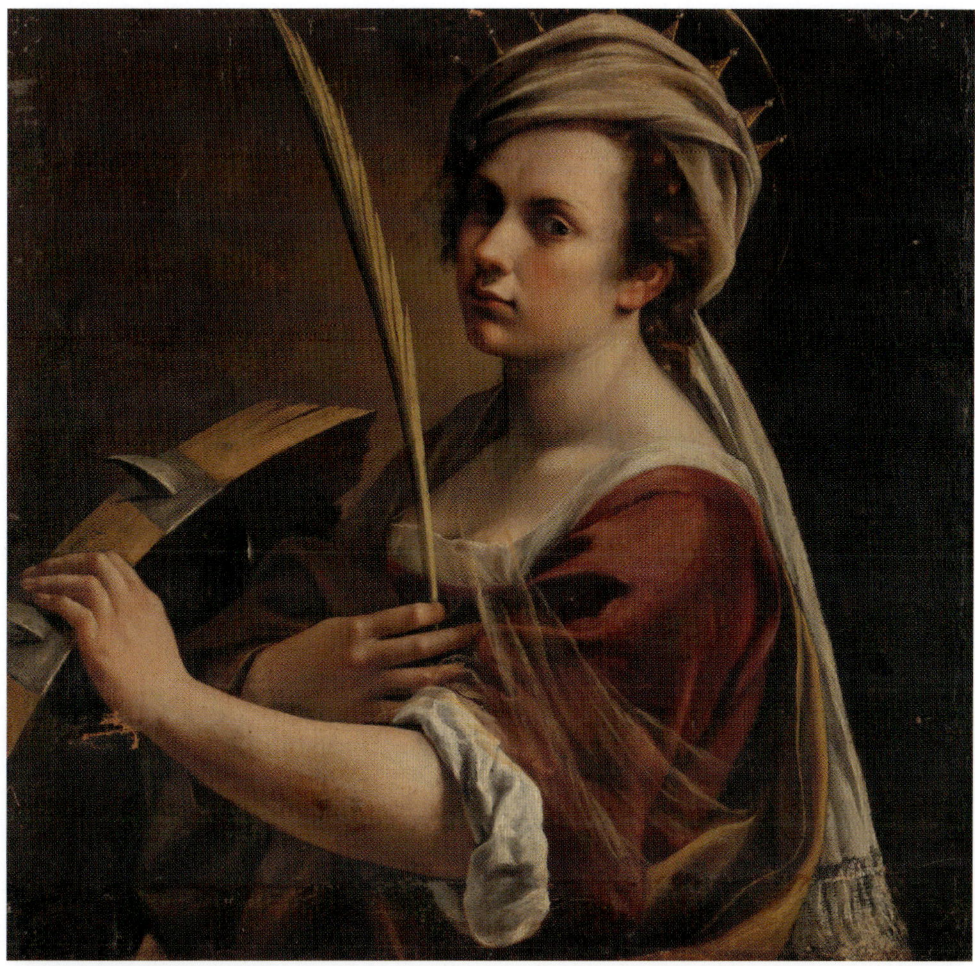

Artemisia Gentileschi. *Self-Portrait as Saint Catherine of Alexandria*, c. 1615–17. Oil on canvas.
National Gallery, London.
Photo: Bridgeman Images

This was brought forward in the exhibition by paintings that are permanently in the UK. The National Gallery's newest acquisition is a *Self-Portrait as St. Catherine of Alexandria*. Acquired in 2018, this is a painting that only recently has been attributed to the artist. In that regard, Artemisia's story is similar to that of Baroque woman painter Sofonisba Anguissola, whose portraits of the Spanish royal family have only recently been reattributed to her. The symbolism of St. Catherine, a woman persevering despite the torture of a spiked wheel, was an image that would have fit perfectly Artemisia's biography and artistic interests.

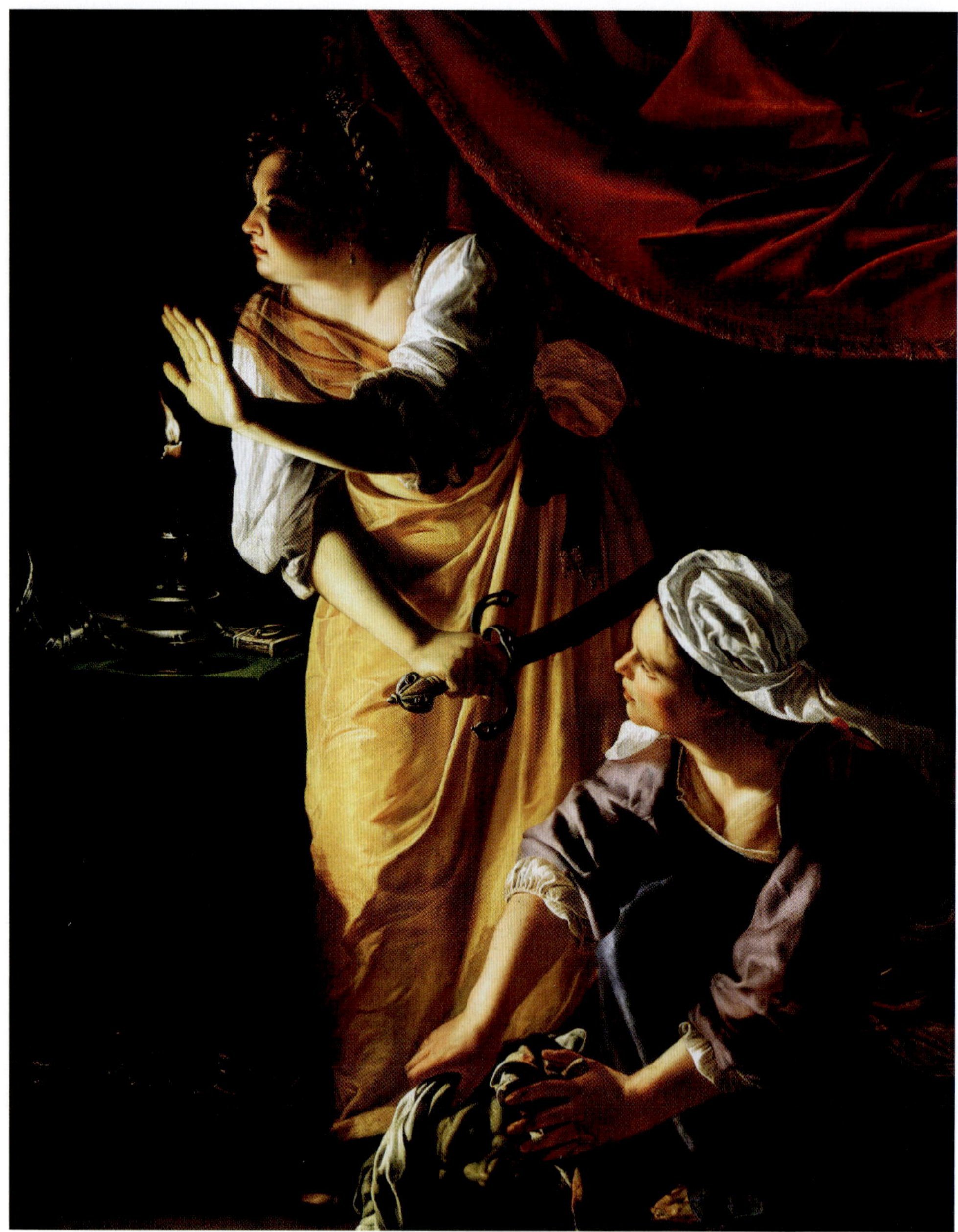

Artemisia Gentileschi. *Judith and Her Maidservant*, c. 1623–25. Oil on canvas.
Detroit Institute of Arts/Gift of Mr. Leslie H. Green.
Photo: Public domain via Wikimedia Commons

In search of patrons and commissions, and perhaps to get away from her wastrel husband, Artemisia traveled a lot. In her later years, she was more or less settled in Naples, except for a stay in London. In 1638, Artemisia traveled to England, joining her father who was then a court painter for King Charles I. Orazio died suddenly a year later, but Artemisia stayed on working for the court for a couple of years. However, political unrest and civil war (which eventually culminated in the king's beheading in 1649) did not provide a safe climate for a foreign woman without protectors, and by 1642, she had returned to Naples.

A delightful yet bold painting from her London period is called *Self-Portrait as the Allegory of Painting* (page 69). A convention of the time would have been to paint such a self-portrait looking at the viewer, with a finished artwork displayed on the easel. This is not the case here. Artemisia paints herself in a complicated pose, engrossed in the act of creation, but the large canvas is tantalizingly bare. This is her face and body (we know how she looked from previous paintings by her and her father), but she is an allegory, an embodiment of the art of painting. The blank canvas is more intriguing and symbolic than had she painted an artist's studio around her. Also, the convention for an allegory of painting (*la Pittura*) would often be to show her with the mouth gagged (because paintings do not speak). Not so in Artemisia's version—this is not an artist who would paint herself being gagged. Instead, we look at a strong woman, in command of her craft, dressed in *cangiante* silk, its green and pink undertones rendered with mastery. Artemisia is indeed a muse of painting in this portrait.

The exhibition at London's National Gallery originally was scheduled to be open to visitors between April 4 and July 26, 2020. This reportage is from the virtual version of the exhibition. The physical show subsequently opened in London on October 3, 2020 and ran through January 24, 2021.

CHAPTER 8

BERTHE MORISOT (1841–1895)

"I do not think any man would ever treat a woman as his equal, and it is all I ask because I know my worth."

~ Berthe Morisot in her notebook

As much or as little as the #MeToo movement has achieved in improving women's lives in the world of male-dominated professions, there is indeed now a larger interest in art museum exhibitions that focus on women artists. There have been recent retrospectives of Cindy Sherman at Broad Museum in Los Angeles, and another one in Paris. Also in Paris, the Musée d'Orsay dedicated a large show in 2019 to a female artist who lived in times even less tolerant of women who wanted to be taken as seriously as men. Berthe Morisot lived in the 19th century, when well-bred young ladies were taught to sing, play some piano, and possibly dabble at watercolors, but with no one expecting them to actually exhibit at professional competitions. Berthe had other ideas.

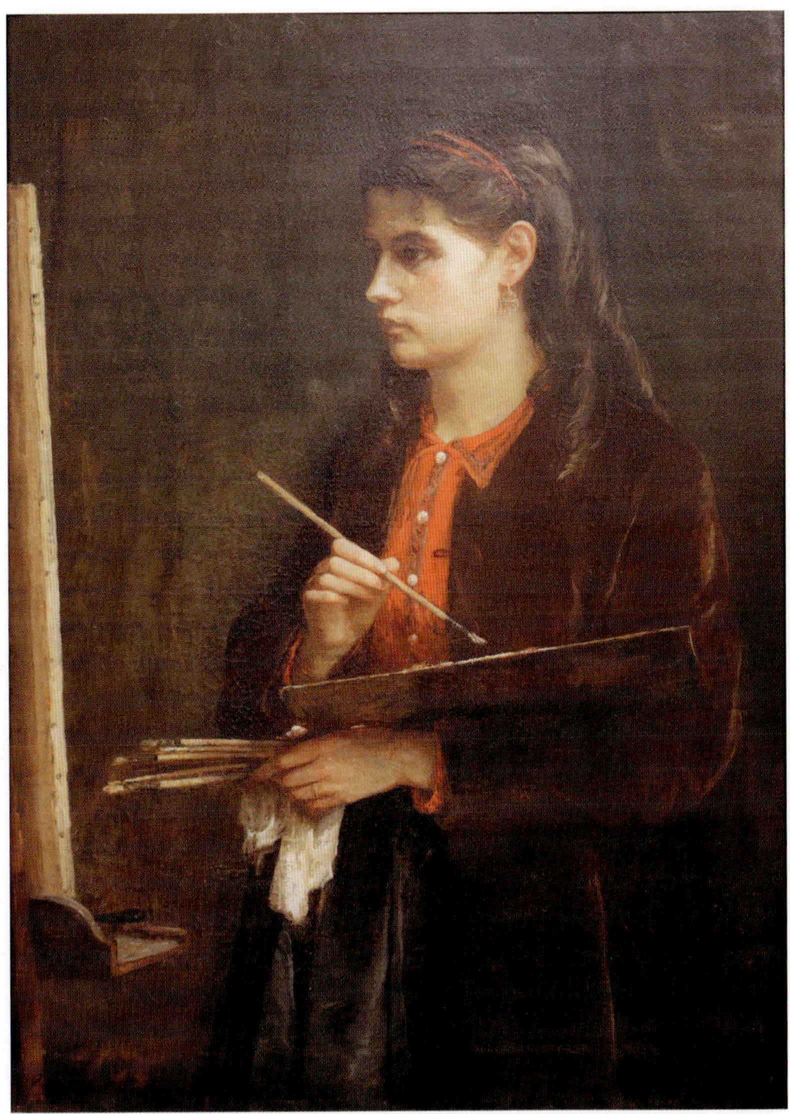

Edma Morisot. *Portrait of her sister Berthe Morisot*, 1865. Oil on canvas.
Private collection.
Photo: Thesupermat, CC BY-SA 4.0 <https://creativecommons.org/licenses/by-sa/4.0>, via Wikimedia Commons

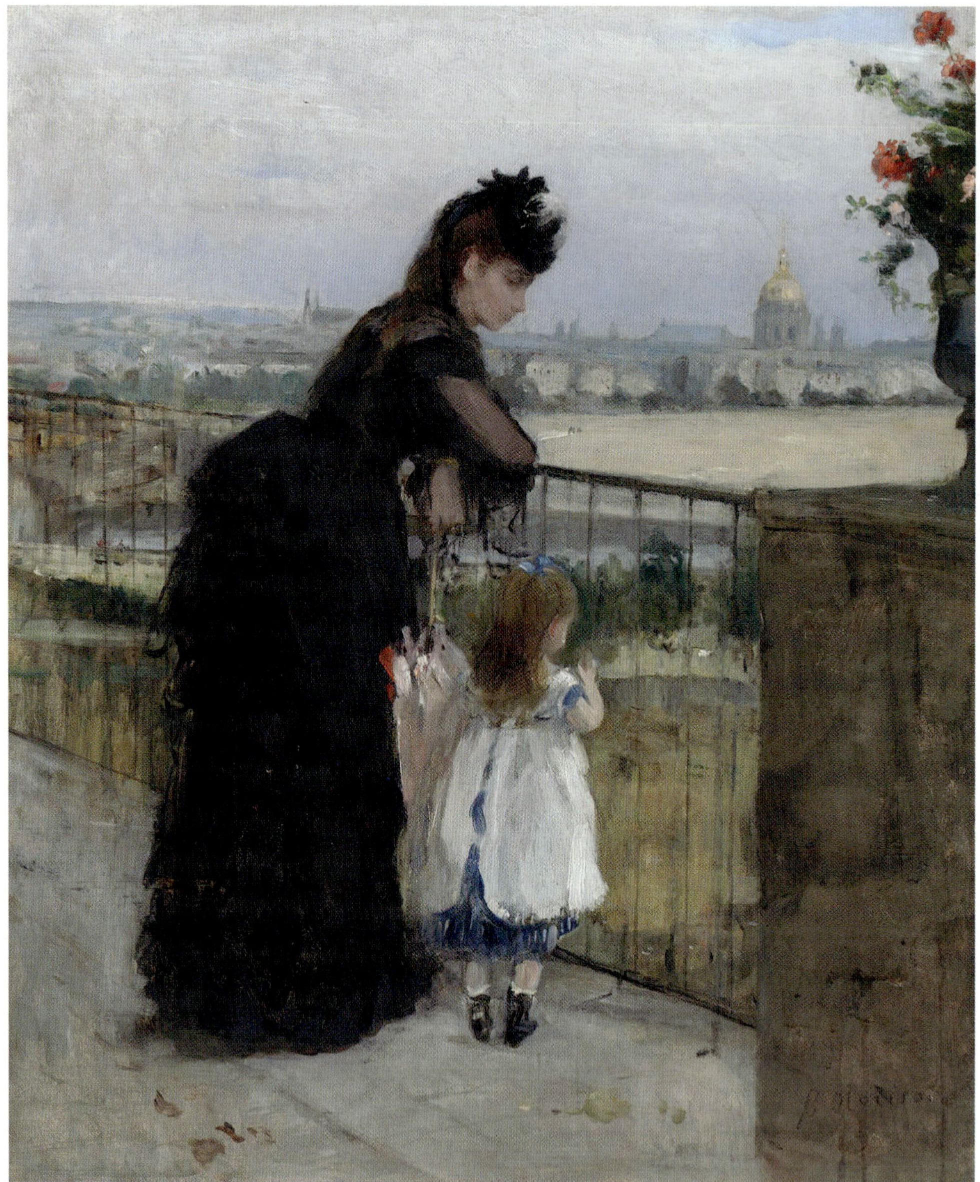

Berthe Morisot. *Woman and Child on a Balcony*, 1872. Oil on canvas.
Private collection.
Photo: Public domain via Wikimedia Commons

It's not that Berthe was not appreciated. Her parents supported both her art studies and her financial needs (she did not marry until she was 33—an extremely advanced marrying age in those days), and Berthe was often praised and encouraged by her friends. Her artistic anguish was more about the fact that she was not appreciated enough—not treated as a "serious" artist the equal of all her male colleagues. In fact, when she started submitting her paintings to the Salon—the ultimate platform to be judged as an artist—her own circle of artists and critics initially tried to dissuade her, including her friend, mentor, and celebrated painter Édouard Manet, who was to become her future brother-in-law.

Exhibitions like this one at the Musée d'Orsay seek to restore the balance of recognition, albeit over 100 years too late for Berthe herself but certainly in time for us to see the bulk of her artistic output. Moreover, since this exhibition was a joint effort of several museums in Canada, the U.S., and France as well as sourced from private collections, the displays could be comprehensively arranged by all themes and periods in Morisot's life.

Berthe, together with her very talented sister Edma, was already placed inside an affluent and artistic milieu when the sisters started in 1860 their serious art studies with no less than Camille Corot, a leading proponent of realistic painting. Four years later, Berthe started exhibiting at the annual exhibitions of the Salon. Edma's portrait of Berthe is sufficient proof of her own gifts, but Edma eventually met with the fate of so many talented women of the era: as soon as she got married and had children, she stopped painting. She never produced any more significant works.

Berthe was praised, albeit somewhat condescendingly—*"The entry into competition of a young girl from a distinguished background is both a salutary example and a singular encouragement"*—but her ambition to be an independent and innovative artist led her away from the academic style to become a co-founder of the Impressionist circle, together with Monet, Pissarro, Cézanne, and Sisley. She exhibited with them at the first famous 1874 exhibition (the one that gave name to the movement as "Impressionism"), and she participated in seven others.

Both Morisot's contemporary artist friends and subsequent art historians and critics have paid much attention to her use of color and her own "poetic" style. French critic Philippe Burty wrote in 1877: *"Here is a delicate colorist who succeeds in making everything cohere into an overall harmony of shades of white which is difficult to orchestrate without lapsing into sentimentality."*

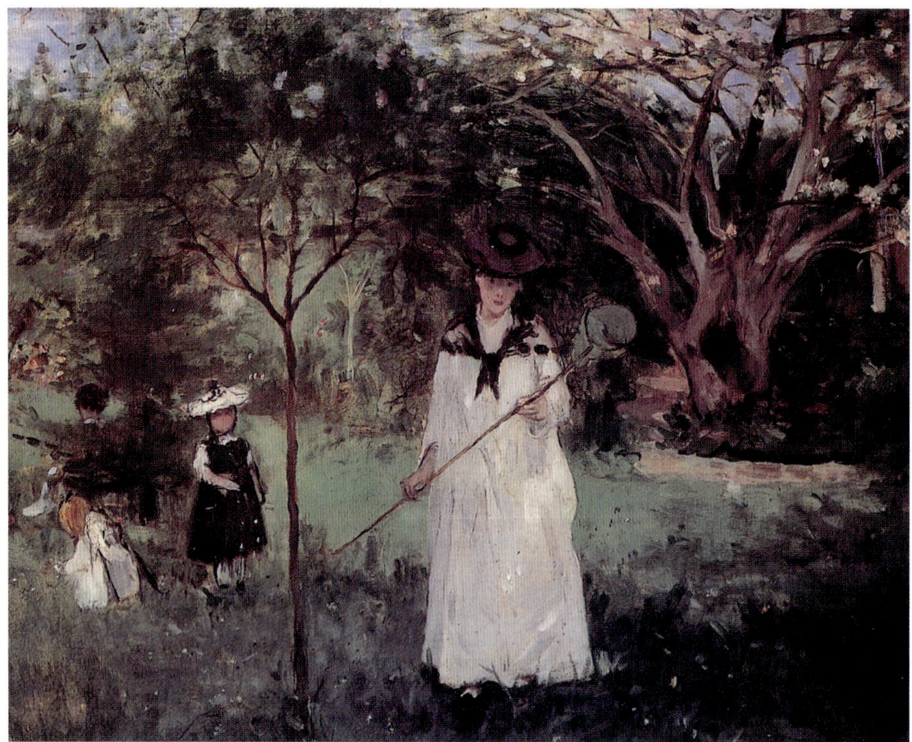

Berthe Morisot. *The Butterfly Hunt (La Chasse aux Papillons)*, 1874. Oil on canvas.
Musée d'Orsay, Paris.
Photo: Public domain via Wikimedia Commons

The Orsay exhibition gives us an insight into all that—the amazing subtlety of shades—a truly Impressionist way to show movement of grass or leaves and the interplay of light and shadow captured at different times in the same open-air location. Ultimately, however, this is not what makes Morisot stand apart. They say that in art, the most important thing is not the subject matter but the way something is presented. In the case of Morisot, this is not entirely true. What is important is precisely what she shows. She was a quiet observer of the lives of the women and children around her, in situations where men would not have been present or observing.

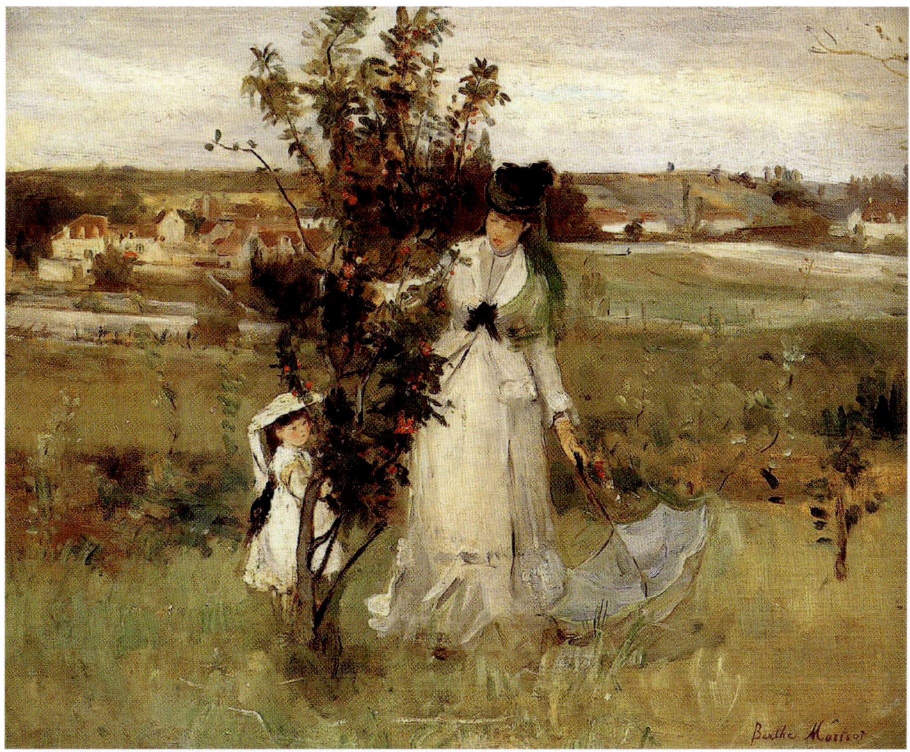

Berthe Morisot. *Hide and Seek (Cache-cache)*, 1873. Oil on canvas.
Private collection.
Photo: Art Heritage/Alamy Stock Photo

At the first Impressionist exhibition in 1874, for example, she exhibited an exquisite painting called *Hide and Seek* (*Cache-cache*, 1873), capturing the sight of a mother playing with her little daughter around a small tree. The mother—dressed in a hat, a jacket, and with a parasol—cannot really "hide" behind a few leaves, but this does not matter to the little one; it's the game of pretend that they both enjoy.

Another and better-known Morisot picture, called *Chasing Butterflies* (*La Chasse aux papillons*, 1874), has a mother and two tots wandering in a garden with a little butterfly net. Again, it is a fleeting moment in a game of pretend with little kids—something that so many mothers would have done over the millennia but that most fathers would not witness.

One of the most beautiful and insightful paintings at the exhibition was *Woman and Child on a Balcony*—the model is Edma with her little girl. This is not a posed portrait—they are looking out at the Parisian Champs de Mars, observing something below them. The little girl's left foot is standing a bit crooked, the way kids tend to fidget a little. Berthe would have spent hours looking at her nieces and then her own daughter, so she knew how kids really look and behave.

Morisot also painted her daughter's nanny and other servants—not as allegorical figures, nor as metaphors of life's hardships, nor even as just studies of color or light. They are just portraits of women at work: picking fruit, doing dishes in the kitchen. These are very feminine insights. Morisot's colleagues tackled sunsets and cathedrals, ballet dancers and card players, but they did not spend too much time noticing women who did dishes or tended to kids.

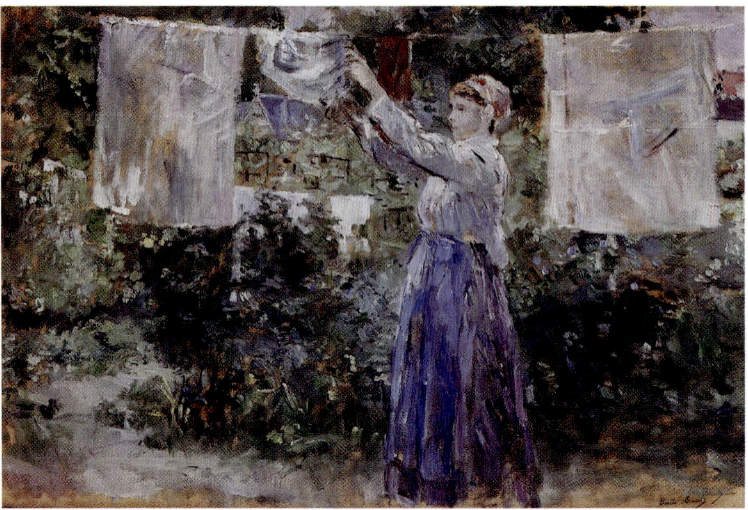

Berthe Morisot. *Woman Hanging Out the Wash (La Blanchisseuse)*, 1881. Oil on canvas.
Ny Carlsberg Glyptotek Museum, Copenhagen.
Photo: Public domain via Wikimedia Commons

The Impressionists' fight with academicians is long gone. Their canvases are now world famous for their use of light and color and the way they captured life scenes. What is still left from that period to be recognized a bit more is the art of someone like Berthe Morisot. She had as much technical talent as her male colleagues, but she had a different way of looking at her subjects precisely because she lived in a world closed to men—that of motherhood, running a household, and providing child care.

This exhibition was a joint effort of the Musée National des Beaux-Arts du Québec, the Barnes Foundation in Philadelphia, the Dallas Museum of Art, and the Musée d'Orsay and Musée de L'Orangerie in Paris.

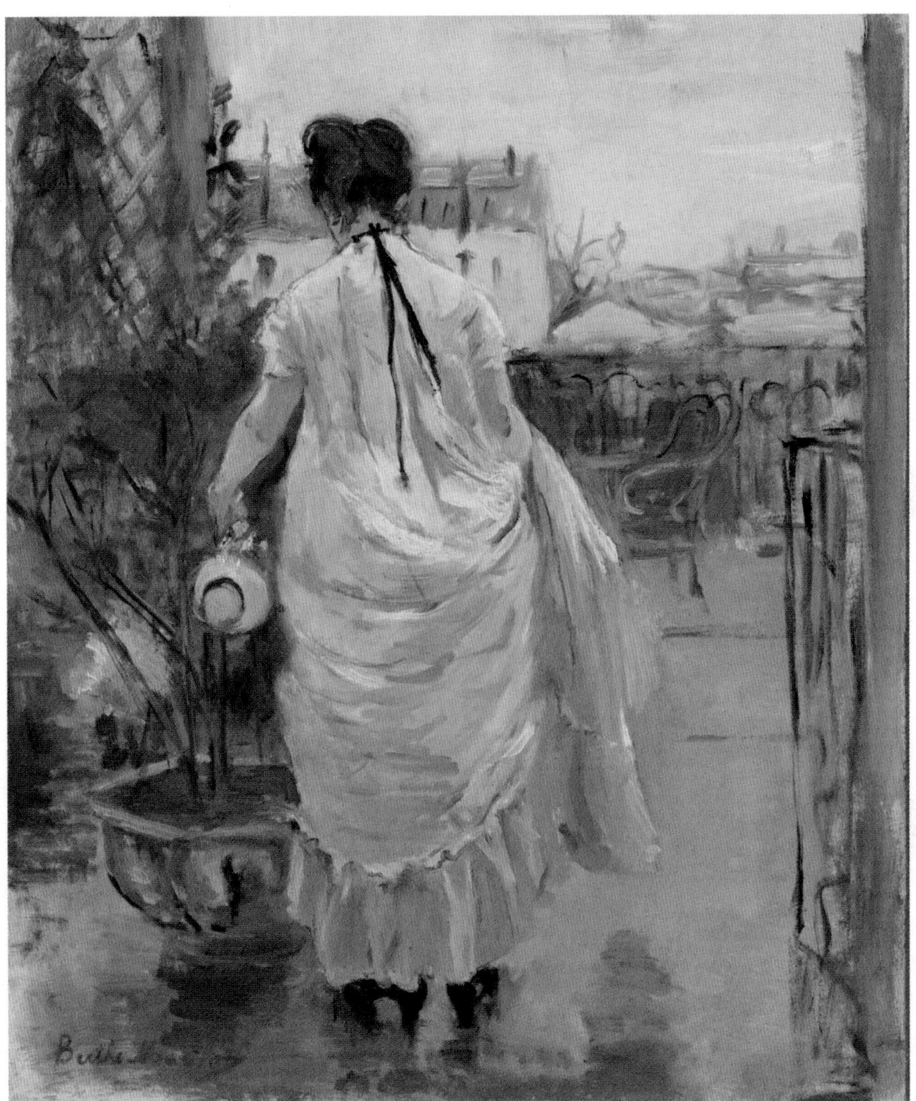

Berthe Morisot. *A Young Woman Watering a Shrub*, 1876. Oil on canvas.
Collection of Mr. and Mrs. Paul Mellon. Virginia Museum of Fine Arts, Richmond, VA.
Photo: Wikimedia Commons

CHAPTER 9

FRIDA KAHLO (1907–1954)

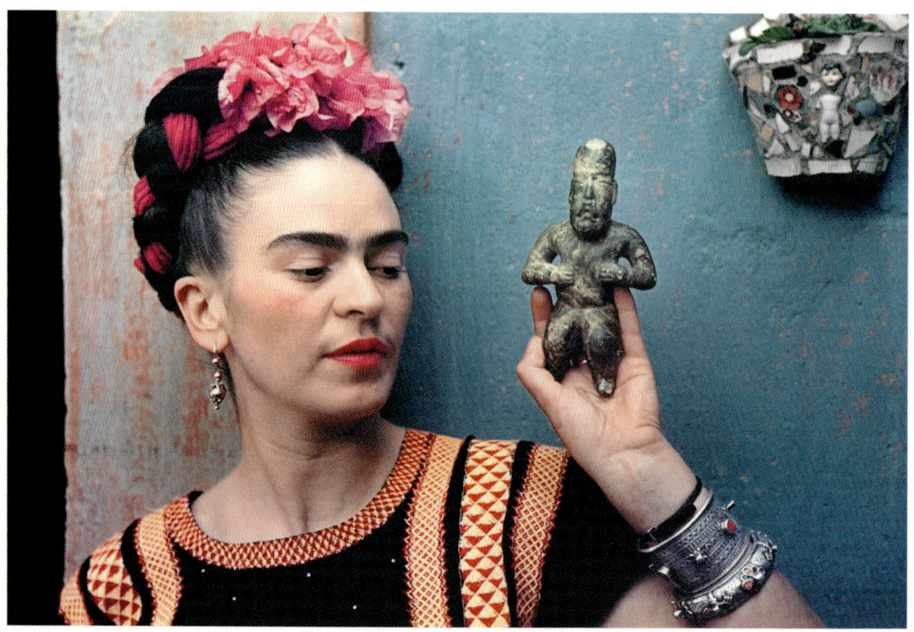

Nickolas Muray. *Frida with Olmeca Figurine, Coyoacán*, 1939. Color carbon print.
Fine Arts Museums of San Francisco.
Photo by Nickolas Muray, © Nickolas Muray Photo Archives

The de Young Museum in San Francisco planned to open an exhibition entitled *Frida Kahlo: Appearances Can Be Deceiving* on March 21, 2020. That week, California went on pandemic lockdown, and the exhibition did not physically open until half a year later. The story below was a reportage from a virtual version of the exhibition. The actual exhibition ran between September 25, 2020 and May 21, 2021.

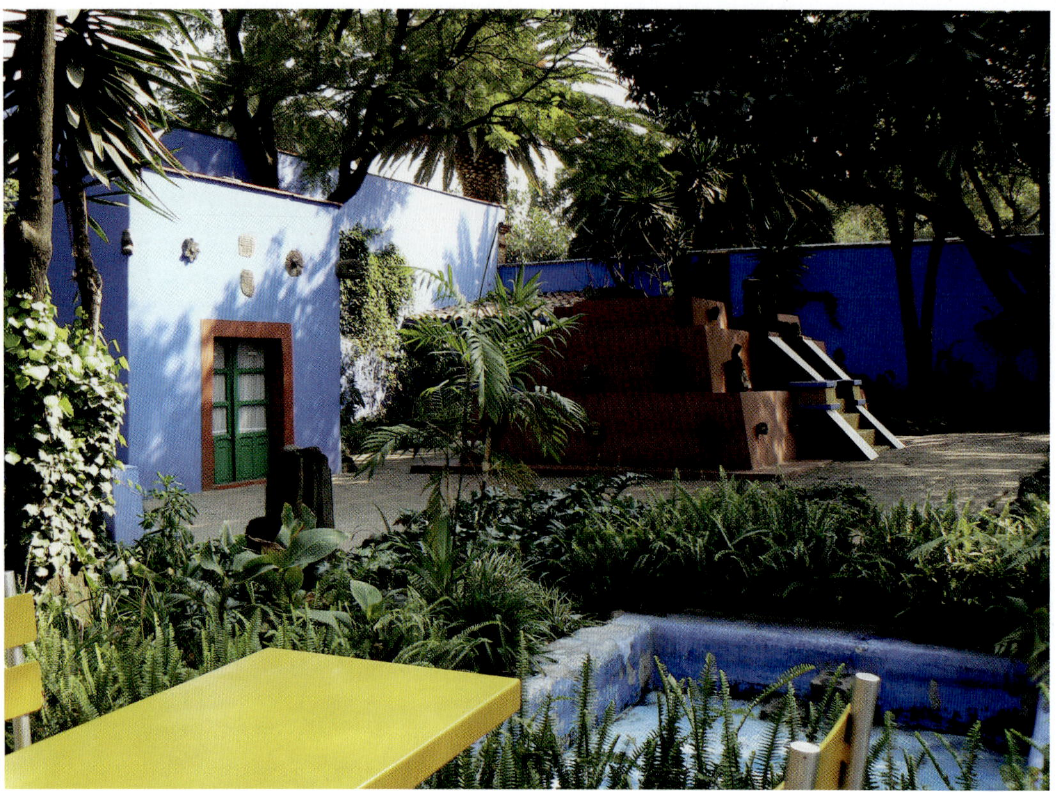

Frida Kahlo's house *Casa Azul* in Coyoacán, Mexico.
Photo: © Janet Mary Cook. All rights reserved 2022/Bridgeman Images

Several years after Kahlo's death in 1954, Diego Rivera donated his wife's famous Blue House (*La Casa Azul*) to the people of Mexico. *La Casa Azul* became the Museo Frida Kahlo, preserving Kahlo's memory. However, some of her personal belongings and mementos were kept in storage for 50 years and only saw the light of day in 2004. The de Young exhibition was aimed at bringing new insights into Kahlo's personal and artistic biography using these recently discovered artifacts—including colorful folk dresses, jewelry, and even her orthopedic corsets.

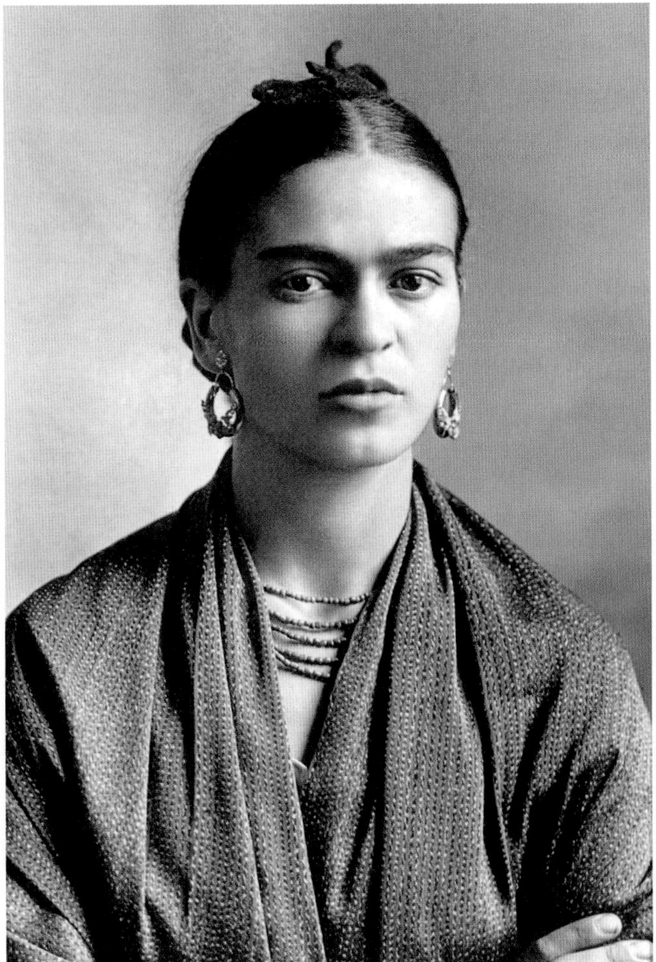

Frida Kahlo photographed by her father Guillermo Kahlo, 1932.
Photo: Bridgeman Images

Even though Frida Kahlo's paintings have a deceiving style of primitive folk art, Frida the artist was actually the result of several sophisticated influences and training. She was the daughter of a photographer who emigrated to Mexico from his native Germany in 1891. He was her first teacher of visual composition and sensitivity, and he taught her the art of photo retouching, which was her first school of painting. She also received some science training at the prestigious National Preparatory School, not to mention the enormous influence of her much older and more famous husband Diego Rivera—the eminent painter and muralist who, together with José Clemente Orozco and David Alfaro Siqueiros, were the three most prominent figures in Mexico's 20th-century art. The Rivera-Kahlo household was an artistic cauldron where everyone mingled and exchanged ideas: artists, politicians (including the anarchist Trotsky with whom Kahlo had an affair and whom Siqueiros tried to assassinate), actors (including Paulette Goddard with whom Rivera had an affair), poets, writers, and composers. It was, therefore, a deliberate aesthetic decision when early in her artistic career Kahlo pivoted from her Modigliani-style paintings toward surrealist and "folk art" style canvases.

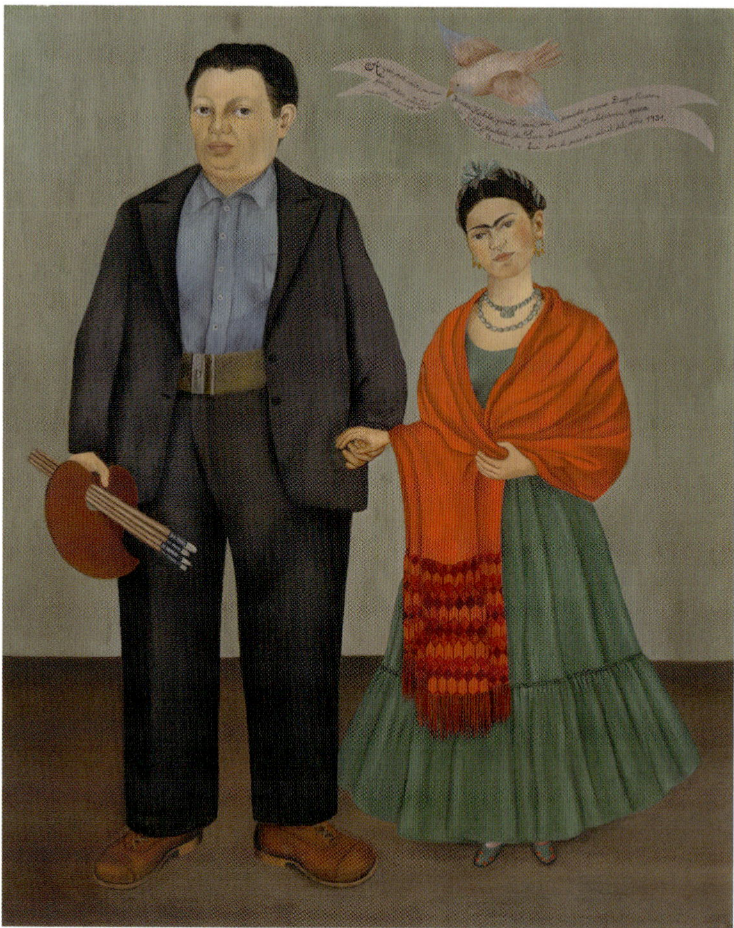

Frida Kahlo. *Frieda and Diego Rivera*, 1931. Oil on canvas.
San Francisco Museum of Modern Art.
Photo: San Francisco Museum of Modern Art/Albert M. Bender Collection, gift of Albert M. Bender/ Bridgeman Images/Artwork © 2022 Banco de México Diego Rivera Frida Kahlo Museums Trust, Mexico, D.F./Artists Rights Society (ARS), New York

Kahlo was inspired by Mexican votive paintings called *retablos* (in her house, she had a collection of 2000 of them), the outlandish and imaginative decorations for the Day of the Dead and other popular street festivals, as well as Aztec figurines and the traditional *Tehuana* dresses with bright shawls and large hair bows that she started to wear instead of modern, flapper-style dresses with Chanel collars.

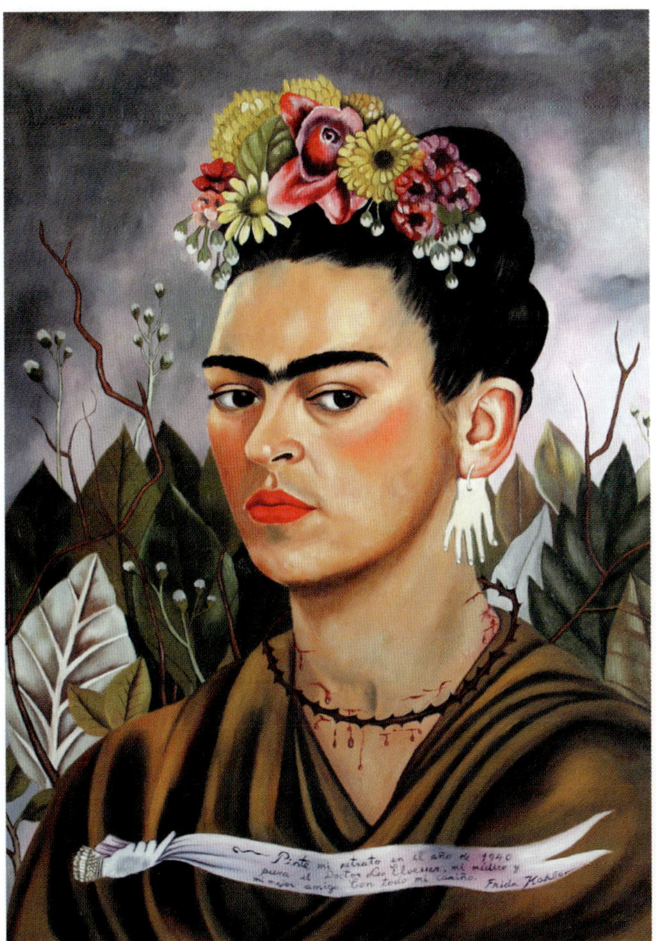

Frida Kahlo. *Self-Portrait Dedicated to Dr. Leo Eloesser*, 1940. Oil on masonite.
Private collection.
Photo: © Pictures from History/Bridgeman Images/Artwork: © 2022 Banco de México Diego Rivera Frida Kahlo Museums Trust, Mexico, D.F./Artists Rights Society (ARS), New York

These days, many female artists create their look to match their artistic persona. If you look at photos of Yoko Ono, Yayoi Kusama, Peggy Guggenheim, Iris Apfel, and many others, they all chose to augment their public personas with eccentric glasses, unusual clothing, stand-out hairdos, or garish accessories. The concept of a holistic artist who lives, wears, and expresses his art 24/7 is a very popular idea, embraced by Andy Warhol, Salvador Dalí, and even Picasso. Kahlo was definitely out there as an artist whose entire life was transformed into art. She included in her paintings everything that affected her life—her incessant suffering (she endured countless surgeries and debilitating treatments on her back and foot), her immersion in the Mexican romantic revival (a movement started in the early 20th century that focused on going back to national roots in relation to the colonial past), and her equally passionate fascination with early Communism (a huge intellectual craze in the 1930s all over the world). This very modern approach to art as a way of life is what still fascinates us in Kahlo, and this is what the exhibition brings into focus.

In 1930, Kahlo made her first trip abroad to "Gringolandia" (as she called the U.S.). In San Francisco, she completed several paintings, including a portrait of her and Rivera where she is wearing a folk dress that would soon become her trademark costume.

"Kahlo used her appearance to express her Mexicanidad, her identity as a Mexican woman at a time when her country was undergoing great political and social change," explained Hillary Olcott, the de Young's Associate Curator of the Arts of Africa, Oceania, and the Americas. *"This became especially important when she left Mexico, and traveled to San Francisco for the first time. She created the double portrait here in the city, which is also where it was first shown outside of Mexico."*

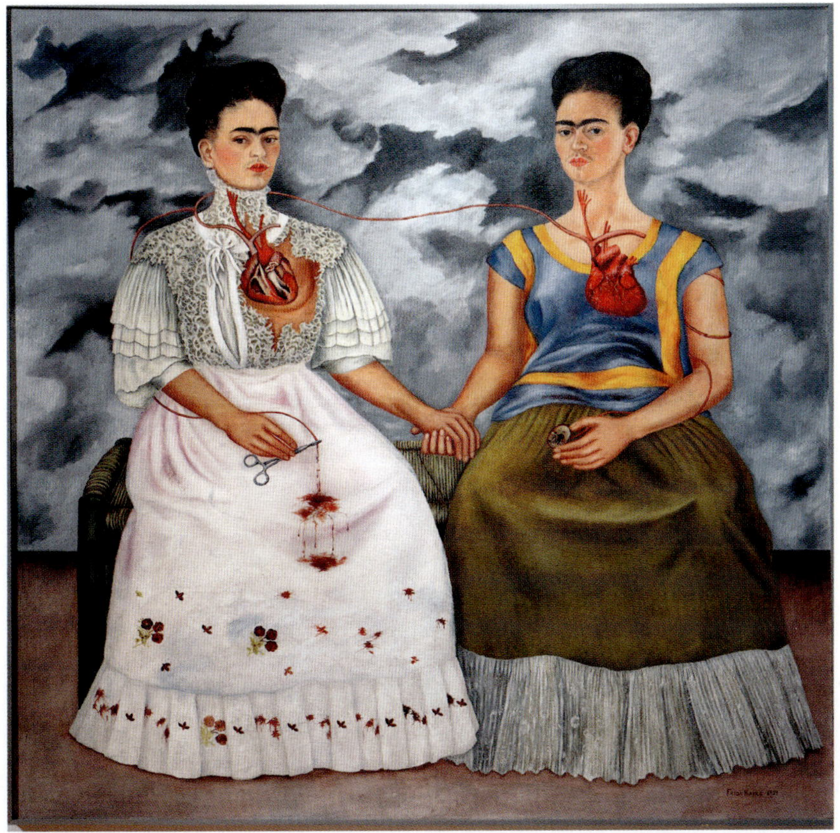

Frida Kahlo. *The Two Fridas*, 1939. Oil on canvas.
Museo de Arte Moderno, Mexico City.
Photo: Luisa Ricciarini/Bridgeman Images/Artwork: © 2022 Banco de México Diego Rivera Frida Kahlo Museums Trust, Mexico, D.F./Artists Rights Society (ARS), New York

The exhibition also displayed about 20 paintings from various periods of Kahlo's life. Over 50 years after her passing, these are her real legacy as an artist, and they are worth examining for their aesthetic value alone rather than just as popular culture icons. For many decades after Kahlo's passing, however, she was not much recognized by the art world outside Mexico. It was only in the 1980s that interest in her grew, but still focusing more on an eccentric female artist with a tragic biography than on Kahlo as a careful creator of artistic output.

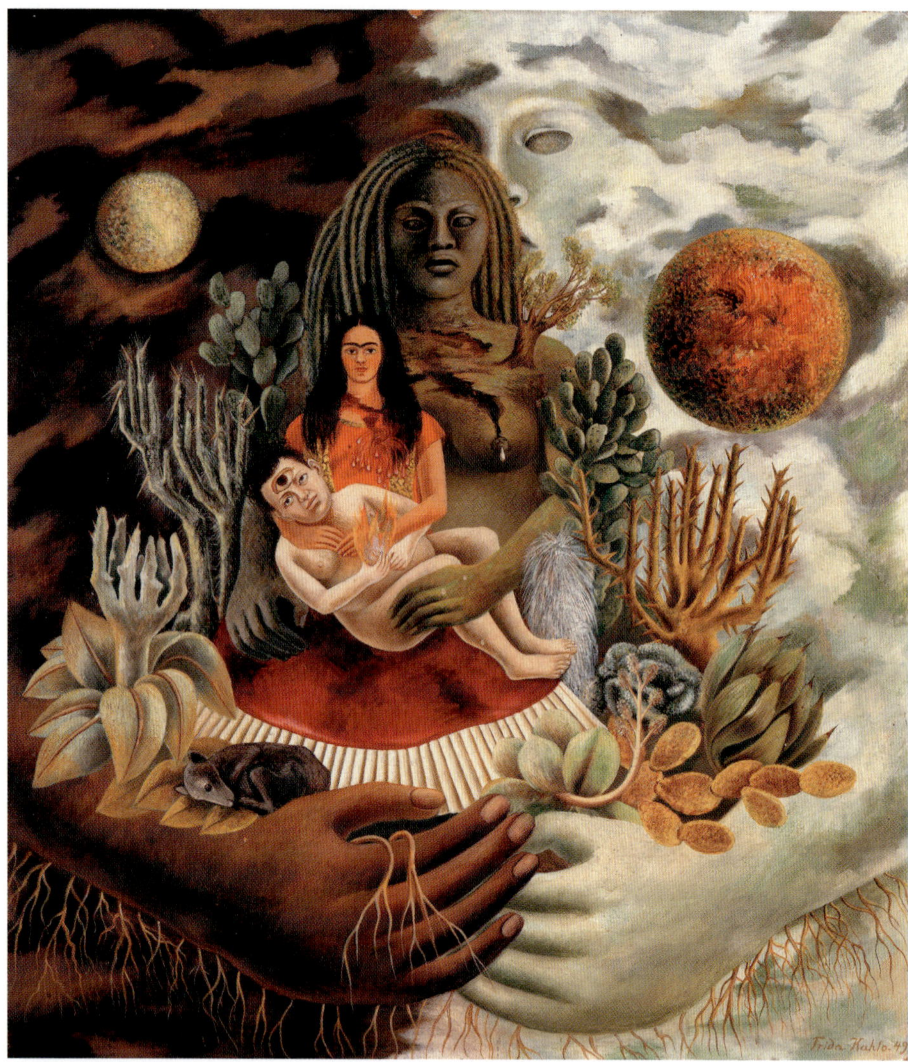

Frida Kahlo. *The Love Embrace of the Universe, the Earth (Mexico), Myself, Diego and Señor Xólotl*, 1949. Oil on cardboard.

Private Collection, Mexico City.

Photo: © Fine Art Images/Bridgeman Images/Artwork: © 2022 Banco de México Diego Rivera Frida Kahlo Museums Trust, Mexico, D.F./Artists Rights Society (ARS), New York

These days, school kids learn about Frida Kahlo. Her colorful self-portraits adorn tote bags, cosmetics, and clothing. There has even been an award-winning movie about her (starring Salma Hayek as Kahlo), as well as several theater plays, and countless art books. It is difficult to separate Frida, the popular icon, from Frida, a genuine artist. She has been endlessly described and analyzed by art critics, feminist writers, and art historians, while being reduced in school essays to merely an example of female contributions in art.

It seems that only the perspective of time can make us understand Kahlo as an early multimedia artist whose paintings, dresses, and personal collections all count as one continuous stream of creativity.

CHAPTER 10

GEORGIA O'KEEFFE (1887–1986)

"I'll paint what I see – what the flower is to me but I'll paint it big and they will be surprised into taking the time to look at it — I will make even busy New Yorkers take time to see what I see of flowers."

~ Georgia O'Keeffe

Georgia O'Keeffe painted flowers for a dozen years in the 1920s and early 1930s. Before that, she painted abstract watercolors, New York skyscrapers, and views of Lake George in upstate New York. After her flower period, she painted the black and red hills of New Mexico, sun-bleached cattle skulls, and the sunset skies of the western United States. But the public will always associate her with those enormous lilacs, irises, and calla lilies.

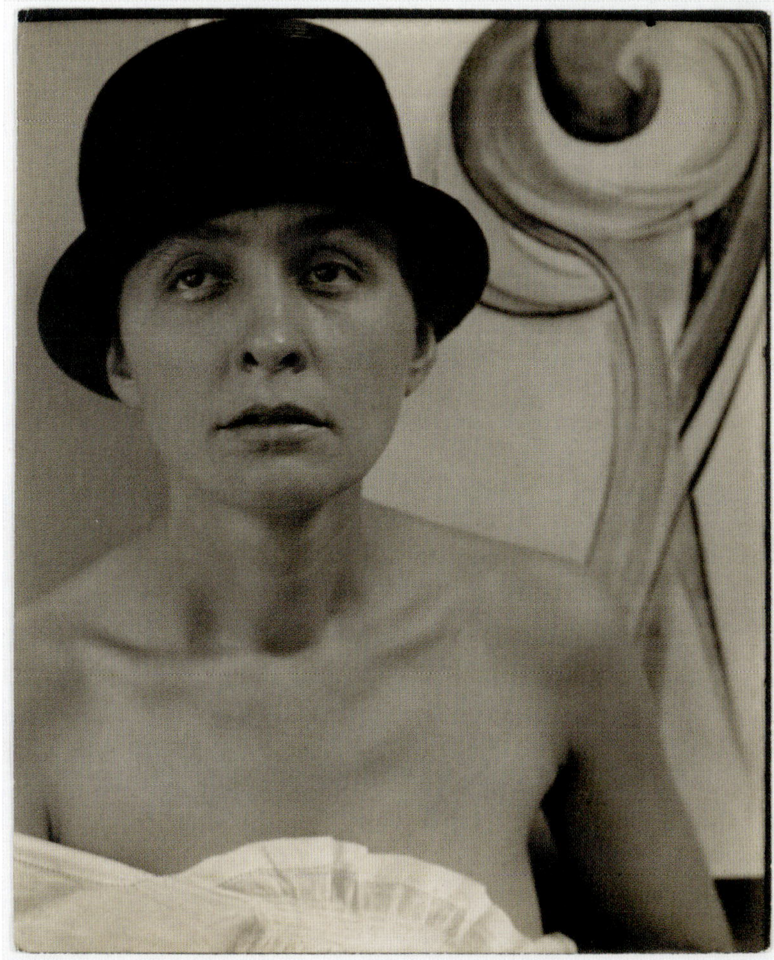

Photo of Georgia O'Keeffe by Alfred Stieglitz, 1918. Palladium print.

Metropolitan Museum of Art, New York/Gift of Georgia O'Keeffe, through the generosity of The Georgia O'Keeffe Foundation and Jennifer and Joseph Duke, 1997.
Photo: Alfred Stieglitz, CC0, via Wikimedia Commons

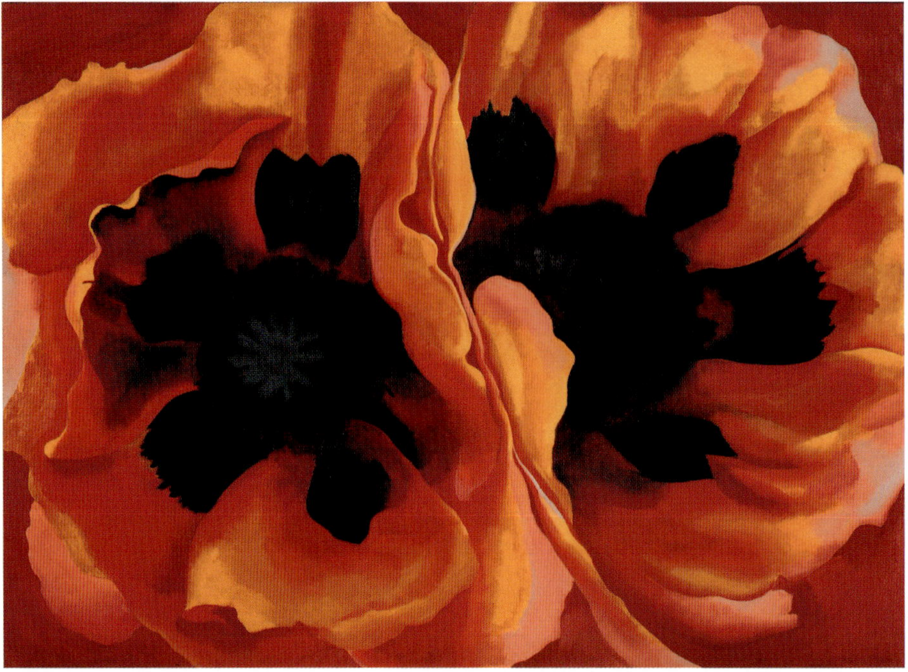

Georgia O'Keeffe. *Oriental Poppies*, 1927. Oil on canvas.
Collection of the Weisman Art Museum at the University of Minnesota, Minneapolis.
Museum purchase. 1937.1.
Photo: Weisman Art Museum at the University of Minnesota, Minneapolis/Artwork
© 2022 Georgia O'Keeffe Museum/Artists Rights Society (ARS), New York

Unlike most artists, O'Keeffe did not really have much of a struggling artist phase. Already in 1910, the twentysomething Georgia was part of the modernist movement in American art, and by 1920 she was a celebrity artist. Her 1916 meeting with New York gallerist and photographer Alfred Stieglitz changed her life and helped to place her in the center of the city's art scene. He accepted her early works for a show in his prestigious gallery (where he exhibited Braque, Matisse, and other masters of modernism), and soon she became his muse (he took over 300 portrait photographs of her), his principal gallery artist, his lover, and eventually his wife in 1924. They stayed together until his death in 1946, living the life of celebrated bicoastal artists (winters in New York, summers first at Lake George and then in New Mexico) working at the forefront of American art.

None of these biographical facts explains O'Keeffe's artistic path, however—the road she took was unique and very much her own. While she was attracted to Art Deco and the abstract styles of her era, O'Keeffe's paintings of New York buildings or her views of the serene Adirondack hills were from her point of view. She showed city towers at sharp and sometimes menacing angles, enveloped in halos of sun or artificial light. Her lake views were also very far from being stereotypically "feminine" depictions of nature—instead, she painted black blocks of barn houses and dark swaths of stormy sky. Even her partner and champion Stieglitz was reluctant to exhibit her more "masculine" works, favoring the ever-popular flowers.

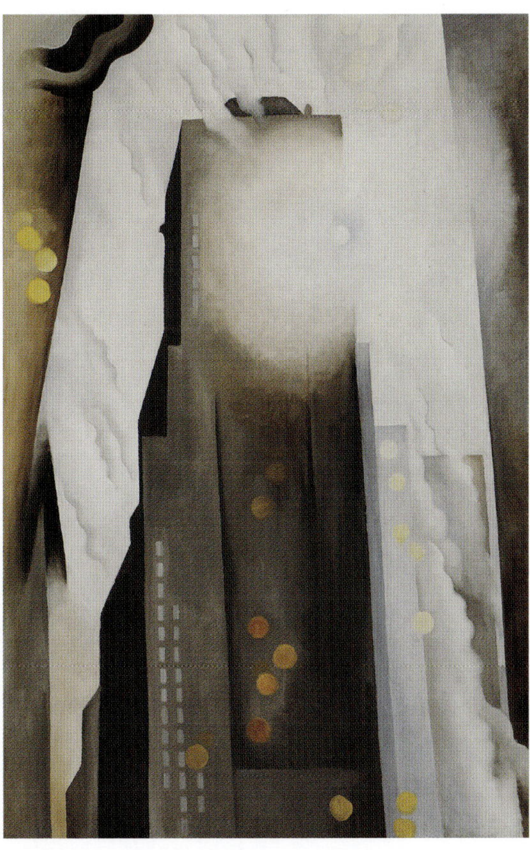

Georgia O'Keeffe.
The Shelton with Sunspots, N.Y., 1926. Oil on canvas.
The Art Institute of Chicago.
Photo: © Art Institute of Chicago/Gift of Leigh B. Block/Bridgeman Images/ Artwork © 2022 Georgia O'Keeffe Museum/Artists Rights Society (ARS), New York

For an American museumgoer, O'Keeffe is a very familiar artist. Her works can be found in many American art institutions; they grace book illustrations and souvenir merchandise, and her biography is taught at schools. In Europe, her artworks are much less common because few of her works are in permanent collections. A 2021 exhibition at Centre Pompidou in Paris was literally the first-ever major solo exhibition of this artist in France. The Modern Art Museum at Centre Pompidou put together an exhibition that aimed to present O'Keeffe not only as a celebrated woman artist and representative of American Modernism but also to show the full scope of her work, far beyond the famous flowers.

Not that there were no flowers in the Paris exhibition. Some of O'Keeffe's most beloved flower compositions made it to Paris from a dozen American museums, illustrating so well the visual shock that is still unleashed on viewers when confronted with these enormous chalices of plants that become a Rorschach test of the viewer's imagination.

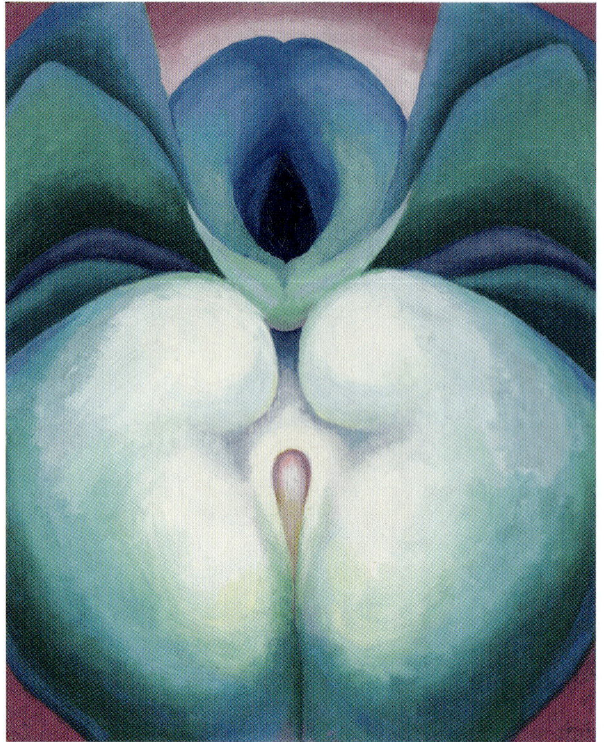

Georgia O'Keeffe. *Series I White & Blue Flower Shapes*, 1919. Oil on board.
Georgia O'Keeffe Museum, Santa Fe/Gift of The Georgia O'Keeffe Foundation.
Photo: Georgia O'Keeffe Museum, Santa Fe/Art Resource, NY/Artwork © 2022 Georgia O'Keeffe Museum/Artists Rights Society (ARS), New York

O'Keeffe's early art, roughly in the period between the two world wars, was at the crossroads of many intellectual and artistic influences. Modern art had been liberated by abstractionists like Wassily Kandinsky and expressionists like August Macke from the burden of a faithful representation of objects. There were also many styles ongoing at the same time—from Surrealism to Fauvism, from Cubism to Futurism, from Art Deco to the sinuous Art Nouveau artwork still popular in advertising. For O'Keeffe to paint her hyperrealist flowers in the 1920s—or in 1924, a sunset that is almost an abstraction in *Red, Yellow and Black Streak*—was proof of her untamed individualism and genuine artistic originality. These days, she is often celebrated as a feminist or at least as a "woman artist." The Pompidou show was more expansive, presenting her art as work created by an exceptionally individual and mature painter who never stopped searching for unique points of view.

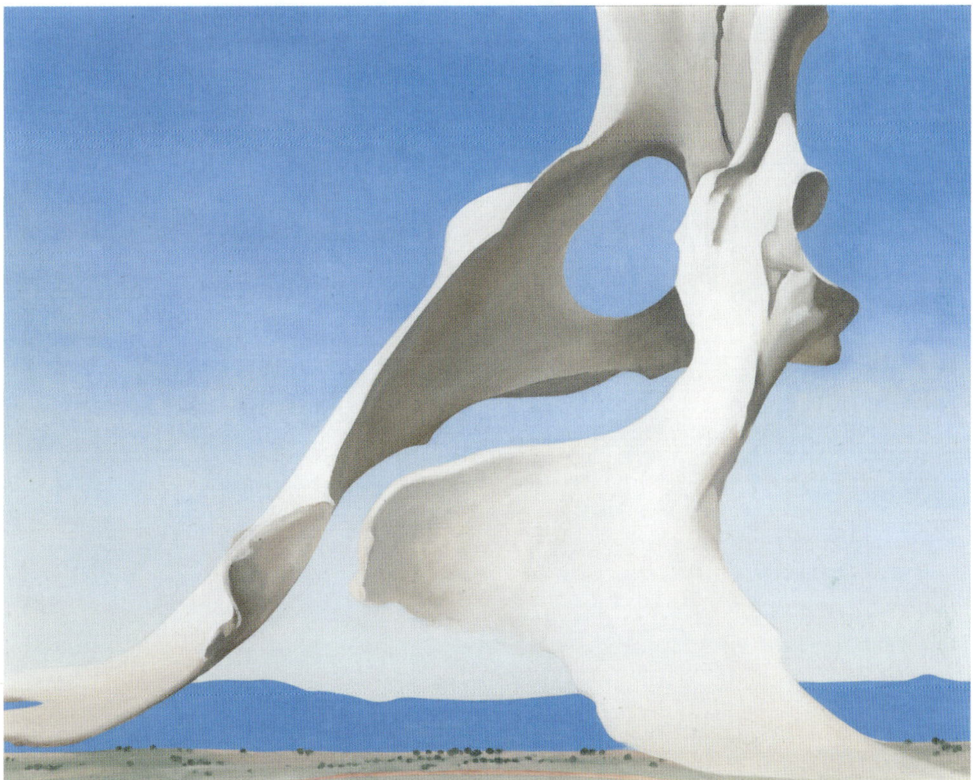

Georgia O'Keeffe. *Pelvis with the Distance*, 1943. Oil on canvas.
Indianapolis Museum of Art, Newfields.
Photo: © Indianapolis Museum of Art/Gift of Anne Marmon Greenleaf in memory of Caroline M Fesler/ Bridgeman Images/Artwork © 2022 Georgia O'Keeffe Museum/Artists Rights Society (ARS), New York

Living on the 30th floor of a Manhattan tower, O'Keeffe naturally turned her gaze on New York's skyscrapers, while her summers at the Stieglitz family property in Lake George resulted in her landscapes with black barns and lush green corn stalks. But these were "not her places," as she once confessed. She found her "own place" in 1929 when she visited an artist colony in Taos, New Mexico. The arid landscapes, the empty rolling hills, Kiowa tribe dances at night, and long walks in a red desert became the environment that nurtured this artist more than the lush but tame vegetation of upstate New York ever could have.

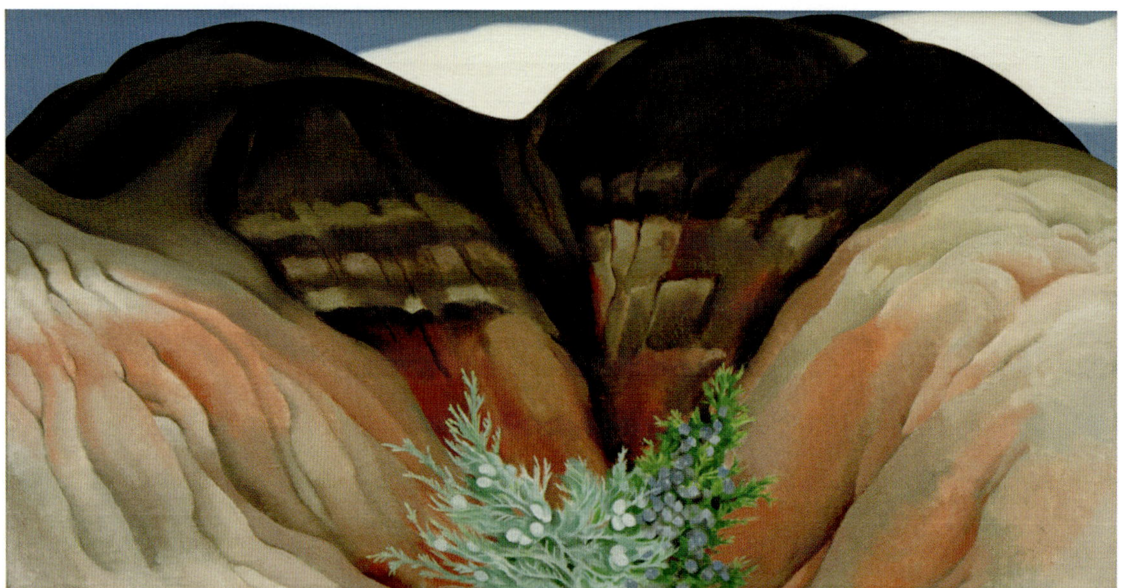

Georgia O'Keeffe. *Black Hills with Cedar*, 1941. Oil on canvas. 16 x 30 in. (40.6 x 76 cm). Hirshhorn Museum and Sculpture Garden, Washington D.C/The Joseph H. Hirshhorn Bequest, 1981. Photo: © akg-images. Artwork © 2022 Georgia O'Keeffe Museum/Artists Rights Society (ARS), New York

For the next five decades, O'Keeffe never tired of the arid and severe landscapes of the American West. Living in a succession of remote adobe houses, she contended with lack of plumbing, stifling heat, solitude, and rattlesnakes—a Wild West environment that likely would have overpowered many an explorer but that stimulated this woman with a pioneer spirit to create more and more sophisticated art.

While the Second World War raged in the world at large, O'Keeffe's austere world of New Mexican deserts inspired her to create a series of paintings depicting animal skulls and bones against the bluest sky of the West. Part meditation on the transitory nature of life and part images of hope (she did, after all, paint the piercingly blue sky beyond), these were bold, modern images that preceded the hyperrealist art movement by decades.

Where some would see lack of water and a hostile, uninhabitable desert, O'Keeffe perceived the grandeur of nature, the softness of the earth, and the stubbornness of desert plants that manage to thrive in a harsh climate. Those empty reddish hills inspired her to create some of her most striking landscapes—images that have remained fresh, modern, and beautiful decades after so many other art styles rolled through the 20th-century art scene.

For a painter, the advantage of living a long life is that there is time for evolution of style and reaching maturity. Who knows what we might have seen develop in the art of Masaccio, Raphael or Frédéric Bazille had they lived on instead of succumbing so early? In O'Keeffe's case, she had time to move beyond the landscapes (and far past her flowers) to the simplicity and elegance of "almost" abstract art.

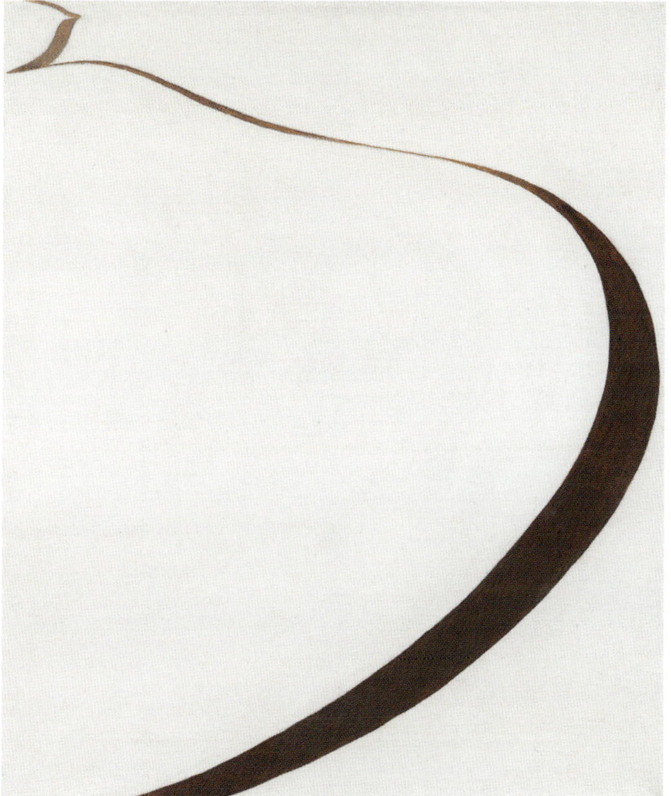

Georgia O'Keeffe. *Winter Road I*, 1963. Oil on canvas.
National Gallery of Art, Washington D.C./Gift of The Georgia O'Keeffe Foundation.
Photo: © Board of Trustees, National Gallery of Art, Washington D.C.

Her *Winter Road*, painted in 1963, is such a picture. It looks like an abstraction—or perhaps some Japanese calligraphy—but it really isn't. It is the artist's way of reducing the landscape to its core element of a winding road. But it is also still a landscape where the emptiness of white canvas can be easily filled with our knowledge of all the hilly roads we have met. The exhibition *Georgia O'Keeffe* ran between September 8 and December 6, 2021 at the Centre Pompidou in Paris.

CHAPTER 11

MAGDALENA ABAKANOWICZ (1930–2017)

"Art does not solve problems but makes us aware of their existence. It opens our eyes to see and our brain to imagine."

~ Magdalena Abakanowicz

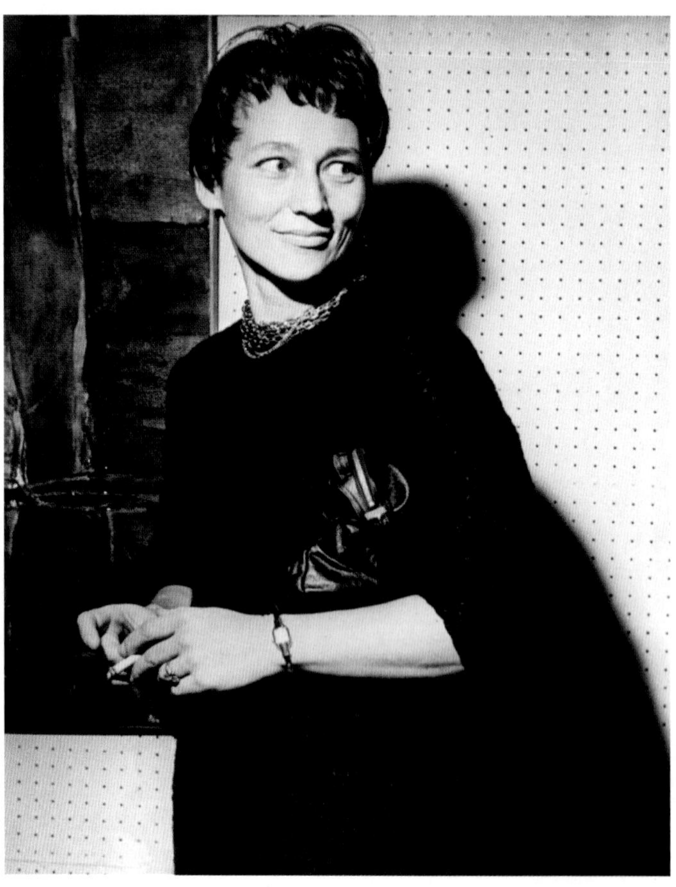

Undated photo of Magdalena Abakanowicz from c. 1960–1969.
Photo: Lebrecht Authors/Bridgeman Images

In 1962, a young woman submitted her abstract *Composition of White Forms*, woven of earth-colored cotton yards, for a competition at the first Tapestry Biennale in Lausanne. This competition entry launched the career of a unique mixed-media artist, and it helped to change the status of textile works from “craft” to “textile art.” That artist was Magdalena Abakanowicz, a fiery young noblewoman from eastern Poland (with ancestry tracing all the way back to a certain Genghis Khan) who liked to use wool yarn, sisal rope, and other industrial fibers in a way that Western artists—raised in the long tradition of tapestry as a flat wall covering that mimics a painting—could not even approach. Her monumental fiber surfaces (kilims? tapestries? gobelins?) were like nothing ever created before.

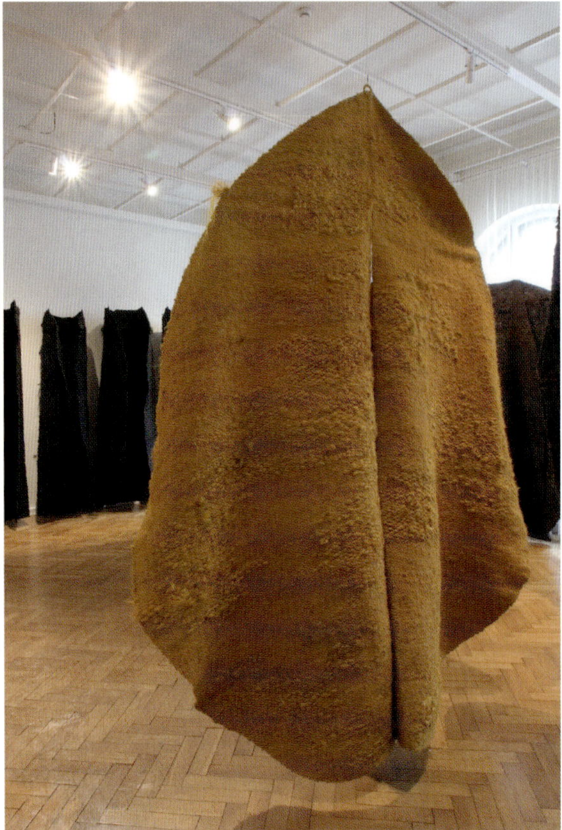

Magdalena Abakanowicz.
Yellow Abakan, 1970–1975.
Mixed media (dyed sisal, metal).
Collection of the National Museum, Wrocław.
Photo: National Museum, Wrocław

The traditional tapestry industry, mostly Belgian and French, was at the time dominated by male artists, who created designs but did not make them—the actual works were executed by manufactories and weavers. With her submission to the Lausanne competition, Abakanowicz went against all of these conventions—a woman designer from eastern Europe whose submission was a huge, almost 20-ft-long vertical abstract composition that she also made by hand herself. Her tapestry won a medal, but the artist herself never attended the event since she lived behind the Iron Curtain in Poland. Traveling abroad required money and a state permit to travel—she had neither. The same thing happened a few years later when her textile composition won a gold medal in Sao Paolo; the artist, again short of money and a travel permit, did not attend. Soon after the Lausanne show, however, grants and show invitations enabled Abakanowicz to travel to the West and establish herself as one of the most inspiring contemporary artists. Since the late 1960s, her fame has spread all over the art world, catapulted by her clear transcendence beyond traditional textile art and her entry into the world of sculpture and abstract art.

Abakanowicz's wool and jute compositions, looking like a cross between multi-dimensional kilims (Turkish rugs or carpets) and textured exotic plants, were featured in a 1969 documentary film titled "Abakans" directed by Jarosław Brzozowski and Kazimierz Mucha. Because her large, fibrous structures did not fit into any existing genre, the filmmakers simply created one from her family name. The name stuck and "*Abakans*" became a perfect, unique moniker for her art.

In 1965, Abakanowicz started to teach tapestry and textile art at the State Graduate School of Art at Poznań University. Even though she acquired a devoted following of students who flocked to her classes from all over the world, she resisted having her creations categorized as textiles or even anything one-dimensional. Moving beyond the two-dimensional "*Abakans*" textile hangings—some of which were exhibited at New York's MoMA and in Chicago in the early 1970s—she started exploring tridimensional, "winged" structures and grew more and more interested in sculpture, or at least in the architectural aspects of what she called "fibrous art."

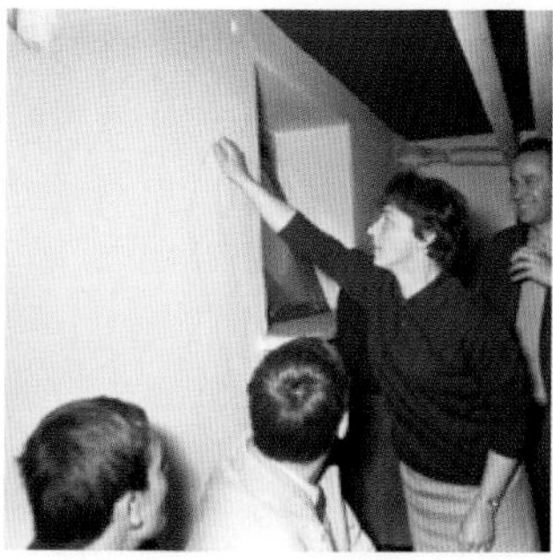

Magdalena Abakanowicz at the State School of Decorative Arts in Poznań (behind her Wacław Twarowski), mid-1960s.
Photo: Jerzy Nowakowski, Collection of Magdalena Abakanowicz University of the Arts in Poznań, Courtesy of Magdalena Abakanowicz University of the Arts in Poznań

A 2021 exhibition held at the Magdalena Abakanowicz University of the Arts in Poznań spotlighted Abakanowicz's artistic transition, not long after the art school was renamed after Abakanowicz (who spent 25 years teaching there). To celebrate this event, the National Museum in Poznań and the University mounted a major show of some of her most famous and seminal works. The exhibition's title is a quote from the artist: "We are fibrous structures." Her early "*Abakans*" are definitely that—fibers that evoke the viscosity and texture of human tissues.

The exhibition showcased not only the famous "*Abakans*" (a major feat since the museum had to assemble these huge, complicated works from faraway museums and private collections while contending with pandemic restrictions) but also the next steps in the artist's development. She once declared: "*My weaving and use of soft materials comes out of my need to protest. A desire to question all the rules and habits connected with the material.*"

In the 1970s, Abakanowicz moved on to abstract structures, like those made out of burlap sacks and sailing ropes.

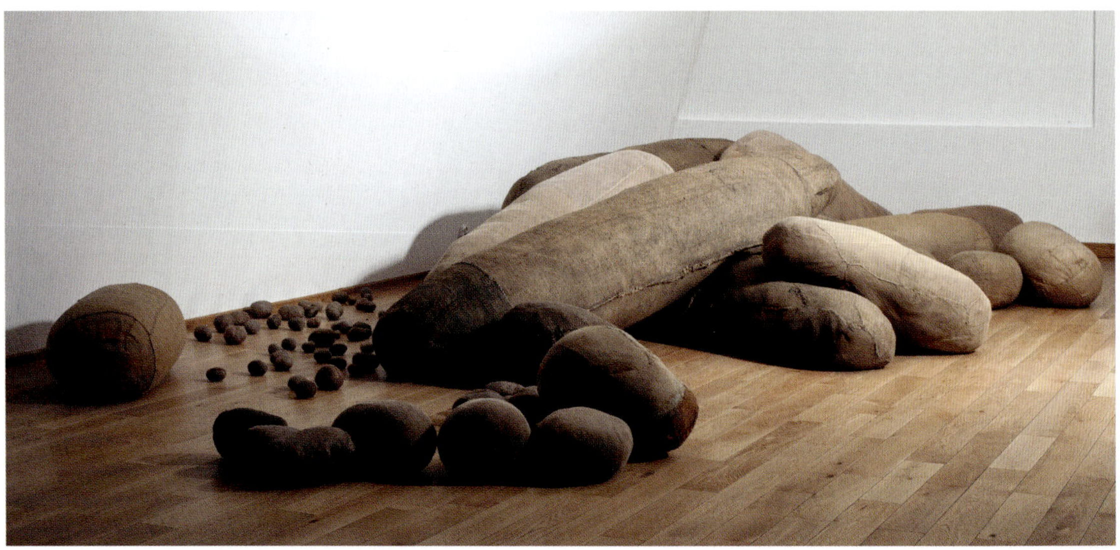

Magdalena Abakanowicz. *Embryology*, 1978–1980. Mixed media (jute fabric, cotton gauze, sisal; filling: mixed material).
Collection of the National Museum, Wrocław.
Photo: National Museum, Wrocław

And then, almost inevitably, she started to explore human figures.

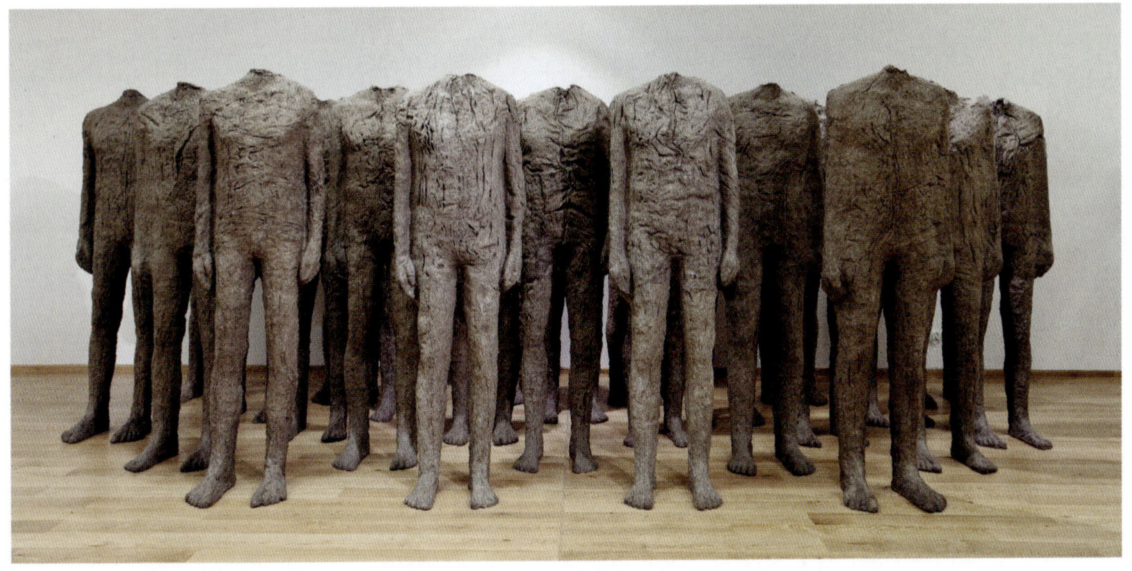

Magdalena Abakanowicz. *Crowd*, 1986–1994. Mixed media (jute fabric, resin).
Collection of the National Museum, Wrocław.
Photo: National Museum, Wrocław

Abakanowicz made her name living in the materially limited world of communist Poland—where even the simplest art materials were hard to obtain, foreign travel was limited, and art was sometimes criticized for suspect political content. Her early works were made from interestingly textured materials at hand: laundry clotheslines, sisal cords, yacht ropes, burlap grain sacs, even some branches found by the roadside. At the same time, the artist struggled against having her work categorized as "decorative art" (as tapestries ordinarily would be); though she was using craft fibers, an affordable and plentiful material, clearly she did so as a means toward the expression of pure art.

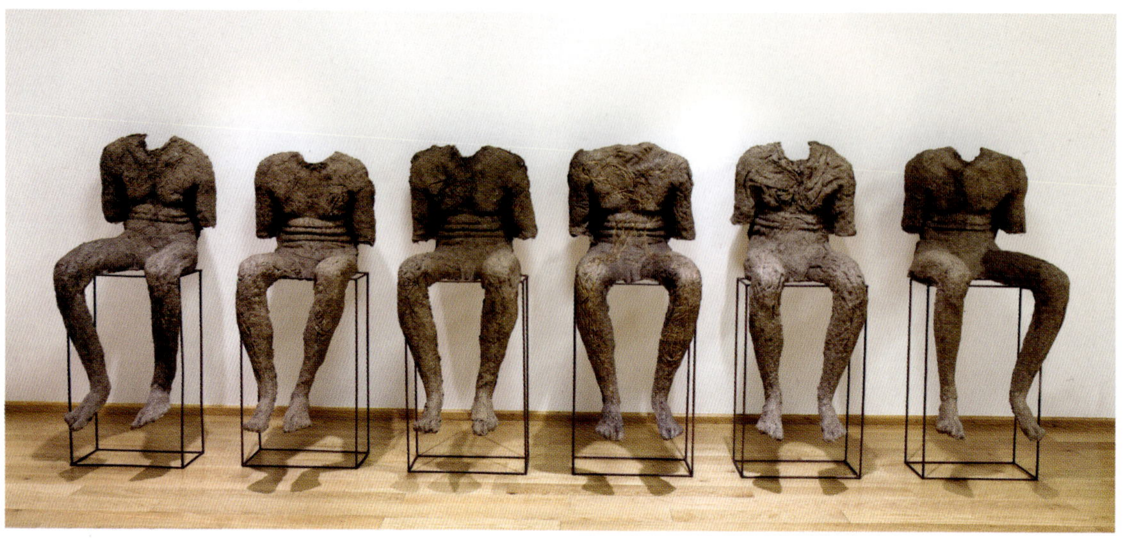

Magdalena Abakanowicz. *Seated Figures*, 1974–1984. Mixed media (jute fabric, resin, metal).
Collection of the National Museum, Wrocław.
Photo: National Museum, Wrocław

Through her "*Abakans*" and then numerous figurative installations, Abakanowicz explored her ideas about what moves or inspires or animates a human body. The relationship of the flesh to consciousness—probed so insightfully in a Zen koan (Hsu Yun's famous "Who is dragging this corpse around?")—seems to be a central tenet of Abakanowicz's later art. She created entire tribes of barely human figures, often headless or misshapen—human and dehumanized at the same time—not unlike the contemporary world that we all live in.

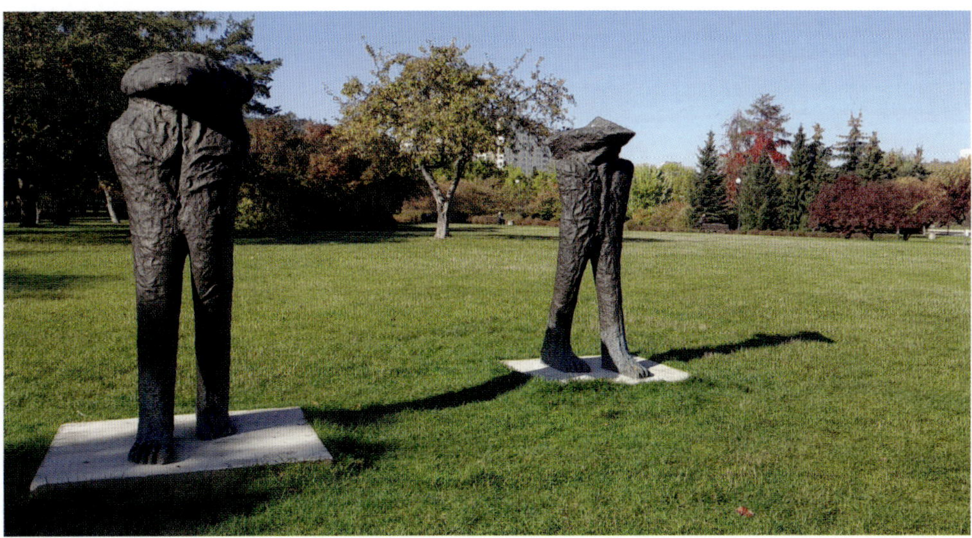

Magdalena Abakanowicz. *Zinaxi and Dolacin*. Bronze.
Installation at Bródno Park, Warsaw, 2021.
Photo: Joanna Barszczewska-Groszek

Moving into figurative art relieved Abakanowicz of the unwelcome label of craft or textile maker and allowed her to use the unconventional medium of fiber to create her disturbing, truncated figures—hunched, headless, anonymous, but powerfully present. Her installations moved outside to park and museum settings. She started creating groups of figures and eventually, like so many sculptors, ended up creating some of them in the most venerated of sculpture mediums—the bronze.

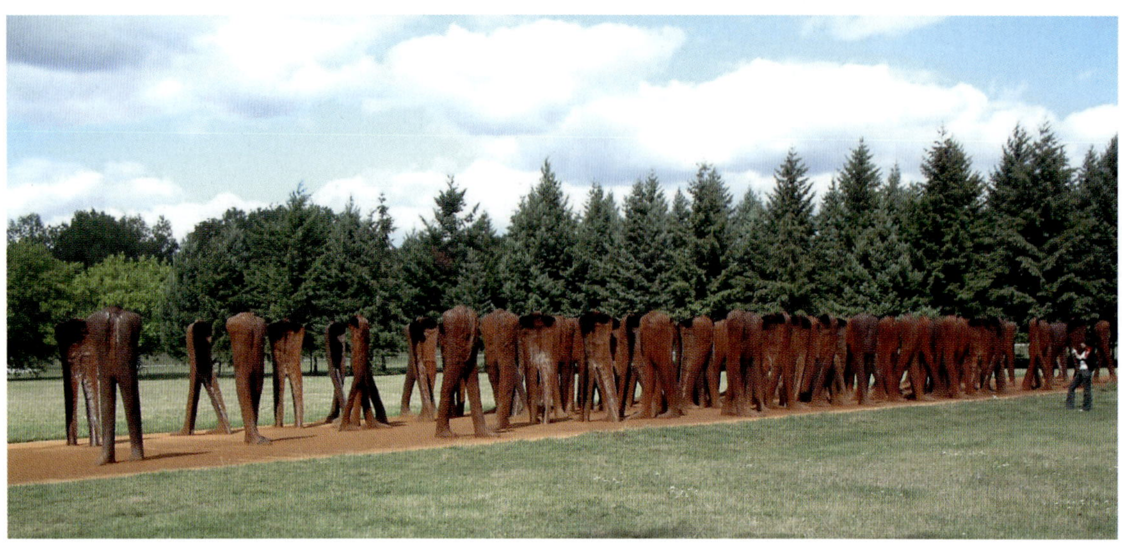

Magdalena Abakanowicz. *Unrecognized/Nierozpoznani* installation, 2002. Bronze.
Poznań Cytadela Park.
Photo: Radomil, CC BY-SA 3.0 <https://creativecommons.org/licenses/by-sa/3.0/>, via Wikimedia Commons

Abakanowicz passed away in 2017, leaving behind an art landscape populated with works made out of any material imaginable by scores of artists who went on to further blur the lines between craft, installation, sculpture, painting, and other mediums of expression. These days, museumgoers routinely encounter objects admired as art that owe something to the pioneering eye of this woman from a remote corner of Europe. Once you have seen an "*Abakan*" or her installation of headless hunched human shapes, all subsequent forays in contemporary art gain a bit more context—you can see where they may have come from, and sometimes they definitely come from the unique world of Magdalena Abakanowicz.

The exhibition *We Are Fibrous Structures* took place at the National Museum in Poznań, Poland between August 8 and October 24, 2021.

PART III

Women at the Studio

CHAPTER 12

ROSALBA CARRIERA (1673–1757)

There are some languages, like German, Polish, and Latin, that have many grammatical cases (so-called declensions) and three genders. You must know exactly what you are going to say before you say your sentence, or it will never come out right. You cannot change your mind halfway. Painting with pastels is a bit like that. You need to know what colors you will use and be sure of your lines because this medium does not really allow mixing pigments or easily painting over the lines in the same way that you might do if you were to change your mind when painting with oils. Painting with pastels is not for hesitant artists.

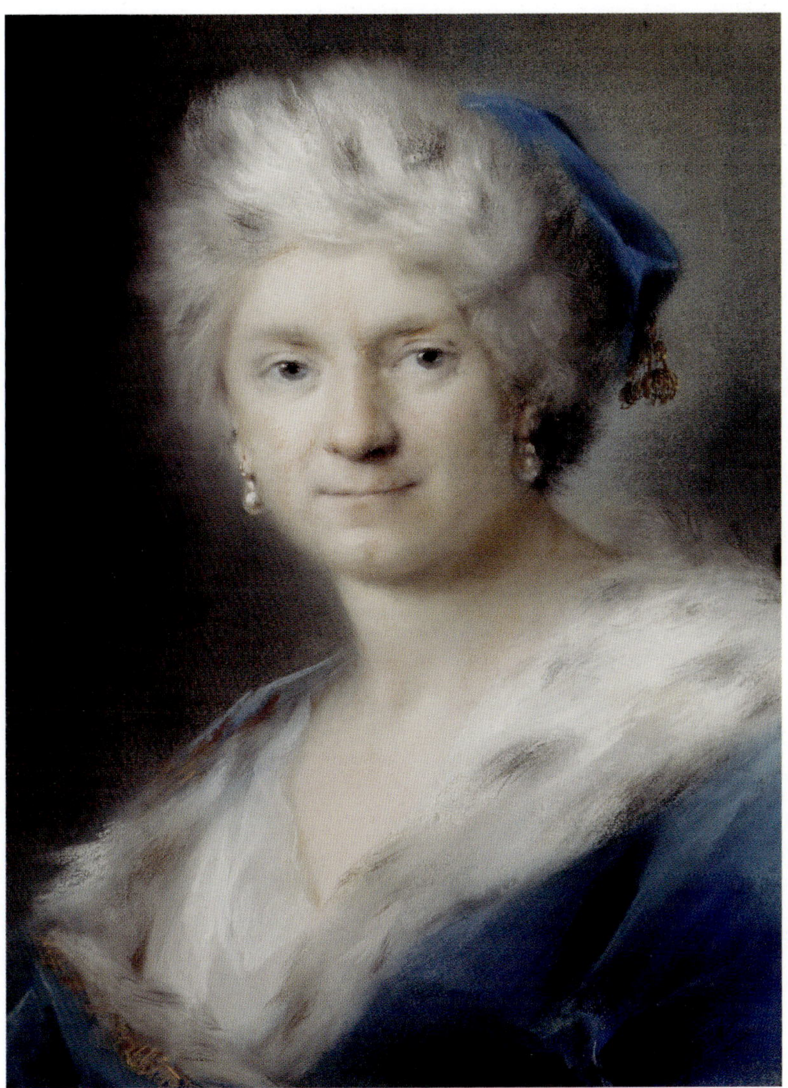

Rosalba Carriera. *Self-Portrait as "Winter,"* 1731. Pastel on paper.
State Art Museum, Dresden.
Photo: Public domain, via Wikimedia Commons

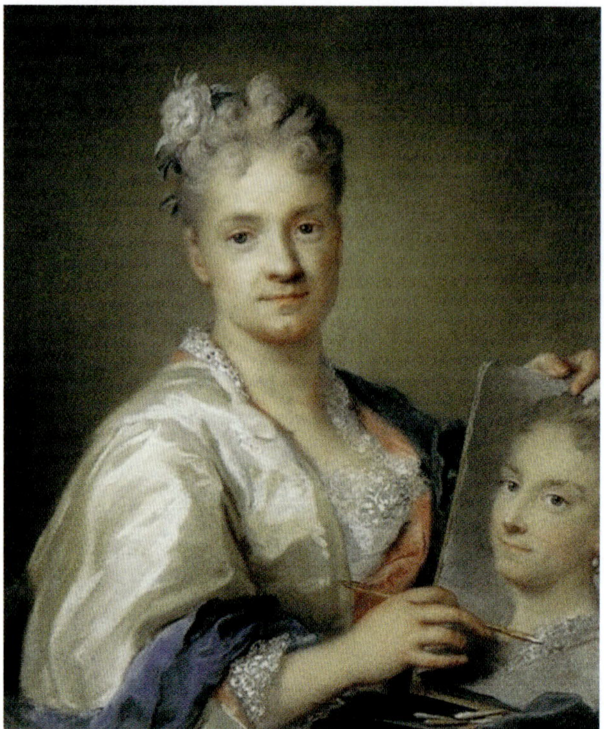

Rosalba Carriera. *Self-Portrait Holding a Portrait of Her Sister*, 1715. Pastel on paper.
Galleria degli Uffizi, Florence.
Photo: Public domain via Wikimedia Commons

The Rococo painter Rosalba Carriera was a pastelist, one of the most famous of her time. Rococo is not a style that appeals strongly to our contemporary sensibilities. It often feels too sweet, kitschy, and insubstantial. It is not easy to have weight in such a style. Only a few artists achieved it, one of them being Carriera, whose chosen medium of pastels was considered by her contemporaries as "suitable for women artists" but whose output was hardly just the pastime of a dilettante.

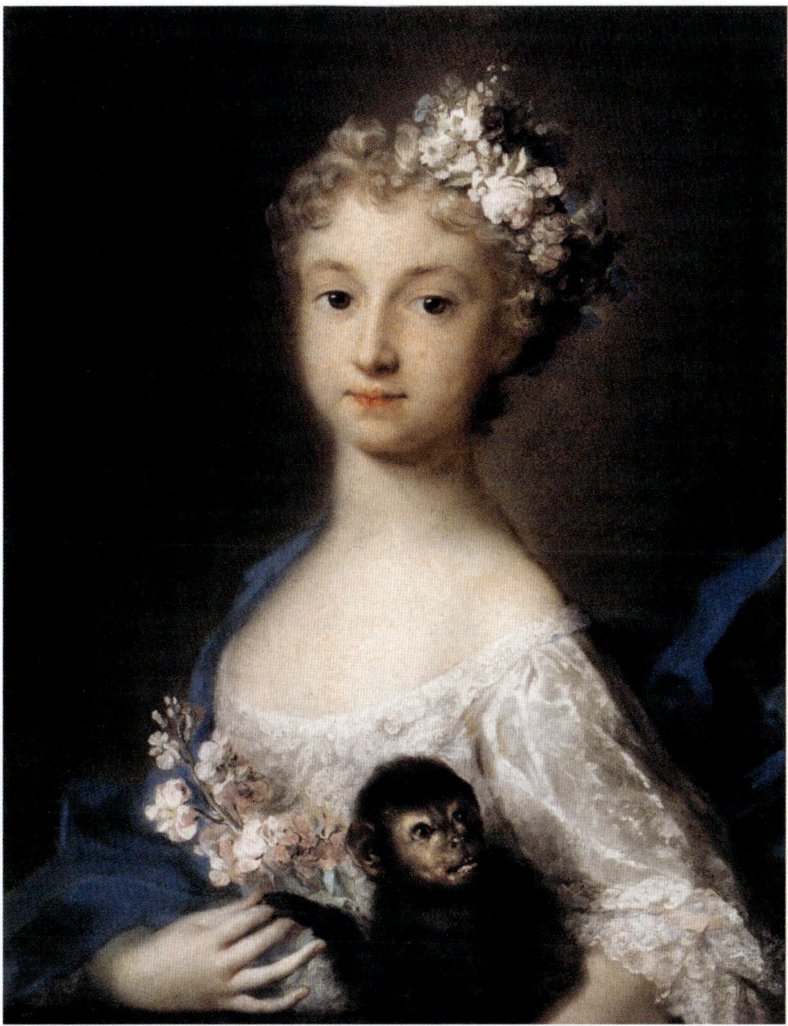

Rosalba Carriera. *Young Girl Holding a Monkey*, c. 1721. Pastel on paper.
The Louvre, Paris.
Photo: Public domain via Wikimedia Commons

Pastels are particularly suitable for rendering fabric surfaces that catch light, and Carriera was the master of this visual treat. She would render silk and embroidery as distinctly and easily as lace and fur. In the portrait *Young Girl Holding a Monkey*, she contrasts the white lace on the girl's sleeve with the fluffy fur of the pet monkey. This is all done with a few scratches of a chalky-colored substance on coarse paper.

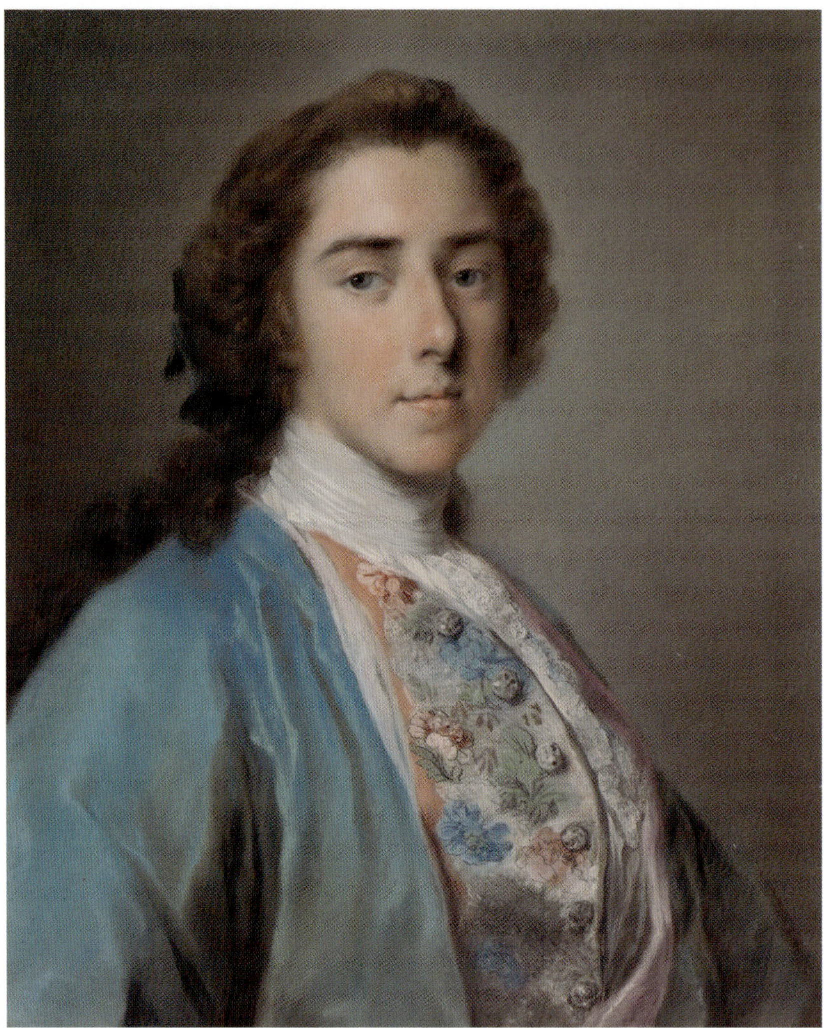

Rosalba Carriera. *Portrait of Henry Fiennes Pelham-Clinton, ninth Earl of Lincoln and second Duke of Newcastle*, 1741. Pastel on paper.
Yale Center for British Art, New Haven.
Photo: Public domain CC0 via Wikimedia Commons

In the aristocratic portrait of the Duke of Newcastle, she draws the lines of intricate embroidery and the alternating shades of blue-yellow shot silk as precisely as if the portrait were a color photo. This was as good as it got in the age before photography (and color photography did not come into widespread use until the late 1960s).

For comparison, here is a look at another Venetian pastelist of the era, Marianna Carlevaris, whose hand was much less accomplished.

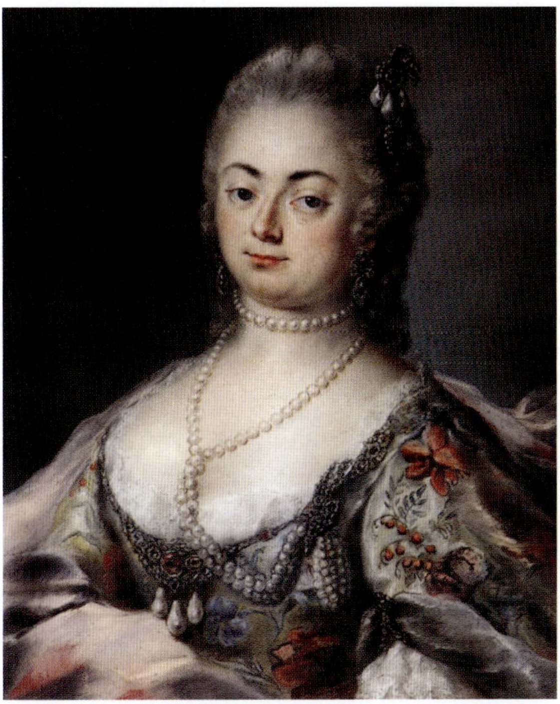

Marianna Carlevaris. *Portrait of Cornelia Froscolo Balbi*, 1740–1742. Pastel on paper.
Ca' Rezzonico, Venice.
Photo: Public domain via Wikimedia Commons

Rosalba Carriera was a Venetian, born at a time when her city was changing from being a shipping and trading superpower to a tourist attraction. By 1600, Venice's domination of sea lanes had declined (mainly due to the opening of western trading routes after Columbus's voyage of 1492 and the decline of the Silk Road after the fall of Constantinople), and there was a need for this once-mighty city to find other sources of revenue. By 1700 when Rosalba was 25 years old, the city was thriving on an early tourist trade and the manufacture of luxury goods. The highborns of Europe, especially England and France, would complete a rite of passage called a Grand Tour, spending a year or two in places such as Venice or Paris before settling down on their home estates and entering politics or commerce. Venice, especially during the carnival, was an obligatory stop on such a tour, which also required the purchase of souvenir paintings and drawings. This is the market in which the young and talented Rosalba thrived. After starting by decorating snuffboxes and painting miniatures, she soon graduated to the quick medium of pastels, providing portraits of traveling aristocrats or daughters of local notables. Even in those commissioned souvenir works, she displayed her mastery.

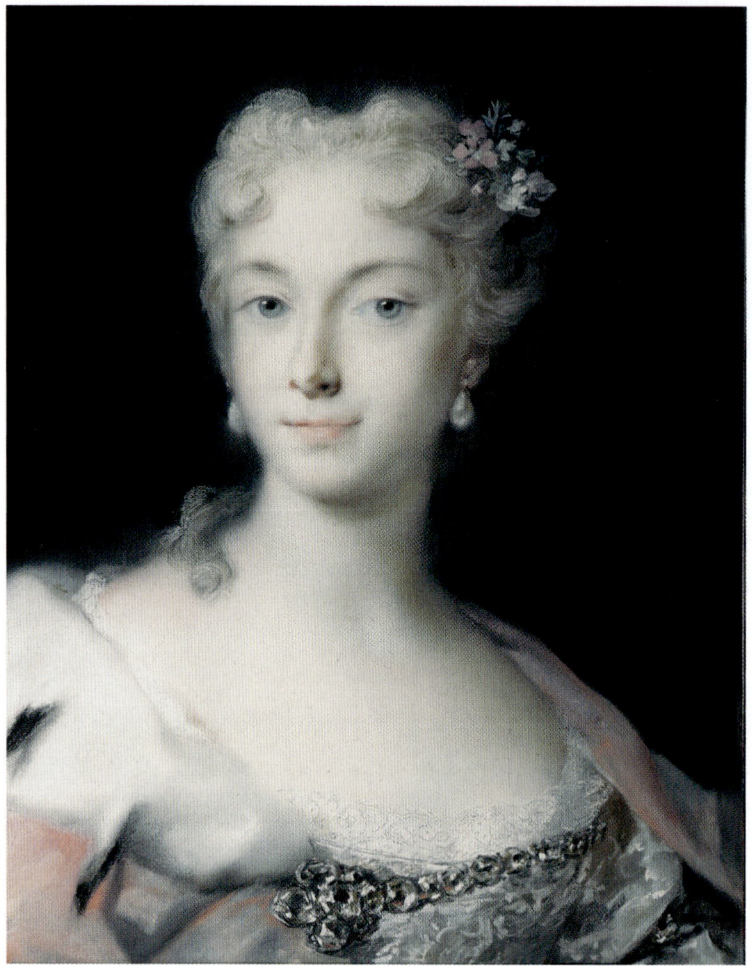

Rosalba Carriera. *Portrait of Maria Theresa of Austria, Archduchess of Habsburg*, 1730. Pastel on paper.
State Art Museum, Dresden.
Photo: Public domain via Wikimedia Commons

In 1720, wealthy banker and collector Pierre Crozat invited Carriera to Paris, precisely at the time when the new boy king Louis XV moved the court to Paris, and French society embraced a new decorative style. Gone was the heavier, gold-dripping, "the-state-is-me" style of Sun King Louis XIV. The new class of urban nobility and the successful, art-collecting bourgeoisie wanted a new decorative style—elegant but lighter and more pleasure-seeking. Carriera only spent a year in Paris, but she is credited with introducing the medium of colorful chalk sticks to France and popularizing Rococo sensibilities in France and even England. Her later followers included Maurice Quentin de La Tour and Elisabeth Vigée Le Brun. Carriera kept busy during her stay in Paris, attending fashionable literary salons and completing many important commissions. She even painted a portrait of the 10-year-old Louis XV (complaining in her correspondence that he was fidgety). Through Crozat, she also met Antoine Watteau, who was very enthusiastic about her art. She paid back the compliment with a great psychological portrait of the French master, who was living on borrowed time, his body being racked with tuberculosis. You can see his pale and melancholy look in this portrait, so different from the rosy-cheeked and flowery portraits of young mademoiselles that Carriera otherwise produced for her noble clients.

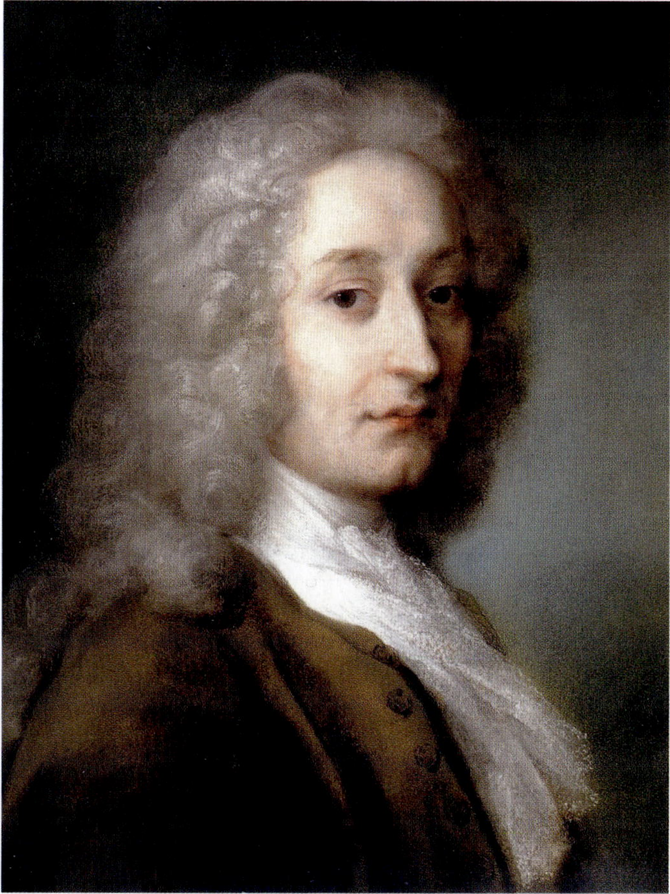

Rosalba Carriera. *Portrait of Antoine Watteau*, 1721. Pastel on paper.
Museum Luigi Balio, Treviso.
Photo: Public domain via Wikimedia Commons

Carriera's exceptional skills also came to the attention of King Augustus II the Strong, the ruler of Saxony who was offered a crown (twice!) by warring factions of Polish nobility. As a result, he traveled a lot between his German lands and Poland, keeping his court in the eastern city of Dresden. He purchased from Carriera a large collection of her pastels for his Dresden gallery (and this collection of about 150 of them is still there). She painted him and his family as well as his offspring with numerous mistresses. One of them was Augustus II's natural daughter, the countess Anna Orzelska.

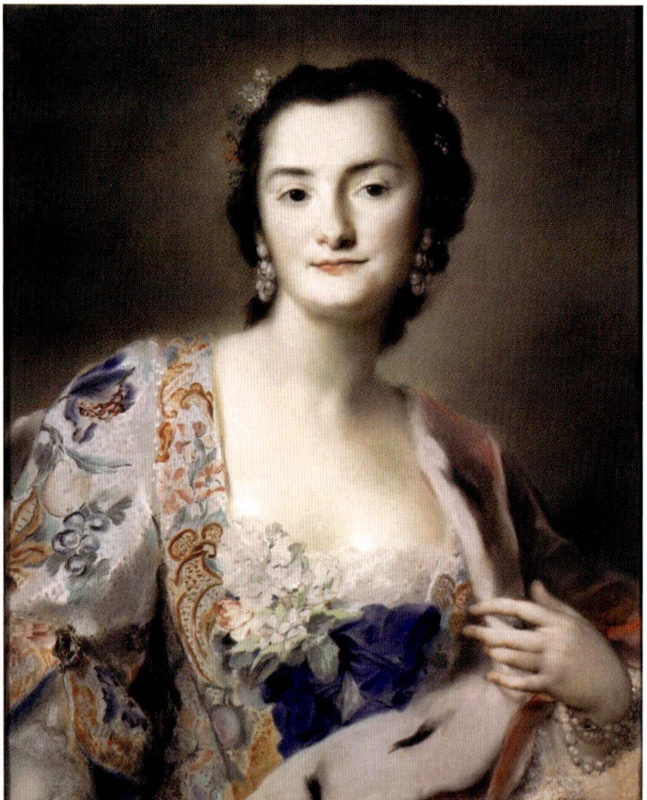

Rosalba Carriera. *Portrait of the Countess Anna Katharina Orzelska*, 1730s. Pastel on paper.
State Art Museum, Dresden.
Photo: Public domain via Wikimedia Commons

This is one of the most naturalistic and "modern-looking" portraits by Carriera. Orzelska, who was famous for her beauty and a freewheeling lifestyle, is shown here as a woman who would look perfect even in a glamorous old Hollywood photo. Carriera's trademark virtuoso rendering of fabric is present as well.

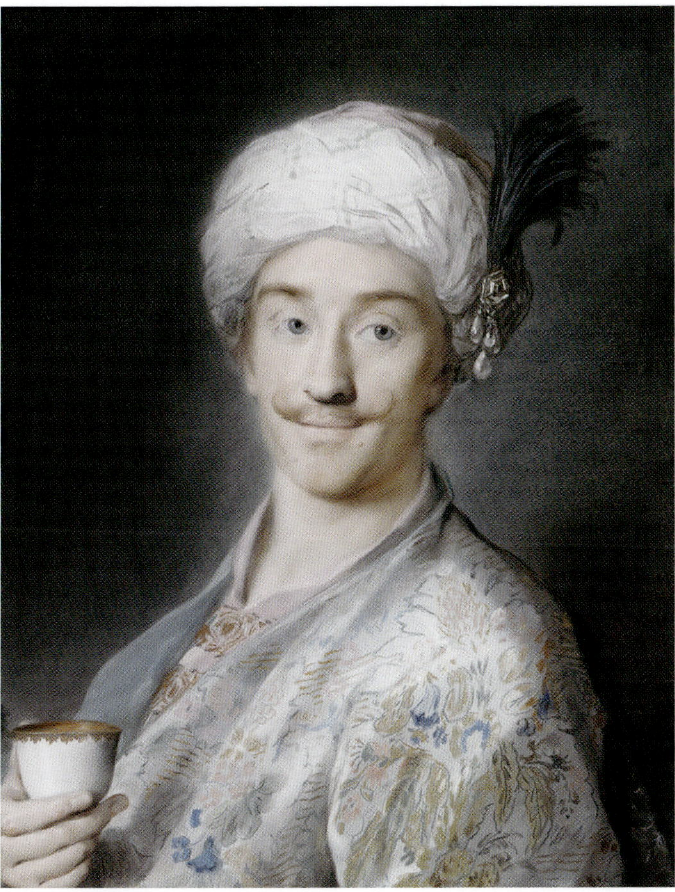

Rosalba Carriera. *The Turk*, c. 1720s. Pastel on paper.
State Art Museum, Dresden.
Photo: Public domain via Wikimedia Commons

The sophisticated European elites of the 18th century were in the grip of "Turkish fashion," with an idealized image of the "Orient" that manifested itself in a passion for coffee or chocolate drinking, orientalized designs in clothing, an unquenchable thirst for silk fabrics and...being painted as "Turks" or even "harem dancers." Mozart's early opera *The Abduction from the Seraglio* was part of the same Turkish craze. Carriera painted several portraits of titled subjects who wanted to look exotic, and *The Turk* is probably the best example. The model is a blue-eyed man, probably French, looking at us with a rakish smile and gripping the obligatory, fashionable cup of chocolate. When Starbucks was introduced to Eastern Europe in the late 2000s, customers started posting photos on social media, holding those green logo cups with similarly excited grins.

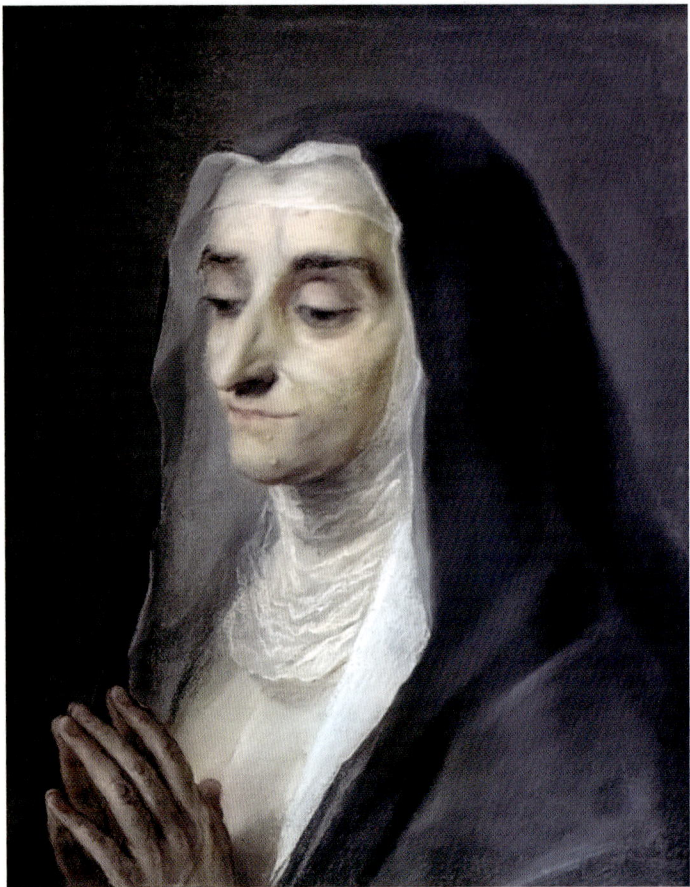

Rosalba Carriera. *Portrait of Sister Maria Caterina Puppi*, 1732. Pastel on paper.
Ca' Rezzonico, Venice.
Photo: Rosalba Carriera, CC BY-SA 4.0 <https://creativecommons.org/licenses/by-sa/4.0>, via Wikimedia Commons/Didier Descouens

Not all of Carriera's paintings were the typical Rococo lace-and-ribbons sweet portraits and allegories. Here, for example, is a very realistic and moving portrait of a nun. Carriera makes her aged face both serene and serious, not hiding any wrinkles or the sagging skin on her hands.

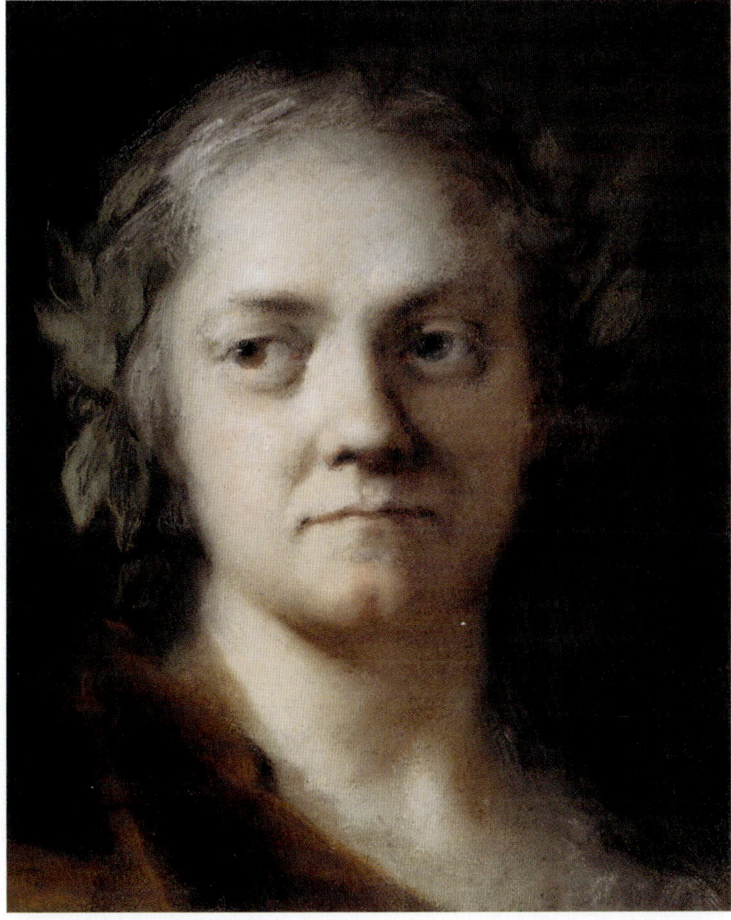

Rosalba Carriera. *Self-Portrait*, c. 1743–1747. Pastel on paper.
Gallerie dell'Accademia, Venice.
Photo: Public domain via Wikimedia Commons

Nor did Carriera have the vanity to hide her own imperfections. Here is a self-portrait of her in middle age—again, with no glossing over of lines and puffiness. She painted what she saw rather than create an idealized smooth portrait so typical of the portraiture of the time.

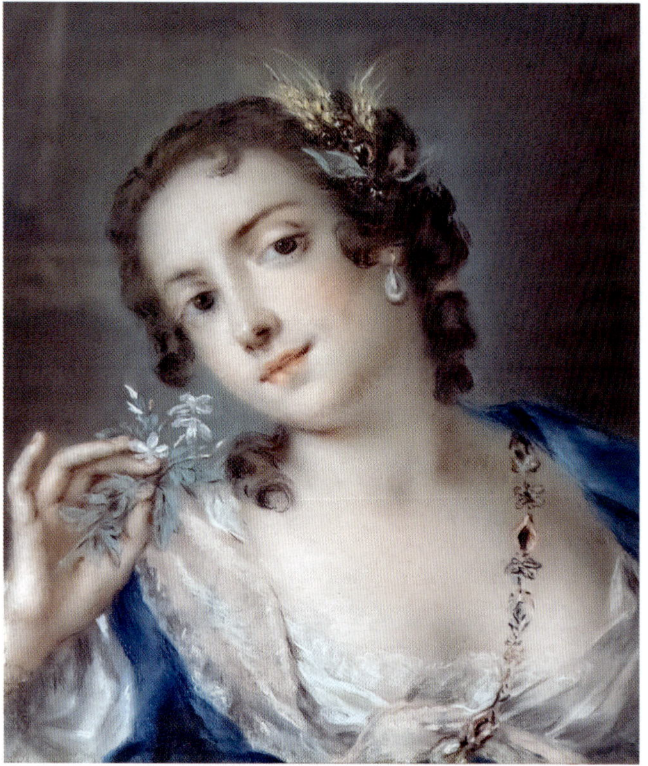

Rosalba Carriera. *Summer*, c. 1725. Pastel on paper.
Fondation Bemberg, Toulouse.
Photo: Public domain, CC BY-SA 4.0 <https://creativecommons.org/licenses/by-sa/4.0>, via Wikimedia Commons/didier descouens

An oil painting never looks as good on a computer screen as in real life—the texture is flattened, the gloss is gone, the brushstrokes are lost. But, strangely enough, pastels seem to gain with the advent of electronic screens—they somehow look richer and more saturated, and the chalky surface becomes smoother. So... Rosalba Carriera, an artist who almost exclusively created in pastels and as a result was relegated in art history to a position of a lesser artist, somehow seems to gain in the age of electronic images and reproductions.

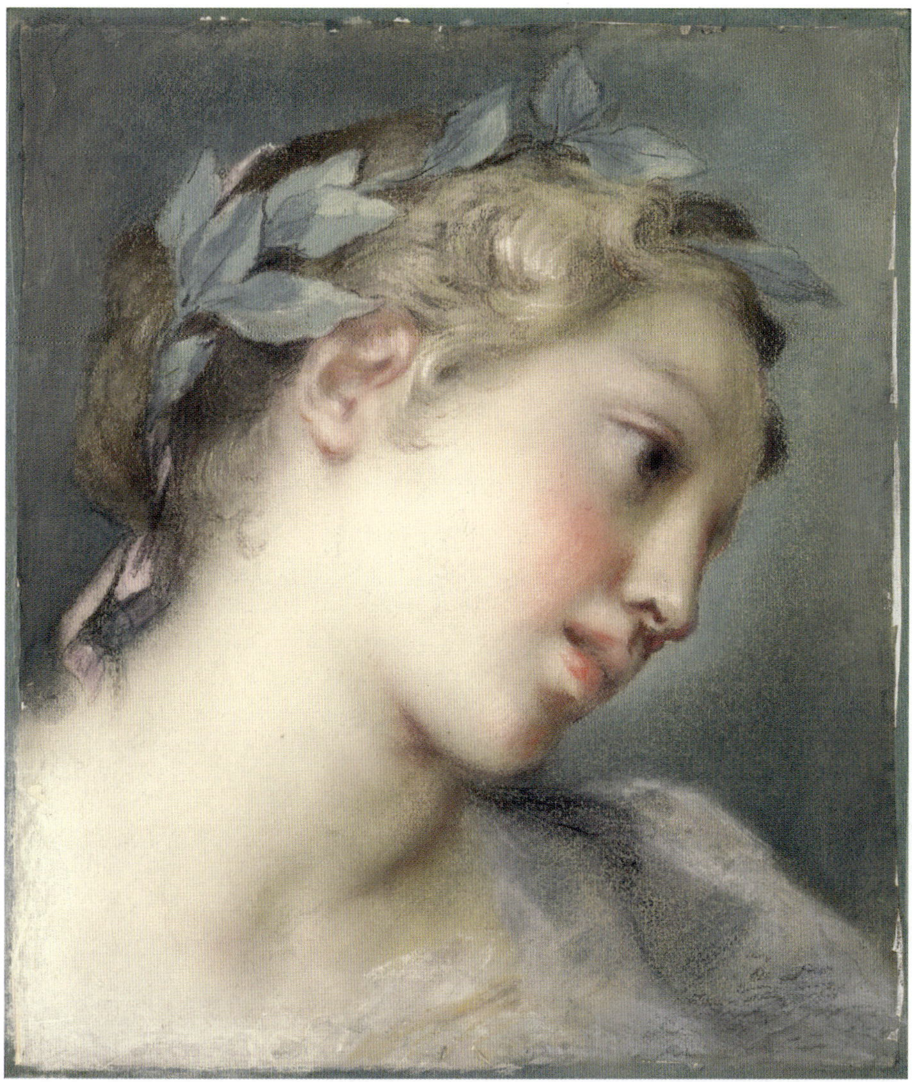

Rosalba Carriera. *A Muse*, c. 1725. Pastel on blue paper.
The J. Paul Getty Museum, Los Angeles.
Photo: Wikimedia Commons

CHAPTER 13

ELISABETH VIGÉE LE BRUN (1755–1842)

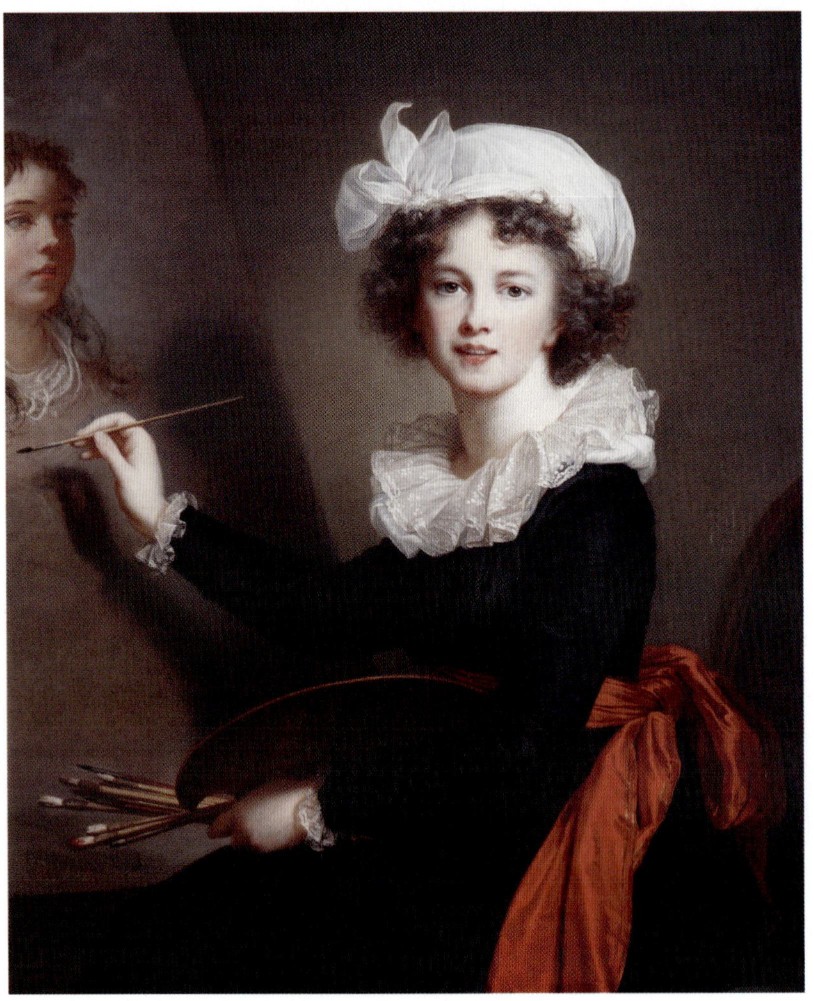

Elisabeth Vigée Le Brun. *Self-Portrait*, 1791. Oil on canvas.
Ickworth House, Suffolk, UK.
Photo: National Trust Photographic Library/Bridgeman Images

When we think of the French upper classes just before the French Revolution, what comes to mind are those impossible panniered gowns, powdered wigs, rouged cheeks, and ostrich feathers. Which is indeed what the aristocrats of the time were wearing, but the winds of change were already blowing, at least in fashion and social ideas. Thanks to Jean-Jacques Rousseau and other social thinkers, the need for less artifice in life started to penetrate the upper echelons of French society. Rousseau advocated being closer to nature and rearing one's young in a different way than the cold-turkey approach of keeping children in faraway nurseries and convents, and having newborns fed by country nursemaids.

Into this changing world of the second part of the 18th century came Elisabeth Vigée Le Brun, the talented daughter of a minor Parisian pastel artist who cherished his daughter's gift and encouraged her painterly education. Though she had a precocious talent and ultimately lived as a friend to royalty all over Europe, she was repeatedly bowled over by circumstances beyond her control. Her mastery of her craft came in handy all too soon when her father died when she was only 12, leaving Elisabeth to earn money for her mother's and younger brother's upkeep. This was the first of many curveballs thrown in her direction by life's circumstances, followed soon by another when her mother's remarriage introduced a cruel stepfather who took all the money that the teenage painter earned.

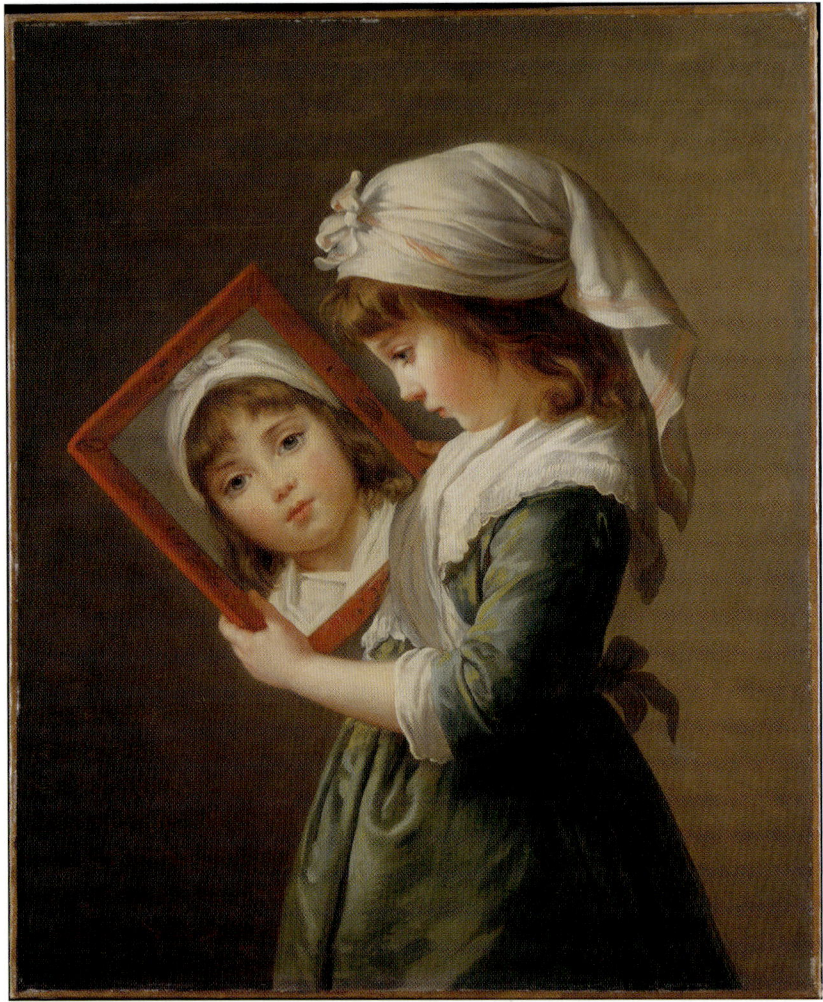

Elisabeth Vigée Le Brun. *Julie Le Brun Looking in a Mirror*, 1787. Oil on canvas.
Metropolitan Museum of Art, New York.
Photo: Metropolitan Museum of Art/Bequest of Mrs. Charles Wrightsman, 2019

Elisabeth overcame this obstacle as well, only to have her studio seized for practicing the craft of painting without a license. At 19, as an established portraitist, she finally managed to get accepted to Académie de Saint-Luc—a guild that legitimized her work status. Two years later, in 1776, she also gained social respectability by marrying an art dealer, Jean-Baptiste-Pierre Le Brun; he gave her a name and a daughter but little else, since he turned out to be a gambler who lived off his wife's growing earnings. They were estranged after a couple of years of marriage and divorced in absentia during the Revolution.

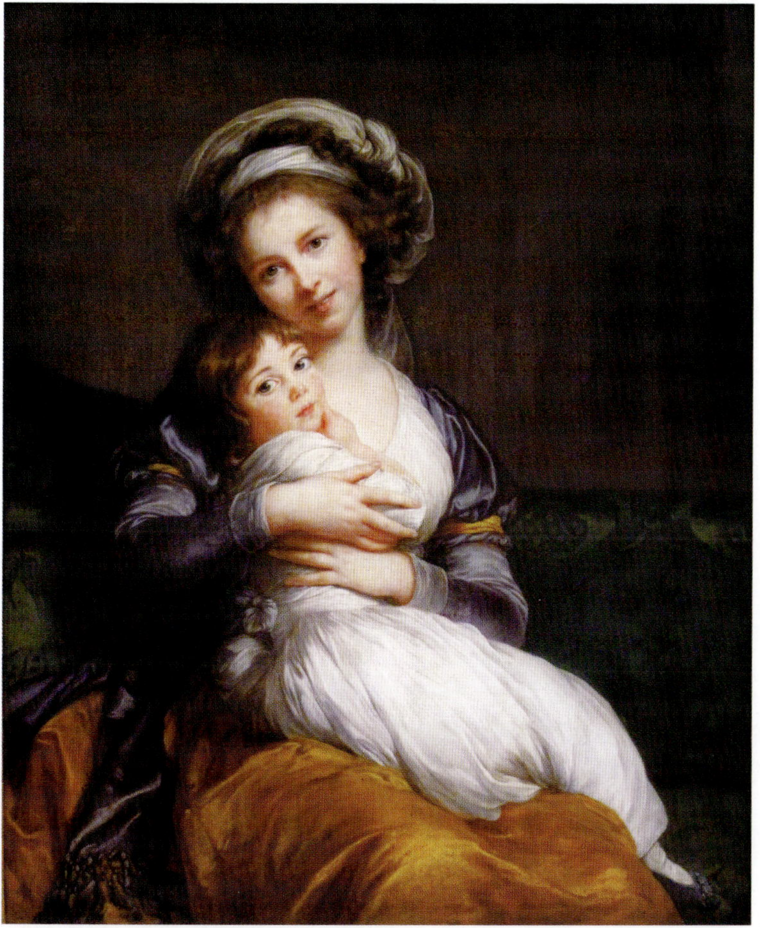

Elisabeth Vigée Le Brun. *Self-Portrait with Her Daughter, Julie*, 1786. Oil on panel.
The Louvre, Paris.
Photo: Public domain via Wikimedia Commons

Elisabeth, very much influenced by Rousseau's ideas, developed a close and loving relationship with her young daughter Julie. Only progressive women of her class would do this at the time; otherwise, children of nobility and the upper bourgeoisie would be sent off to a wet nurse at birth and then be seen by their parents only at formal occasions. There is a charming and clever portrait of Julie Le Brun when she was about five; the girl is not only exquisitely painted but also interestingly portrayed en face through the mirror and directly in profile. Elisabeth's self-portrait with Julie painted a year later caused a scandal when it was exhibited at the Salon of 1787. It featured the artist smiling and showing her teeth—a look acceptable perhaps in a genre painting but not in nobility portraiture.

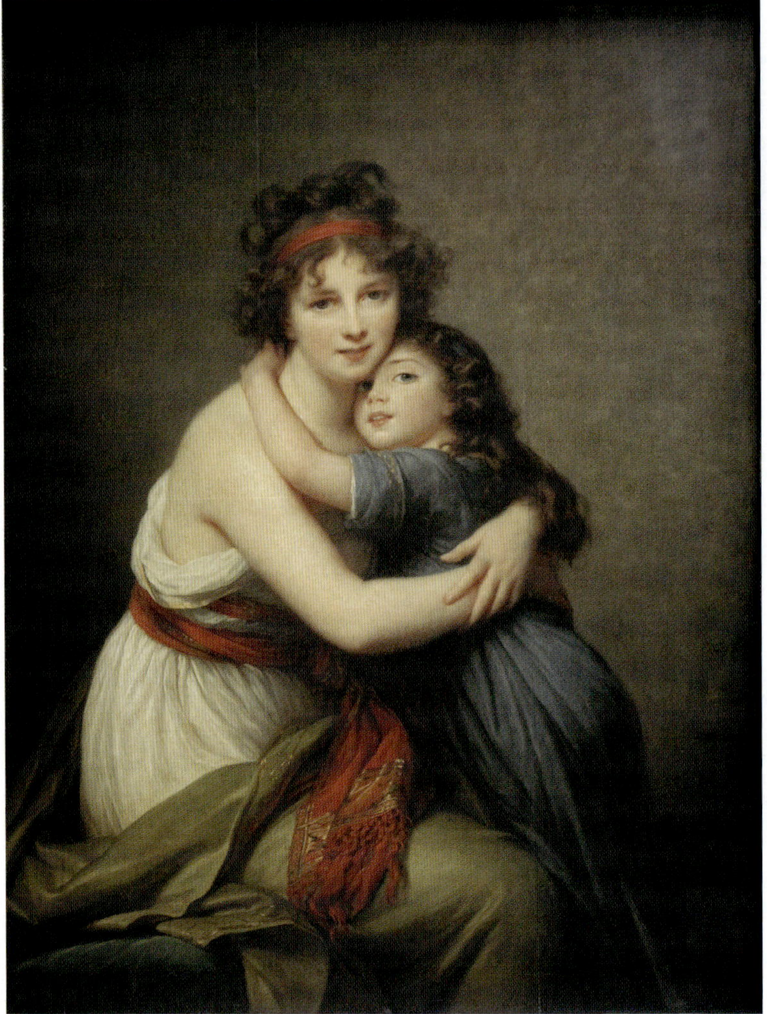

Elisabeth Vigée Le Brun. *Self-Portrait with Her Daughter*, 1789. Oil on canvas.
The Louvre, Paris.
Photo: Public domain via Wikimedia Commons

There is another equally famous and charming portrait of Elisabeth tenderly holding her child. This one is perhaps more conventional, except that this deliberate pose evokes Raphael's *The Small Cowper Madonna*.

Elisabeth's output was not limited to portraying her child. Professionally and socially, she was climbing. In 1781, she went on a journey to Holland and Flanders —places that were a painter's paradise, full of works by Rembrandt, Rubens, and other masters of the Northern Baroque.

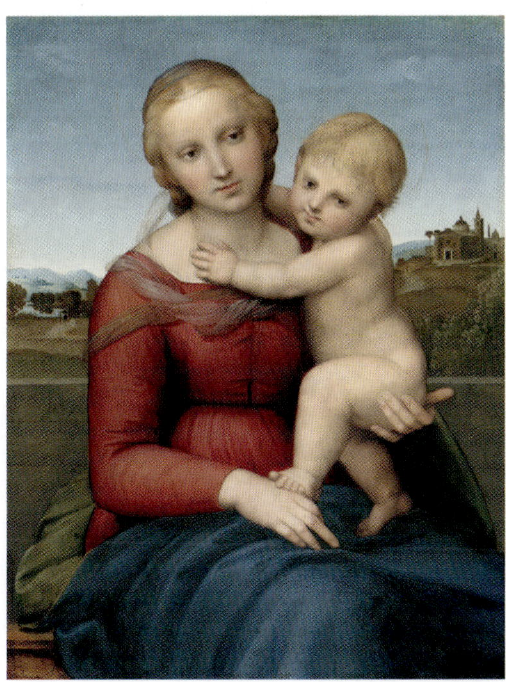

Raphael.
The Small Cowper Madonna,
c. 1505. Oil on panel.
Widener Collection/National Gallery of Art, Washington D.C.
Photo: Widener Collection/National Gallery of Art, Washington D.C.

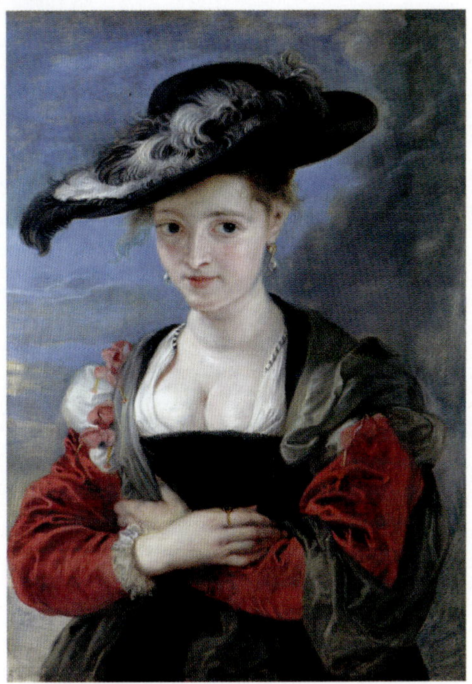

Peter Paul Rubens.
Portrait of Susanna Lunden,
c. 1622–1625. Oil on oak panel.
National Gallery, London.
Photo: Bridgeman Images

She saw there the famous *Portrait of Susanna Lunden*, also known as *The Straw Hat*—a panel by Rubens that inspired her greatly. This image, together with the rising, Rousseau-inspired fashion for "country lifestyle," resulted in one of her most famous canvases, *Self-Portrait in a Straw Hat*. This was painted when the predominant, official portraiture style represented women in powdered wigs, corseted dresses, and pyramidal silk hats. This painting not only promoted a new "shepherdess" look but was also the artist's commentary on the Rubens painting (which shows a woman in a hat that, despite its title, is actually made of fabric). "This is what a real straw hat looks like!" Elizabeth seems to say with her self-portrait.

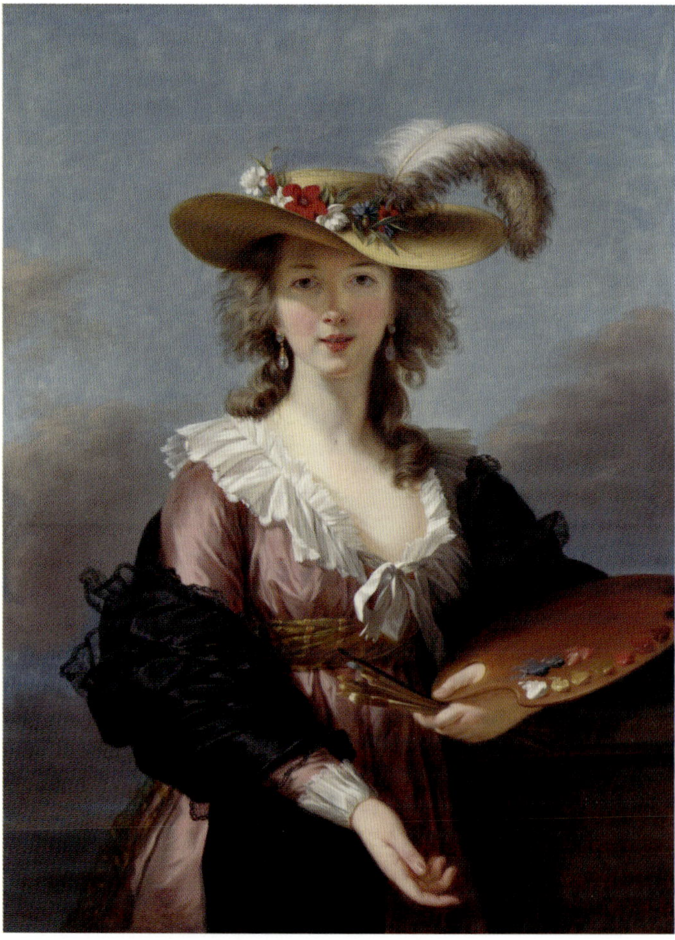

Elisabeth Vigée Le Brun. *Self-Portrait in a Straw Hat*, after 1782. Oil on canvas.
National Gallery, London.
Photo: Danvis Collection/Alamy Stock Photo

A few years earlier, Elisabeth's social skills and outstanding talent earned her the highest level of patronage—she became a favorite portraitist of Marie Antoinette, the queen of France and wife of King Louis XVI. In an early portrait of Marie Antoinette, the artist portrayed her in full ancient régime regalia, conforming to the imagery style of the court.

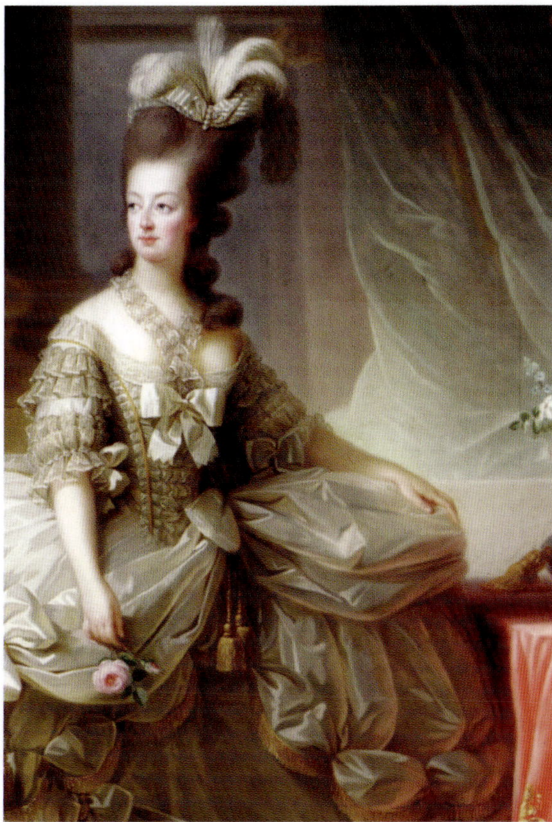

Elisabeth Vigée Le Brun. *Marie Antoinette in Court Dress*, 1778. Oil on canvas.
Kunsthistorisches Museum, Vienna.
Photo: Public domain via Wikimedia Commons

However, a few years after this formal, old-style portrait, both the sitter and the artist had moved on to the new look of straw hats, free-flowing muslin dresses, and long hair freed from the powdered wigs. While Marie Antoinette had famously created a bucolic retreat around the Petit Trianon at Versailles, Elisabeth made her name and fortune painting aristocratic women dressed in diaphanous gauzes and straw hats covering wind-swept hair.

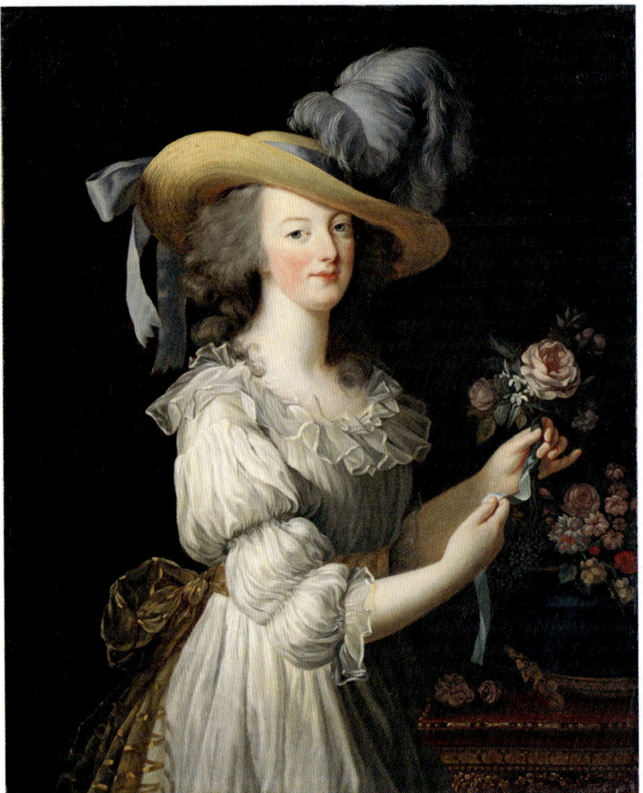

Elisabeth Vigée Le Brun. *Marie Antoinette in a Muslin Dress*, before 1783. Oil on canvas.
Hessian House Foundation/Wolfsgarten Castle, Hesse.
Photo: Public domain via Wikimedia Commons

The original painting of *Marie Antoinette in a Muslin Dress* is housed in a German castle, but the Western public is probably more familiar with its copy in Washington, DC's National Gallery. We know it was painted before 1783 because it was exhibited at the Paris Salon of that year, causing a great social stir.

For a few years, Elisabeth had everything—a royal patroness who helped her to get accepted into the Royal Academy, important commissions from noble patrons, a lovely daughter, and substantial earnings and prestige. Elisabeth painted 33 portraits of the queen and a dozen other important works. At the pinnacle of her career and influence, she had a golden life...until she didn't. Life threw her another curveball, as her royal patroness lost her freedom (and eventually her head), and Paris was engulfed in the flames of the Revolution. Elisabeth and her young daughter had to flee in disguise in a public coach, carrying with her 80 gold coins —all that her husband would give her.

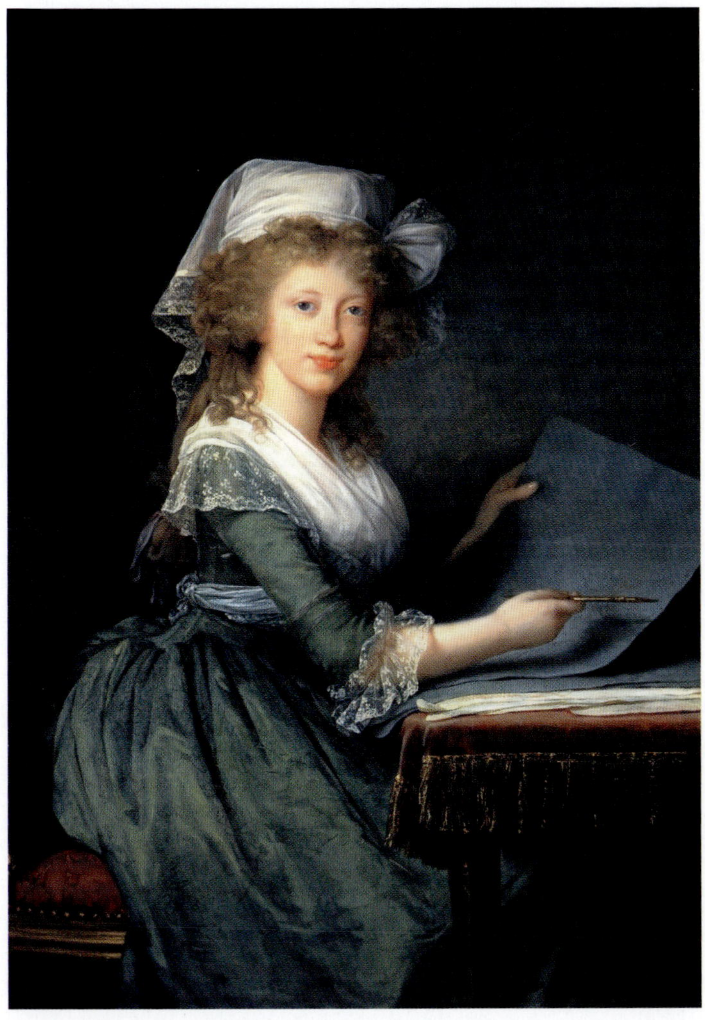

Elisabeth Vigée Le Brun. *Maria Luisa di Borbone, Princess of the Two Sicilies*, 1790.
Oil on canvas.
Museo di Capodimonte, Naples.
Photo: Public domain via Wikimedia Commons

Elisabeth started a 12-year exile, with long stays in Italy, Austria, and Russia. The only thing the artist had to ease the hardship of her sudden emigration was her exceptional skill at painting. Here is an example of a painting she executed in Italy. According to Elisabeth's memoirs, her model Maria Luisa, princess of Sicily, was "extremely ugly, and pulled such faces that I was most reluctant to finish her portrait." We have other portraits of this much-painted princess with which to compare. Here is one by Filippo Lucci, currently at the Uffizi in Florence.

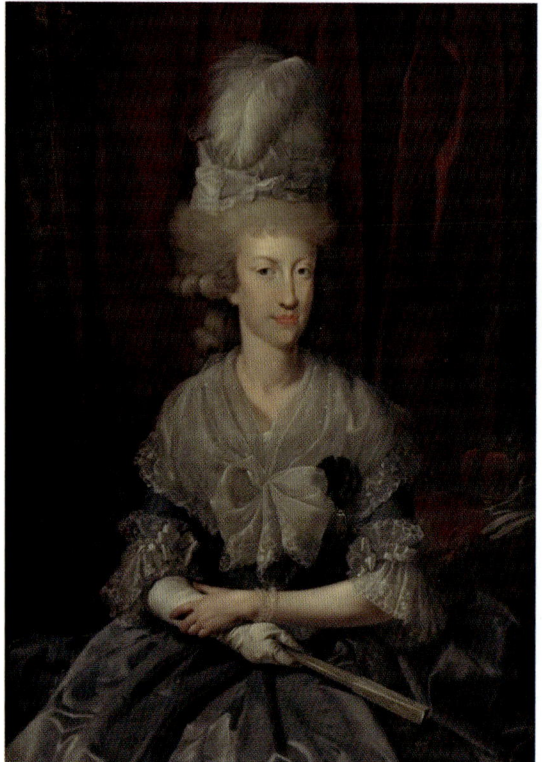

Filippo Lucci. *Luisa Maria Amalia di Borbone Granduchessa di Toscana*, 1792–1794.
Oil on canvas.
Galleria degli Uffizi, Florence.
Public domain via Wikimedia Commons

If we compare Lucci's more naturalistic version with the flattering portrait by Elisabeth, it is clear why her romanticized, lively portraits were all the rage among her titled sitters. The long-faced princess Luisa looks—in Elisabeth's portrait—like a pretty, sophisticated woman with some artistic talent to boot. Meanwhile, Elisabeth, who had more artistic talent than most, was still dependent on commissions and invitations to court. When an invitation came from Empress Catherine the Great of Russia, the artist packed up her brushes and her teenage daughter, and off they went through the snows of northern Europe. During her six years in Russia, she made many friends among Russian and Polish aristocrats and painted some of her most exquisite works.

Among Elisabeth's Russian-period paintings, the most famous and most accomplished is her *Portrait of Countess Golovina*, but here are two that come from that period that are a bit less known.

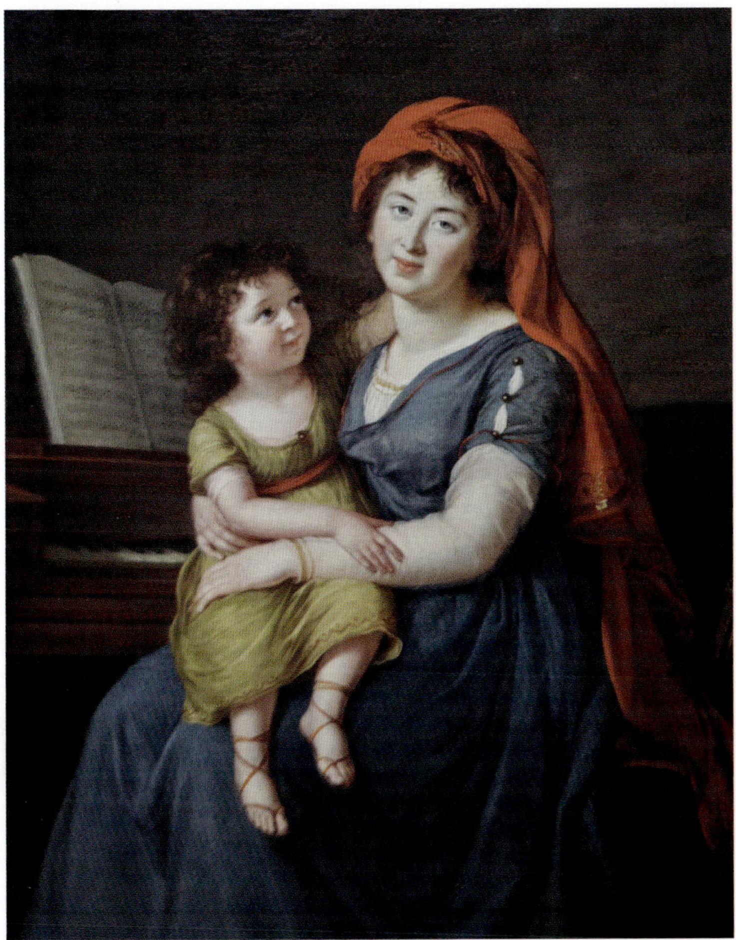

Elisabeth Vigée Le Brun. *Princess Ekaterina Nikolaevna Mienshikova*, 1795. Oil on canvas.
National Gallery of Armenia.
Photo: Mariano Garcia/Alamy Stock Photo

Princess Ekaterina Nikolaevna Mienshikova offers proof of Elisabeth's unerring skill in making any woman look exceptionally beautiful and endowed with desirable qualities—here as a tender mother and cultured person. In real life, Princess Ekaterina must have had a fuller figure and perhaps she was not as musical as the sheet music indicates. But in this painting, she is a mother in a loving embrace with her cute little daughter while at the same time looking ethereal and romantic. Elisabeth knew how to make women feel good about themselves when looking at their portraits.

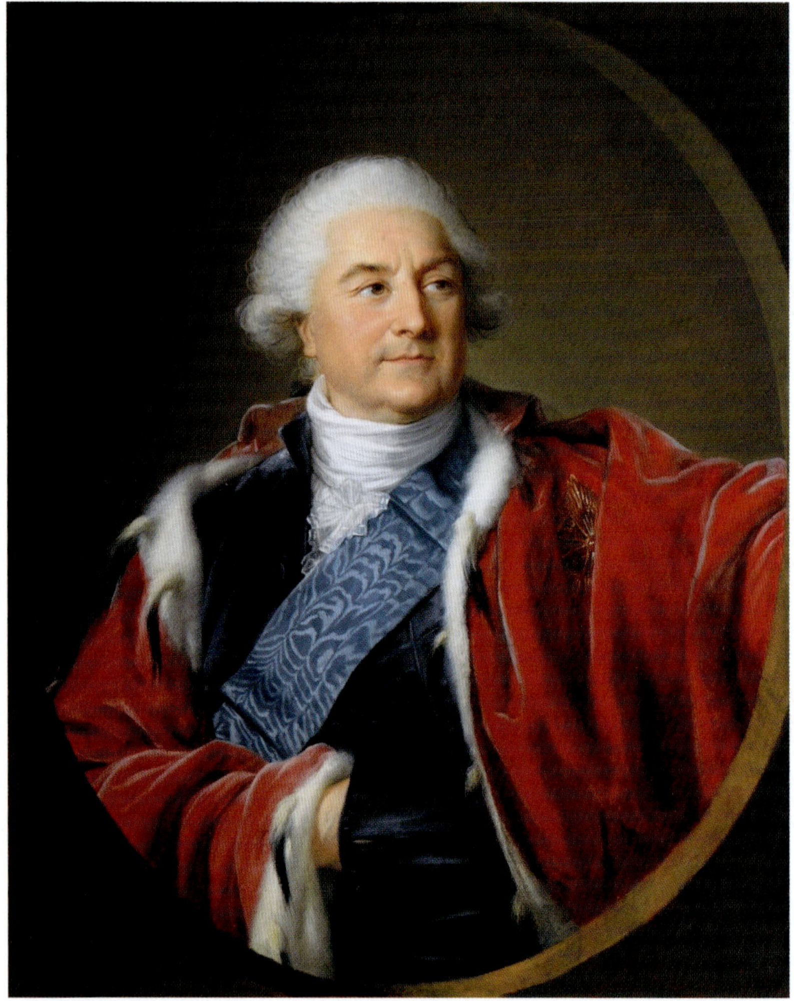

Elisabeth Vigée Le Brun. *Stanisław August Poniatowski, King of Poland*, 1797. Oil on canvas. Palace of Versailles.
Photo: Public domain via Wikimedia Commons

Although Elisabeth mostly painted women, her male portraits are some of the most accomplished ones of the era, even if they are less appreciated than those made by her male contemporaries (like Fragonard or David). In St. Petersburg, she befriended another exile, a collector who for years tried to buy a painting of hers but failed due to the high price (he bought a miniature by Angelica Kauffmann instead). This fan of Elisabeth was the last king of Poland, Stanisław August Poniatowski. In 1779, the king had just been released by the Russian emperor Paul I from a two-year home exile near Grodno (today's Belarus) and was forced to live in St. Petersburg under strict supervision (even though the king himself was hoping to retire to Rome). He was at the end of his royal ambitions (he was first put on the throne and then forced to abdicate by Catherine the Great). The exiled ex-king and Elisabeth became close friends, meeting in the third year of Elisabeth's Russian exile at social events (such as Princess Kurakina's birthday party, where Elisabeth organized and performed in live pictures, a typical home entertainment of the era). The artist painted two of his portraits—the more known one is the one in an ermine cloak—memorializing a regal look and stance that would remind the world that he was once a king of Poland before both he and the country lost their independence.

Unfortunately, during the Russian years, Elizabeth also experienced a disastrous falling out with her beloved Julie. As any mother of a teenage daughter can attest, the moment when a girl starts looking at boys is not the easiest one in mother-daughter relationships. Twenty-year-old Julie, spoiled and coddled by her mother, set her eyes on a ne'er-do-well, Gaétan-Bernard Nigris, a secretary at the imperial court. After many fights, Elisabeth relented, obtained a marriage permission from her ex-husband (mothers had zero power in those days), and threw Julie a sumptuous wedding. Two weeks later, her stubborn daughter was in tears since the marriage was over. Julie's disastrous marriage carved an irreparable rift between Elisabeth and her child.

After six years of Russian winters, Elisabeth was done with that part of the world. She was able to return to France to restart her life again. Although she lost her Academy membership—because revolutionary France abolished this right for women (presumably as part of revolutionary social progress)—Elisabeth was slowly able to pick up commissions. Julie came back to France, too, but she remained estranged from her mother, lived in poverty, had a string of bad relationships, contracted either TB or syphilis or perhaps both (there aren't enough records), and only reconciled with her mother on her deathbed. Elisabeth, meanwhile, outlived her daughter, her ex-husband, her younger brother, and most of her friends and confidantes. Over her lifetime, she witnessed several monarchies (Louis XVI, Bonaparte, Charles X, Louis Philippe I) and the rise and fall of the Revolution, and she was a friend of royals, artists, writers, and politicians (Voltaire, Talleyrand, Franklin, Lafayette). Elisabeth Vigée Le Brun died at the age of 86, well into the 19th century, a symbol of old monarchies and new post-Rococo portraiture, leaving behind 600 works.

CHAPTER 14

ROSA BONHEUR (1822–1899)

There is a reason why the traditionally dressed Victorian lady in the portrait here is resting her hand on a bull instead of a chair or some other conventional prop. While the lady, Rosa Bonheur, was painted by the portraitist Édouard Louis Dubufe, Bonheur herself painted in the bull after deciding that a "boring chair" would not be appropriate for any description of her as an artist. And she could not have been more right.

Rosa Bonheur had an unconventional childhood, followed by an even less conventional life. Her father, a minor painter, taught her and her three younger brothers the craft. He was not just an artist but a free spirit, a man seduced by the egalitarian and feminist ideas of Henri de Saint-Simon; as such, he was not fazed by the fact that Rosa was a tomboy or that she was thrown out of a girls' school for unladylike behavior. He tutored his unruly but extremely talented daughter himself, sent her to the Louvre to copy masterpieces, and allowed her to keep a menagerie of animals at their Paris residence. This highly unconventional schooling paid off, for by the age of 19, Rosa's first animal paintings were accepted to the Salon of 1841.

Rosa did not paint what other Victorian-era ladies tended to paint—such as flowers and landscapes—and did not even paint portraits all that much. She was only interested in animals. She would roam forests and visit farms, and then she started attending slaughterhouses and animal fairs to study animal anatomy.

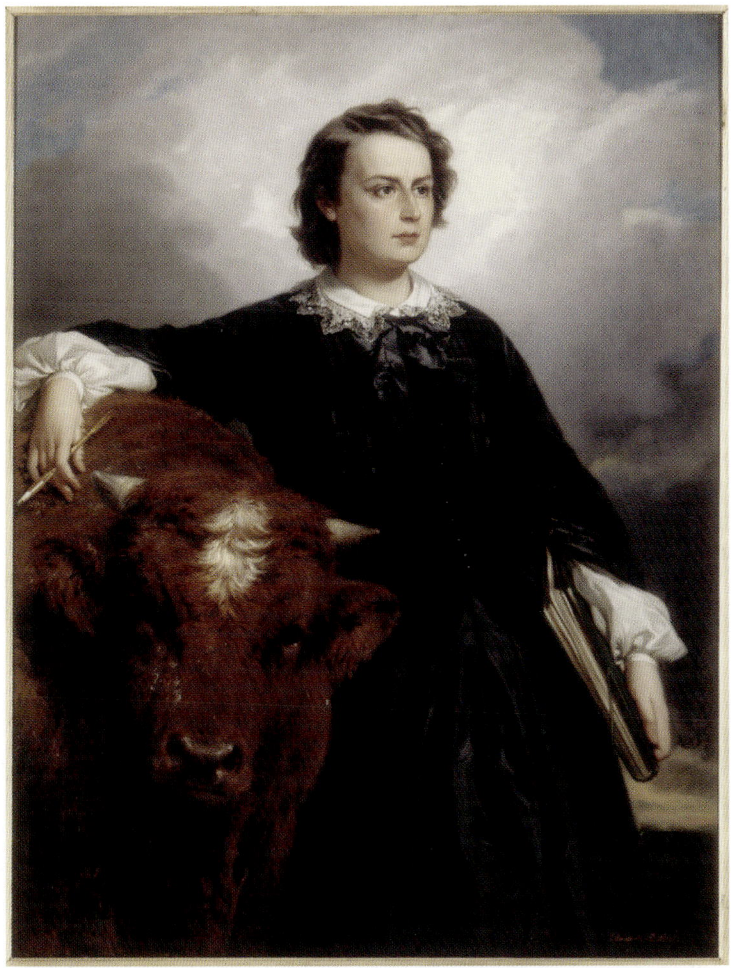

Édouard Louis Dubufe. *Portrait of Rosa Bonheur* (the bull was painted by Bonheur), 1857. Oil on canvas.

Palace of Versailles.
Photo: Public domain via Wikimedia Commons

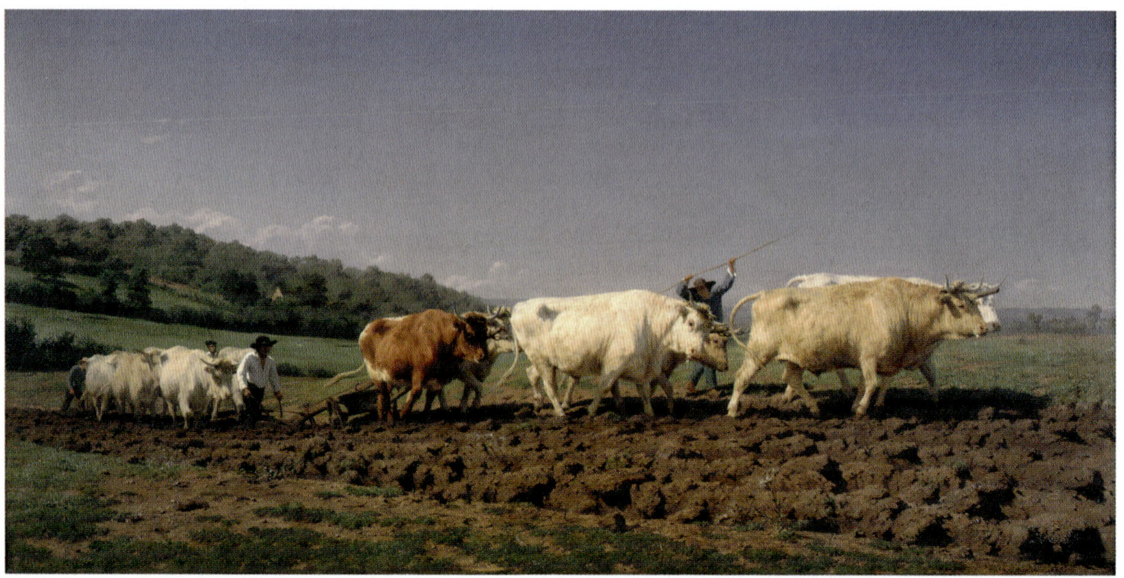

Rosa Bonheur. *Ploughing in the Nivernais* or *The First Dressing*, 1849. Oil on canvas.
Musée d'Orsay, Paris.
Photo: Public domain via Wikimedia Commons

Ploughing in the Nivernais, painted right after the 1848 Springtime of the Peoples (a wave of nationalistic uprisings and social revolts that swept through Europe and shook French society), was considered by critics a metaphor of the rebirth of the French nation; it also brought Bonheur acclaim as an outstanding realist painter of nature. While farm scenes were common in the 19th century's realist canvases, they typically focused on the beauty of a landscape or perhaps the toil of peasants. *Ploughing in the Nivernais*, on the other hand, is all about the group of muscled oxen marching through an autumn field, cutting through the buttery earth and looking strong, almost majestic. Whereas their human overseers are anonymous, with their faces hidden by wide-brimmed hats, the animals are more individualized —with a different color, gait, and expression for each of the huge beasts. Bonheur's focus, both in composition and in technique, is on the animals. Interestingly, when London's National Gallery did a restoration of their version of her famous canvas *The Horse Fair*, they discovered that while Bonheur used broad strokes for the sky and earth, she used minute strokes of a very fine brush to render the horses' coats.

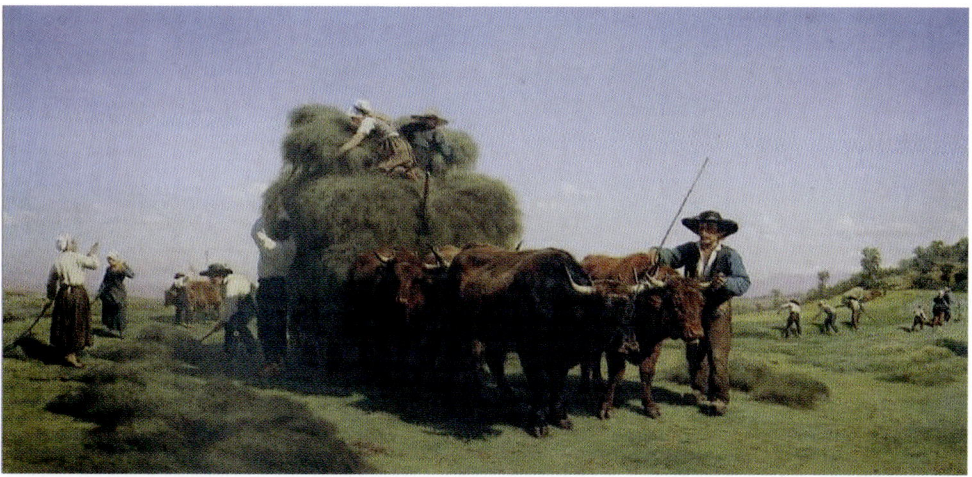

Rosa Bonheur. *Haymaking in Auvergne (La Fenaison)*, 1855. Oil on canvas.
Musée d'Orsay, Paris.
Photo: Rosa Bonheur, CC BY-SA 4.0 <https://creativecommons.org/licenses/by-sa/4.0>, via Wikimedia Commons

The success of *Ploughing in the Nivernais* was the beginning of Bonheur's fame as the most accomplished animal painter in France. It marked a period of huge strides as an artist but also a period of personal happiness. A few years earlier, Rosa had encountered Nathalie Micas, a painting model of her father's, with whom she formed an instantaneous and unbreakable bond (even Nathalie's father blessed this bond on his deathbed a year later). Nathalie stayed at Bonheur's side as her life partner, business manager, and artistic assistant until her death over 40 years later.

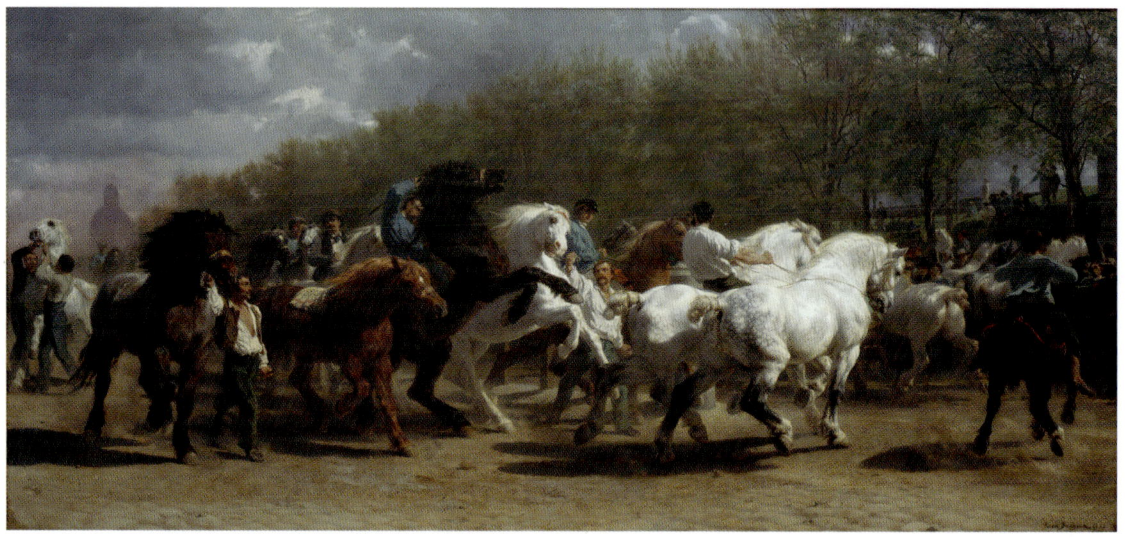

Rosa Bonheur. *The Horse Fair*, 1852–55. Oil on canvas.
The Metropolitan Museum of Art, New York.
Photo: Public domain via Wikimedia Commons

Bonheur's most famous painting is the enormous canvas titled *The Horse Fair*. She had prepared for this work for 18 months by attending, twice a week, a horse-trading market in Paris. She even obtained a police permit to be able to dress in pants when sketching and observing at the market. That saved her the harassment of horse traders who would not have ignored a young woman in a crinoline and bonnet, but it was also probably a relief for the unconventional Bonheur to be able to move around freely. Later, pants became her trademark painting attire to the point that the French president insisted that she receive him wearing them so that he could see "how the artist worked."

The massive 8 x 16 feet (244 x 506 cm) artwork depicts a scene at the Paris horse market (the dome of La Salpêtrière hospital is visible in the background). Exhibited in the Salon of 1853, the scene of bucking Percherons tossing their heads with flying manes and straining their enormous muscles excited the crowds of viewers and brought Bonheur to the heights of fame and recognition.

There are two versions of *The Horse Fair*, but neither version of the artist's most famous painting resides in her native country. The American one was purchased by Cornelius Vanderbilt and then offered to the Met; the other, smaller one is at the National Gallery in London. Bonheur initially offered the painting to the city of Bordeaux, but the offer was rejected. Instead, her dealer Ernst Gambart purchased it and came up with a clever marketing campaign. He re-sold the painting for the huge sum of 40,000 francs, but only after reserving the right to tour the painting for three years (including in England and the U.S.) and to strike engravings that made the canvas famous and the entrepreneur rich.

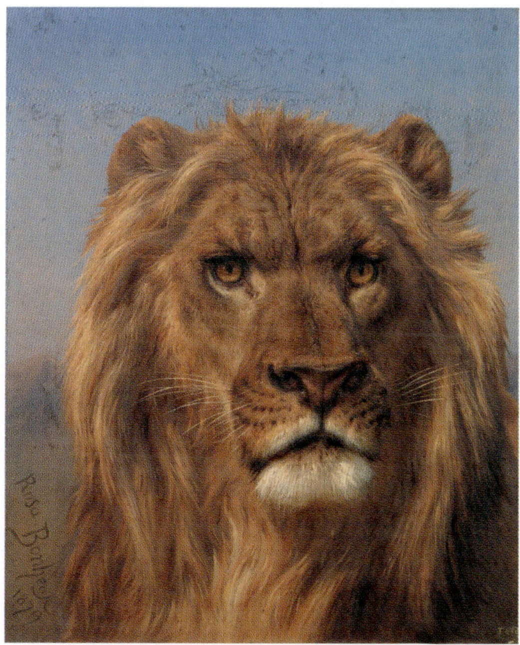

Rosa Bonheur. *El Cid*, 1879. Oil on canvas.
Museo del Prado, Madrid.
Photo: Public domain via Wikimedia Commons

To Bonheur, animals were people—creatures with individualized expressions and great faces to be painted. One of the most famous animal portraits is at the Prado Museum in Madrid. This majestic head of a lion is named *El Cid* (implying both the name of a valiant Castilian knight and the term for a "lord" or even a "prince"). It was donated by Bonheur's dealer to the museum. Bonheur always had a fondness for lions; in fact, she even kept a pair in her private zoo on her property of Château de By near Fontainebleau. Not all Bonheur portraits were of exotic creatures, however, as evidenced by the tender portrait of a hound named Brizo.

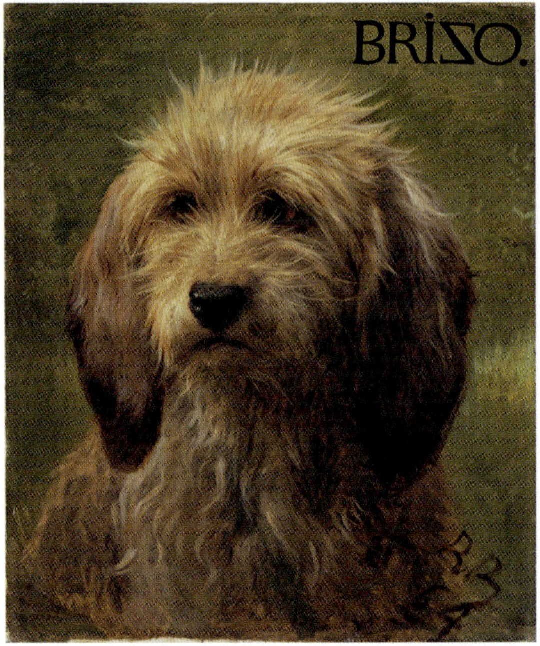

Rosa Bonheur. *Brizo the Shepherd's Dog*, 1864. Oil on canvas.
The Wallace Collection, London.
Photo: Public domain via Wikimedia Commons

Bonheur was (excuse the pun) lionized by the public and royalty alike. French Empress Éugenie, after a spontaneous visit to Bonheur's residence, returned there a year later and pinned on her a Légion d'Honneur medal—with Bonheur becoming the first woman to be awarded this distinction in the arts. Queen Victoria requested and enjoyed a private viewing of *The Horse Fair* when the painting was touring Britain. Bonheur also received medals from the king of Spain and the hapless Emperor Maximilian of Mexico, as well as invitations to royal courts all over Europe. She also got rave reviews in America.

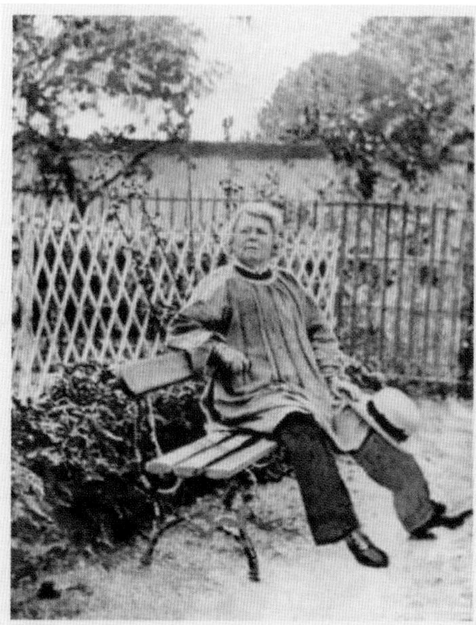

Photo of Rosa Bonheur, 1890s.
Photo: Public domain via Wikimedia Commons

Interestingly, none of her titled patrons nor art critics seem to have minded the fact that Bonheur openly lived in relations with women (first with Nathalie, and after the latter's passing, with American artist Anna Klumpke), wore pants (even if permitted by police), kept her hair short, smoked cigars, and generally ignored all the rules of appropriate behavior for women in rigorous "polite society." As Empress Éugenie declared, "genius has no gender." Bonheur's passion and admiration for the animals she portrayed seems to have swept away any social objections.

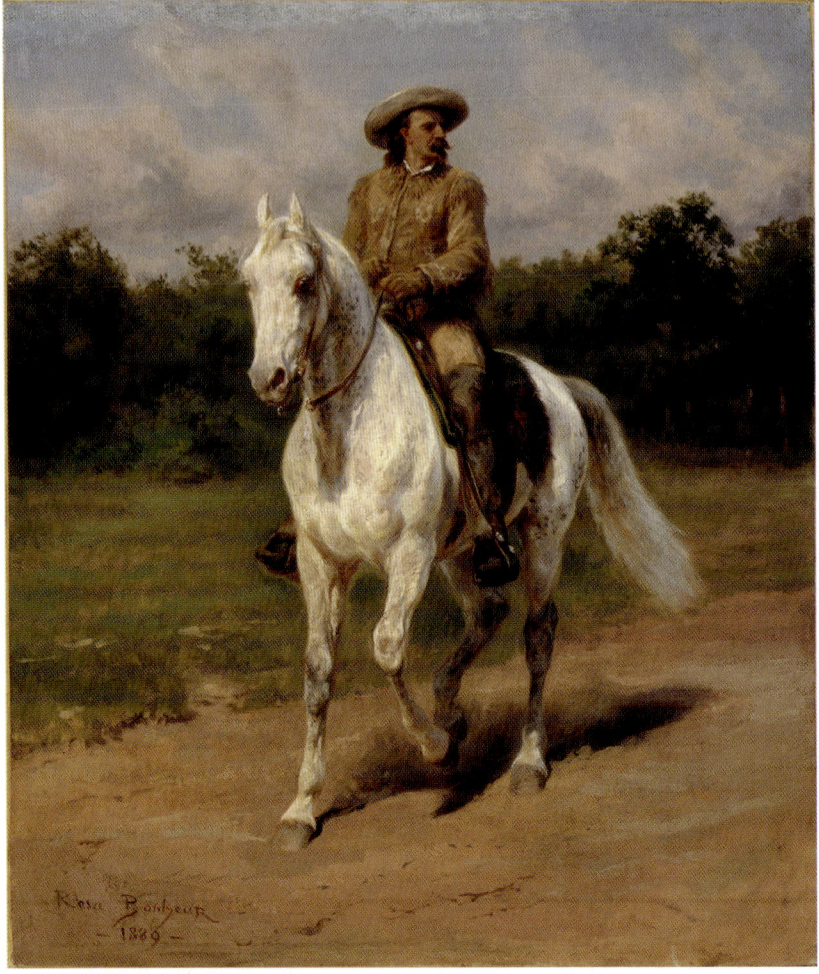

Rosa Bonheur. *Portrait of Col. William F. Cody*, 1899. Oil on canvas.
Buffalo Bill Center of the West, Cody.
Photo: Public domain via Wikimedia Commons

Even toward the end of her life, Bonheur lost neither her amazing skill at portraying animals nor her curiosity about the unconventional. Buffalo Bill enthralled Europeans with his Wild West exhibition when he took it to Paris for the *Exposition Universelle* in 1889. Bonheur visited the grounds of Cody's Wild West attraction to sketch the exotic American animals and the Indian warriors with their families. Cody, in turn, accepted her invitation to visit her château near Fontainebleau, where she painted his portrait. For Bonheur, the colorful character of Col. Cody seems to have embodied the freedom and independence of the United States, a young country so different from codified and formal France. In this painting, however, she shows Col. Cody as a somewhat distant figure gazing away, while his white steed faces front and is painted with minute detailed attention to his spots and fine hair. Again, it is the horse that is the ultimate star of the painting.

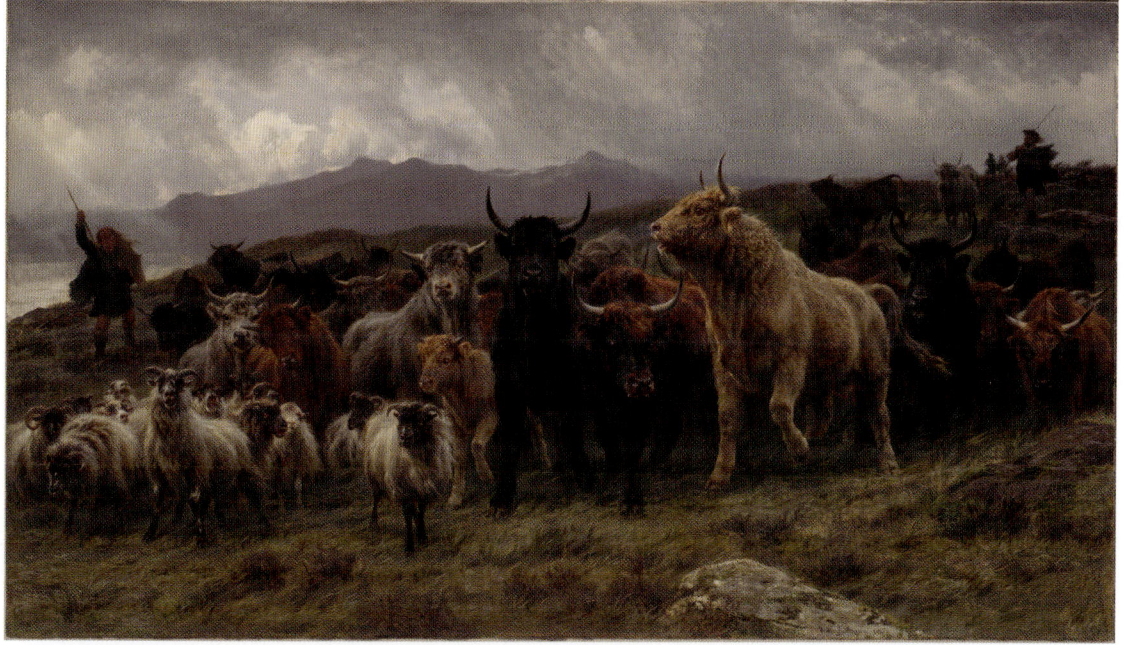

Rosa Bonheur. *The Highland Raid*, 1860. Oil on canvas.
National Museum of Women in the Arts, Washington D.C./Gift of Wallace and Wilhelmina Holladay.
Photo: Public domain via Wikimedia Commons

It is ironic that one of the most popular painters of the 19th century eventually became one of the most unfashionable ones. Even within the realistic style, Bonheur's genre of animal pictures eventually was overshadowed by academic art of historical scenes and the landscapes of the Barbizon school. By the 1870s, Impressionism had begun challenging realistic paintings, and by the time Bonheur passed away in 1899, art, especially in France, had moved in a myriad of different directions, none of which included her kind of painting. Even Bonheur's Château de By fell into disrepair after the death of her last companion Anna Klumpke in the 1940s. Only very recently did a French businesswoman and her daughters purchase the property; they are in the process of restoring it and bringing back Bonheur's memory. This will perhaps help to move Bonheur from being just a poster child for early emancipation to an artist recognized for her unique, emotional paintings.

CHAPTER 15

OLGA BOZNAŃSKA (1865–1940)

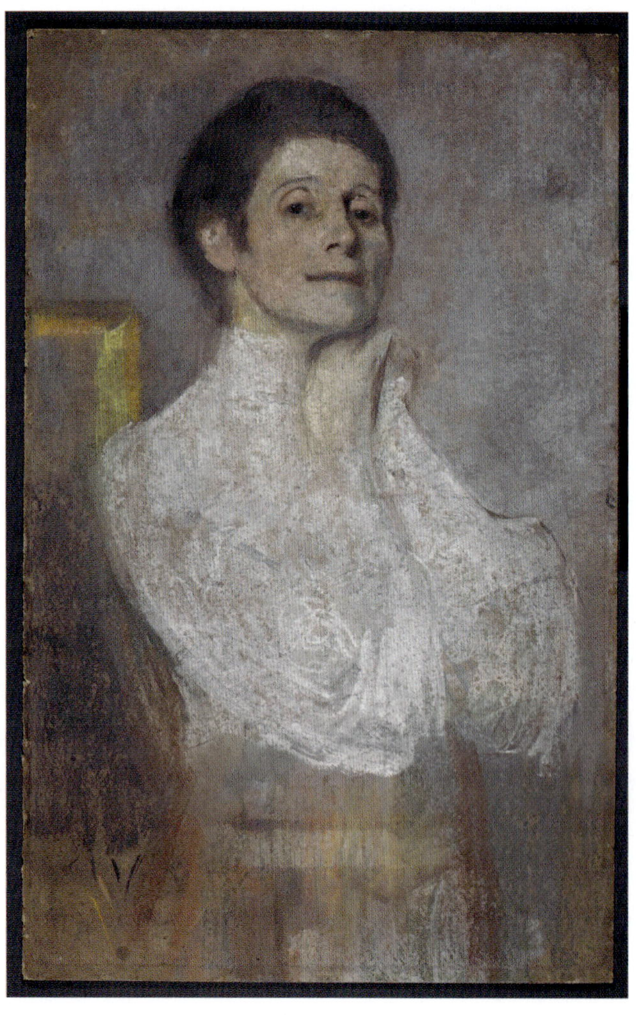

Olga Boznańska. *Self-Portrait*, 1908. Pastel, gouache on cardboard.
National Museum, Warsaw.
Photo: Public domain via Wikimedia Commons

Even casual museumgoers are familiar with such female artists as Georgia O'Keeffe or Mary Cassatt—celebrated painters whose art is prominently displayed in major Western galleries. Fewer art lovers are familiar with someone like Olga Boznańska, even though she was very active in the early 20th century, working not only in her native Kraków but also in Munich and then for over 40 years in Paris. In her native Poland, she has been famous for a long time—but, typically, more appreciated after her death in 1940 (she died alone, forgotten, in German-occupied Paris) than during her lifetime. Though her painting style echoes the Impressionists' loose brushwork, she was disdainful of landscapes: "You cannot sit the landscape down on a sofa and ask it to come back to the studio for a dozen sittings," she would say. So, she limited herself to painting people and sometimes flowers. One of her early portraits of her favorite subject—a child—has been considered a masterpiece ever since she painted it in 1894 in Munich, the city of her greatest artistic achievements.

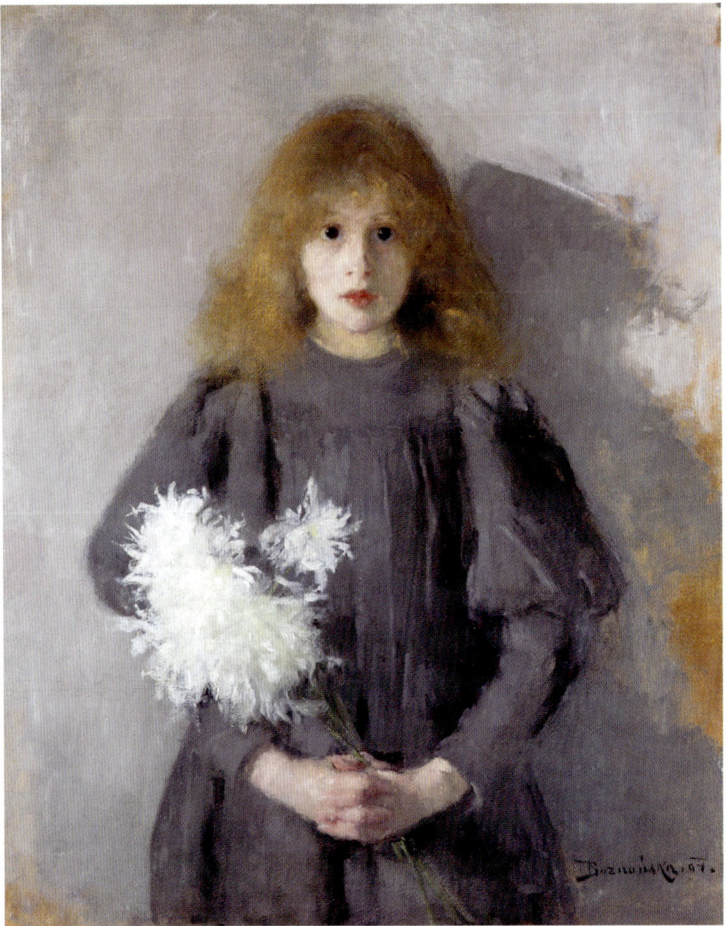

Olga Boznańska. *Girl with Chrysanthemums*, 1894. Oil on cardboard.
National Museum, Kraków.
Photo: Public domain via Wikimedia Commons

Girl with Chrysanthemums seems to have been influenced by James McNeill Whistler (compare it with his *Harmony in Grey and Green*) in the sense of style and color palette; however, those enormous dark eyes and the model's serious expression are Boznańska's own contribution to portraiture. There is gravity and even perhaps mystery in this posed, formal image. The girl's somber expression clashes with the fluffy flowers she is holding...or perhaps they are not entirely out of place because white chrysanthemums are traditionally placed at gravesites in Poland and some other European countries. They are not given as cheerful bouquets. There is certainly a sad vibe of anxiousness or even bereavement in this painting.

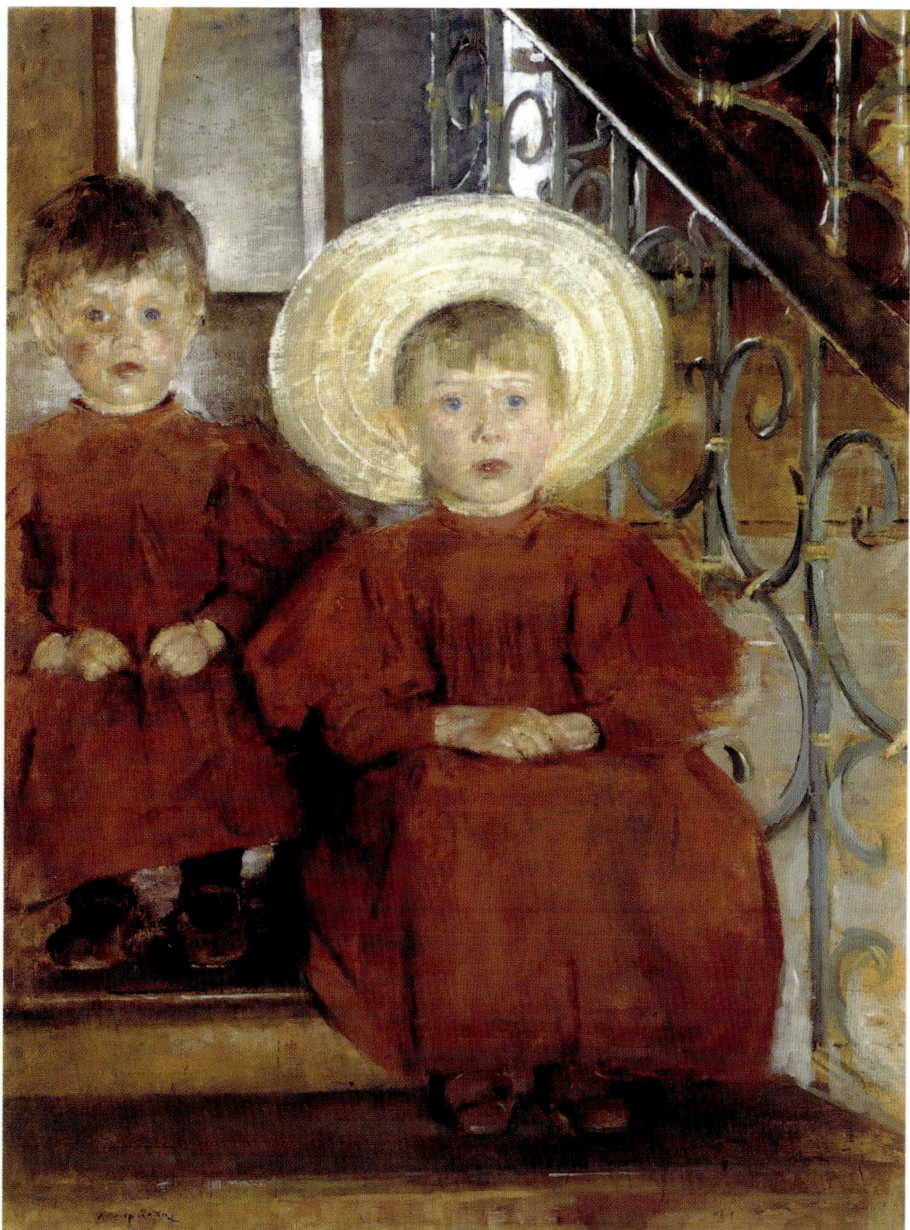

Olga Boznańska. *Children Sitting on the Stairs (Dzieci Siedzące na Schodach)*, 1898.
Oil on cardboard.
National Museum, Poznań.
Photo: Public domain via Wikimedia Commons

Not all of Boznańska's famous portraits of children were so sad, but her little sitters always look unnaturally serious, as if she needed to reach into a sitter's soul—and any socially expected smiling would stand in the way. *Children Sitting on the Stairs* was painted during her artistically most fecund period in Munich. She lived there for a decade, making huge strides in crafting her individual style—one that was in opposition to the pompous historical paintings that dominated Mitteleuropa at the time. The two kids are arranged in identical poses, and they are wearing the same red smocks; one has a cute straw hat that looks almost like a halo in an Italian Renaissance altar panel. The ornate green ironwork provides a contrasting backdrop. Everything in this picture would be almost too cute if not for the masterly application of color and light—and the serious facial expressions that were the artist's hallmark.

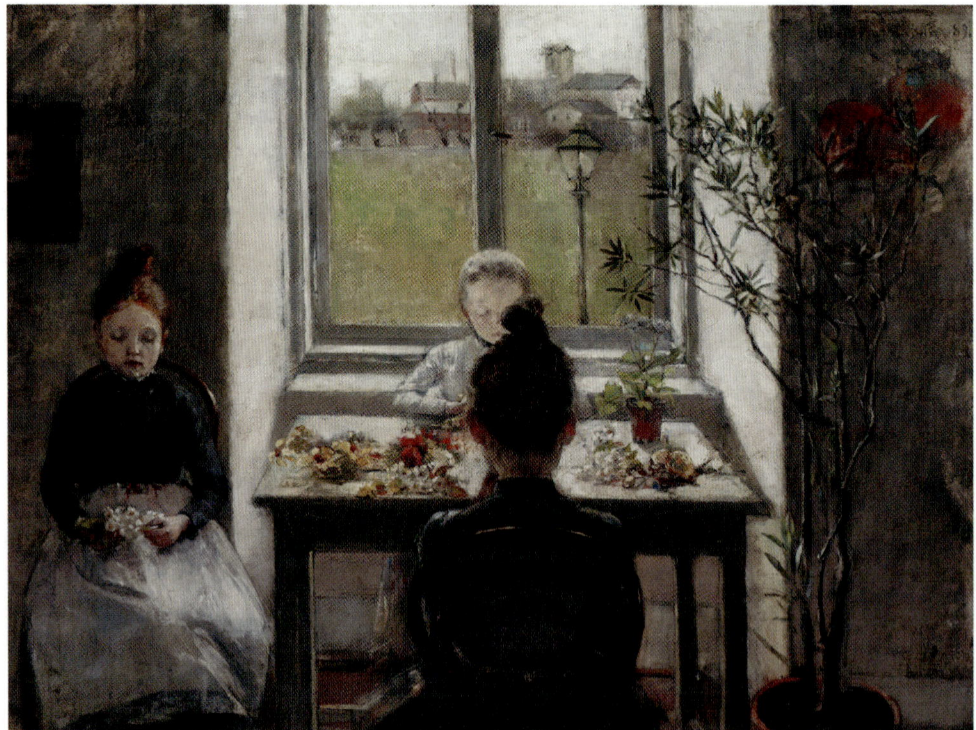

Olga Boznańska. *Florist Girls (Kwiaciarki)*, 1889. Oil on canvas.
National Museum, Kraków.
Photo: Public domain via Wikimedia Commons

One more example of Boznańska's approach to painting youngsters comes from a period when she was just starting out. *Florist Girls* is a fantastic composition, with a central bay window providing an outside view that opens up the picture and, at the same time, furnishes a brightly lit focal point for the three figures. This picture looks like a reinterpretation of Dutch Baroque paintings of women working in interiors. Given that this was early in Boznańska's artistic career, the figures are not yet perfect, but the folds of the apron and the light on the central figure already are. The telltale serious expressions on the girls' faces are here as well.

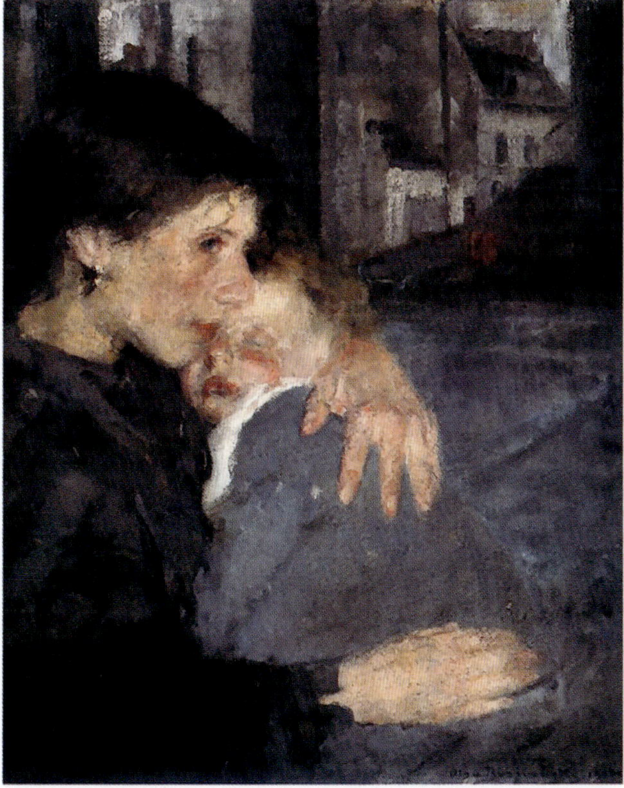

Olga Boznańska. *Maternity*, 1902. Oil on cardboard.
Private collection.
Photo: Art Collection 4/Alamy Stock Photo

Even when she painted the popular theme of a mother holding a child, Boznańska's paintings were different from Berthe Morisot's or Mary Cassatt's tender portraits of mothers caring for their little ones. Boznańska's *Maternity* seems to be telling some disturbing story. The mother has a questioning look on her face, and she is clutching the child in an extremely protective way. There is also a strange streetscape behind her, suggesting that she might be sitting on the doorstep or a veranda of a house. Is she about to lose her home? She is wearing jewelry, so perhaps not. Is she sitting at an open window? Why does she look slightly anxious—is she worried about the future? Was the child born out of wedlock perhaps, or is she just thinking serious thoughts? The artist is telling some story here (or maybe even illustrating some literary work), but of course, viewers can construct their own tale and spend hours pondering the poetry of this picture.

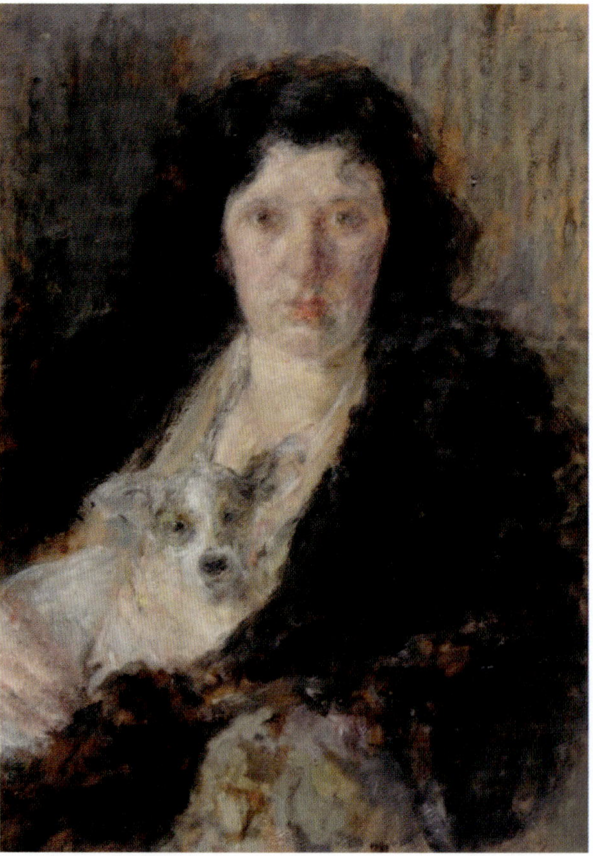

Olga Boznańska. *Portrait of Włodzimiera Lipońska*, 1931. Oil on cardboard.
National Museum, Kielce.
Photo: Public domain via Wikimedia Commons

Many of Boznańska's portraits were painted as commissions, often requested by prominent Polish artists, politicians, or landed gentry of the period. But even when painting commissioned works, her artist's eye sought the psychological truth of the person painted. In *Portrait of Włodzimiera Lipońska*, she paints her sitter with a serious if slightly unsure expression, as if this woman was a bit reluctant to pose or needed some security lacking in her life. Maybe the warm fur stole around her arm provides some confidence, along with the dog who is clearly so self-assured that he is sitting for a portrait as well. He is not an accessory—he has an individualized expression and an important placement in this composition. Or perhaps he is just a very friendly pet of the artist, happy to serve as a model? Here is a photograph of Boznańska with her favorite canine companion, called Boby, who looks almost exactly like the one in this painting.

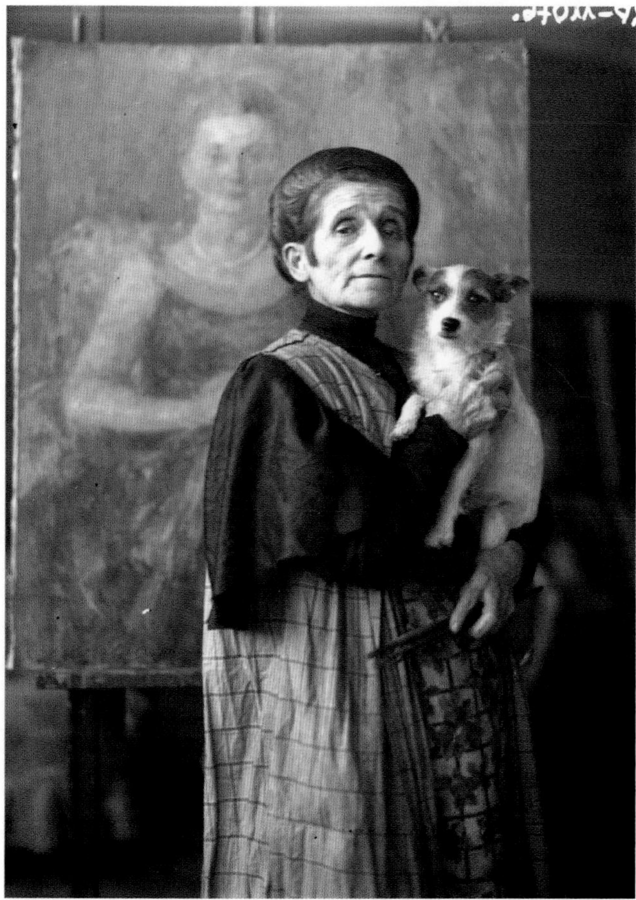

Photo of Olga Boznańska in her studio, c. 1930–31.
National Digital Archive, Poland.
Photo: Narodowe Archiwum Cyfrowe, Public domain via Wikimedia Commons.

In a portrait entitled *Yearning*, the psychology of the sitter is again as important as the choice of color and brushstrokes. In 1900 when this was painted, formal frontal portraits of real people rarely presented someone with an open mouth. This portrait does, because this is above all a painting of a feeling.

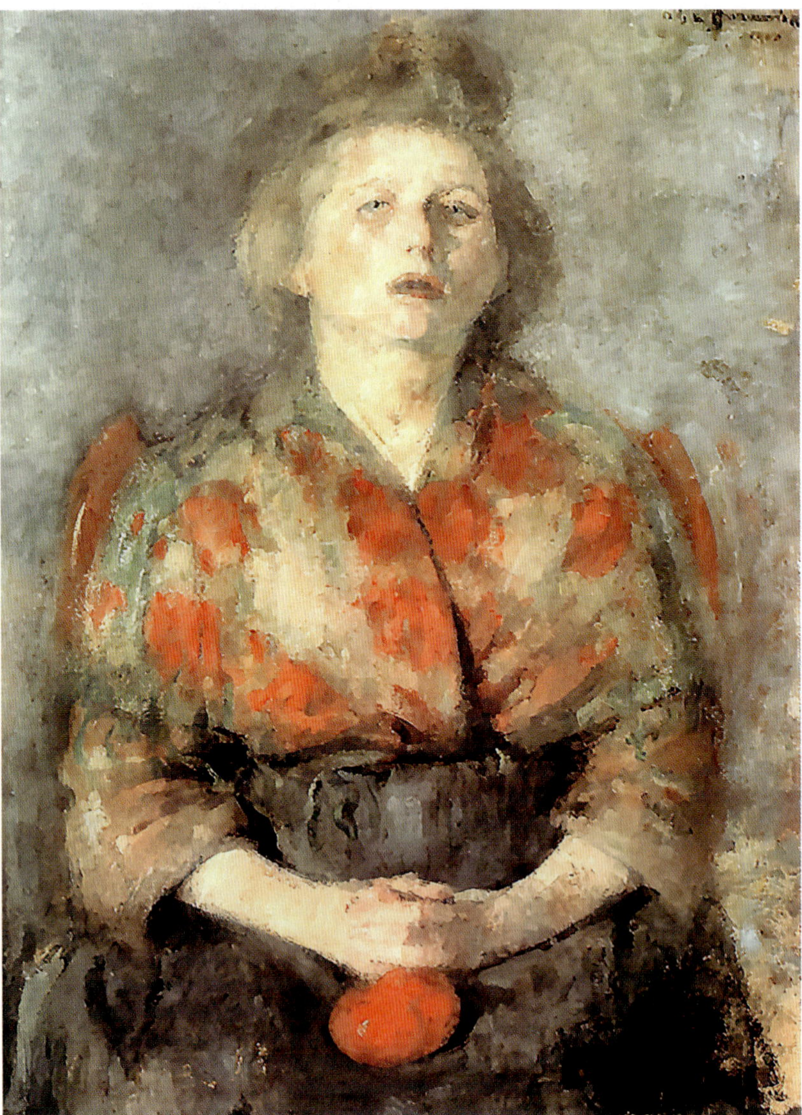

Olga Boznańska. *Yearning (Tęsknota)*, 1900. Oil on cardboard.
Private collection.
Photo: Artepics/Alamy Stock Photo

This woman, not very elegantly dressed (perhaps a housekeeper in Paris, a city to which the artist had moved two years prior), has an expression of anxiety and a gaze that reaches far beyond. The title, which can be translated as "yearning" or "longing," suggests that the artist wanted to capture some unrealized wish or desire—for a person, or for something to happen? The style might be Impressionist or even Post-Impressionist, but the psychology here is more that of the Secession (Freud, Jung, Klimt, Munch, Steiner)—all the mucking around the soul and mind that was en vogue at the time.

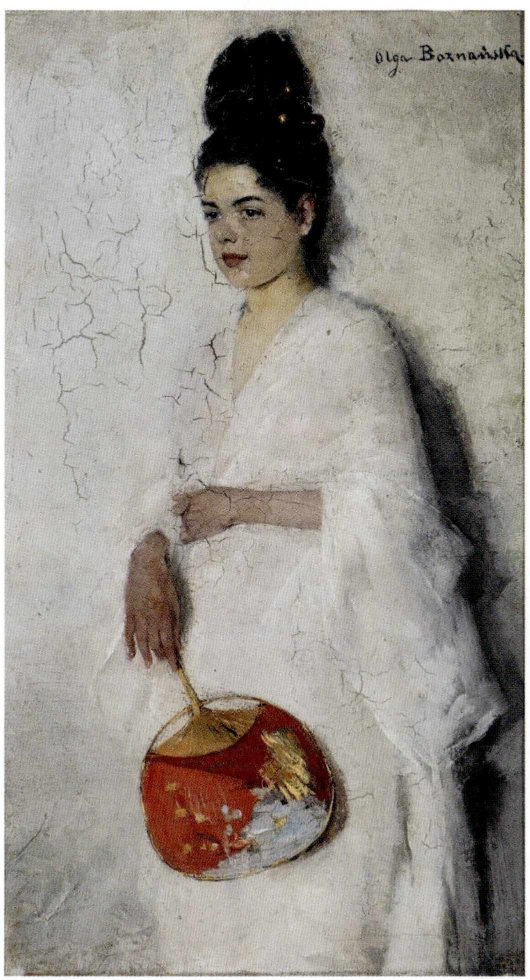

Olga Boznańska. *A Japanese Woman (Japonka)*, 1889. Oil on oak panel.
National Museum, Warsaw.
Photo: Public domain via Wikimedia Commons

Europe discovered Japanese art and style in the mid-19th century, and Boznańska was fascinated by Japanese costume and design as well. She painted her own self-portrait with a Japanese parasol, while in this portrait, she dressed a young model in a Japanese costume. The paint in this work has not weathered time well, but it still retains some of the original luminosity. Unfortunately, Boznańska's later paintings do not look as radiant and intriguing as her early work; they have a much darker palette, and many of them yellowed with time because they were painted on cardboard that sucked oil out of paint.

Not a single of Boznańska's self-portraits shows her with a brush and a palette—she did not need to document her profession as many female artists before her did. She lived her own way. She had several long relationships but never married; she stuck to her style despite many revolutionizing changes in art around her; and she always maintained a distinguished "regal" posture and manners (the press called her "the First Lady of Polish painting") rather than embrace the bohemian, artistic lifestyle that was so fashionable at the time.

Sadly, Western art books rarely mention Olga Boznańska, not even those ubiquitous and trendy anthologies of female artists. You can find stories on second-rate debutants but nothing on this mature, accomplished artist with a body of work that spans decades. A lot of her portraits are in private hands, and only a few museums have some samples of her work. Boznańska is still almost as unappreciated outside her native country as she was 100 years ago.

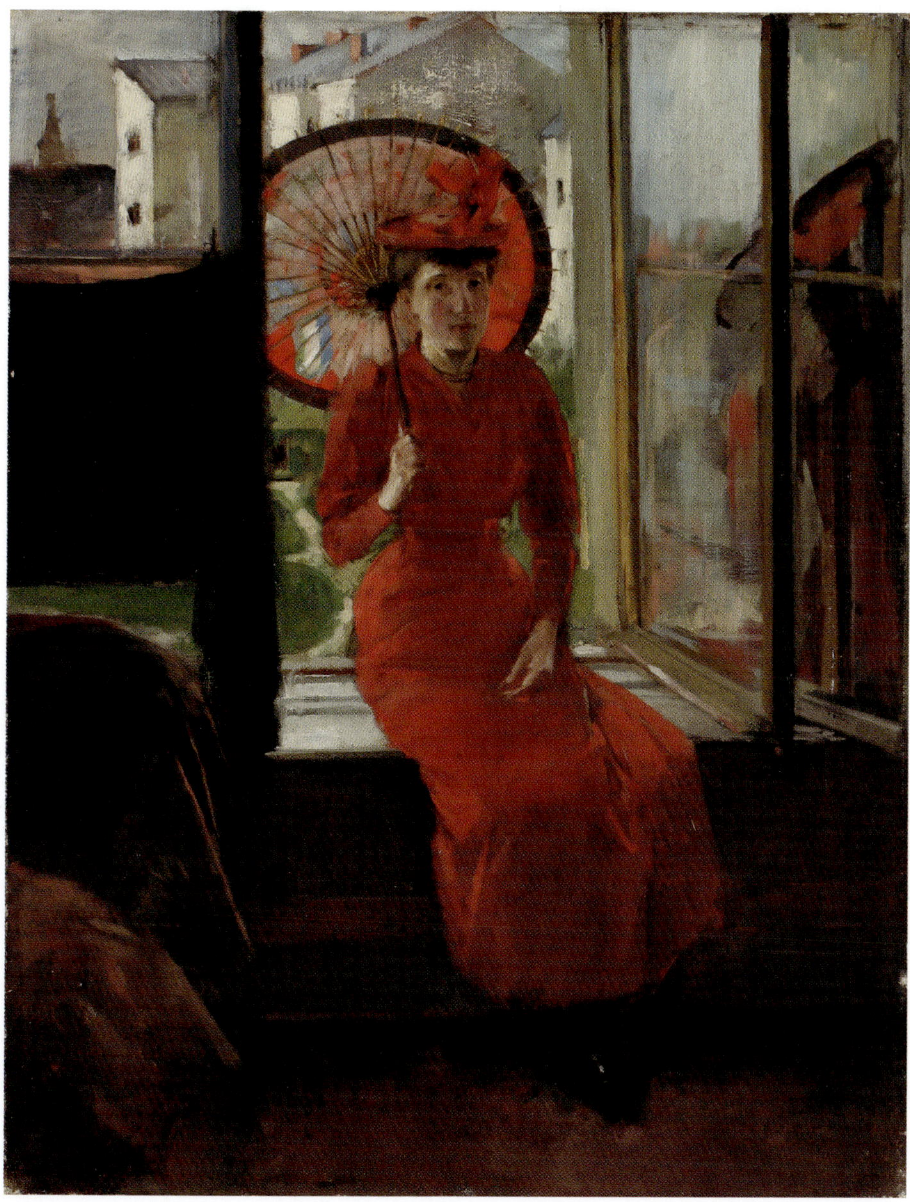

Olga Boznańska. *Japanese Self-Portrait*, 1892. Oil on cardboard.
Collection of the National Museum, Wrocław.
Photo: Arkadiusz Podstawka/National Museum, Wrocław

CHAPTER 16

HILMA AF KLINT (1862–1944)

The fact that painter Hilma af Klint has been unknown in the history of modern art is not that surprising. That even now she remains fairly unknown is a bit more controversial.

There are several reasons for Hilma's artistic obscurity everywhere, including in her native Sweden. During her active years in the early part of the 20th century, she exhibited only once, and most of her artwork was kept in storage not just during her lifetime but for decades afterwards. As a woman and a spiritualist, she was also shunned by mainstream art and cultural authorities. She still remains relatively unknown because almost all her important paintings are kept together by her family foundation, outside any major museums. In other words—since her paintings aren't owned by any modern art museums and are not available for purchase by collectors, Hilma's art remains obscure even though studying her art would possibly entirely revise the history of art.

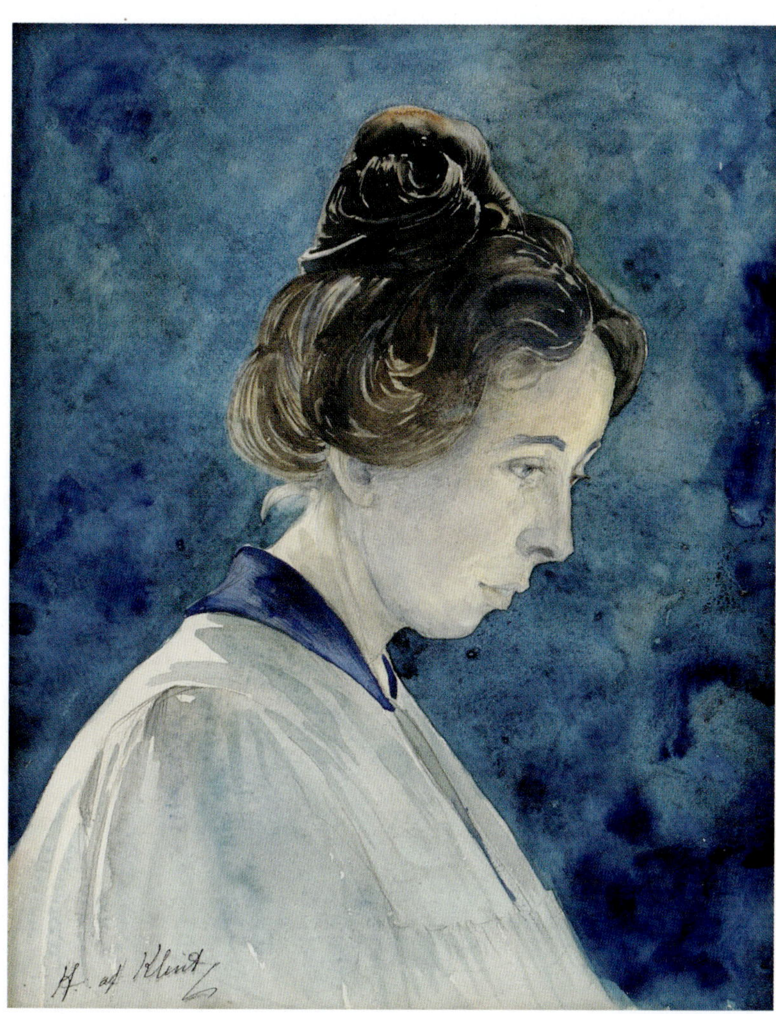

Hilma af Klint. *Self-Portrait*, date unknown. Oil on canvas.
Hilma af Klint Foundation.
Photo: Public domain via Wikimedia Commons

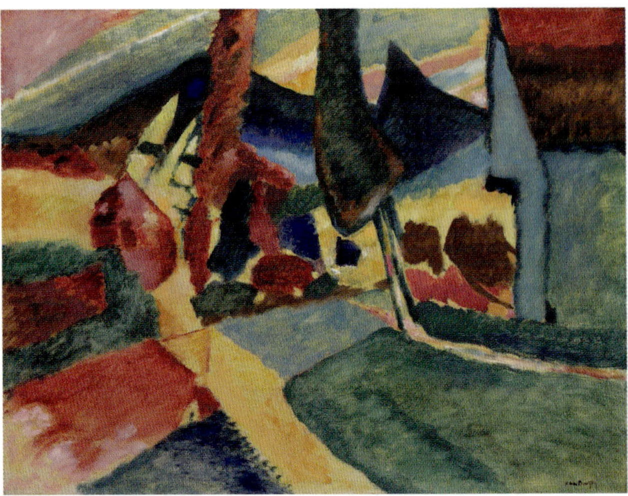

Wassily Kandinsky. *Landscape with Two Poplars*, 1912. Oil on canvas.
Art Institute of Chicago.
Photo: Public domain via Wikimedia Commons

If you ask art historians about abstract art, they will often point to Wassily Kandinsky and 1911 as the pivotal year when this artist shifted from modern but figurative paintings (such as paintings of a horse, a factory, or even a comet) to images that were devoid of recognizable depictions. The color and line compositions for which Kandinsky is so famous immediately inspired scores of artists and schools, such as the Italian Futurists, French Cubists, and, well, all Abstractionists. In 1935, Kandinsky wrote about his (lost) 1911 abstract painting: "Indeed, it's the world's first ever abstract picture, because back then not one single painter was painting in an abstract style. A 'historic painting,' in other words." Smart lawyer that he was, he must have wanted to record his place in art history as the first abstractionist ever. Except that he wasn't.

Hilma, living quietly in the backwater of European art centers, went from *Late Summer* in 1903 to *Primordial Chaos*, three years later.

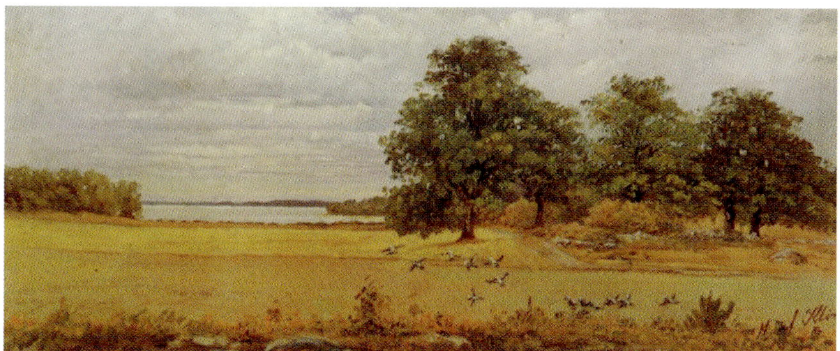

Hilma af Klint. *Late Summer*, 1903. Oil on canvas.
Hilma af Klint Foundation.
Photo: Public domain via Wikimedia Commons

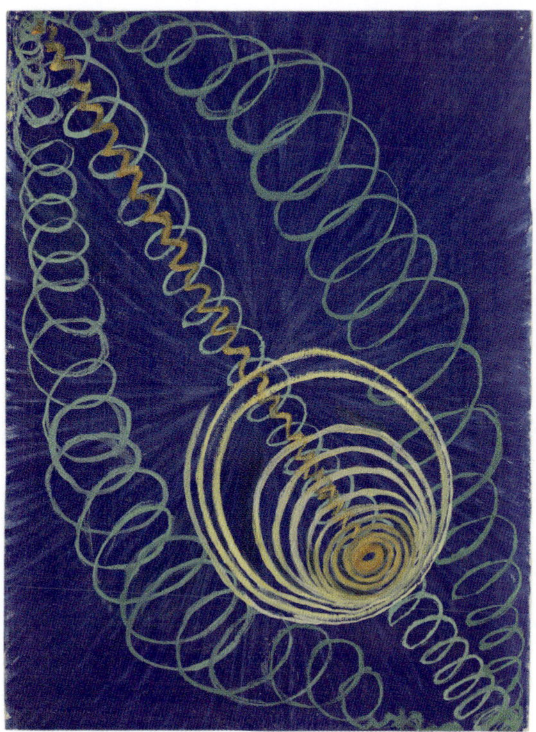

Hilma af Klint. *Primordial Chaos, No. 16 from The WU/ROSEN Series Group 1*, 1906–07. Oil on canvas.
Hilma af Klint Foundation.
Photo: Public domain via Wikimedia Commons

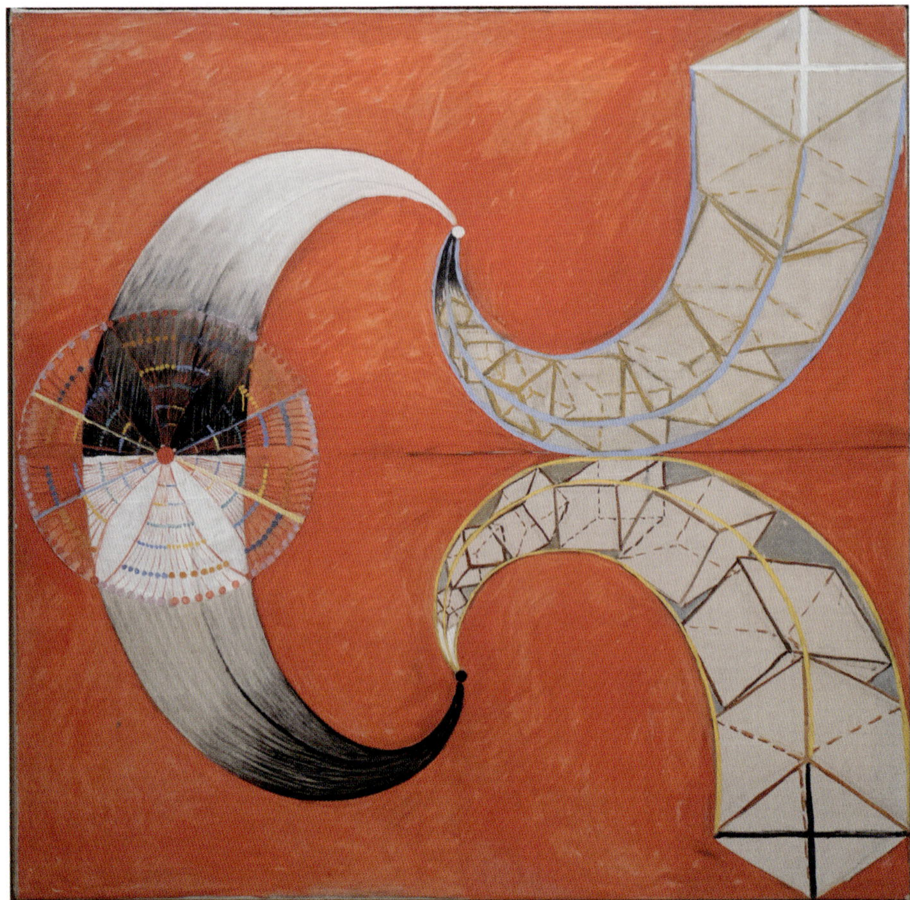

Hilma af Klint. *Group IX SUW, The Swan No. 9*, 1915. Oil on canvas.
Hilma af Klint Foundation.
Photo: Public domain via Wikimedia Commons/Rhododendrites

What happened? Hilma was inspired by her study of theosophy and by the writings of Madame Blavatsky and Rudolf Steiner. This was a popular spiritual direction for educated female seekers at the end of the 19th century. Theosophy and similar movements of the time provided an outlet for women seeking paths to spiritual growth not offered by traditional religions. Medium-led séances and theosophical study were popular all over Europe and America. But Hilma went beyond treating these interests as a fashionable pastime. In her own words, recorded in hundreds of meticulously kept notebooks, her spiritual studies led her to an opening of enormous creativity. She channeled her mystic experiences into complex abstract paintings in a place and time that had not seen anything like them before: "The pictures were painted directly through me, without any preliminary drawings, and with great force. I had no idea what the paintings were supposed to depict; nevertheless I worked swiftly and surely, without changing a single brush stroke."

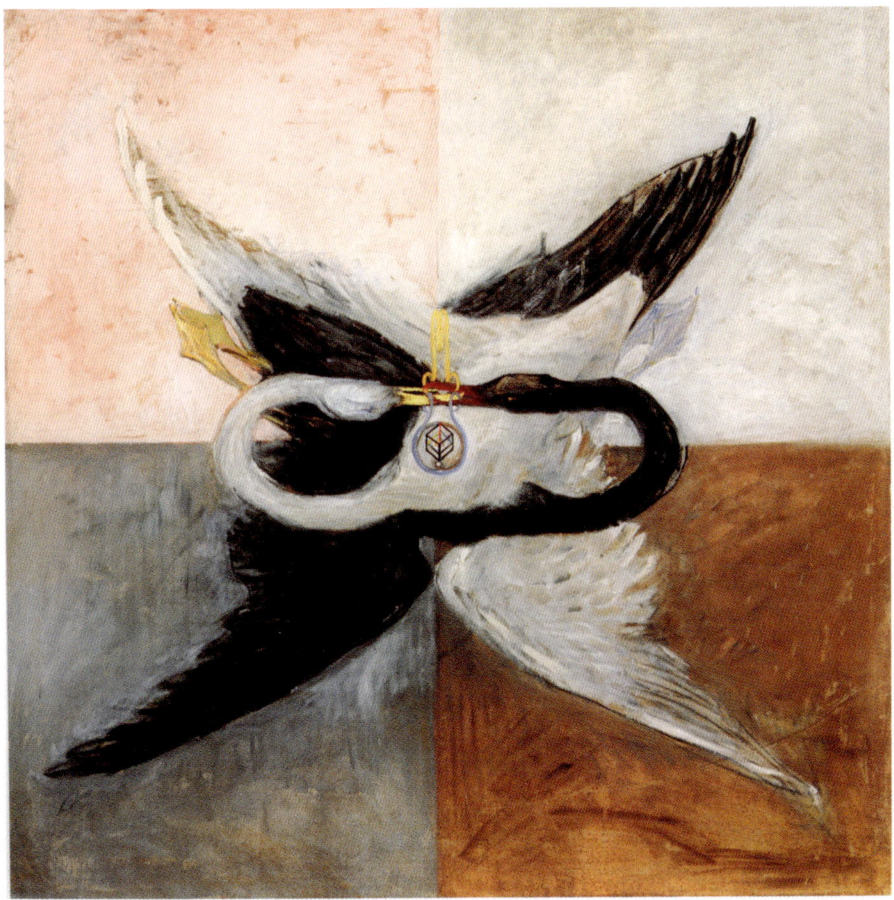

Hilma af Klint. *The Swan*, 1914. Oil on canvas.
Hilma af Klint Foundation.
Photo: Public domain via Wikimedia Commons

Like many artists, from Monet to Picasso, Hilma painted in series. Her earliest and most impressive was the cycle of large-scale *Paintings for the Temple Decorations* that included ten large works and another 183 paintings that were to represent, in an abstract form, "immortal aspects of man." While this remains her most important work of the period until 1915, she also produced other cycles including *Primordial Chaos*, a blue abstract series, and many paintings of swans—from some more or less realistic (albeit conceptually positioned) to complete abstractions such as the one on page 172.

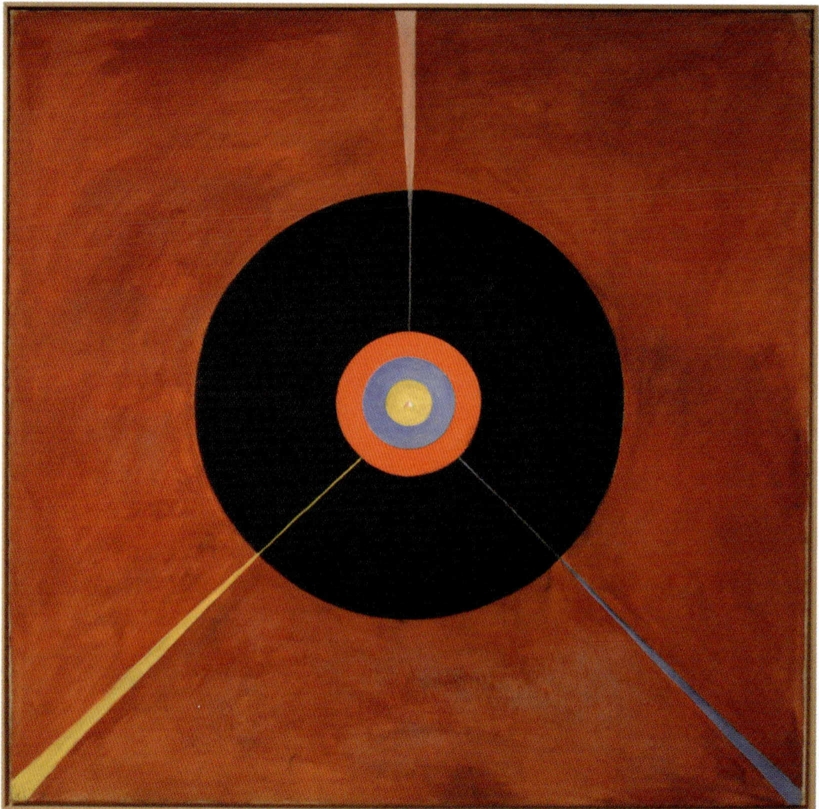

Hilma af Klint. *The Swan No. 18*, 1915. Oil on canvas.
Hilma af Klint Foundation.
Photo: Public domain via Wikimedia Commons

Hilma came from a family that traditionally provided Sweden with many naval captains and admirals, so the precocious girl grew up in the world of precise lines and shapes of naval maps as well as a scientific approach to information. She perfected her drawing skills at the Royal Academy in Stockholm, where she forged lifelong friendships with women artists who would later support her creative path. After graduation in 1877, she spent a few years painting traditional portraits and florals—her nature and anatomical illustrations are masterfully precise. One of her paintings from this era was sold to the Louvre, leaving no doubt that she could have continued on the respectable and profitable path of a professional portraitist and nature illustrator. Her restless mind led her first to detailed studies of nature (she wrote in her notebooks of her plans to catalog all the Swedish water flora and fauna, moving on to trees and wood creatures), and then to her more profound studies on the origins of human consciousness.

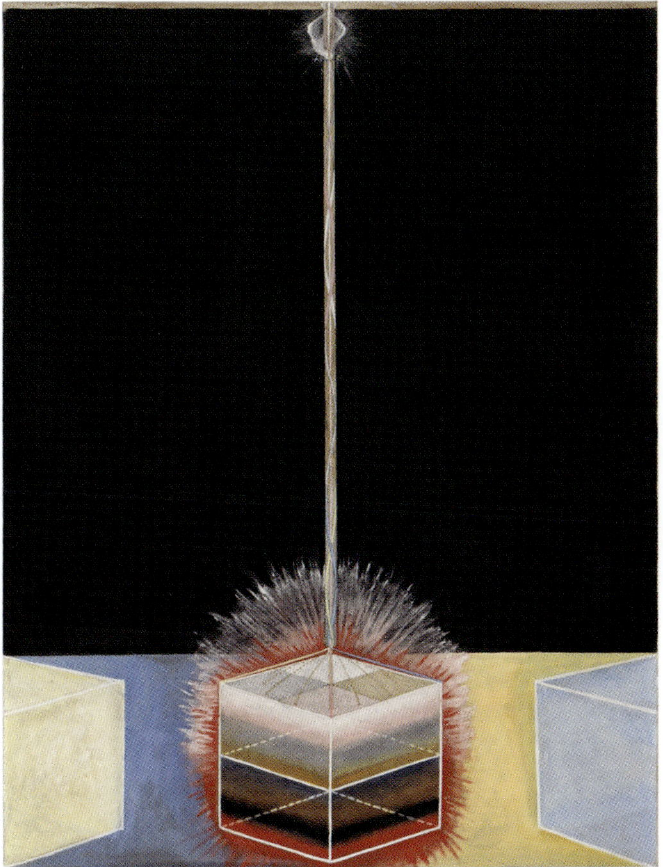

Hilma af Klint. *The Dove, No. 3, Group IX/UW, The SUW/UW Series*, 1915. Oil on canvas.
Hilma af Klint Foundation.
Photo: Public domain via Wikimedia Commons

The turn of the last century was an age of shocking and revolutionary discoveries—radioactivity, the atom, the theory of relativity, genetics. For a curious and bold mind, these discoveries upended all the then-prevailing ideas about the surrounding reality and raised new questions. For example, if most of the world is invisible, how do you show this invisible play of forces of light, rays, waves, and particles? What is soul? What is spirit? How are things interconnected? Are humans, plants, and earth elements all just expressions of the same matter? These questions lay at the foundation of Hilma's images, which were truly like nothing ever before invented in fine art.

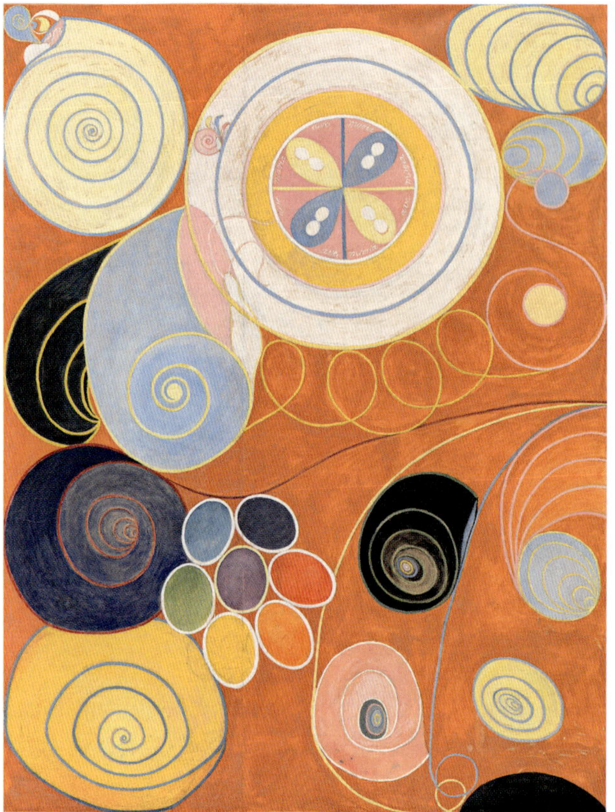

Hilma af Klint. *The Ten Largest No. 3 – Youth*, 1907. Tempera on paper, mounted on canvas. Hilma af Klint Foundation.
Photo: Public domain via Wikimedia Commons

Between 1906 and 1907, Hilma painted 10 large-scale paintings; the paper sheets are approximately 10 feet by 8 feet (320 x 240 cm). She used oil and tempera paints that held their vivid oranges and blues extremely well. These images, which she called "the key to all works," were a result of séances where a spirit guide directed her to create them as decorations for a theosophical temple. They were intended to express insights about human development and the holistic view of interconnectivity. The New Age ideas of the 20th century may be old hat to us now, but at the dawn of that century, Hilma must have had a lot of artistic conviction to express these unconventional ideas in her bold, huge paintings. Today, we would call them "psychedelic," but what could they have been named decades before the hippie era? The world around Hilma—especially in austere, Protestant Sweden—was Victorian: conventional, tangible, realistic. Her paintings were nothing of the sort.

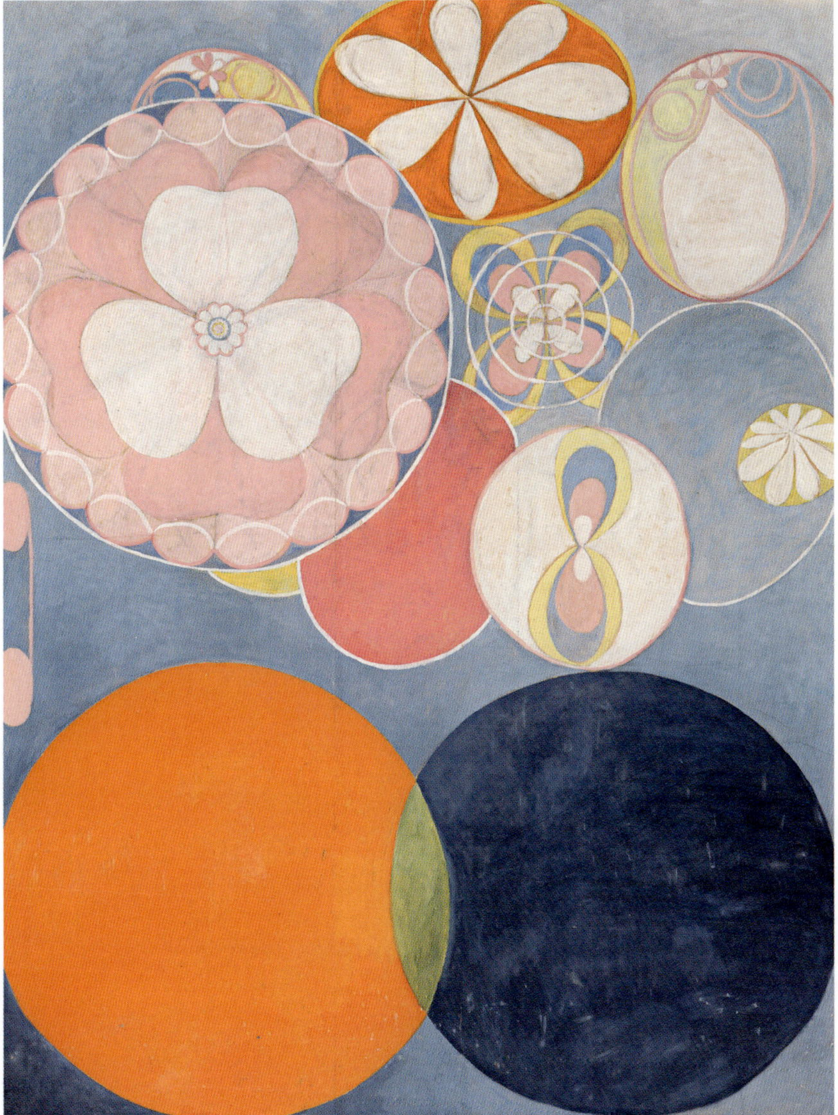

Hilma af Klint. *The Ten Largest No. 2 – Childhood*, 1907. Tempera on paper, mounted on canvas.
Hilma af Klint Foundation.
Photo: Public domain via Wikimedia Commons

The tragedy for both Hilma and art history is that her pioneering creativity was never recognized during her lifetime. She exhibited just once (or possibly twice), despite her numerous attempts to connect with gallerists, artists, and thinkers outside Sweden. A recent theory suggests that photographs of her abstract paintings (painted between 1906 and 1910) were shown to Wassily Kandinsky, whose own artistic evolution moved, from 1911 on, to this kind of purely abstract imagery. So... maybe he was not entirely unaware of the abstract revelations of this woman living in a city far away from the artistic center of Paris? Hilma tried unsuccessfully to popularize her art and her theosophical insights, but as a woman artist and someone who dared to proclaim her spiritualism as a source of inspiration, she was not taken very seriously. Eventually, she locked up all of her art and stipulated in her will that the paintings were not to be exhibited for 20 years, leaving about 1300 artworks and notebooks locked in a family attic for decades. Only recently did her descendants start bringing her art out into the limelight, including an exhibition in Los Angeles in 1986. An exhibition in Stockholm drew over a million visitors. Some international museums like the Tate have shown her work, and the Guggenheim exhibited her work in 2018.

For the most part, however, Hilma's inspired, colorful, holistic images remain unknown, and she is non-existent in textbooks on modern art or in anthologies of abstract artists—even if she was literally the first one.

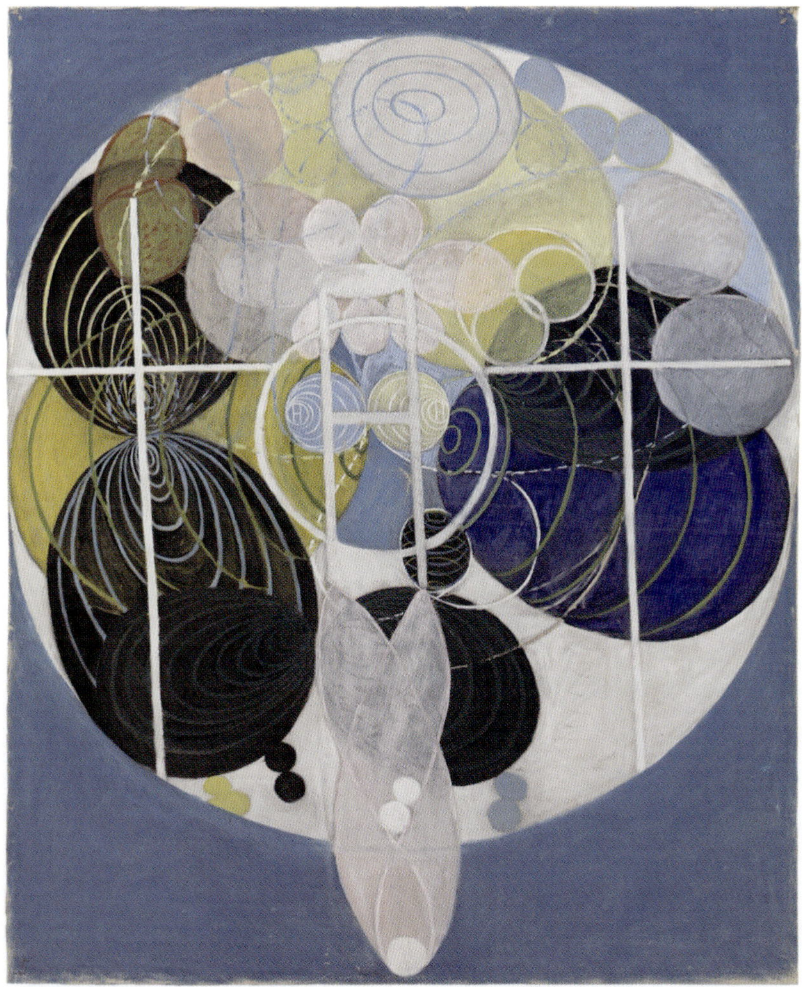

Hilma af Klint. *The Large Figure Paintings, No. 5, The Key to All Works to Date, Group III, The WU/Rosen Series*, 1907. Tempera on paper, mounted on canvas.
Hilma af Klint Foundation.
Photo: Public domain via Wikimedia Commons/Albin Dahlström/Moderna Museet

CHAPTER 17

BARBARA HEPWORTH (1903–1975)

Imagine that you are a mother of a five-year-old boy as well as newborn, underweight triplets. You are staying in a damp, badly heated flat in 1930s London. The father of the triplets is a renowned painter who is away in Paris to visit his legal wife and their children. On top of these challenges, you are yourself an artist who cannot live without sculpting, but carving in stone among boiling cloth diapers and screaming infants is not really an option.

This is not some theoretical situation—this was the impasse of a young sculptor named Barbara Hepworth in 1934 in Hampstead, London. Juggling work and motherhood has always been a dilemma for women, but Hepworth's case was just a bit more extreme. She was an artist whose principal medium was stone, and who wanted to create despite the constraints of convention and expectations regarding motherhood. While she made extraordinary artistic achievements, she has been criticized in some biographies for her unconventional life choices, such as a divorce (a socially questionable move in the 1930s) and the fact that she did not devote the entirety of her time to caring for her children.

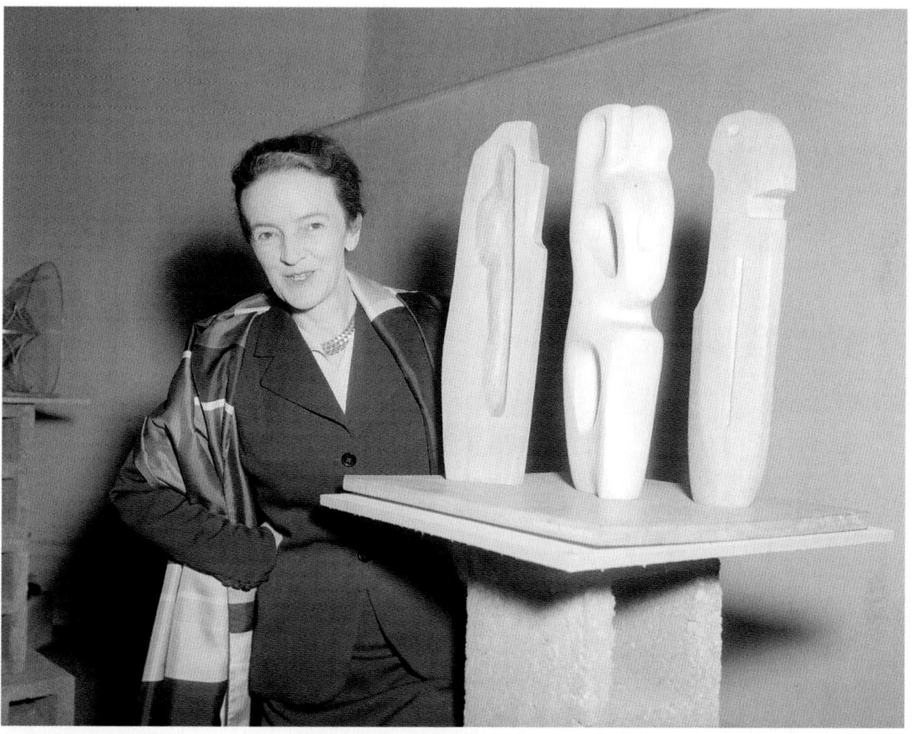

Barbara Hepworth with *The Unknown Political Prisoner*, 1953. Wood.
Barbara Hepworth © Bowness.
Photo: Alamy Stock Photo/Mirrorpix/Trinity Mirror.

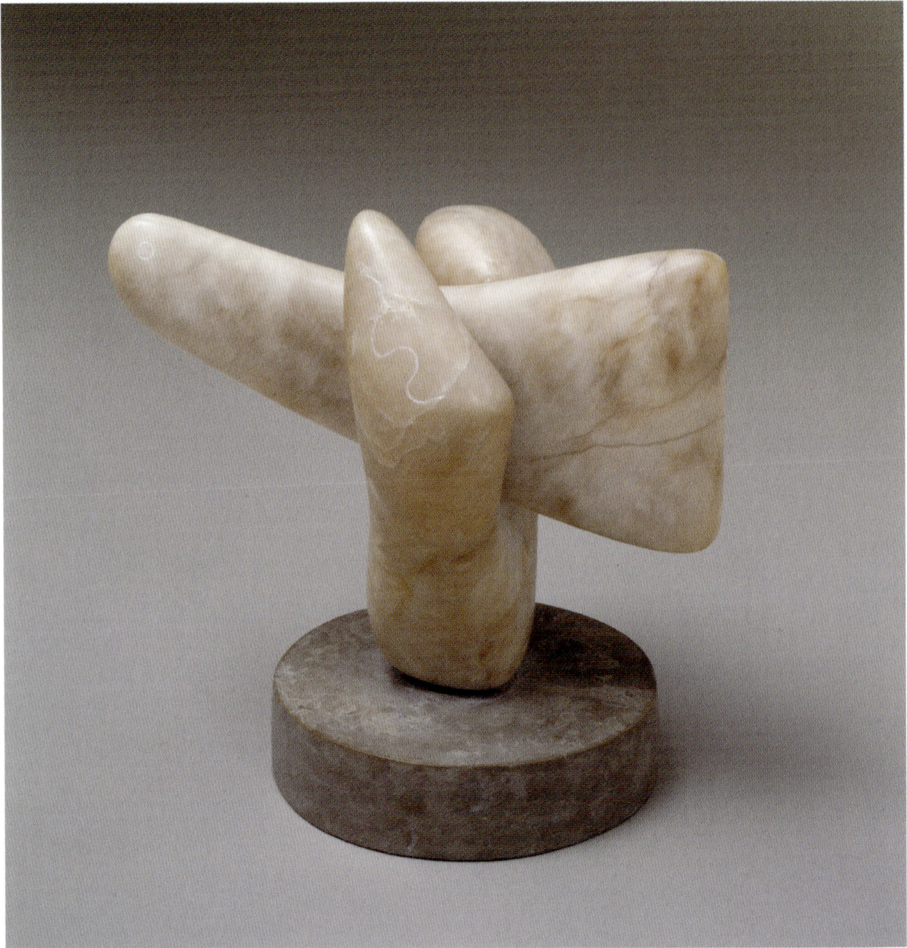

Barbara Hepworth. *Two forms*, 1933. Alabaster on limestone base.
Tate T07123. Barbara Hepworth © Bowness.
Photo: © Tate

Hepworth, born in 1903 to the family of a civil engineer in Yorkshire, knew already as a child that she wanted to be a sculptor. This was hardly an appropriate goal for a demure woman in Edwardian England. She prevailed, however, attending art schools (where she studied alongside another outstanding British sculptor, Henry Moore), traveling to Italy and eventually marrying in Florence her fellow artist John Skeaping. Italy influenced Hepworth enormously. In her 1952 autobiographical writings entitled *Carvings and Drawings*, she talked about her discovery of southern light—so different from her England experiences—and the joy of carving in marble: *"A chance remark by Ardini, an Italian master carver whom I met there [in Rome], that 'marble changes colour under different people's hands' made me decide immediately that it was not dominance which one had to attain over material, but an understanding, almost a kind of persuasion, and above all greater co-ordination between head and hand."*

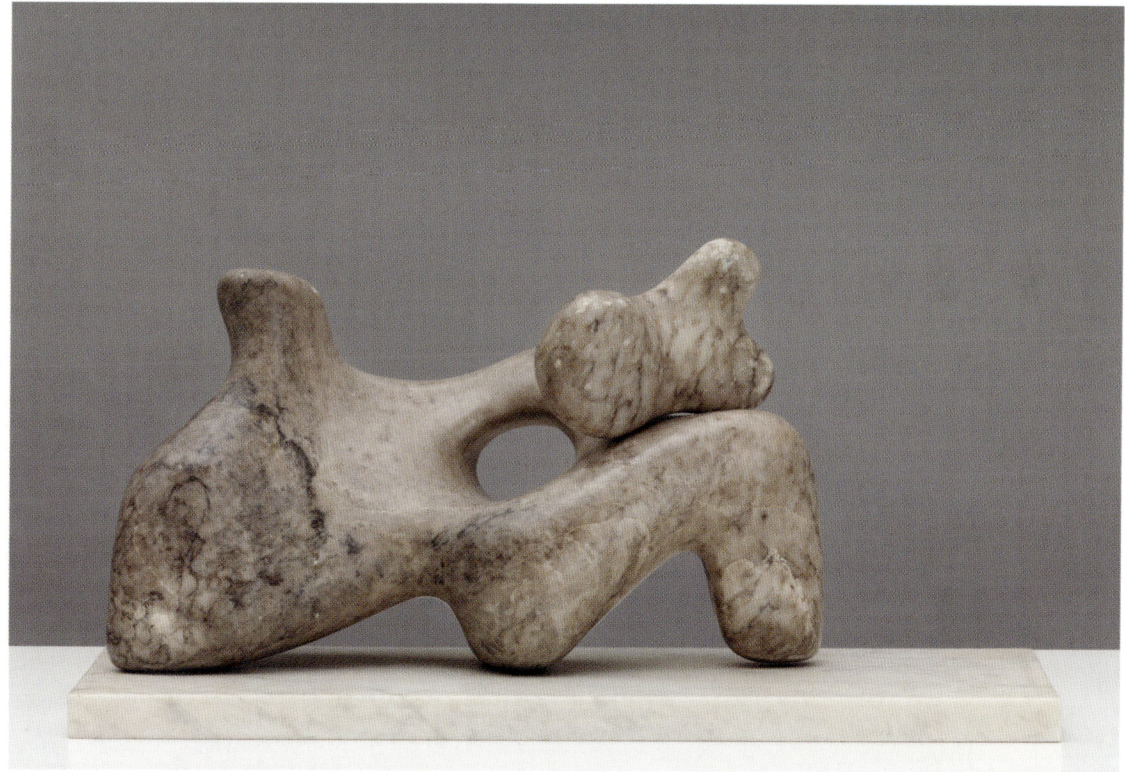

Barbara Hepworth. *Mother and Child*, 1934. Cumberland alabaster on marble base.
Tate T06676. Barbara Hepworth © Bowness.
Photo: © Tate

The end of the 1920s and the beginning of the 1930s was a period of rapid changes in Hepworth's personal life and a period of major artistic growth. On their return from Italy, Hepworth and Skeaping settled in London, where Hepworth bore their son Paul and started carving in earnest. However, a few years after Paul's birth, she started attending plein air gatherings in Norfolk with fellow artists. One of them was an abstract painter named Ben Nicholson. In 1931, they started a relationship, and she divorced Skeaping the same year. Three years later, her triplets were born. She most likely suffered from postpartum depression, since she later described in detail her bouts of uncontrollable crying during this period. The burdens of caring for five-year-old Paul and the newborns were so great that for a while she had to have the babies cared for in a nursery home. It took a good few years before the incompatibility of ordinary life mixed with art eased somewhat in her life.

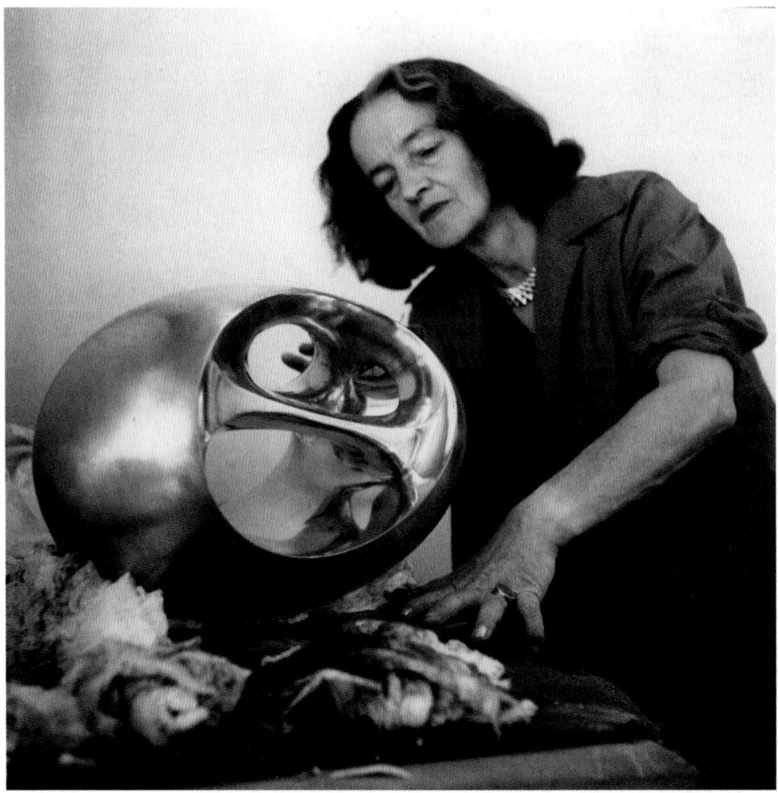

Barbara Hepworth examining her 1943 artwork *Oval Sculpture* (photo taken in 1958).
© The Estate of Tom Picton. Artwork Barbara Hepworth © Bowness.
Photo: © Tate

Artistically, this was Hepworth's period of invention and perfecting the medium (stone carving at the time was less popular than sculpting). She started carving stones and wood with pierced holes, creating compositions that included an abstract shape and empty space, both of which would complement and define the other. She was carving what Picasso rendered in paint and Calder in wire—the relationship between an empty and a filled space. Nicholson—a leading abstract modernist in Britain—also influenced her lifelong devotion to abstract art.

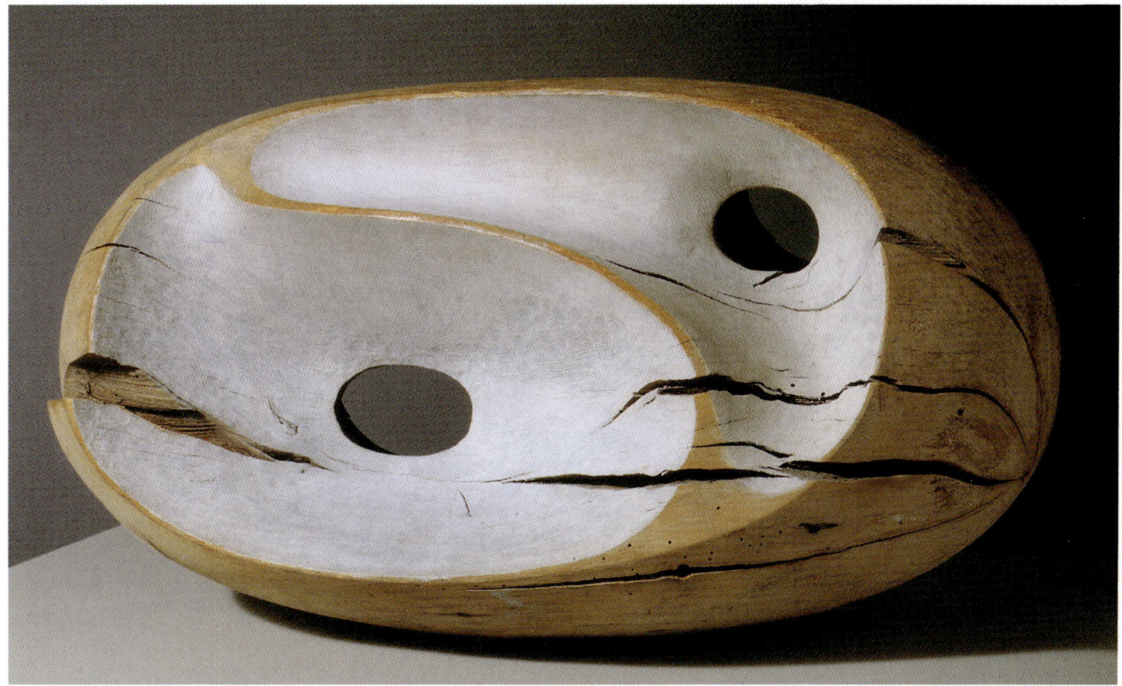

Barbara Hepworth. *Tides I*, 1946. Holly wood.
Tate T02008. Barbara Hepworth © Bowness.
Photo: © Tate

Despite recognition in the form of some gallery shows, Hepworth and Nicholson lived in relative poverty. City life was not very conducive to creativity, and they started spending more time away from London. Hepworth wrote: *"I have gained very great inspiration from the Cornish land – and seascape, the horizontal line of the sea and the quality of light and colour which reminds me of the Mediterranean light and colour which so excites one's sense of form; and first and last there is the human figure which in the country becomes a free and moving part of a greater whole. This relationship between figure and landscape is vitally important to me. I cannot feel it in a city."*

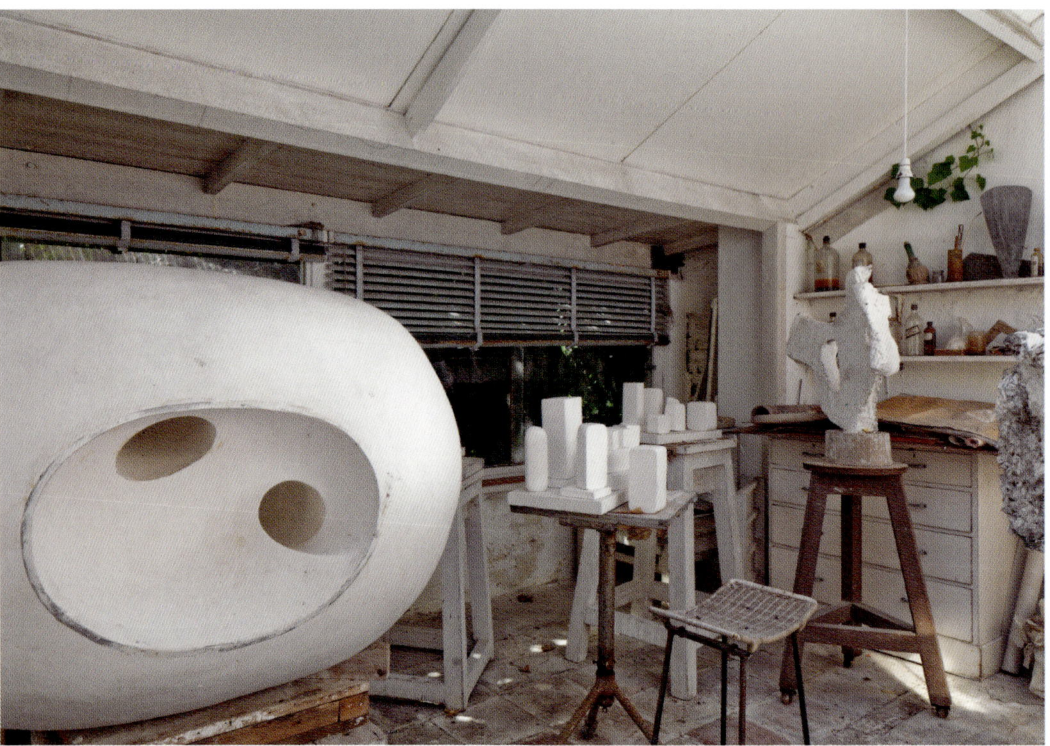

Interior of plaster workshop at Trewyn Studio, Barbara Hepworth Museum and Sculpture Garden, St Ives.
Artwork Barbara Hepworth © Bowness.
Photo © Tate (Marcus Leith & Andrew Dunkley) 2011

In 1939, a few days before England entered WWII, Hepworth and Nicholson found themselves in the artists' colony of St. Ives in Cornwall. Blitzed London was unsafe for the children, and the war years were not very art-friendly either, so this part of England became their permanent home. During the war years, the couple created their own art while inspiring and helping other artists, some of them wartime refugees. Their life in St. Ives launched a very fertile period in both artists' biographies. While Nicholson eventually left Cornwall and the couple separated, Hepworth stayed there for life, purchasing land around her Trewyn studio to create an ever-expanding, open-air display of her large sculptures.

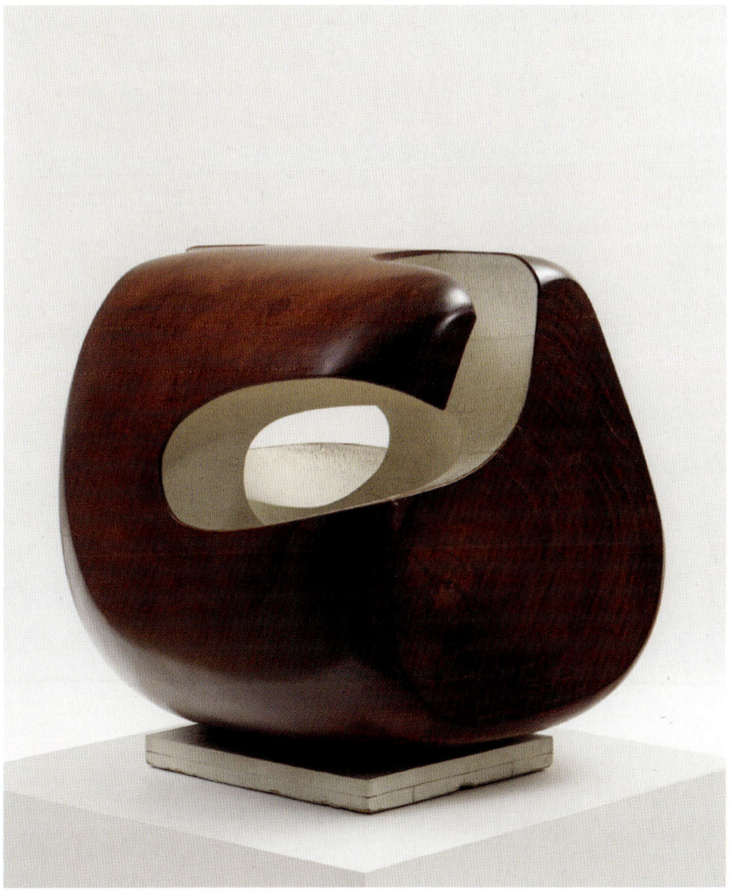

Barbara Hepworth. *Corinthos*, 1954–55. Guarea wood, paint, wooden base.
Tate T00531. Barbara Hepworth © Bowness.
Photo: © Tate

Hepworth's sculptures were rarely figurative, but she did create one in 1954, a figure entitled *Madonna and Child*, a sort of modernist Madonna that is now placed at St. Ives parish church. This unusual carving was prompted by the tragic death of Hepworth's son Paul in a flight accident in 1953. The following year, she traveled through Greece to get over her grief, and on her return, she started carving some of her loveliest pieces inspired by landscape and architecture of that land. *Corinthos* is carved from Nigerian guarea wood and painted white inside to contrast better with the brown hue of the outside. It reminds me of a freshly fallen chestnut when the brown nut skin is still shiny and incredibly smooth. Unlike the large stone and bronze public sculptures, this piece is intimate—it seduces the viewer into wanting to touch it and run a hand over it.

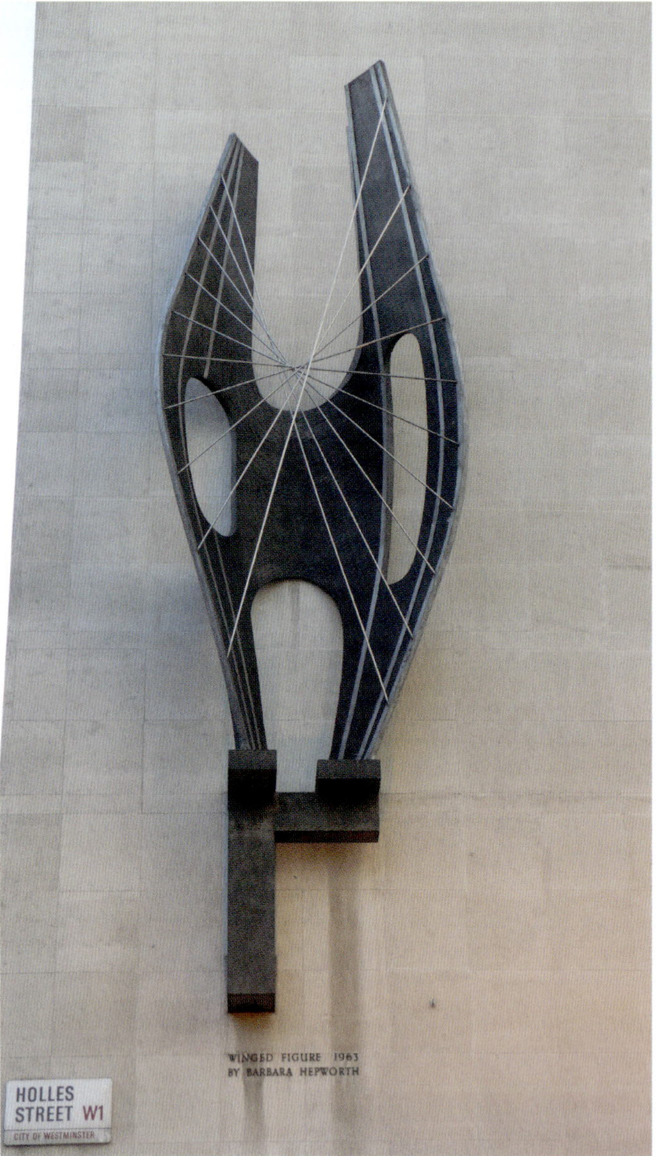

Barbara Hepworth. *Winged Figure*, 1963. Aluminum and steel rods. John Lewis building, London.

Barbara Hepworth © Bowness.
Photo: Wikimedia Commons/Justinc

Many of Hepworth's sculptures, especially in her postwar years, were created as public or private commissions. In 1961, for example, John Lewis, the Oxford Street department store, reached out to several British sculptors requesting proposals for a large sculpture to enliven the beige Portland stone façade of their flagship building in central London. Hepworth's design won; it was manufactured in aluminum and steel and installed in 1963. The commission was supposed to express "the idea of common ownership and common interests in a partnership of thousands of workers." This abstract construction is certainly impressive and a popular London landmark, even if it is debatable whether the crisscrossing steel rods actually signify a "partnership of workers."

One of Hepworth's most famous public commissions was her *Single Form* (1964), installed in front of the United Nations headquarters in New York.

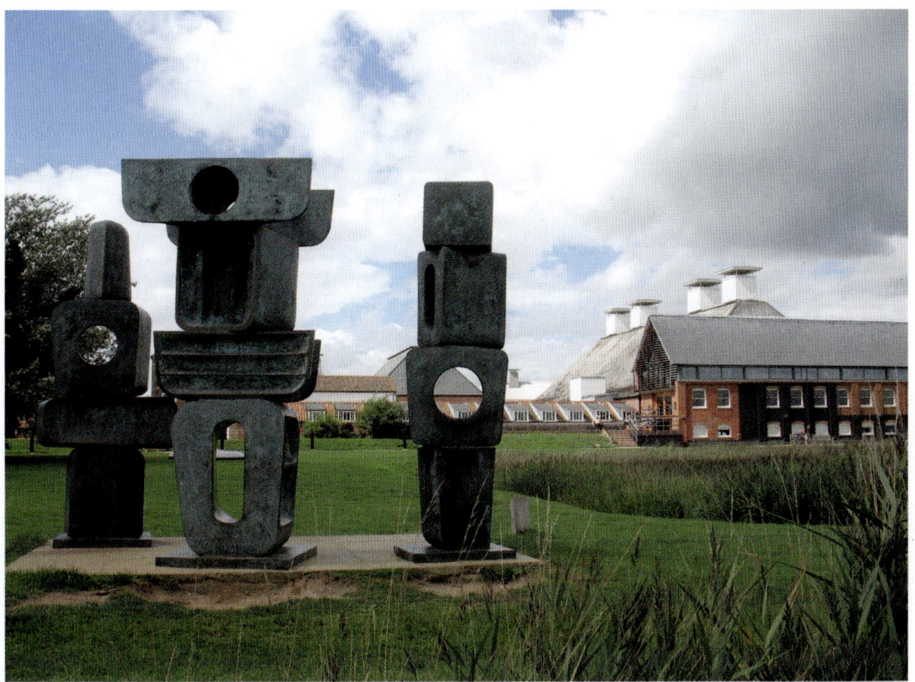

Barbara Hepworth. Three of the nine figures from *The Family of Man*, 1970. Bronze.
Fitzwilliam Museum, Cambridge on loan to Britten Pears Arts, permanently sited at Snape Maltings, UK.
Barbara Hepworth © Bowness.
Photo: Alan Stanton, CC BY-SA 2.0 <https://creativecommons.org/licenses/by-sa/2.0>, via Wikimedia Commons

Considered her masterpiece, Hepworth created *The Family of Man* as a group of nine, 5-to-10-foot bronzes (with the individual figures given titles such as *Ancestor II*, *Young Girl*, *Parent 1*, *Youth*, and so on). One complete set is displayed at Yorkshire Sculpture Park in the UK, while the other set is in a private collection. It was one of the last major works by Hepworth before her demise in 1975 (she died tragically in a studio fire started by her cigarette).

After her passing, Hepworth's carving studio in St. Ives was transformed into a museum, where many of her memorable sculptures from different decades are displayed in the surrounding garden that was her creative oasis for so many years. This is where she lived, where her beloved pet cats wandered, and where she created her unique, sinuous abstractions in stone and bronze.

Another location where you can see a collection of Hepworth's art is a museum in her native city of Wakefield in Yorkshire. The Hepworth Wakefield held a retrospective exhibition titled *Barbara Hepworth Art & Life* to celebrate the tenth anniversary of the gallery from May 21, 2021 through February 27, 2022.

PART IV

Women Who Made It Happen

CHAPTER 18

GERTRUDE VANDERBILT WHITNEY

(1875–1942)

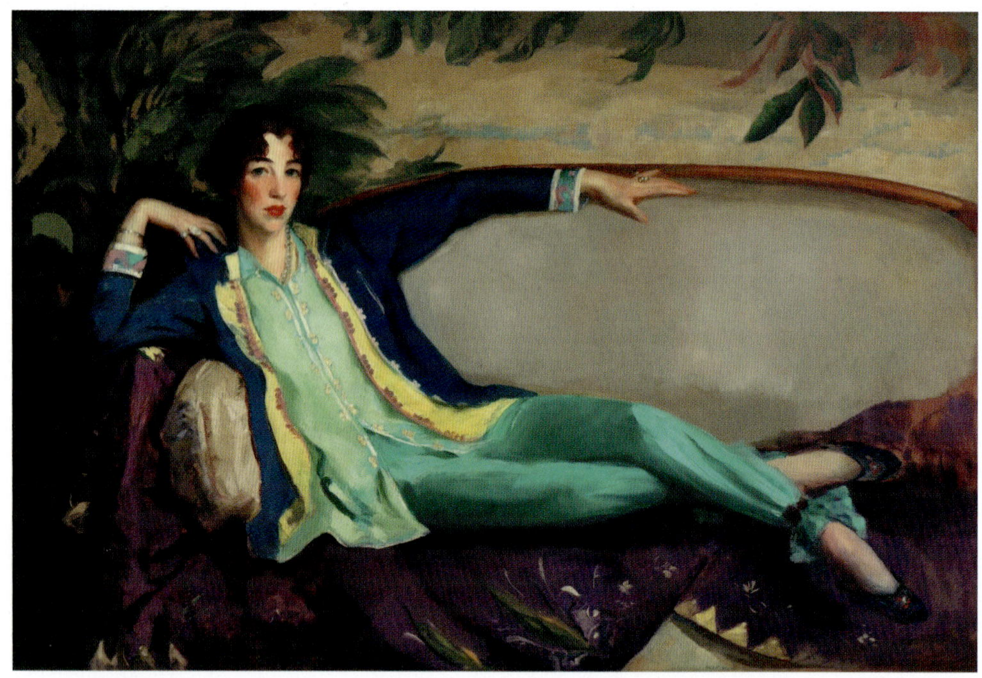

Robert Henri. *Gertrude Vanderbilt Whitney*, 1916. Oil on canvas, 49 15/16 × 72 in. (126.8 × 182.9 cm).

Whitney Museum of American Art, New York; gift of Flora Whitney Miller 86.70.3.
Photo: Public domain via Wikimedia Commons

In a press release issued in 1930, Gertrude Vanderbilt Whitney announced that she was launching a museum of American art because *"...not only can the visiting foreigner find no adequate presentation of the growth and development of the fine arts in America under a single roof; the same difficulty faces the native who wants to get what American art is all about."*

By the time she embarked on this pioneering venture, heiress Gertrude Whitney already had numerous other accomplishments to her name: as a book author, a WWI hero (for founding a field hospital in France), and an accomplished professional sculptor with statues gracing many public spaces.

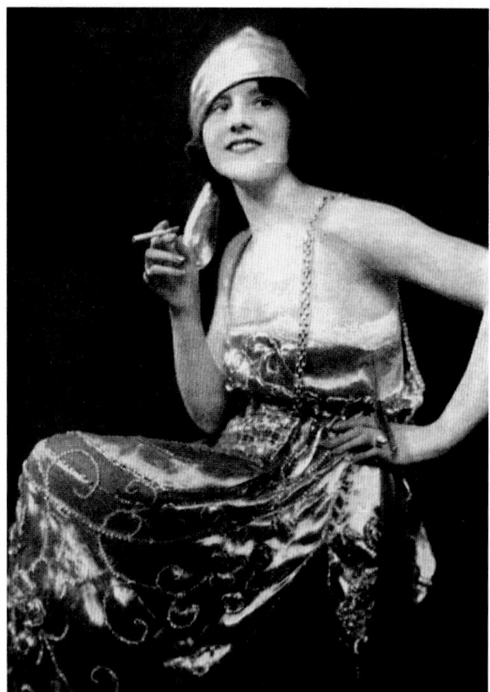

Photo of Gertrude Whitney from September 1921 edition of *Tatler*.
Photo: Public domain via Wikimedia Commons/Alfred Cheney Johnston

As a daughter of the billionaire Vanderbilt shipping family, Gertrude was never "like anyone else." An heiress raised during the American Gilded Age, she was fully aware that she would always be in the spotlight, with responsibilities that came along with the privileges of wealth. She also was subject to a myriad of conventions (such as not being able to attend her cousin Consuelo's wedding of the century to the Duke of Marlborough simply because Consuelo's parents were divorced) and expectations to marry right, attend the correct balls, and be a prominent New York socialite. By age 25, married to Harry Payne Whitney (a childhood friend from a distinguished old family), she had three children, and...a restlessness that led her to study sculpture.

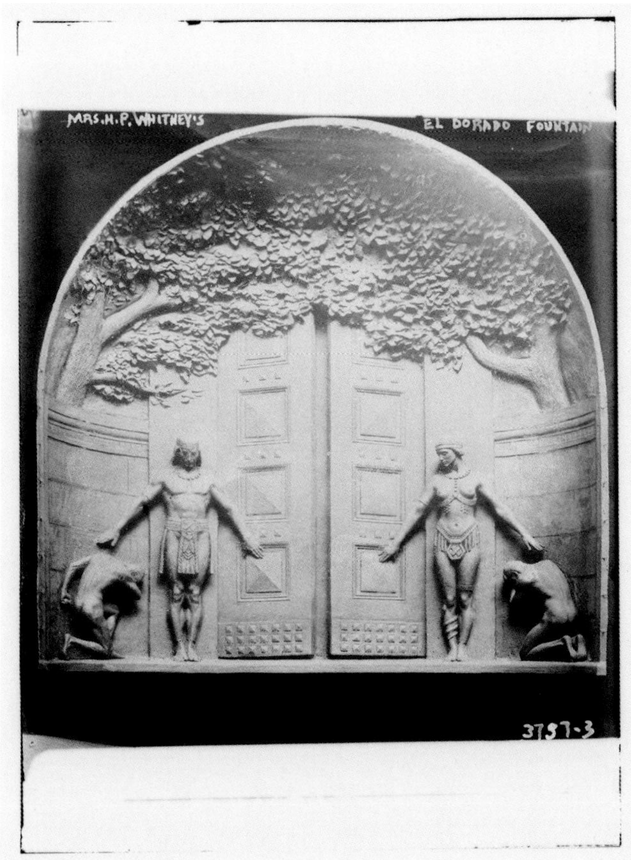

Gertrude Whitney. *El Dorado Fountain*—photo detail of the sculpture at the Pan-Pacific Exposition, San Francisco, 1915. Marble.
Photo: Bain News Service/United States Library of Congress Prints and Photographs Division, Washington, D.C./Public domain

By the early 1900s, sculpting and writing travel books took up more of her time than a marriage that had settled into one of convenience. For the next 15 years, Gertrude produced numerous large sculptures, such as the El Dorado Fountain that graced the 1915 World Exposition in San Francisco and the Titanic Memorial. The Memorial, designed by Gertrude in 1914 but not erected until 1931, in Washington, DC, was commissioned as an initiative of women survivors to honor men who died in the Titanic disaster. As the inscription on the monument says, it was dedicated to "the brave men who perished in the wreck of the Titanic, April 15, 1912. They gave their lives that women and children might be saved." Gertrude's powerful design of a man stretching his arms inspired the famous pose of the couple on the bow of the doomed ship in the 1997 movie "Titanic".

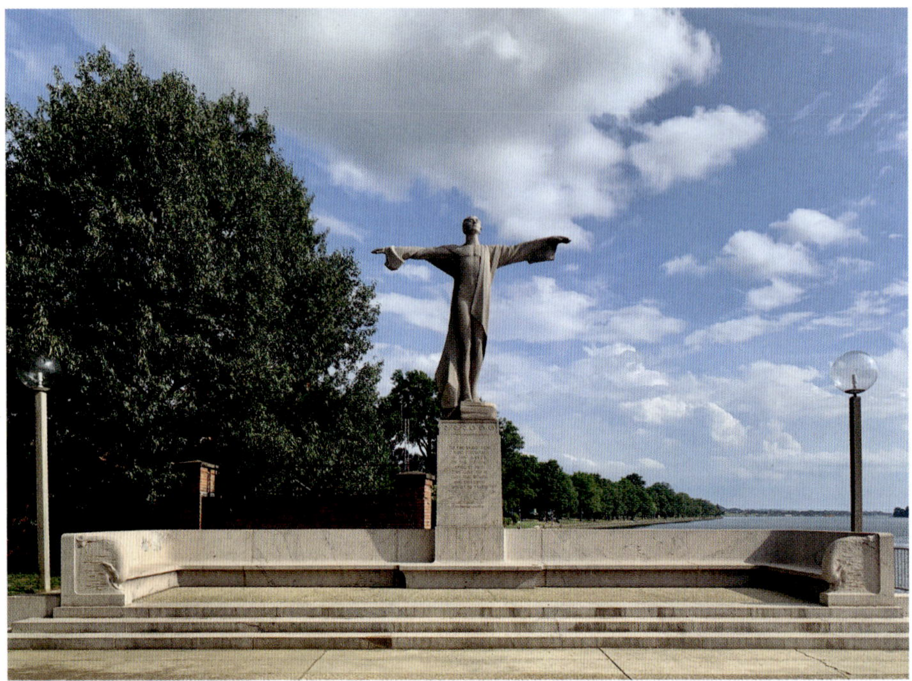

Gertrude Whitney. *Titanic Memorial*, 1931. Granite. Washington, D.C.
Photo: APK, CC BY-SA 4.0 <https://creativecommons.org/licenses/by-sa/4.0>, via Wikimedia Commons

While her husband mostly pursued horse breeding, polo playing, and yachting, Gertrude sculpted in all seriousness while also getting involved in many humanitarian causes. One of her causes was supporting the WWI war effort from the start by providing funds of an estimated quarter of a million (in 1914 dollars) to establish a field hospital on the European front. With this gesture, Gertrude wanted to repay the years of happiness that France had given her before the war, when she would spend months each year working on her sculptures at her Paris studio, going to museums, and traveling to French resorts. Her commitment to the field hospital did not just include securing the enormous funds, organizing a team of medical personnel, and shipping supplies to France—she also traveled herself a few times to war-torn France to supervise the hospital's set-up. In 1926, she completed her last public commission: a statue of an American soldier intended to commemorate America's support of France during WWI. That symbol of the American-French alliance overlooked a harbor in Saint-Nazaire in Brittany until it was dynamited and destroyed in 1941 by the German army.

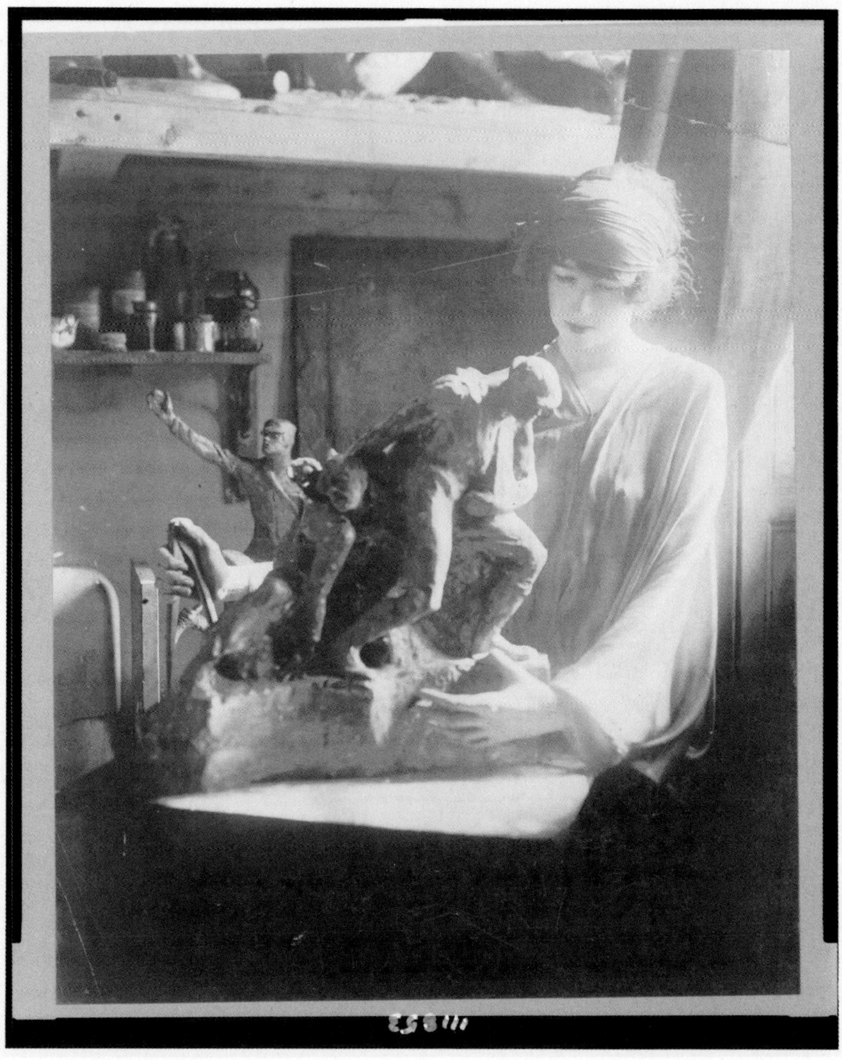

Gertrude Whitney standing with her statue of soldiers, 1920. Photographic print.
Photo: United States Library of Congress Prints and Photographs Division, Washington, D.C./Public domain

Throughout the 1920s, Gertrude supported art events and individual artists. She also started dreaming of creating a place where contemporary American painters and sculptors could exhibit their works. At the time, there was little respect or financial recognition for American artists in their homeland. In 1907, for example, when Renoir's *La Famille Charpentier* sold to New York's Metropolitan Museum of Art (the "Met") for $18,480, a painting by a living American artist would have fetched only about $1500.

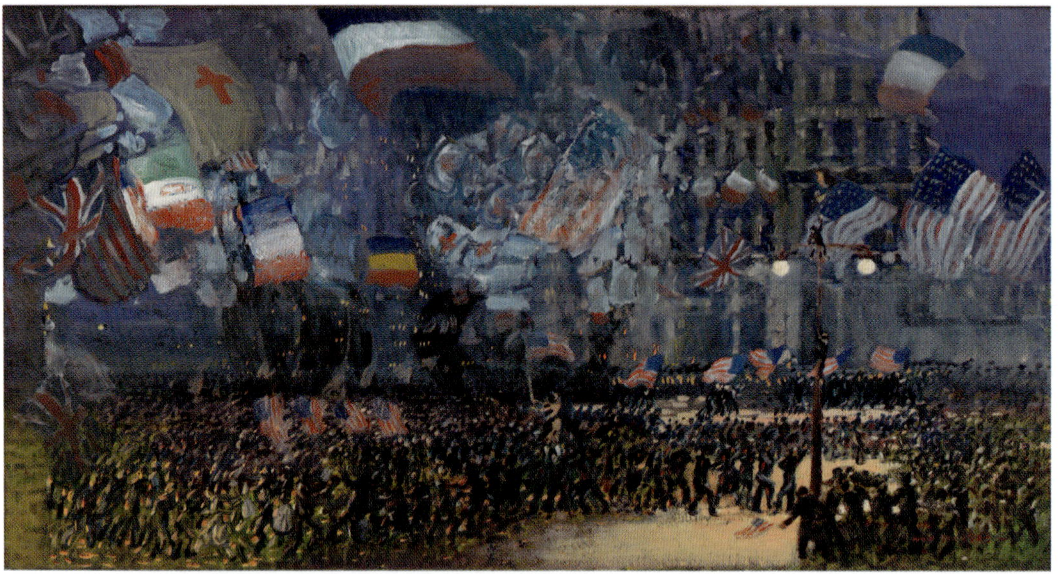

George Benjamin Luks. *Armistice Night*, 1918. Oil on canvas.
Whitney Museum of American Art, New York.
Photo: Public domain via Wikimedia Commons

In those days, supporting the arts also meant supporting artists. Gertrude did it all —including paying artists' overdue rent or doctor bills, sponsoring trips to Paris, or helping with solo exhibitions. She also set up the Whitney Studio Club, an organization to promote the education, support, and presentation of contemporary artists. In 1916, the first show at Whitney Studio Club was called *Modern American and Foreign Artists*. Many painters, such as John Sloan and Edward Hopper, had their first shows at the Club. Notably, out of 400 club members, more than a quarter were women artists, at a time when women—artists or not—had a hard time being admitted to many public organizations.

Being an artist herself, Gertrude was more than a rich collector of art—she bought the works of new artists, and she opened the doors of other galleries for many debutants. By 1929, she had a serious collection of about 600 works and a mission to make them known to the American public. But when she offered her collection to the Met, even proposing to endow a special wing to house it, the museum's director Edward Robinson immediately refused the offer, since the American art did not rate high enough in his eyes. Out of that refusal was born the Whitney Museum of American Art.

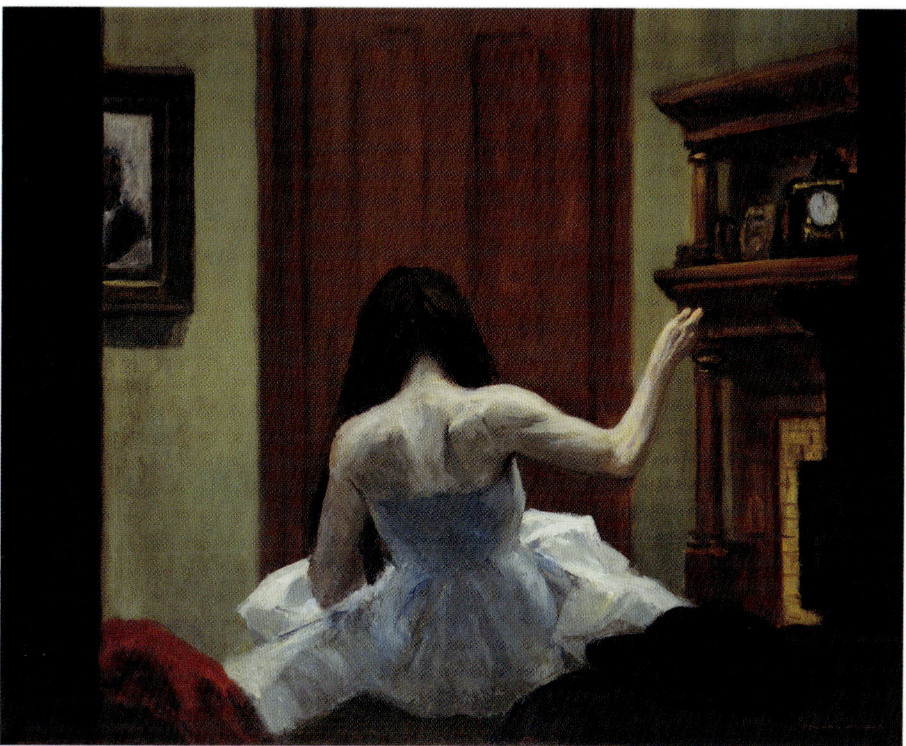

Edward Hopper. *New York Interior*, 1921. Oil on canvas.
Whitney Museum of American Art, New York.
Photo: © Fine Art Images/Bridgeman Images. Artwork: © 2022 Heirs of Josephine N. Hopper/Licensed by Artists Rights Society (ARS), NY

The Whitney Museum's beginnings were modest. Although several thousand guests showed up for the opening, the initial collection reflected Gertrude's personal preference of realist paintings and included few of the future greats of other styles in American art. With the museum's creation, a first step was taken, however —for the first time, there was concrete recognition that American artists deserved their own dedicated institution, even while all other New York museums were still filled with mostly European art.

Gertrude's legacy was not only the founding of a museum that no one else deemed it worthwhile to establish; she also ensured that her daughter and granddaughter would continue her commitment. Her devotion to a museum as a focal point for artists was also reinforced by the fact that the first three curators of the Whitney—Edmund Archer, Karl Free, and Hermon Moore—who served all the way until 1958, were artists themselves.

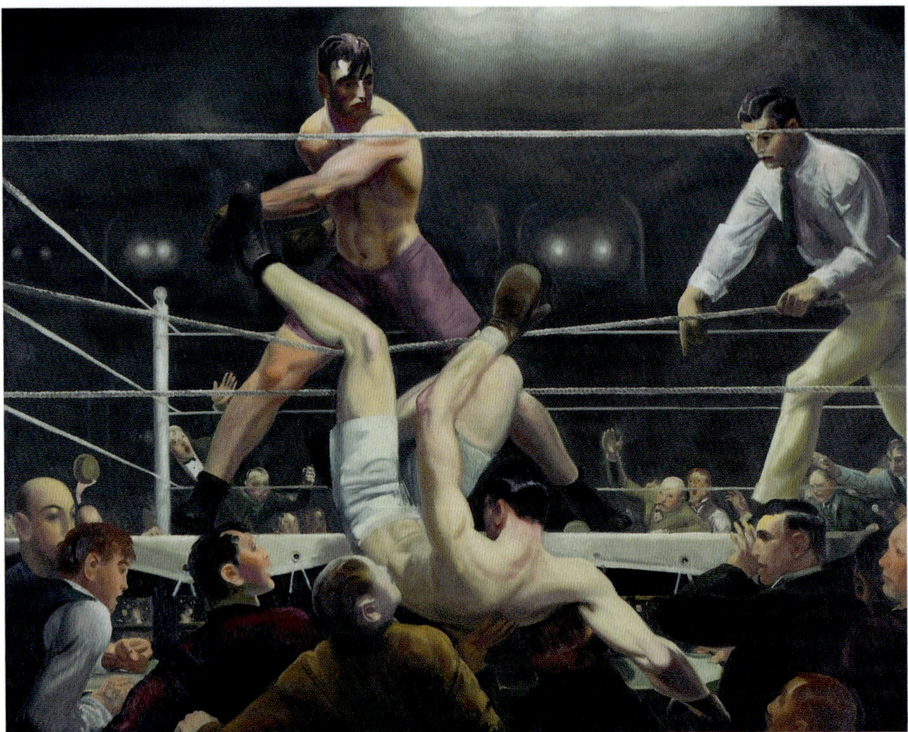

George Bellows. *Dempsey and Firpo*, 1924. Oil on canvas.
Whitney Museum of American Art, New York.
Photo: Public domain via Wikimedia Commons

Thanks to generations of Whitney women, the museum has continued to thrive. First, there was Gertrude, who had the idea to create one place devoted to American artists and the fortitude to carry out this idea. Then there was her daughter, Flora Whitney Miller, who not only maintained the museum's mission but also, resisting financial pressures, declined to have the Whitney folded into the Met in 1948; instead, she expanded the museum's gifting policies to enable artists, patrons, and trusts to endow the Whitney with more art. Her daughter (and Gertrude's granddaughter), Flora Miller Biddle, continued on the board of the museum and presided over the creation of the new Bauer Building. Meanwhile, the museum evolved in many ways, changing location a couple of times, moving from collecting primarily realist art to acquiring all new styles and genres (which brought the museum exciting modern art masterpieces ranging from Abstract Expressionist to Pop and Post-Modern), and increasing its collection to the current 25,000 works.

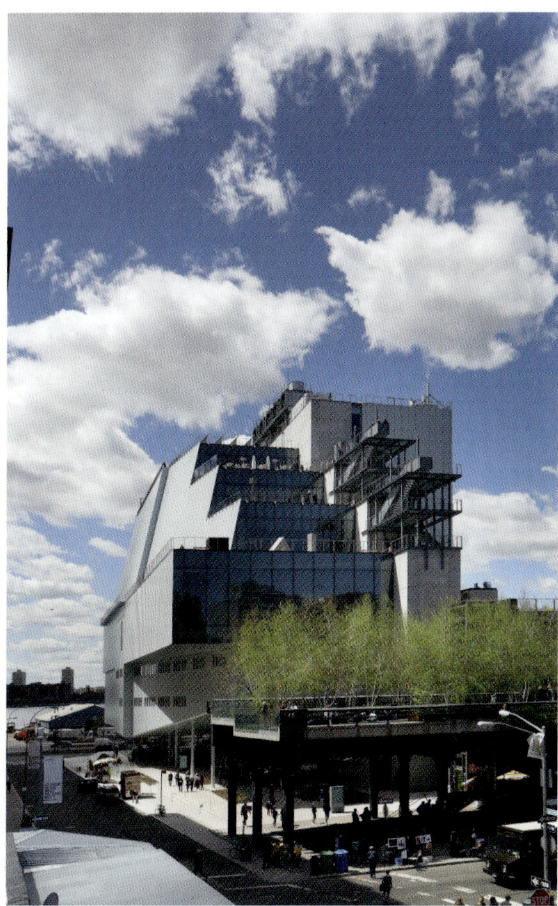

View of the Whitney Museum of American Art from Gansevoort Street.
Photo: Ed Lederman, 2015. © Whitney Museum of American Art, New York.

Today, the Whitney Museum of American Art is firmly established as one of the most exciting and beautiful world depositories of modern art, but it is often overlooked that this supermodern building on the Hudson River had its modest beginnings in the vision of one woman—Gertrude Vanderbilt Whitney.

CHAPTER 19

ISABELLA STEWART GARDNER (1840–1924)

March 18, 1990 was the St. Patrick's Day holiday in Boston. The streets were full of revelers, and the police had their hands full with traffic control. Two mustachioed policemen who knocked on the doors of the Isabella Stewart Gardner Museum on Fenway Street were readily admitted by two nightguards when the policemen announced they were checking on some disturbance. The guards were not much in the way of guards anyway—one of them was a music school student moonlighting in the evenings as a security guard. The cops were not really cops either—as soon as they were admitted to the museum, the robbers tied up the two guards and started hacking at picture frames. By the end of that night, three of the most famous paintings in the world—Rembrandt's *The Storm on the Sea of Galilee*, Vermeer's *The Concert*, and Manet's *Chez Tortoni*—along with ten other major works of art had disappeared. To this day, the largest and most damaging art theft of the 20th century has never been solved and the paintings have never been recovered, nor has the mystery of who ordered the well-planned heist ever been revealed.

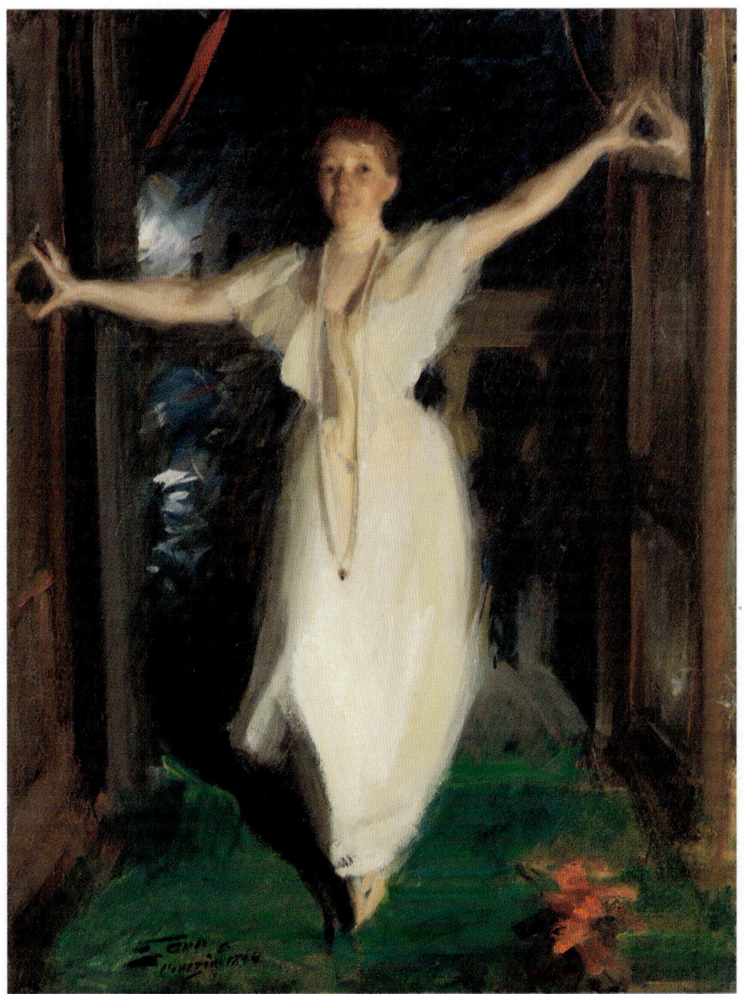

Andres Zorn. *Isabella Stewart Gardner in Venice*, 1894. Oil on canvas.
Isabella Stewart Gardner Museum, Boston.
Photo: Public domain via Wikimedia Commons

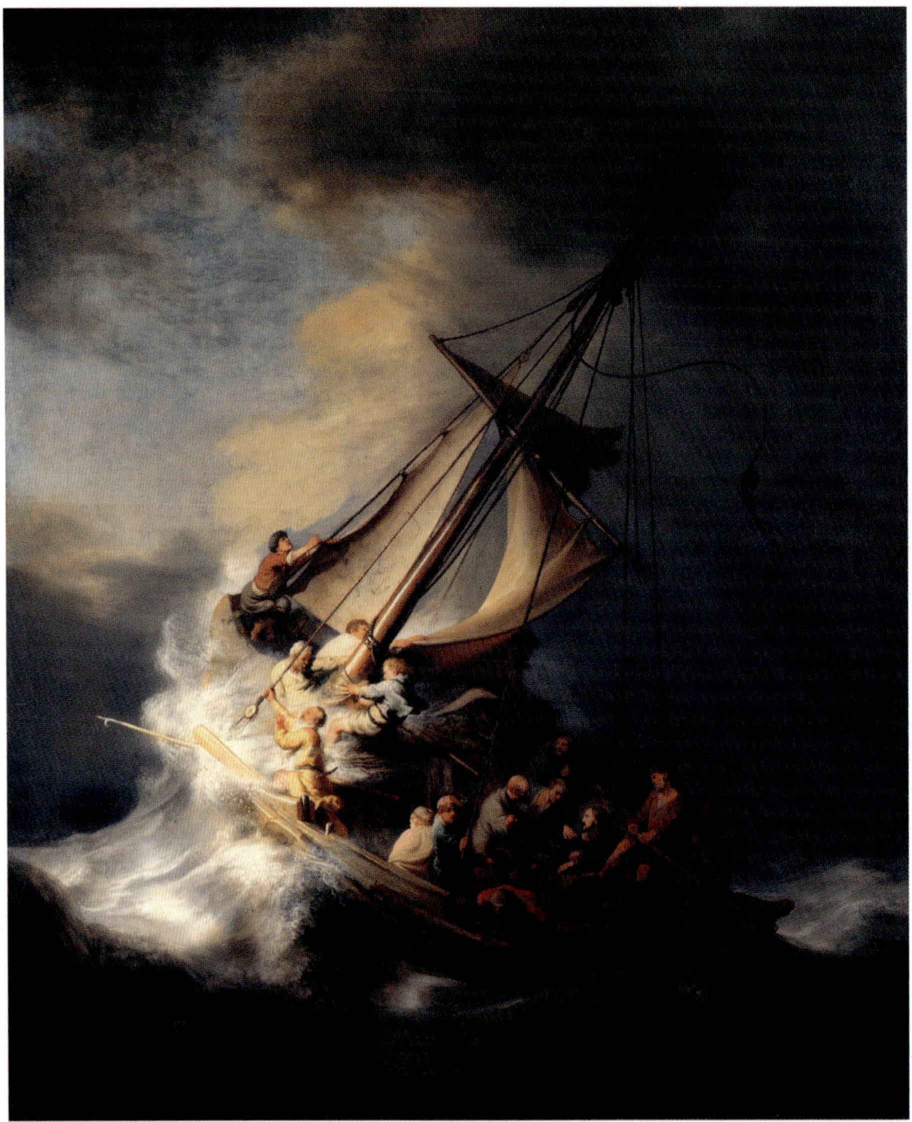

Rembrandt van Rijn. *The Storm on the Sea of Galilee*, 1633. Oil on canvas.
Stolen from Isabella Stewart Gardner Museum, Boston in 1990.
Photo: Public domain via Wikimedia Commons

It is unfortunate that for many current and future museum patrons, the name of Isabella Stewart Gardner is now associated more with the daring 1990 heist than with the story of the unusual woman behind one of the most sophisticated fine art collections in America.

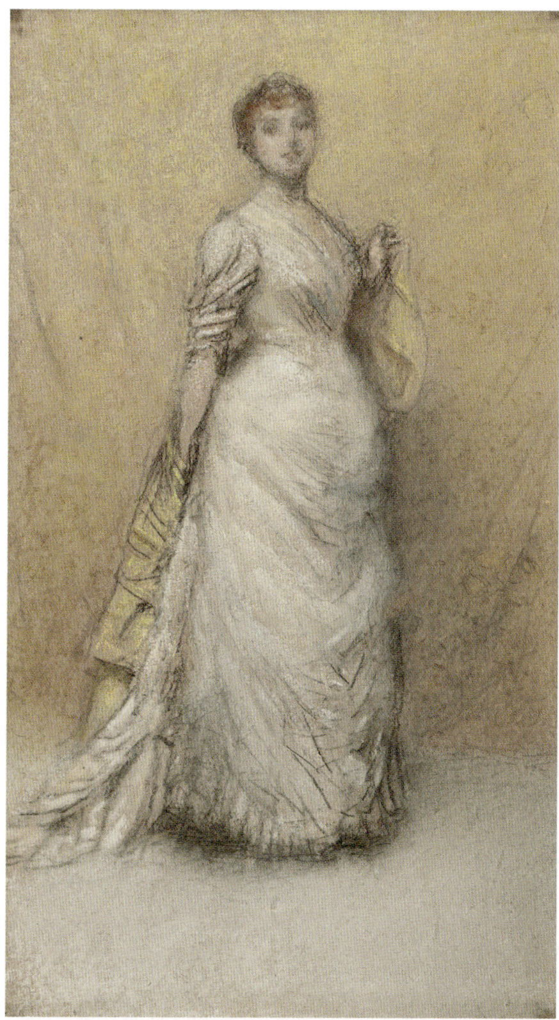

James McNeill Whistler. *The Little Note in Yellow and Gold*, 1866.
Chalk and pastel on cardboard.
Isabella Stewart Gardner Museum, Boston.
Photo: Public domain via Wikimedia Commons

Gardner started out in the conventional, patrician circles of the East Coast society of the Victorian era as a young bride, married off in 1860 to the scion of the Boston Brahmins, John "Jack" Lovell Gardner, Jr. A series of misfortunes—the death of her two-year-old son, a miscarriage that rendered her unable to have more children, a severe depression, and a marriage that descended into a union of convenience—contributed to the transformation of this patrician lady into "Mrs. Jack"—an eccentric, scandalizing, formidable patroness of the arts and artists.

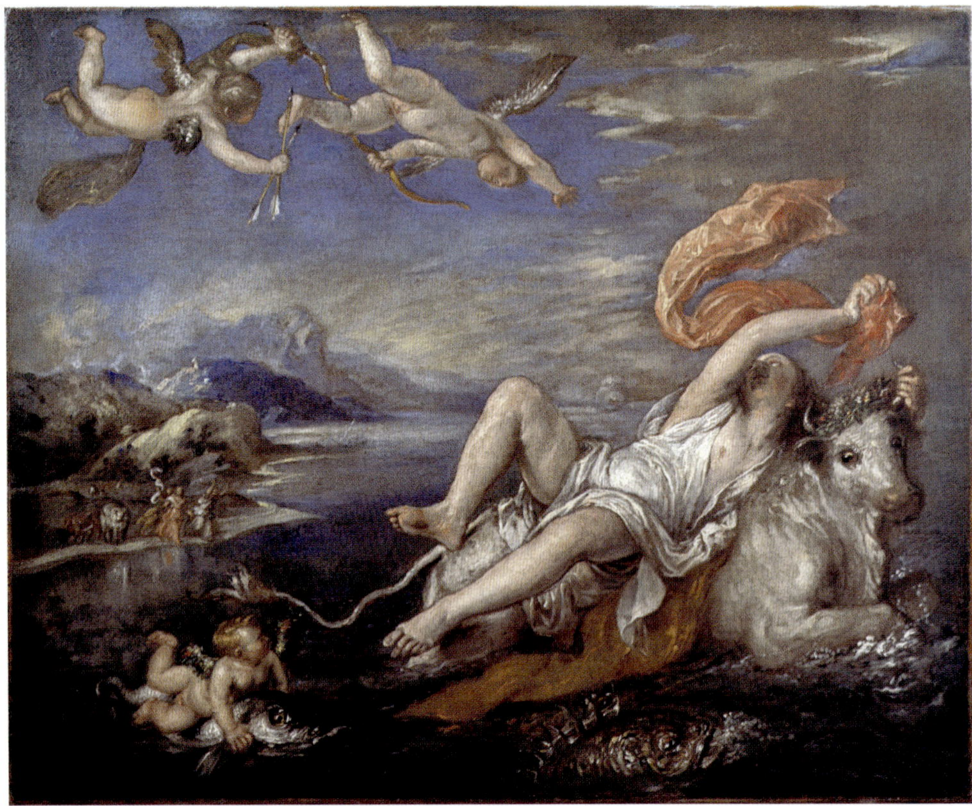

Titian. *The Rape of Europa*, 1551. Oil on canvas.
Isabella Stewart Gardner Museum, Boston.
Photo: Public domain via Wikimedia Commons

Paradoxically, one way to tell the story of this woman who was more colorful and willful than anyone in her world of Boston high society is through the relationships she had with men in her life. This does not mean that she was their victim or even much of a dependent—these were men, including her father and her husband, who either supported her or who were dominated by her, financially or psychologically. Her father David Stewart was a wealthy businessman from whom she inherited a fortune that was independent from her husband's property and which enabled her to spend freely on her art hunts. "Jack" Gardner, her husband, was very indulgent of his wife's eccentricities (such as walking around the city streets with a tame lion) and her friendships with people who traditional Boston society would not normally accept (for example, men who were either gay, Jewish, or impoverished artists—or all three at the same time).

Above all, though, Gardner's intellectual life was influenced by three men outside her family circle—all three of whom were cultured, refined, and towered over others in their respective fields. They may have all profited from their association with Gardner and her financial support, but they also gave her in return the princely gifts of artistic immortality.

First, there was "the Writer." Gardner's deep and complex friendship with Henry James resulted in her being portrayed in his writings (most notably in the novel *The Wings of the Dove*). James also provided her with a long-standing opportunity for intellectual development, as evidenced in their correspondence, as well as a crucial introduction to another key male figure in her life: "the Painter."

John Singer Sargent, an American expat who spent more time in Venice and North Africa than on the East Coast, met Gardner in London in 1886. He was already famous and infamous at the same time for painting the scandalizing *Portrait of Madame X*.

Gardner, with her penchant for creating an outraged buzz in high society, would have liked nothing more than to be the subject of an equally shocking likeness from Sargent. However, this commission had to wait for both of them to be in Boston at the same time, since they tended to be busy roaming the world, from Asia (Gardner) to Africa (Sargent). When she finally posed for him in 1887, the result was startling.

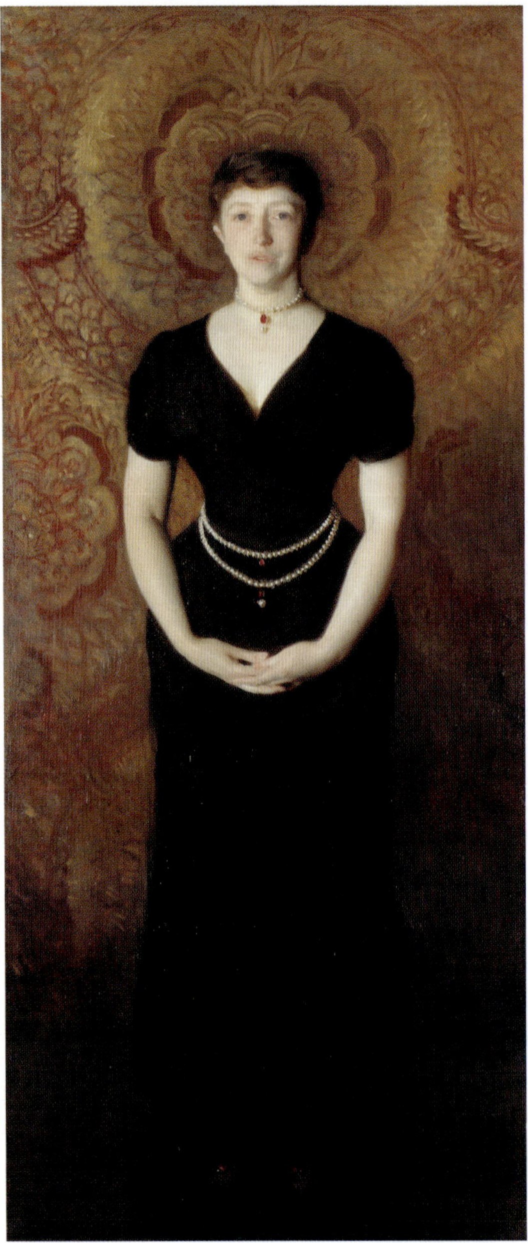

John Singer Sargent.
Portrait of Isabella Stewart Gardner, 1888. Oil on canvas.
Isabella Stewart Gardner Museum, Boston.
Photo: Public domain via Wikimedia Commons

Sargent's *Portrait of Isabella Stewart Gardner* showed her in an indecently deep décolleté, with priceless pearls casually serving as a belt and with her head surrounded by a radiating halo like a Byzantine Madonna. The picture was exhibited only once, at Sargent's first American one-man show in Boston in 1888. After that,

Gardner's husband, usually more philosophical about his wife's ebullience, forbade the portrait to be displayed during his lifetime. He would not even assent to lending it for a Salon exhibition in Paris. However, not only did Sargent remain Gardner's artistic friend and a house guest (he painted the famous double portrait of Gretchen Osgood Warren and her daughter in one of the rooms of Fenway Court) but also her portraitist.

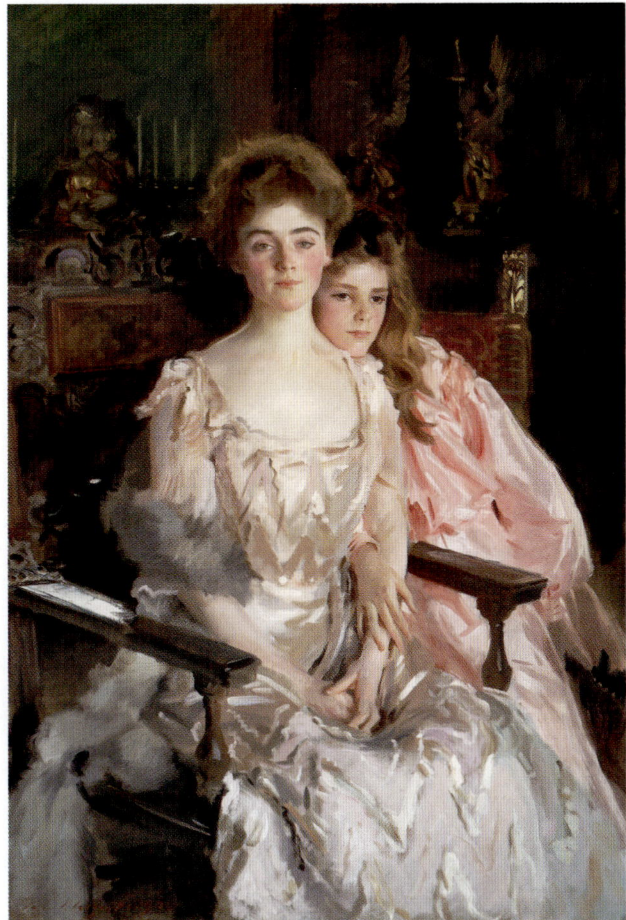

John Singer Sargent. *Mrs. Fiske Warren (Gretchen Osgood) and Her Daughter Rachel*, 1903. Oil on canvas.
Museum of Fine Arts, Boston.
Photo: Public domain via Wikimedia Commons

Sargent's last portrait of his patroness and friend, *Mrs. Gardner in White,* was painted in 1922, a couple of years before Gardner's death. It shows her as an ethereal being, all swaddled in white muslin gauze shawls and almost fading into the bedding. This is a painful but truthful image of a once invincible woman slowly passing away.

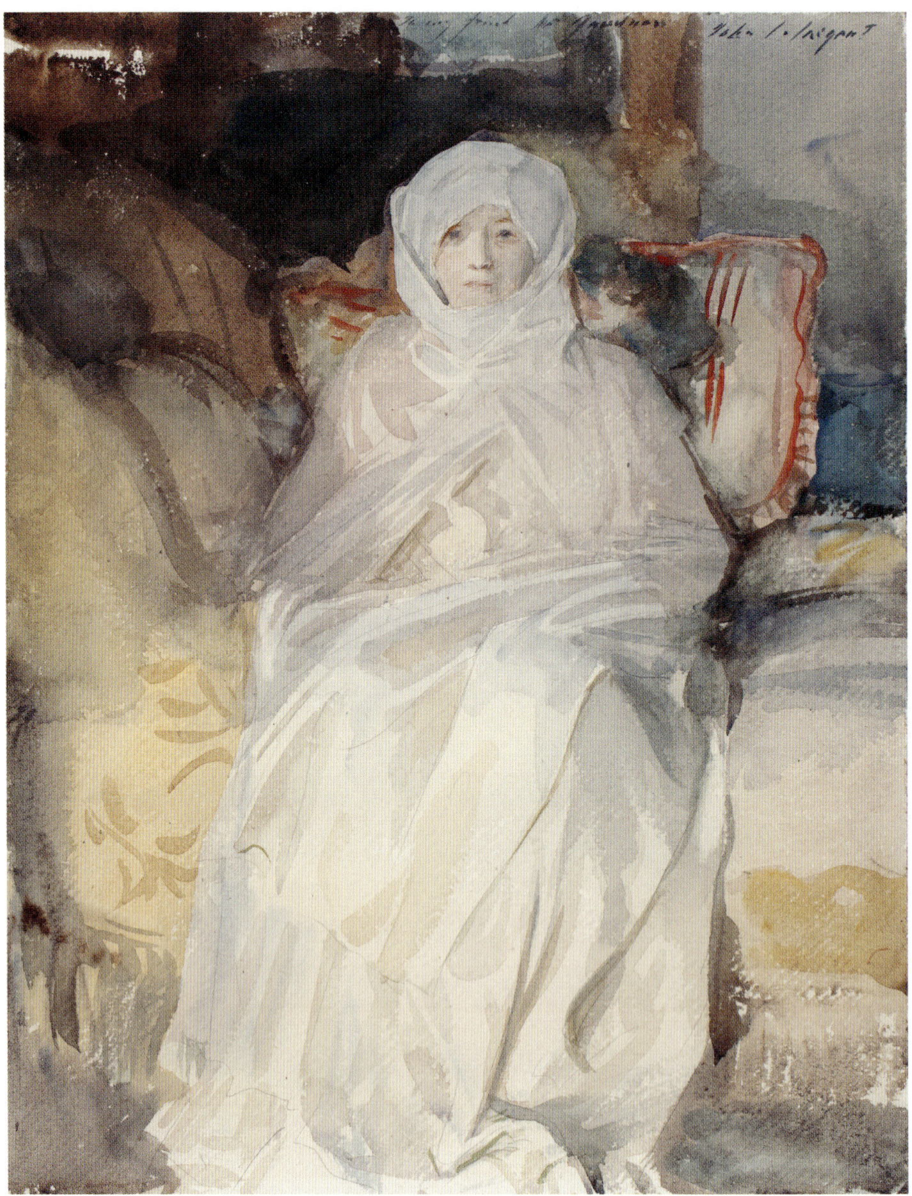

John Singer Sargent. *Mrs. Gardner in White*, 1922. Watercolor on paper.
Isabella Stewart Gardner Museum, Boston.
Photo: Public domain via Wikimedia Commons

The third man who changed Gardner's life and her place in history can be dubbed "the Collector." Bernard Berenson was a Harvard-educated Jewish historian who made it possible for his friend and client to assemble an astounding treasury of Old Masters.

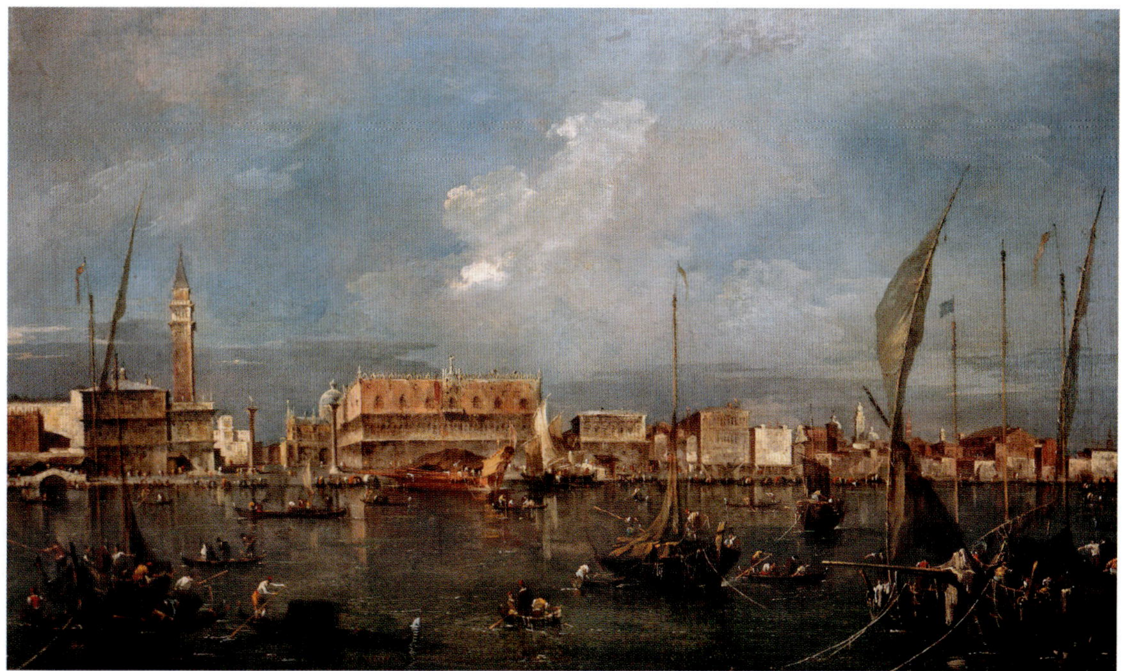

Francesco Guardi. *View of the Riva degli Schiavoni and the Piazzetta from the Bacino di San Marco*, 1760s. Oil on canvas.
Isabella Stewart Gardner Museum, Boston.
Photo: Public domain via Wikimedia Commons

Berenson, whose professional knowledge was unsurpassed at the time (he would research the provenance and authenticity of artworks using modern methods such as paint analysis and style comparisons), was also a shrewd dealer who managed to trump the collecting efforts of such competitors as the Rockefellers, the Morgans, William Randolph Hearst, and Henry E. Huntington—all the American billionaires who were actively shopping for European art treasures with pockets much deeper than Mrs. Gardner.

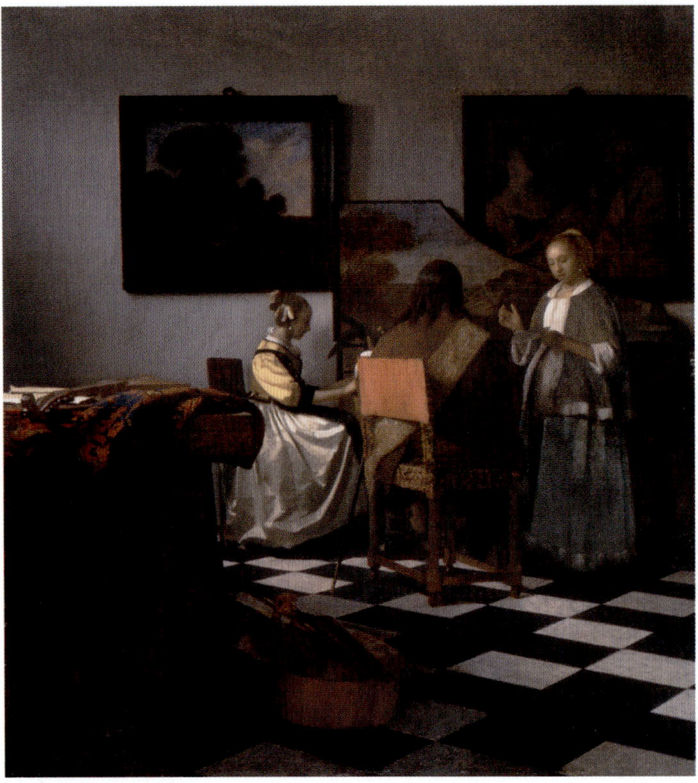

Johannes Vermeer. *The Concert*, 1663–66. Oil on canvas.
Stolen from Isabella Stewart Gardner Museum, Boston in 1990.
Photo: Public domain via Wikimedia Commons

Gardner had already entered the art-buying arena with her 1892 purchase of Vermeer's *The Concert*, beating out bids from the Louvre and the National Gallery. She soon topped this auspicious debut when Berenson started assisting her in locating, authenticating, and securing some unique gems of European painting. In the 1890s, the art of art research, so to speak, was still in its infancy. Louisine Havemeyer, the wife of a "sugar baron" and another famous, dedicated, and rich collector, assembled at the same time a much more expensive trove of Titian and Raphael artworks, advised by Mary Cassatt. However, Cassatt, while a great painter, was clearly not a Renaissance art researcher, and her counsel did not protect Mrs. Havemeyer from a disaster—many of the Italian "Old Master" paintings she collected turned out to be fakes. In all fairness, the Havemeyers acquired superb French 19th-century art with Cassatt's assistance, which formed part of an astounding and historic 2000-piece bequest donated by Louisine in 1929 to the Metropolitan Museum of Art.

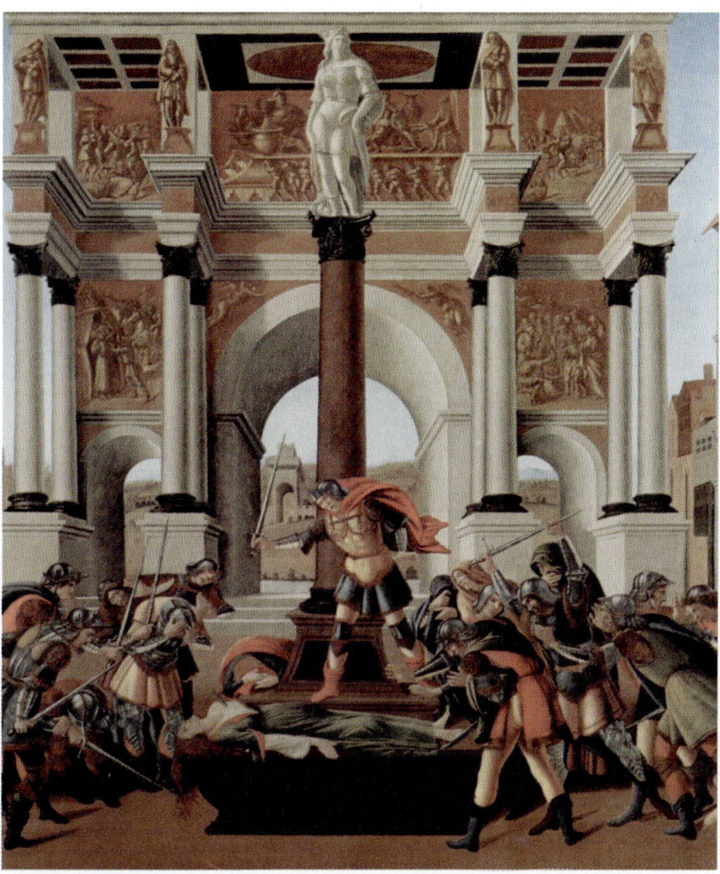

Sandro Botticelli. *The Story of Lucretia*, 1496–1504. Tempera and oil on wood.
Isabella Stewart Gardner Museum, Boston.
Photo: Public domain via Wikimedia Commons

One of the first paintings acquired by Gardner in 1894 with Berenson's guidance was Botticelli's *The Story of Lucretia*. For followers of the Italian Renaissance, a typical Botticelli work is a sinuous Madonna or perhaps an equally sweet-faced *Aphrodite* or *Primavera*. *Lucretia*, however, is a different type of Botticelli painting from a group of religious or historical scenes that were visually inspired by architectural discoveries of antiquity. It is also a strong statement about revolt against tyranny—not the usual mythological or religious subject of the majority of Botticelli's works. It is, therefore, not only beautiful and visually arresting—it is also an important milestone in the artist's legacy. This spectacular Gardner acquisition was followed in short order by a great Rembrandt self-portrait, Titian's *The Rape of Europa*, and Francesco Guardi's *View of the Riva degli Schiavoni*. In fact, between 1894 and

1903, Gardner spent most of her fortune—close to nine million in 1900s dollars—on exquisite and rare art.

By the time Gardner launched the construction of her museum, she was in her fifties—the age at which most women of her time would already have been viewed as matronly grandmothers in their sunset years. Gardner was not a grandmother since she had no children, she hardly looked matronly, and from 1898 on, she had no husband anymore. What she did have was a determination to devote all the time and funds she had to the creation of a place of wonder such as Boston had never seen.

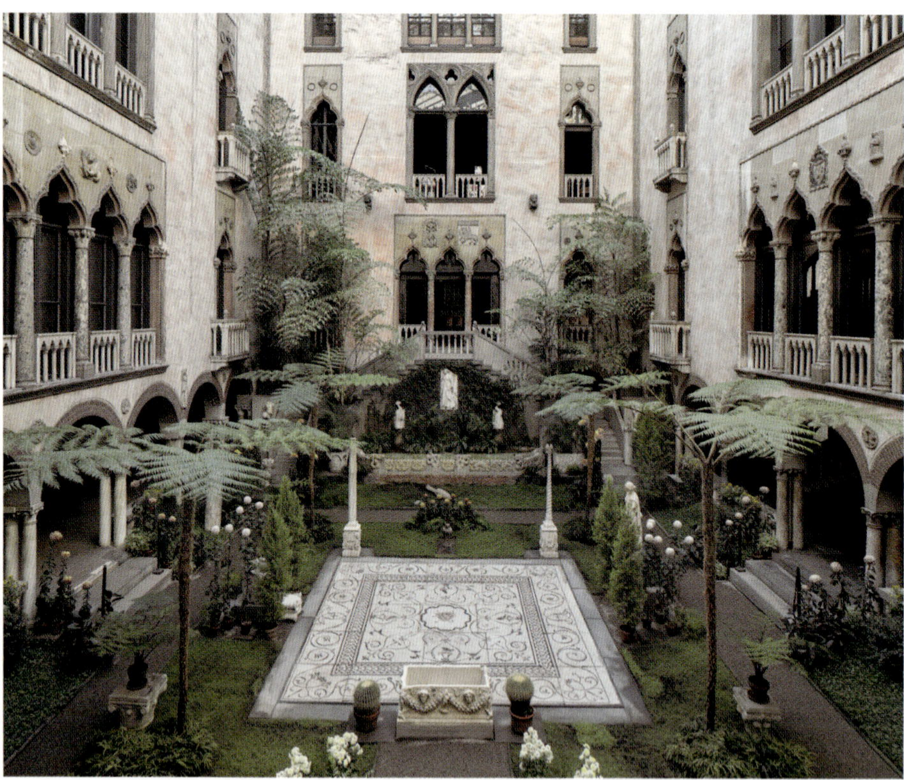

View of the courtyard of the Isabella Stewart Gardner Museum, Boston.
Photo: © Isabella Stewart Gardner Museum/Photo © Sean Dungan/Bridgeman Images

Fenway Court was entirely Gardner's vision. With the help of architect Willard T. Sears, she imagined and created a version of a Venice palazzo. The exterior fits the fickle Boston weather—muddy-colored brick and little external decoration. The enchantment is reserved for the interior. Once you enter Gardner's world of art, you are greeted by columns, mosaics, and lattice stonework surrounding a glass-covered garden of flowers, ferns, and southern plants. Inside, room after room is arranged thematically, showcasing art masterpieces, sculptures, and tapestries, all in dialogue with each other.

Gardner chose to design the interiors around the art she carefully arranged, rather than just fill the existing walls with pictures. A case in point is one of Sargent's early masterpieces called *El Jaleo.* This theatrical composition shows a Spanish dancer in a white underskirt that catches the light during the woman's turn. It is a beguiling composition of light and shadow. The painting was originally purchased by Bostonian statesman Jefferson Coolidge, and it took Gardner years to convince Coolidge to part with it.

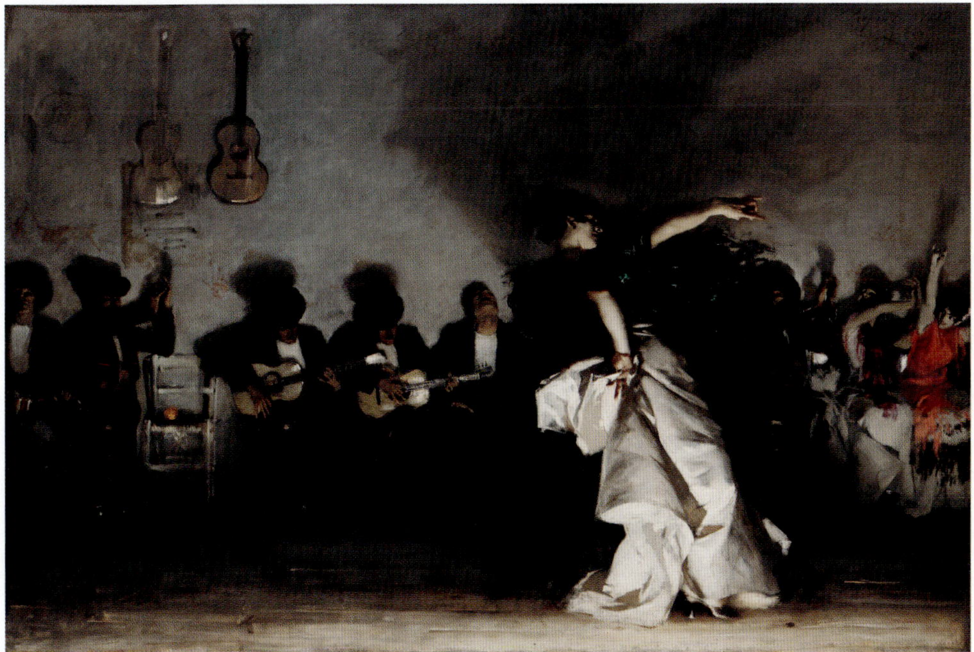

John Singer Sargent. *El Jaleo*, 1882. Oil on canvas.
Isabella Stewart Gardner Museum, Boston.
Photo: Public domain via Wikimedia Commons

The clincher was the way Gardner designed a space for the painting in her Spanish Cloister. Not only did she have a Moorish-style niche built for the painting, but she also devised side lighting to highlight the dancing scene. In 1914, when she finally acquired the painting, electrical lighting was not yet ubiquitous, much less the idea of lighting an art object from underneath.

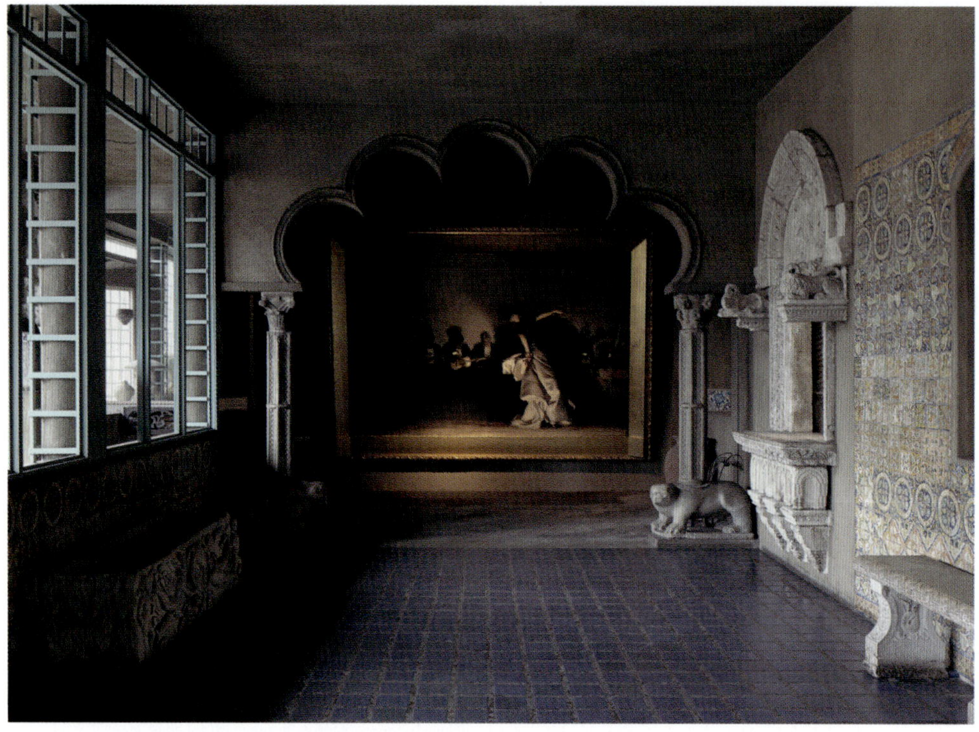

John Singer Sargent's *El Jaleo* in the Spanish Cloister.
Isabella Stewart Gardner Museum, Boston.
Photo: © Isabella Stewart Gardner Museum/Photo © Sean Dungan/Bridgeman Images

Gardner's life cannot be properly judged from the perspective of the 21st century, with its emphasis on political correctness and inclusivity, its feminist overtones, and the frequent condemnation of anything to do with social or material privilege. Gardner was the product of a different era, when the American high society of the Gilded Age was run by wealthy European descendants of patrician families. They were refined, and they loved art, but they were also very restricted by convention. It is what Gardner achieved despite this rigid society that counts today. She could easily have lived like every other woman who married into a Boston Brahmin family—perhaps just becoming the patron of an occasional exhibition or artist for her salon—but instead she created one of the most accomplished and original museums in North America. Despite the barbarous 1990 theft, the Isabella Stewart Gardner Museum remains a unique depository of fine art in the U.S.

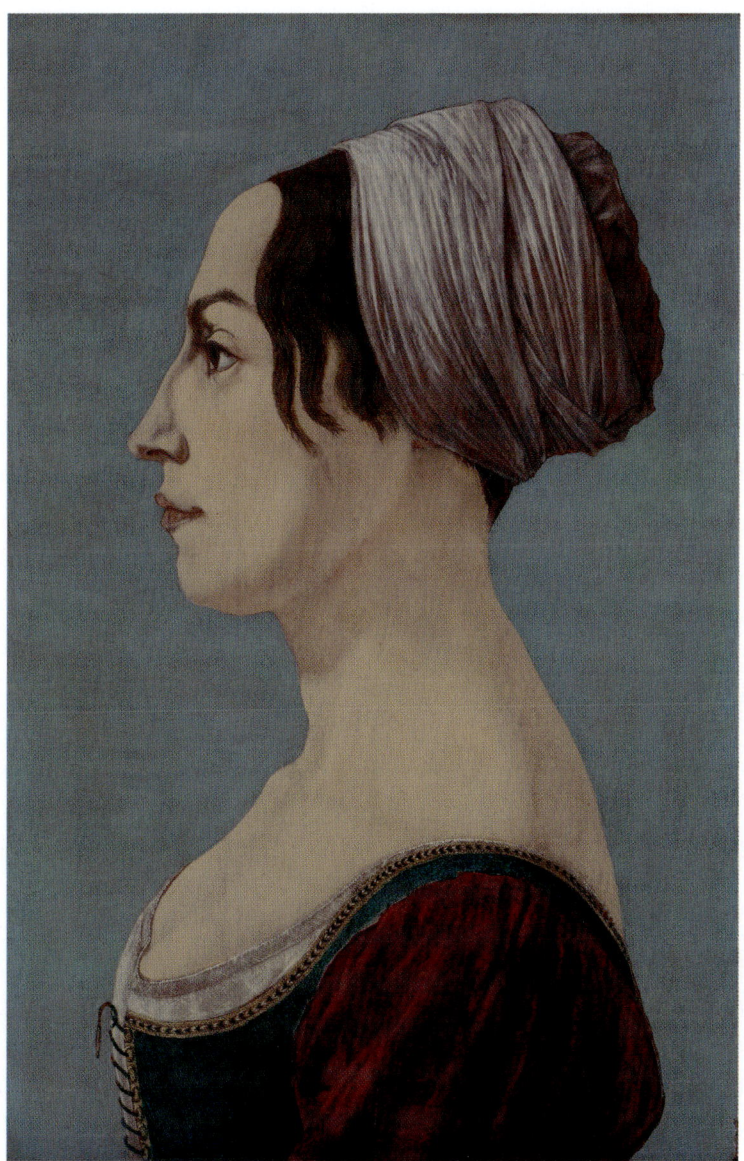

A picture acquired by Gardner through Bernard Berenson in 1907.
(Attr.) **Piero della Pollaiuolo**. *A Woman in Green and Crimson*, c. 1490–99. Oil on panel.
Isabella Stewart Gardner Museum, Boston.
Photo: Public domain via Wikimedia Common

CHAPTER 20

WOMEN WHO GAVE US VAN GOGH

Paris at the end of the 19th century was packed with sophisticated men who loved art. They were making it, discussing it, and selling it. There were those who created new styles—like Monet, Gauguin, or Cézanne. Others excelled as art dealers, like *marchand* Paul Durand-Ruel, who handled sales of over 1000 Monets, 1500 Renoirs, and 800 Pissarros. There were also art journalists and connoisseurs whose writings could make or break a career, like Émile Zola or Louis Leroy, who was the first to use the term "Impressionism" when he disparaged the new style. It is, therefore, most ironic that in the case of Vincent van Gogh, his greatest early recognition and support came from three women mostly ignored by art history.

"Life beats down and crushes the soul and art reminds you that you have one."

~ Stella Adler

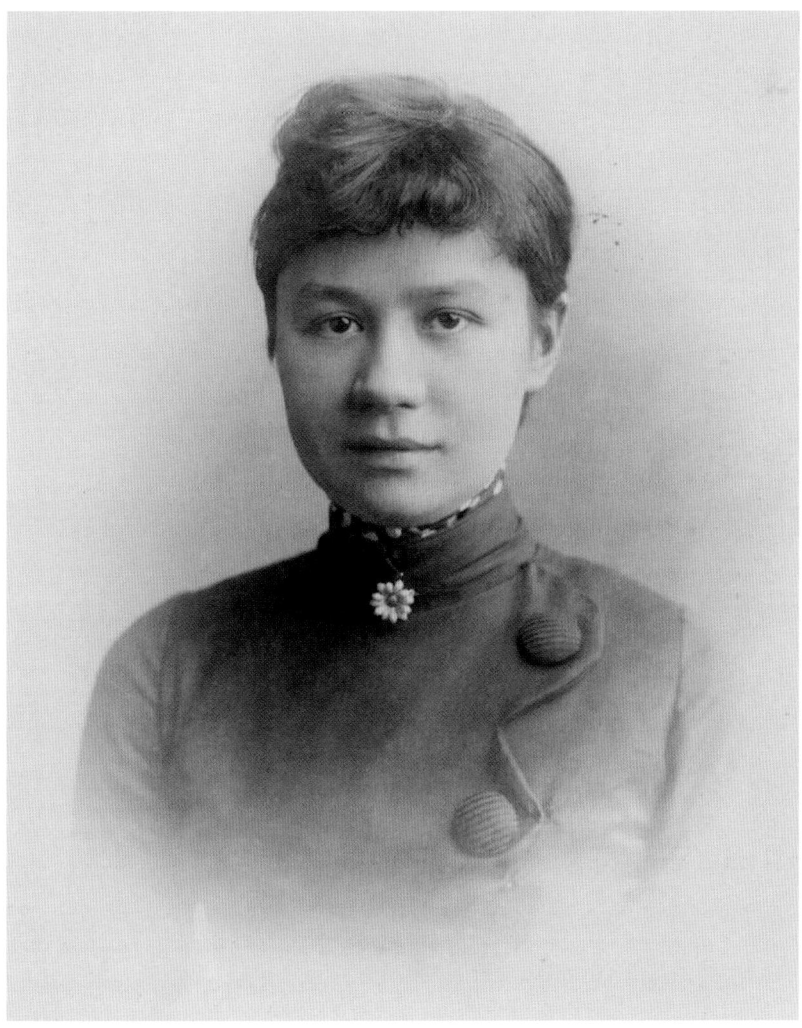

Johanna Bonger in April 1899. Studio photo by Woodbury & Page.
Photo: Woodbury & Page/National Library of The Netherlands/Public domain via Wikimedia Commons

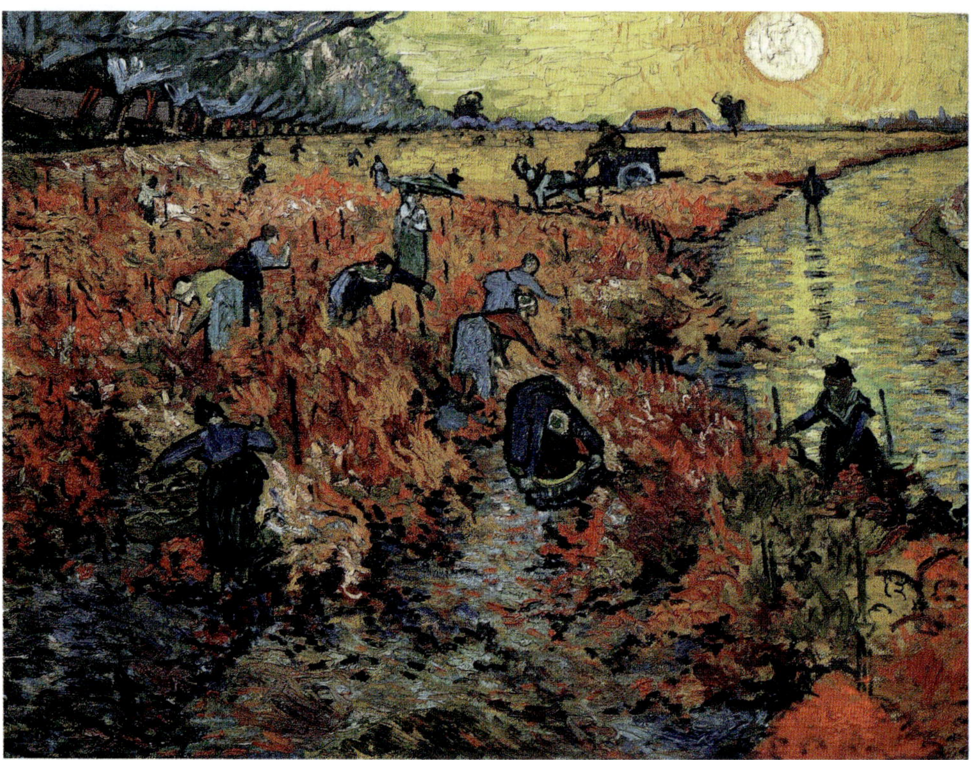

Vincent van Gogh. *Red Vineyards at Arles*, 1888. Oil on canvas.
Ivan Morozov Collection, Pushkin Museum of Fine Art, Moscow.
Photo: Public domain via Wikimedia Commons

The first of these women was Anna Boch, a Belgian artist and a friend of Vincent's brother Theo, who purchased *Red Vineyards at Arles* in February 1890 from an exhibition in Brussels. This sale was the first and only one to take place during van Gogh's lifetime, because he died at the end of that year. There are no records of any other artworks that either Vincent or Theo managed to sell commercially. Anyone who has stood in front of any major canvas by van Gogh today cannot help but be astonished at how pictures that convey so much life force and beauty could have failed to beat out all the dun-colored landscapes of the era, but clearly, Paris was not ready for this art during van Gogh's short life. Consequently, Boch's aesthetic preference remains an important moment in art history—she was the first to express her appreciation of van Gogh's paintings with her wallet.

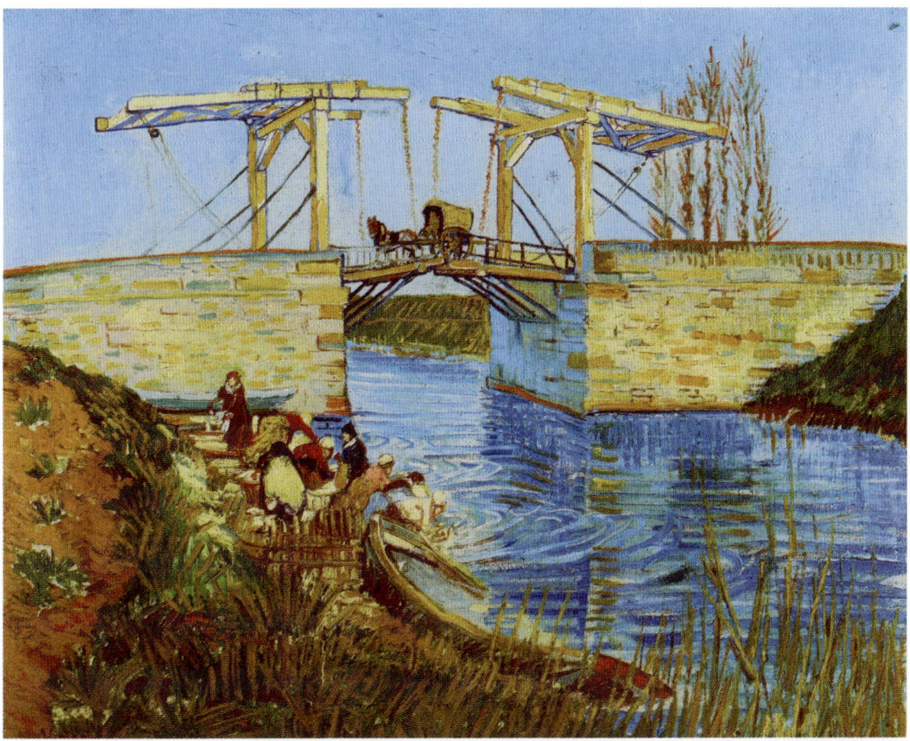

Vincent van Gogh. *The Langlois Bridge at Arles with Women Washing*, 1888. Oil on canvas.
Kröller-Müller Museum, Otterlo.
Photo: Public domain via Wikimedia Commons

The second woman whose prescient recognition of van Gogh's art contributed to his posthumous fame was heiress Helene Kröller-Müller. The daughter of a fabulously wealthy German industrialist, Kröller-Müller married a Dutch tycoon and learned about fine art from a connoisseur named HP Bremmer. When she started to buy art, she decided *"to collect only those pieces that will stand the test of the future."* In her eyes—even if not yet in the eyes of van Gogh's countrymen—Vincent's art met this criterion. Between 1908–1929, she bought 90 paintings and 180 drawings by van Gogh. To house her collection, in 1938 she opened a museum of modern art near Otterlo, in a remote part of the Netherlands. When she died the following year, she left a disposition to display her coffin for the funeral service in front of her most favorite van Gogh paintings. (*The Langlois Bridge at Arles with Women Washing* was her favorite canvas.) Helene donated her entire collection to the Dutch people. Today, the Kröller-Müller Museum has the second largest collection of van Gogh art in the world and is a popular center for modern art.

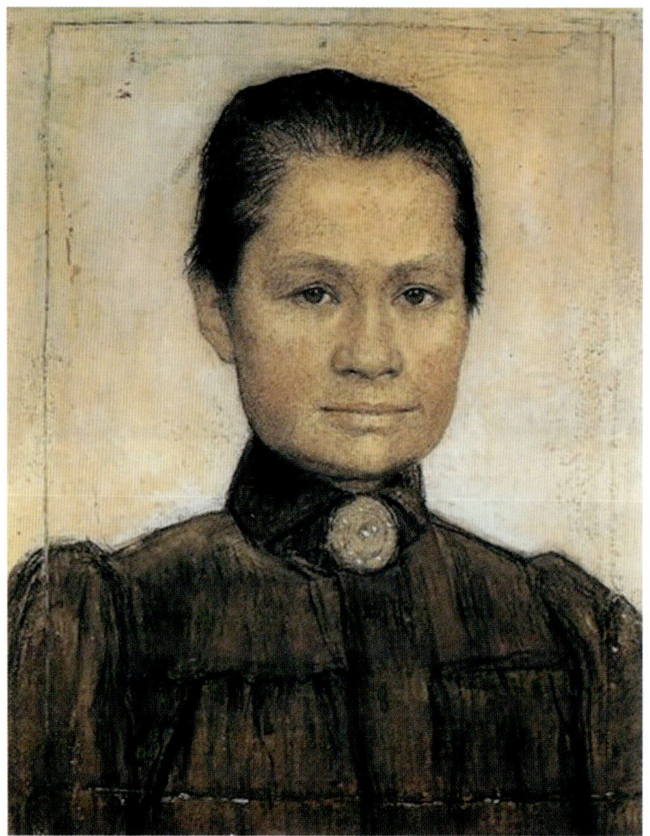

Johan Cohen Gosschalk. *Portrait of Johanna Bonger*, 1905. Chalk and watercolor on paper.
Drents Museum, Assen.
Photo: The History Collection/Alamy Stock Photo

We have all heard of Theo van Gogh, the artist's brother, enabler, supporter, and confidant—and addressee of hundreds of letters that provide us with insights into Vincent's soul and mind as well as his creative inspirations and tastes. What is less well known is that these letters between the brothers (all 902 of them) were preserved and published by the only person to have had access to the legacy of both men—Theo's wife Johanna.

Theo's demise from syphilitic dementia followed Vincent's death by a few short months, leaving Johanna Bonger van Gogh to raise her small son alone, find a means of financial survival, and cope with a double dose of family grief. In her diary, she wrote: *"As well as the child, he has left me another task—Vincent's work—getting it seen and appreciated as much as possible—keeping all the treasures that Theo and Vincent had collected intact for the child—that, too, is my work."*

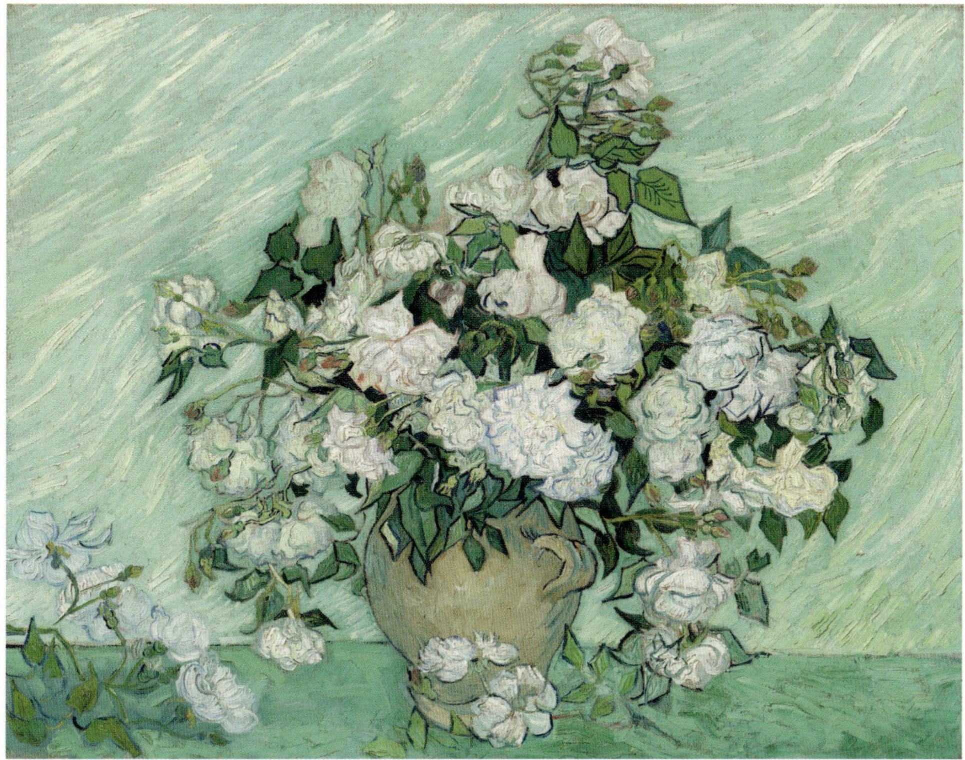

Vincent van Gogh. *Roses*, 1890. Oil on canvas.
National Gallery of Art, Washington, D.C./Gift of Pamela Harriman in memory of W. Averell Harriman.
Photo: Courtesy National Gallery of Art/Public Domain Open Access CC0

Painter Émile Bernard at least tried to honor his friend by organizing a posthumous exhibition of van Gogh's canvases in his own apartment, as well as writing a short biography and then publishing their letters in 1911. Paul Gauguin was less kind. Shortly after the death of Theo, in his letters to Bernard, Gauguin opposed any idea of promoting Vincent's art. He wrote, *"It is completely out of place to remember Vincent and his madness,"* stating that to arrange another exhibition is "*IDIOTIC*" (his capitalization, not mine).

Thus, it primarily fell to Johanna to popularize van Gogh's paintings through exhibitions and sales. Throughout the 1890s, sales of van Gogh canvases supported Johanna and her son while serving as a way of spreading his name all over the world. Slowly, some museums (starting with one in Vienna and one in Helsinki) and some collectors (Russian industrialists and the indomitable Helene Kröller-Müller) started buying. In 1905, Johanna organized an exhibition in Amsterdam of 474 artworks—the largest display of van Gogh art that has ever taken place.

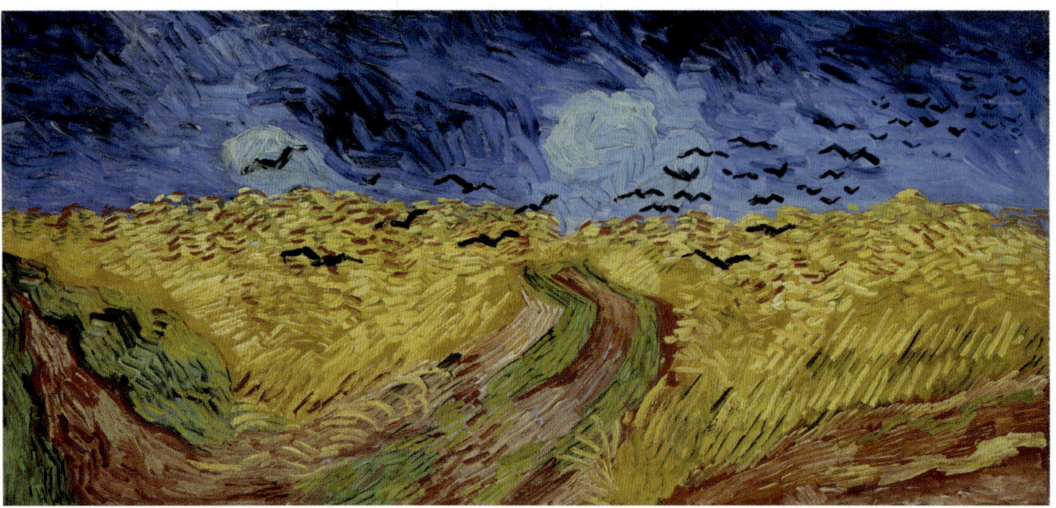

Vincent van Gogh. *Wheatfield with Crows*, 1890. Oil on canvas.
Van Gogh Museum, Amsterdam.
Photo: Public domain via Wikimedia Commons

Throughout the first decade of the 20th century, the pioneering Russian collectors Sergei Shchukin and Ivan Morozov brought many exquisite van Gogh canvases to Russia (including *Red Vineyards at Arles*, which Morozov bought in 1909 in Belgium), introducing the Post-Impressionist style to that part of the world. They were some of the first collectors and among the most refined, appreciating both van Gogh and Matisse well before the French public and museums did. By 1910, however, artists, dealers, and collectors had begun flocking in to start collecting or praising van Gogh's paintings. In 1913, an *International Exhibition of Modern Art* in New York introduced van Gogh to American viewers.

It took Johanna a long time to decide to edit and publish the voluminous correspondence between her husband and Vincent. Although less than 100 letters from Theo were found among Vincent's possessions, Theo had meticulously preserved more than 800 of Vincent's missives to him. In her diary, Johanna asked herself, "Who will write that book about Vincent?" It turned out that, in a way, she was the first to undertake this task, releasing in 1914 a three-volume set of the van Gogh brothers' letters (she also managed to translate more than half of them into English before her passing in 1925). Even if by that date there had already been van Gogh biographers, collectors, and critics, it was this compilation of the artist's own writings that allowed for some of the deepest insights into the creative process ever to emerge in the history of art. Very few other major artists had left anything as personal and revealing as van Gogh's letters. Between his letters to Theo and other letters to friends like Bernard, van Gogh offered a wealth of information on what he did, what he painted (and why), and what he thought of various landscapes, styles, artists, and himself.

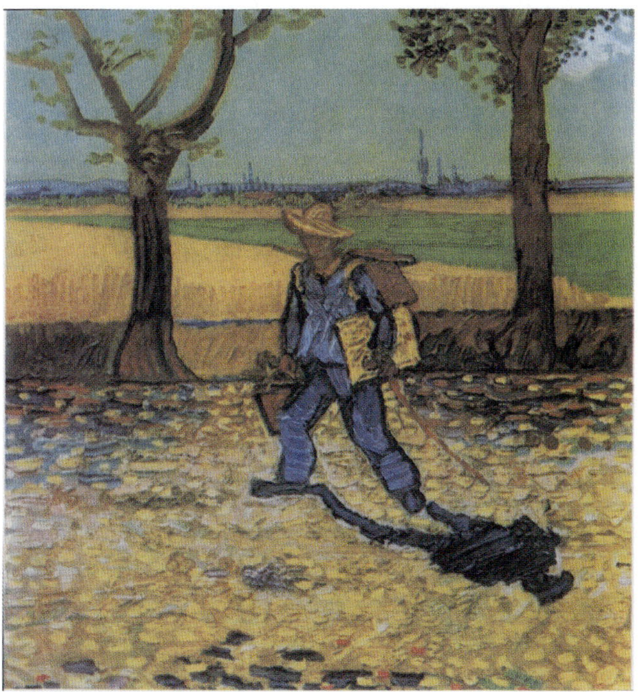

Vincent van Gogh. *Painter on His Way to Work*, 1888. Oil on canvas.
Destroyed during WWII.
Photo: Public domain via Wikimedia Commons

When another Dutch painter, Johannes Vermeer, died in 1675, his paintings were sold or destroyed (only about 34 survived until our time), and he was entirely forgotten for 200 years. Thanks to Johanna Bonger, not only did the paintings of van Gogh survive and almost immediately find their way into the most prestigious collections, but interest in his life—both artistic and personal—has grown with each generation that reads his letters.

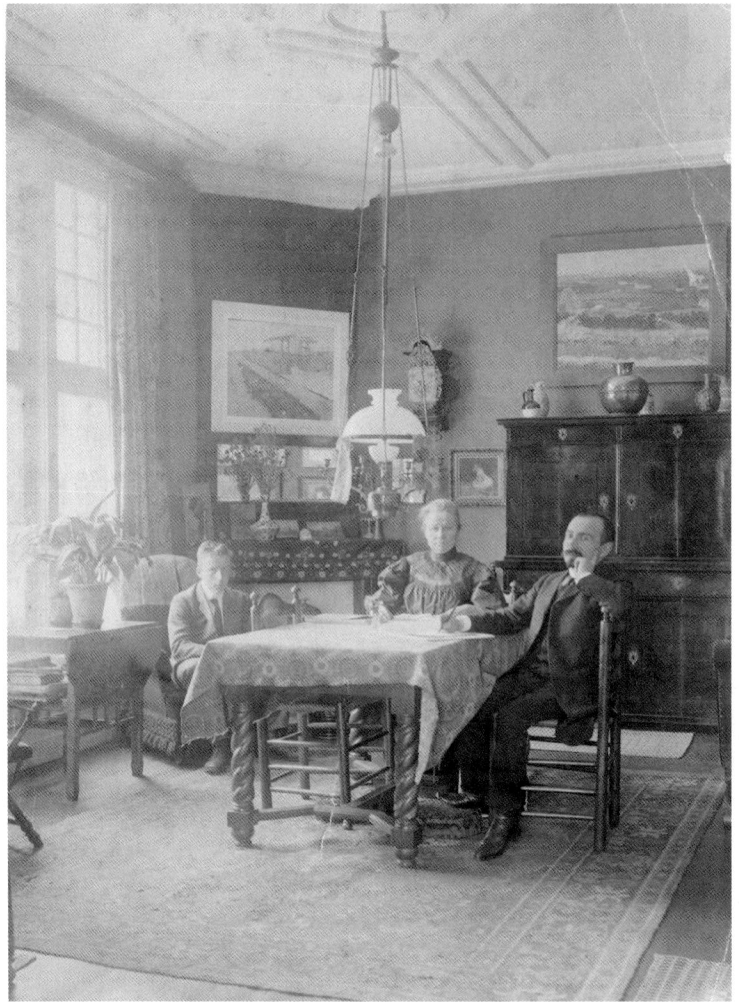

Bernard Eilers. Vincent Willem van Gogh, Jo Cohen Gosschalk-Bonger and Johan Cohen Gosschalk (from left to right) in the Dining Room of the House at Koninginneweg 77, Amsterdam, 1910–1911. Print on paper.

Photo credit: Van Gogh Museum, Amsterdam (Vincent van Gogh Foundation)

As a teenager, Johanna wrote in her diary: *"I would think it dreadful to have to say at the end of my life, 'I've actually lived for nothing, I have achieved nothing great or noble.'"* In her case, this was not just the angst of a young person contemplating the future. Far from "living for nothing," she achieved something unique and great. So far, art history has not been very kind to Johanna Bonger, but perhaps this century will bring her the respect and recognition that she was not given 100 years ago.

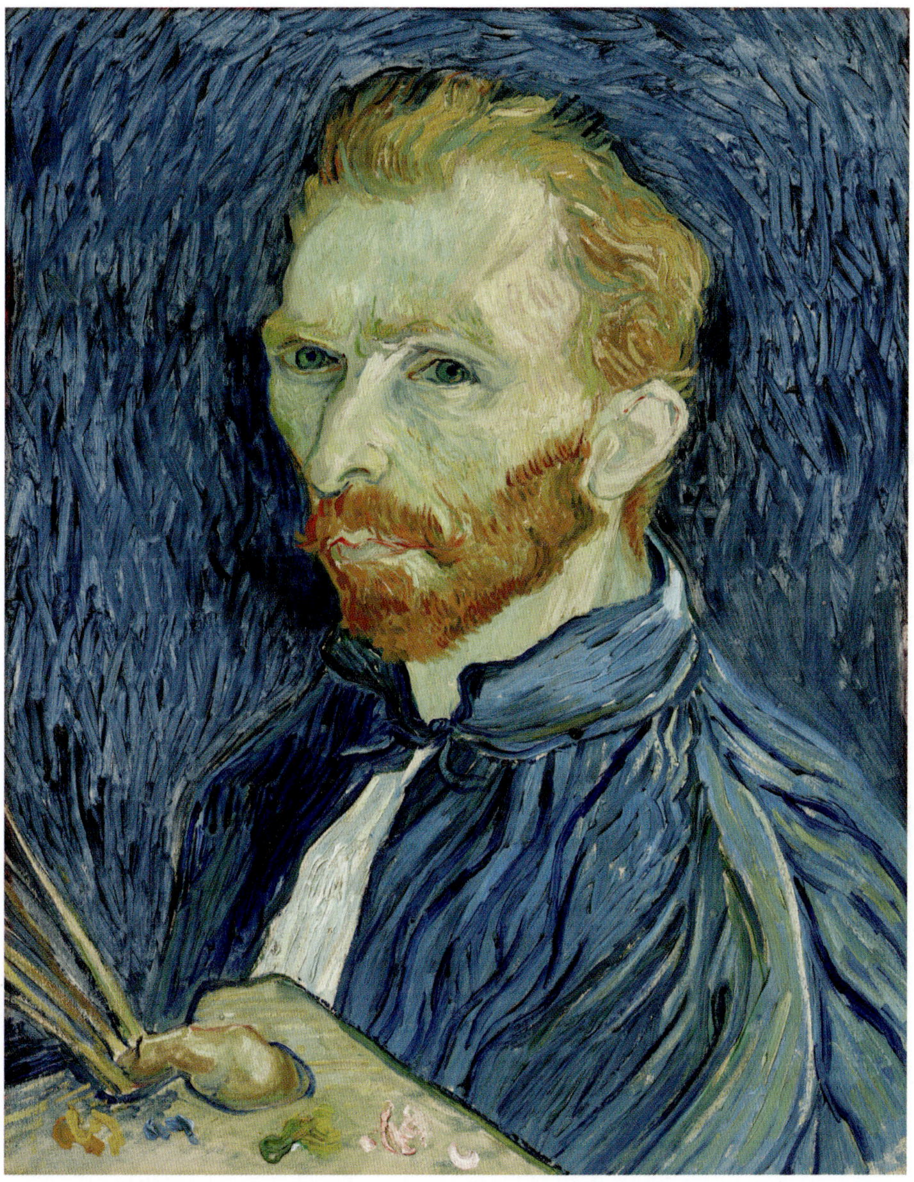

Vincent van Gogh. *Self-Portrait*, 1889. Oil on canvas.
National Gallery of Art, Washington, D.C./Collection of Mr. and Mrs. John Hay Whitney.
Photo: Courtesy National Gallery of Art/Public Domain Open Access CC0

FOOD FOR THE SOUL

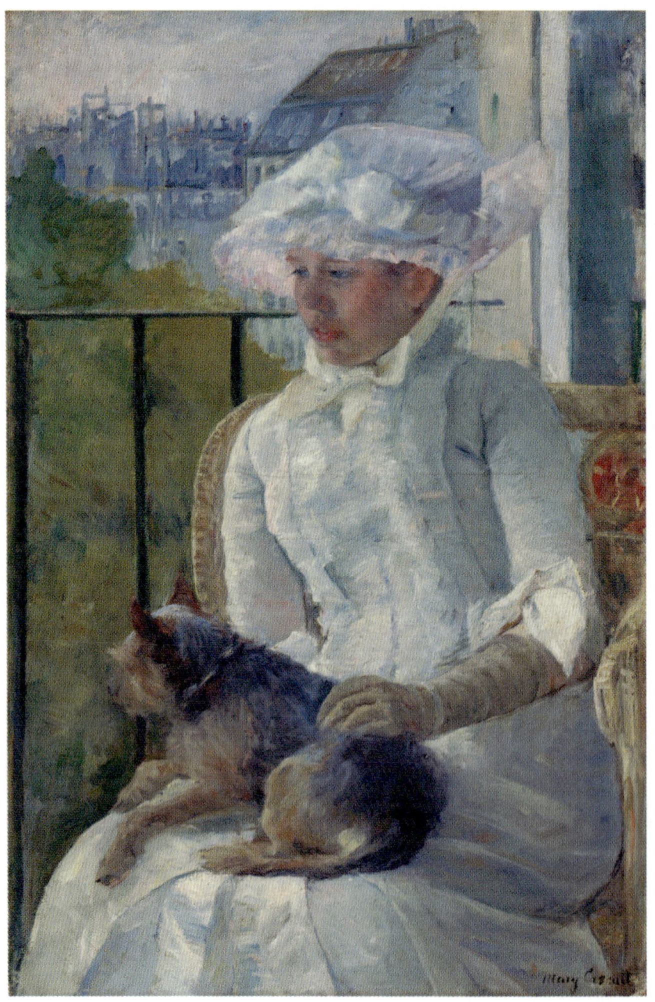

Mary Cassatt. *Young Girl at a Window*, c. 1883–84. Oil on canvas.
National Gallery of Art, Washington, D.C./Corcoran Collection (Museum Purchase, Gallery Fund). Photo: Courtesy National Gallery of Art/Public Domain Open Access CC0

To write my biweekly postings about art, I have named the website *Food for the Soul*. In the same way that a body needs nourishment, the immaterial part of us—no matter if we call it spirit, intellect, or soul—also needs sustenance. Art as therapy for the stress and pain of daily life is not a new concept, but it is not utilized enough.

Many people may have been told at some point in time that fine art demands specialized knowledge. Yes—to write an exhibition catalog. No—to enjoy oneself and to nourish the yearning for beauty and positive emotions. All you need is to go to a museum and look at paintings or sculptures—at least some of them might resonate with you. You do not need to know too much about art to enjoy it.

I would love for my art tales to inspire you to look at fine art as much as possible. Visit museums whenever you can, share the experience with kids, teach art if you are homeschooling, try doing art if you feel creative, and look at good art when and where you find it. It feeds the soul.

ACKNOWLEDGMENTS

I owe the existence of this book, as well as all the articles that originally appeared at my Food for the Soul site, to one person whose vision, optimism, intellectual scope, integrity...and faith in me...are boundless: Catherine Austin Fitts. She created a successful magazine and publishing company out of nothing and despite powerful obstacles. Although her domain is finance and geopolitics (two subjects as alien to me as life on Mars), we found a common language in our love of Culture—the one with a capital "C." We are united in our desire to make fine art accessible, understandable, and pleasurable for people—including the younger generations—who might otherwise regard art as something elitist, hard to comprehend, or perhaps just boring.

The inspiration for the book came from Robert Dupper, designer of the beautifully produced quarterly issues of the Solari Report, who first proposed turning my online stories into a tangible, traditional art book. I also owe a debt of gratitude to Claire Viadro for her patient, cheerful, and insightful proofreading and editorial suggestions—the book would be impossible without her professionalism. As for the images in this book, none of them would ever have appeared in these pages if not for the expertise, tenacity, and professional reputation of photo researcher *extraordinaire* Lorraine Beck. I know which paintings I love, but Lorraine knows how to bring them to you. Finally, the book would not look the way it does without the printing and design expertise of Paul Howson, whose patience, creativity, and persistence are evident on every page.

My list of thanks also includes Solari team members Nita Lax, Jeroen van Straaten, Hans de Vries, and especially my digital gurus Darlene Heckman and Mark Gilmore. Huge thanks to Nancy Ong for her insightful comments and support while I was editing this book.

I would like to thank Ms. Sophie Bowness, the granddaughter of sculptor Barbara Hepworth, for her patience, generosity, and invaluable factual corrections to my chapter on Hepworth's art and life.

The book is dedicated to all the women in my life—my late mother Hu Pei Fang (Irena Slawińska), my daughters Alexandra and Victoria, as well as all the female mentors and friends who have been my inspiration and support.

SELECTED BIBLIOGRAPHY

B

Bailey, Martin. *Van Gogh's Finale: Auvers & the Artist's Rise to Fame*. London: Frances Lincoln, Quarto Publishing, 2021.

Bal, Mieke (ed.). *The Artemisia Files: Artemisia Gentileschi for Feminists and Other Thinking People*. Chicago: The University of Chicago Press, 2006.

Beard, Mary. *How Do We Look: The Body, the Divine, and the Question of Civilization.* New York: Liveright Publishing Corporation, 2018.

Beckett, Sister Wendy. *The Story of Painting*. London: Dorling Kindersley Ltd., 2001.

Benke, Britta*, O'Keeffe*. Köln: Taschen GmbH, 2018.

Biddle, Flora Miller. *The Whitney Women and the Museum They Made: A Family Memoir*. New York: Arcade Publishing, 2017.

Bowness, Sophie. *Barbara Hepworth: The Sculptor in the Studio*. London: Tate Publishing, 2017.

Brook, Timothy. *Vermeer's Hat: The Seventeenth Century and the Dawn of the Global World*. New York: Bloomsbury Press, 2008.

C

Cesati, Franco. *The Medici: Story of a European Dynasty*. Florence: Mandragora SRL, 2018.

Chadwick, Whitney. *Women, Art, and Society*. New York: Thames & Hudson, 2020.

Charney, Noah. *The Museum of Lost Art*. New York: Phaidon Press, 2018.

D

Dzikowska, Elżbieta. *Polacy w Sztuce Świata/ Polish Artists on the World Arts Scene*. Warsaw: Rosikon Press, 2001.

F

Farthing, Stephen. *1001 Paintings You Must See Before You Die*, Updated Edition. London: Hachette, 2018.

Frankopan, Peter. *The Silk Roads: A New History of the World*. New York: Vintage Books, 2017.

Frelinghuysen, Alice Cooney; Tinterow, Gary; Stein, Susan Alyson; Wold, Gretchen, Meech, Julia. *Splendid Legacy: The Havemeyer Collection*. New York: The Metropolitan Museum of Art, 1993.

Friegieri, Flavia. *Women Artists*. New York: Thames & Hudson, 2019.

Fuga, Antonella. *Artists' Techniques and Materials*. Los Angeles: The J. Paul Getty Museum, 2006.

G

Gentou, Albertine. *Rosa Bonheur: Une femme au service de l'art*. Paris: L'Harmattan, 2018.

Gombrich, E.H. *The Story of Art*. New York: Phaidon, 1995.

Gomez, Leticia Ruiz (ed.). *A Tale of Two Women Painters. Sofonisba Anguissola and Lavinia Fontana*. Madrid: Museo del Prado, 2019.

Guide to the Louvre. Paris: Musée du Louvre Editions, 2015.

H

Hale, Sheila. *Titian. His Life*. New York: HarperCollins Publishers, 2012.

Hazan, Fernand (ed.). *Dictionnaire de la peinture moderne*. ADGP: Paris, 1963.

Houpt, Simon. *Museum of the Missing: A History of Art Theft*. New York: Madison Press Books, 2006.

Hughes, Robert. *Goya*. New York: Alfred A. Knopf, 2003.

J

Jones, Roger and Nicholas, Penny. *Raphael*. New Haven and London: Yale University Press, 1983.

K

Kahng, Eik (ed.). *Through Vincent's Eyes: van Gogh and his Sources*. New Haven and London: Yale University Press, Columbus Museum of Art and Santa Barbara Museum of Art, 2021.

Kluszczyński, Ryszard Jeremi. *Od Michałowskiego do Fangora*. Kraków: WBC, 2016.

M

MacGregor, Neil. *A History of the World in 100 Objects*. New York: Penguin Books, 2013.

Malinowski, Jerzy. *Malarstwo polskie XIX wieku*. Toruń: Wydawnictwo DiG, 2003.

Mariani, Massimo. *Light in Art: Perception and the Use of Light in the History of Art*. Barcelona: Hoaki Books SL, 2022.

McQuillan, Melissa. *Van Gogh*. London: Thames & Hudson, 1997.

Mettais, Valerie. *Louvre. 7 Centuries of Painting*. Versailles: Art Lys, 2002.

Miller, Dana (ed.). *Whitney Museum of American Art. Handbook of the Collection*. New York: Yale University Press for Whitney Museum of American Art, 2015.

Mohun, Janet (senior ed.) *Art: The Definitive Visual Guide*. New York: Dorling Kindersley Ltd., 2008.

O

Ottinger, Didier and Hiddleston-Galloni, Anna. *Georgia O'Keeffe*. Paris: Centre National d'Art et de Culture Georges Pompidou, 2021.

Hazan, Fernand (ed.). *Nouveau Dictionnaire de la Peinture Moderne*. ADGP: Paris, 1963.

Q

Quinn, Bridget. *Broad Strokes: 15 Women Who Made Art and Made History (in That Order)*. San Francisco: Chronicle Books, 2017.

P

Pomarède, Vincent (ed.), and Grebe, Anja. *The Louvre: All the Paintings*. New York: Black Dog & Leventhal Publishing, 2011.

R

Rey, Jean-Dominique. *Berthe Morisot*. Paris: Flammarion, 2018.

Roginsky, Gwen; High, Rachel; Morrill, Rebecca; and Fortenberry, Diane (eds.). *Art = Discovering Infinite Connections in Art History*. New York: Phaidon and The Metropolitan Museum of Art, 2020.

Rose, Barbara. *Magdalena Abakanowicz*. New York: Harry N. Abrams, Inc. 1994.

Ryszkiewicz, Andrzej. *Polska sztuka współczesna*. Warszawa: Arkady, 1981.

S

Saint Bris, Gonzague. *Rosa Bonheur: Liberté est son nom*. Paris: Edition Robert Laffont, 2012.

Shand-Tucci, Douglass. *The Art of Scandal: The Life and Times of Isabella Stewart Gardner*. Harvard: Back Bay Historical, 2016.

Schutz, Karl. *Vermeer: The Complete Works*. Köln: Taschen, 2018.

T

Tarabra, Daniela. *European Art of the Eighteenth Century*. Los Angeles: The J. Paul Getty Museum, 2008.

Thompson, Jon. *How to Read a Modern Painting : Lessons from the Modern Masters*. Belgium: Ludion and New York: Abrams, 2006.

Treuherz, Julian. *Victorian Painting*. London: Thames & Hudson, 1997.

V

Vircondelet, Alain. *Les couples mythiques de l'art*. Paris: Beaux Arts Éditions, 2011.

W

Weidemann, Christiane; Larass, Petra; Klier, Melanie. *50 Women Artists You Should Know*. New York: Prestel Verlag, 2018.

Wilton, Andrew. *Five Centuries of British Painting: From Holbein to Hodgkin*. London: Thames & Hudson, 2001.

Z

Zuffi, Stefano. *European Art of the Sixteenth Century*. Los Angeles: The J. Paul Getty Museum, 2006; Italian edition 1961.

LIST OF IMAGES

Cover: Olga Boznańska. *Japanese Self-Portrait*, 1892. Oil on cardboard. Collection of the National Museum, Wrocław. Photo: Arkadiusz Podstawka/National Museum, Wrocław

pvii

Angelica Kauffmann. Self-portrait in *The Artist Hesitating Between Painting and Music*, 1794. Oil on canvas. Nostell Priory, West Yorkshire. Photo: National Trust Photographic Library/John Hammond/Bridgeman Images

p2

Domenico Ghirlandaio. *Birth of the Virgin*, 1479–85. Fresco. Santa Maria Novella, Florence. Photo: Public domain via Wikimedia Commons
https://commons.wikimedia.org/wiki/File:Domenico_Ghirlandaio_-_Birth_of_Mary_-_WGA8830.jpg

p5

Francisco de Zurbarán. *The Birth of the Virgin*, 1629. Oil on canvas. Norton Simon Museum, Pasadena. Photo: Public domain via Wikimedia Commons
https://commons.wikimedia.org/wiki/File:Francisco_de_Zurbar%C3%A1n_018.jpg

p6

Diego Velázquez. *The Spinners or The Fable of Arachne/Las Hilanderas,* c. 1655–60. Oil on canvas. Museo del Prado, Madrid. Photo: Public domain via Wikimedia Commons
https://commons.wikimedia.org/wiki/File:Velazquez-las_hilanderas.jpg

p8

Titian. *Venus of Urbino*, 1538. Oil on canvas. Galleria degli Uffizi, Florence. Photo: Public domain via Wikimedia Commons
https://commons.wikimedia.org/wiki/File:Venere_di_Urbino.jpg

p9 (top)

Giorgione. *The Sleeping Venus*, 1508–10. Oil on canvas. Staatliche Kunstsammlungen Dresden. Photo: Public domain via Wikimedia Commons
https://commons.wikimedia.org/wiki/File:Giorgione_-_Sleeping_Venus_-_Google_Art_Project_2.jpg

p9 (bottom)

Édouard Manet. *Olympia*, 1863. Oil on canvas. Musée d'Orsay, Paris. Photo: Public domain via Wikimedia Commons
https://commons.wikimedia.org/wiki/File:Edouard_Manet_-_Olympia_-_Google_Art_ProjectFXD.jpg

p10

Tintoretto. *The Last Supper*, 1594. Oil on canvas. Church of San Giorgio Maggiore, Venice. Photo: Public domain, via Wikimedia Commons
https://commons.wikimedia.org/wiki/File:Jacopo_Tintoretto_-_The_Last_Supper_-_WGA22649.jpg

p13

Nicolaes Maes. *A Young Woman Sewing*, 1655. Oil on canvas. Harold Samuel Collection, Guildhall Art Gallery, City of London. Photo: Guildhall Art Gallery/Harold Samuel Collection/Bridgeman Images

p14

Diego Velázquez. *Old Woman Cooking Eggs*, 1618. Oil on canvas. Scottish National Gallery, Edinburgh. Photo: Public domain via Wikimedia Commons

https://commons.wikimedia.org/wiki/File:Diego_Velazquez_-_An_Old_Woman_Cooking_Eggs_-_Google_Art_Project.jpg

p15

Nicolaes Maes. *The Account Keeper*, 1656. Oil on canvas. Saint Louis Art Museum. Photo: Public domain via Wikimedia Commons

https://commons.wikimedia.org/wiki/File:Nicolaes_Maes_-_The_Account_Keeper.jpg

p15

Johannes Vermeer. *A Maid Asleep*, 1656–57. Oil on canvas. Metropolitan Museum of Art, New York. Photo: Public domain via Wikimedia Commons

https://commons.wikimedia.org/wiki/File:Vermeer_young_women_sleeping.jpg

p19

Berthe Morisot. *In the Dining Room*, 1886. Oil on canvas. Chester Dale Collection, National Gallery of Art, Washington. Photo: Courtesy National Gallery of Art, Washington, D.C. Public domain.

https://www.nga.gov/collection/art-object-page.46660.html

p21

Édouard Vuillard. *A Woman Sweeping*, 1899–1900. Oil on cardboard mounted on cradled panel. The Phillips Collection, Washington D.C. Photo: The Phillips Collection, Washington D.C./Acquired 1939/Bridgeman Images

p23

Pierre Bonnard. *The Letter*, c. 1906. Oil on canvas. Chester Dale Collection, National Gallery of Art, Washington D.C. Photo: Public domain via Wikimedia Commons

https://commons.wikimedia.org/wiki/File:Pierre_Bonnard,_c.1906,_La_Lettre,_oil_on_canvas,_National_Gallery_of_Art.jpg

p25

Manly Edward MacDonald. *Land Girls Hoeing*, 1918–19. Oil on canvas. Canadian War Museum, Ottawa. Photo: Public domain via Wikimedia Commons

https://commons.wikimedia.org/wiki/File:Manly_Edward_MacDonald_-_Land_Girls_Hoeing_CWM_19710261-0370.jpg

p26

Copy of Barthélemy d'Eyck miniature (attrib). *Mortification of the Vain Pleasure/Le mortifiement de vaine plaisance*, c. 1455. Illumination on parchment. Bibliothèque municipale de Metz. Photo: Public domain via Wikimedia Commons https://commons.wikimedia.org/wiki/File:Muehle_1470.jpg

p27

Emanuel de Witte. *Adriana van Heusden and Daughter at the Fishmarket*, c. 1662. Oil on canvas. National Gallery, London. Photo: © NPL - DeA Picture Library/Bridgeman Images

p29

Émile Charles Dameron. *Visiting the Farm*, 1908. Oil on canvas. Private Collection. Photo: Public domain via Wikimedia Commons

https://commons.wikimedia.org/wiki/File:Emile_Charles_Dameron_Besuch_am_Bauernhof.jpg

p51

Adam Elsheimer. *Saint Elizabeth of Hungary Bringing Food for the Inmates of a Hospital*, c. 1598. Oil on copper. Wellcome Collection, London. Photo: Wellcome Collection/ NonCommercial 4.0 International (CC BY-NC 4.0)

https://wellcomecollection.org/works/qw34f3vs

p53

Raphael. *The Fire in the Borgo*, 1516. Fresco. Stanza dell'Incendio di Borgo, Apostolic Palace, Vatican Museums and Galleries, Vatican City. Photo: Public domain via Wikimedia Commons

https://commons.wikimedia.org/wiki/File:Raphael_-_Fire_in_the_Borgo.jpg

p54

Raphael. Detail from *The Fire in the Borgo*, 1516. Fresco. Stanza dell'Incendio di Borgo, Apostolic Palace, Vatican Museums and Galleries, Vatican City. Photo: Public domain via Wikimedia Commons

https://commons.wikimedia.org/wiki/File:Incendio_di_borgo_07.jpg

p59

Sofonisba Anguissola. *Self-Portrait at the Easel*, 1556–57. Oil on canvas. Muzeum Zamek, Łańcut. Photo: Public domain via Wikimedia Commons

https://commons.wikimedia.org/wiki/File:Self-portrait_at_the_Easel_Painting_a_Devotional_Panel_by_Sofonisba_Anguissola.jpg

p60

Sofonisba Anguissola. *Portrait Group with the Artist's Father Amilcare Anguissola and Her Siblings Minerva and Astrubale,* c. 1559. Oil on canvas. Nivaagards Malerisamling, Niva. Photo: Public domain CC0 1.0 Universal Public Domain Dedication, via Wikimedia Commons

https://commons.wikimedia.org/wiki/File:Sofonisba_Anguissola,_Portr%C3%A6tgruppe_med_kunstnerens_fader_Amilcare_Anguissola_og_hendes_s%C3%B8skende_Minerva_og_Astrubale,_ca._1559,_0001NMK,_Nivaagaards_Malerisamling.jpg

p62

Sofonisba Anguissola. *The Chess Game*, 1555. Oil on canvas. The Raczyński Foundation at the National Museum, Poznań. Photo: Public domain via Wikimedia Commons

https://commons.wikimedia.org/wiki/File:The_Chess_Game_-_Sofonisba_Anguissola.jpg

p63

Sofonisba Anguissola. *Queen Anne of Austria,* c. 1573. Oil on canvas. Museo del Prado, Madrid. Photo: Public domain via Wikimedia Commons

https://commons.wikimedia.org/wiki/File:La_reina_Ana_de_Austria,_por_Sofonisba_Anguissola.jpg

p64

Lavinia Fontana. *Self-Portrait at the Spinet,* 1577. Oil on canvas. Accademia Nazionale di San Luca, Rome. Photo: © Fine Art Images/Bridgeman Images

p65

Lavinia Fontana. *Noli Me Tangere*, 1581. Oil on canvas. Galleria degli Uffizi, Florence. Photo: Bridgeman Images

p67

Lavinia Fontana. *Mars and Venus,* c. 1595. Oil on canvas. Fundación Casa de Alba, Madrid. Photo: Heritage Images/Fine Art Images/akg-images

p69

Artemisia Gentileschi. *Self-Portrait as the Allegory of Painting (La Pittura), c.* 1638–39. Oil on canvas. The National Gallery, London. Photo: Royal Collection Trust/© His Majesty King Charles III, 2022/Bridgeman Images

p70

Artemisia Gentileschi. *Judith Beheading Holofernes,* 1612–13. Oil on canvas. Museo di Capodimonte, Naples. Photo: Public domain via Wikimedia Commons
https://commons.wikimedia.org/wiki/File:Gentileschi_Artemisia_Judith_Beheading_Holofernes_Naples.jpg

p71

Caravaggio. *Judith Beheading Holofernes, c.* 1598–99. Oil on canvas. Palazzo Barberini, Rome. Photo: incamerastock/Alamy Stock Photo

p72

Artemisia Gentileschi. *Judith Beheading Holofernes*, c.1620. Oil on canvas. Galleria degli Uffizi, Florence. Photo: Public domain via Wikimedia Commons
https://commons.wikimedia.org/wiki/File:Artemisia_Gentileschi_-_Giuditta_decapita_Oloferne_-_Google_Art_Project-Adjust.jpg

p73

Artemisia Gentileschi. *Judith and Her Maidservant,* 1614–20. Oil on canvas. Galleria Palatina, Palazzo Pitti, Florence. Photo: Public domain via Wikimedia Commons
https://commons.wikimedia.org/wiki/File:Gentileschi_judith1.jpg

p74

Artemisia Gentileschi. *Susanna and the Elders,* 1610. Oil on canvas. Schönborn Collection, Pommersfelden. Photo: Public domain via Wikimedia Commons
https://commons.wikimedia.org/wiki/File:Susanna_and_the_Elders_(1610),_Artemisia_GentileschiFXD.jpg

p75

Artemisia Gentileschi. *Susanna and the Elders*, 1649. Oil on canvas. Moravian Gallery, Brno. Photo: Domenico Gargiulo, CC BY-SA 4.0 <https://creativecommons.org/licenses/by-sa/4.0>, via Wikimedia Commons
https://commons.wikimedia.org/wiki/File:Artemisia_Gentileschi,_Zuzana_a_starci,_1649.jpg

p76

Artemisia Gentileschi. *Susanna and the Elders*, 1652. Oil on canvas. Private collection. Photo: Public domain via Wikimedia Commons
https://commons.wikimedia.org/wiki/File:Artemisia_Gentileschi_-_Susanna_and_the_Elders_near_a_Balcony.jpg

p77

Artemisia Gentileschi. *Self-Portrait as Saint Catherine of Alexandria, c.* 1615–17. Oil on canvas. National Gallery, London. Photo: Bridgeman Images

p78

Artemisia Gentileschi. *Judith and Her Maidservant,* c. 1623–25. Oil on canvas. Detroit Institute of Arts/Gift of Mr. Leslie H. Green. Photo: Public domain via Wikimedia Commons
https://commons.wikimedia.org/wiki/File:Artemisia_Gentileschi_Judith_Maidservant_DIA.jpg

p81

Edma Morisot. *Portrait of her sister Berthe Morisot,* 1865. Oil on canvas. Private collection. Photo: Thesupermat, CC BY-SA 4.0 <https://creativecommons.org/licenses/by-sa/4.0>, via Wikimedia Commons
https://commons.wikimedia.org/wiki/File:Edma_Morisot_-_Berthe_Morisot_-_vers_1865_-_001.jpg

p82

Berthe Morisot. *Woman and Child on a Balcony,* 1872. Oil on canvas. Private collection. Photo: Public domain via Wikimedia Commons

https://commons.wikimedia.org/wiki/File:Berthe_morisot_femme_et_enfant_au_balcon.jpg

p84

Berthe Morisot. *The Butterfly Hunt (La Chasse aux Papillons),* 1874. Oil on canvas. Musée d'Orsay, Paris. Photo: Public domain via Wikimedia Commons

https://commons.wikimedia.org/wiki/File:Morisot_-_the-butterfly-hunt-1874.jpg

p85

Berthe Morisot. *Hide and Seek (Cache-cache)*, 1873. Oil on canvas. Private collection. Photo: Art Heritage/Alamy Stock Photo

p86

Berthe Morisot. *Woman Hanging Out the Wash (La Blanchisseuse),* 1881. Oil on canvas. Ny Carlsberg Glyptotek Museum, Copenhagen. Photo: Public domain via Wikimedia Commons

https://commons.wikimedia.org/wiki/File:Berthe_Morisot_-_Woman_Hanging_Out_the_Wash.jpg

p87

Berthe Morisot. *Young Woman Watering a Shrub*, 1876. Oil on canvas. Virginia Museum of Fine Arts, Richmond, VA/Collection of Mr. and Mrs. Paul Mellon. Photo: Public domain via Wikimedia Commons

https://commons.wikimedia.org/wiki/File:Morisot_-_Jeune_Femme_arrosant_un_arbuste,_1876.jpg

p88

Nickolas Muray. *Frida with Olmeca Figurine, Coyoacán*, 1939. Color carbon print. Fine Arts Museums of San Francisco. Photo by Nickolas Muray, © Nickolas Muray Photo Archives

p90

Frida Kahlo's house *Casa Azul* in Coyoacán, Mexico. Photo: © Janet Mary Cook. All rights reserved 2022/Bridgeman Images

p91

Frida Kahlo photographed by her father Guillermo Kahlo, 1932. Photo: Bridgeman Images

p92

Frida Kahlo. *Frieda and Diego Rivera,* 1931. Oil on canvas. San Francisco Museum of Modern Art. Photo: San Francisco Museum of Modern Art/Albert M. Bender Collection, gift of Albert M. Bender/Bridgeman Images/Artwork © 2022 Banco de México Diego Rivera Frida Kahlo Museums Trust, Mexico, D.F./Artists Rights Society (ARS), New York

p93

Frida Kahlo. *Self-Portrait Dedicated to Dr. Leo Eloesser,* 1940. Oil on masonite. Private collection. Photo: © Pictures from History/Bridgeman Images/Artwork: © 2022 Banco de México Diego Rivera Frida Kahlo Museums Trust, Mexico, D.F./Artists Rights Society (ARS), New York

p95

Frida Kahlo. *The Two Fridas*, 1939. Oil on canvas. Museo de Arte Moderno, Mexico City. Photo: Luisa Ricciarini/Bridgeman Images/Artwork: © 2022 Banco de México Diego Rivera Frida Kahlo Museums Trust, Mexico, D.F./Artists Rights Society (ARS), New York

p96

Frida Kahlo. *The Love Embrace of the Universe, the Earth (Mexico), Myself, Diego and Señor Xólotl,* 1949. Oil on cardboard. Private Collection, Mexico City. Photo: © Fine Art Images/

Bridgeman Images/Artwork: © 2022 Banco de México Diego Rivera Frida Kahlo Museums Trust, Mexico, D.F./Artists Rights Society (ARS), New York

p99

Photo of Georgia O'Keeffe by Alfred Stieglitz, 1918. Palladium print. Metropolitan Museum of Art, New York/Gift of Georgia O'Keeffe, through the generosity of The Georgia O'Keeffe Foundation and Jennifer and Joseph Duke, 1997. Photo: Alfred Stieglitz, CC0 1.0 Universal Public Domain Dedication, via Wikimedia Commons
https://commons.wikimedia.org/wiki/File:Georgia_O%27Keeffe_MET_DT227433.jpg

p100

Georgia O'Keeffe. *Oriental Poppies*, 1927. Oil on canvas. Collection of the Weisman Art Museum at the University of Minnesota, Minneapolis. Museum purchase. 1937.1. Photo: Weisman Art Museum at the University of Minnesota, Minneapolis/Artwork © 2022 Georgia O'Keeffe Museum/Artists Rights Society (ARS), New York

p101

Georgia O'Keeffe. *The Shelton with Sunspots, N.Y.,* 1926. Oil on canvas. The Art Institute of Chicago. Photo: © Art Institute of Chicago/Gift of Leigh B. Block/Bridgeman Images/Artwork © 2022 Georgia O'Keeffe Museum/Artists Rights Society (ARS), New York

p102

Georgia O'Keeffe. *Series I White & Blue Flower Shapes,* 1919. Oil on board. Georgia O'Keeffe Museum, Santa Fe/Gift of The Georgia O'Keeffe Foundation. Photo: Georgia O'Keeffe Museum, Santa Fe/Art Resource, NY/Artwork © 2022 Georgia O'Keeffe Museum/Artists Rights Society (ARS), New York

p103

Georgia O'Keeffe. *Pelvis with the Distance*, 1943. Oil on canvas. Indianapolis Museum of Art, Newfields. Photo: © Indianapolis Museum of Art/Gift of Anne Marmon Greenleaf in memory of Caroline M Fesler/Bridgeman Images/Artwork © 2022 Georgia O'Keeffe Museum/Artists Rights Society (ARS), New York

p104

Georgia O'Keeffe. *Black Hills with Cedar,* 1941. Oil on canvas. 16 x 30 in. (40.6 x 76 cm). Hirshhorn Museum and Sculpture Garden, Washington D.C/The Joseph H. Hirshhorn Bequest, 1981. Photo: © akg-images. Artwork © 2022 Georgia O'Keeffe Museum/Artists Rights Society (ARS), New York

p105

Georgia O'Keeffe. *Winter Road I,* 1963. Oil on canvas. National Gallery of Art, Washington D.C./ Gift of The Georgia O'Keeffe Foundation. Photo: © Board of Trustees, National Gallery of Art, Washington D.C.

p106

Undated photo of Magdalena Abakanowicz from 1960–1969. Photo: Lebrecht Authors/ Bridgeman Images

p108

Magdalena Abakanowicz. *Yellow Abakan*, 1970–1975. Mixed media (dyed sisal, metal). Collection of the National Museum, Wrocław. Photo: National Museum, Wrocław

p109

Magdalena Abakanowicz at the State School of Decorative Arts in Poznań (behind her Wacław Twarowski), mid-1960s. Photo: Jerzy Nowakowski, Collection of Magdalena Abakanowicz

University of the Arts in Poznań, Courtesy of Magdalena Abakanowicz University of the Arts in Poznań

p110

Magdalena Abakanowicz. *Embryology*, 1978–1980. Mixed media (jute fabric, cotton gauze, sisal; filling: mixed material). Collection of the National Museum, Wrocław. Photo: National Museum, Wrocław

p111

Magdalena Abakanowicz. *Crowd*, 1986–1994. Mixed media (jute fabric, resin). Collection of the National Museum, Wrocław. Photo: National Museum, Wrocław

p112

Magdalena Abakanowicz. *Seated Figures*, 1974–1984. Mixed media (jute fabric, resin, metal). Collection of the National Museum, Wrocław. Photo: National Museum, Wrocław

p113

Magdalena Abakanowicz. Zinaxi and Dolacin. Bronze. Installation at Bródno Park, Warsaw, 2021. Photo: Joanna Barszczewska-Groszek

p114

Magdalena Abakanowicz. *Unrecognized/Nierozpoznani* installation, 2002. Bronze. Poznań Cytadela Park. Photo: Radomil, CC BY-SA 3.0 <https://creativecommons.org/licenses/by-sa/3.0/>, via Wikimedia Commons

https://commons.wikimedia.org/wiki/File:Abakany_Cytadela_Poznan_2.jpg

p117

Rosalba Carriera. *Self-Portrait as "Winter,"* 1731. Pastel on paper. State Art Museum, Dresden. Photo: Public domain, via Wikimedia Commons

https://commons.wikimedia.org/wiki/File:Rosalba_Carriera_-_Self-Portrait_as_%22Winter%22_-_Google_Art_Project.jpg

p118

Rosalba Carriera. *Self-Portrait Holding a Portrait of Her Sister,* 1715. Galleria degli Uffizi, Florence. Photo: Public domain via Wikimedia Commons

https://commons.wikimedia.org/wiki/File:Rosalba_Carriera_Self-portrait.jpg

p119

Rosalba Carriera. *Young Girl Holding a Monkey*, c. 1721. Pastel on paper. The Louvre, Paris. Photo: Public domain via Wikimedia Commons

https://commons.wikimedia.org/wiki/File:Rosalba_Carriera_-_Young_Girl_Holding_a_Monkey_-_WGA04508.jpg

p120

Rosalba Carriera. *Portrait of Henry Fiennes Pelham-Clinton, ninth Earl of Lincoln and second Duke of Newcastle*, 1741. Pastel on paper. Yale Center for British Art, New Haven. Photo: Rosalba Carriera, CC0 1.0 Universal Public Domain Dedication, via Wikimedia Commons

https://commons.wikimedia.org/wiki/File:Rosalba_Carriera_-_Portrait_of_Henry_Fiennes_Pelham-Clinton,_ninth_Earl_of_Lincoln_and_second_Duke_of_Newcastle_-_B2018.5_-_Yale_Center_for_British_Art.jpg

p121

Marianna Carlevaris. *Portrait of Cornelia Froscolo Balbi*, 1740–1742. Pastel on paper. Ca' Rezzonico, Venice. Photo: Public domain via Wikimedia Commons

https://commons.wikimedia.org/wiki/File:Marianna_Carlevaris_-_Portrait_of_Cornelia_Foscolo_Balbi_-_WGA04241.jpg

p122

Rosalba Carriera. *Portrait of Maria Theresa of Austria, Archduchess of Habsburg*, 1730. Pastel on paper. State Art Museum, Dresden. Photo: Public domain via Wikimedia Commons

https://commons.wikimedia.org/wiki/File:Rosalba_Carriera_-_Maria_Theresa,_Archduchess_of_Habsburg_(1717-1780)_-_Google_Art_Project.jpg

p123

Rosalba Carriera. *Portrait of Antoine Watteau*, 1721. Pastel on paper. Museum Luigi Balio, Treviso. Photo: Public domain via Wikimedia Commons

https://commons.wikimedia.org/wiki/File:Rosalba_Carriera_Portrait_Antoine_Watteau.jpg

p124

Rosalba Carriera. *Portrait of the Countess Anna Katharina Orzelska*, 1730s. Pastel on paper. State Art Museum, Dresden. Photo: Public domain via Wikimedia Commons

https://commons.wikimedia.org/wiki/File:Rosalba_Carriera_-_Anna_Orzelska.jpg

p125

Rosalba Carriera. *The Turk*, c. 1720s. Pastel on paper. State Art Museum, Dresden. Photo: Public domain via Wikimedia Commons

https://commons.wikimedia.org/wiki/File:Rosalba_Carriera_-_Ein_T%C3%BCrke.jpg

p126

Rosalba Carriera. *Portrait of Sister Maria Caterina Puppi*, 1732. Pastel on paper. Ca' Rezzonico, Venice. Photo: Rosalba Carriera, CC BY-SA 4.0 <https://creativecommons.org/licenses/by-sa/4.0>, via Wikimedia Commons/Didier Descouens

https://commons.wikimedia.org/wiki/File:Ca%27_Rezzonico_Sala_dei_pastelli_-_Ritratto_di_Suor_Maria_Caterina_Puppi_(Venezia,_1651-1722)_-_Rosalba_Carriera_44x35.jpg

p127

Rosalba Carriera. *Self-Portrait*, c. 1743–1747. Pastel on paper. Gallerie dell'Accademia, Venice. Photo: Public domain via Wikimedia Commons

https://commons.wikimedia.org/wiki/File:Rosalba_Carriera_-_Self-Portrait_-_WGA04503.jpg

p128

Rosalba Carriera. *Summer*, c. 1725. Pastel on paper. Fondation Bemberg, Toulouse. Public domain, CC BY-SA 4.0 <https://creativecommons.org/licenses/by-sa/4.0>, via Wikimedia Commons/didier descouens

https://commons.wikimedia.org/wiki/File:Bemberg_Fondation_Toulouse_-_L%27%C3%A9t%C3%A9_-_Rosalba_Carriera_-_inv_1064.jpg

p129

Rosalba Carriera. *A Muse*, c. 1725. Pastel on blue laid paper. The J. Paul Getty Museum, Los Angeles. Photo: Photo: Public domain via Wikimedia Commons

https://commons.wikimedia.org/wiki/File:Rosalba_Carriera_-_A_Muse_(ca._1725).jpg

p130

Elisabeth Vigée Le Brun. *Self-Portrait*, 1791. Oil on canvas. Ickworth House, Suffolk, UK. Photo: National Trust Photographic Library/Bridgeman Images

p132

Elisabeth Vigée Le Brun. *Julie Le Brun Looking in a Mirror*, 1787. Oil on canvas. Metropolitan Museum of Art, New York. Photo: Metropolitan Museum of Art/Bequest of Mrs. Charles Wrightsman, 2019. Public domain.

https://www.metmuseum.org/art/collection/search/438132

p133

Elisabeth Vigée Le Brun. *Self-Portrait with Her Daughter, Julie*, 1786. Oil on panel. The Louvre, Paris. Photo: Public domain via Wikimedia Commons

https://commons.wikimedia.org/wiki/File:Madame_Vigee-Lebrun_and_her_daughter,_Jeanne_Lucia_(Julie).jpg

p134

Elisabeth Vigée Le Brun. *Self-Portrait with Her Daughter*, 1789. Oil on canvas. The Louvre, Paris. Photo: Public domain via Wikimedia Commons

https://commons.wikimedia.org/wiki/File:Self-portrait_with_Her_Daughter_by_Elisabeth-Louise_Vig%C3%A9e_Le_Brun.jpg

p135 (top)

Raphael. *The Small Cowper Madonna*, c. 1505. Oil on panel. Widener Collection/National Gallery of Art, Washington D.C., Photo: Photo: Widener Collection/National Gallery of Art, Washington D.C. Public domain.

https://www.nga.gov/collection/art-object-page.1196.html

p135 (bottom)

Peter Paul Rubens. *Portrait of Susanna Lunden*, c. 1622–1625. Oil on oak panel. National Gallery, London. Photo: Bridgeman Images

p136

Elisabeth Vigée Le Brun. *Self-Portrait in a Straw Hat,* after 1782. Oil on canvas. National Gallery, London. Photo: Danvis Collection/Alamy Stock Photo

p137

Elisabeth Vigée Le Brun. *Marie Antoinette in Court Dress*, 1778. Oil on canvas. Kunsthistorisches Museum, Vienna. Photo: Public domain via Wikimedia Commons

https://commons.wikimedia.org/wiki/File:Marie-Antoinette_en_robe_de_cour_1778.jpg

p138

Elisabeth Vigée Le Brun. *Marie Antoinette in a Muslin Dress*, before 1783. Oil on canvas. Hessian House Foundation/Wolfsgarten Castle, Hesse. Photo: Public domain via Wikimedia Commons

https://commons.wikimedia.org/wiki/File:MA-Lebrun.jpg

p139

Elisabeth Vigée Le Brun. *Maria Luisa di Borbone, Princess of the Two Sicilies*, 1790. Oil on canvas. Museo di Capodimonte, Naples. Photo: Public domain via Wikimedia Commons

https://commons.wikimedia.org/wiki/File:Luisa_Maria_Amelia_Teresa_di_Borbone-Due_Sicilie_V2.jpg

p140

Filippo Lucci. *Luisa Maria Amalia di Borbone Granduchessa di Toscana*, 1792–1794. Oil on canvas. Galleria degli Uffizi, Florence. Public domain via Wikimedia Commons

https://commons.wikimedia.org/wiki/File:Lucci,_Filippo_-_Luisa_Maria_Amalia_di_Borbone,_granduchessa_di_Toscana_1792-94.jpg

p141

Elisabeth Vigée Le Brun. *Princess Ekaterina Nikolaevna Menshikova*, 1795. Oil on canvas. National Gallery of Armenia. Photo: Mariano Garcia/Alamy Stock Photo

p142

Elisabeth Vigée Le Brun. *Stanisław August Poniatowski, King of Poland*, 1797. Oil on canvas. Palace of Versailles. Photo: Public domain via Wikimedia Commons

https://commons.wikimedia.org/wiki/File:Vigee_Stanislaw_Augustus.jpg

p157

Olga Boznańska. *Children Sitting on the Stairs (Dzieci Siedzące na Schodach)*, 1898. Oil on cardboard. National Museum, Poznań. Photo: Public domain via Wikimedia Commons

https://commons.wikimedia.org/wiki/File:Olga_Bozna%C5%84ska_1898_Dzieci_na_schodach.jpg

p158

Olga Boznańska. *Florist Girls (Kwiaciarki)*, 1889. Oil on canvas. National Museum, Kraków. Photo: Public domain via Wikimedia Commons

https://commons.wikimedia.org/wiki/File:Olga_Bozna%C5%84ska_1889_Kwiaciarki.jpg

p159

Olga Boznańska. *Maternity*, 1902. Oil on cardboard. Private collection. Photo: Art Collection 4/ Alamy Stock Photo

p160

Olga Boznańska. *Portrait of Włodzimiera Lipońska*, 1931. Oil on cardboard. National Museum, Kielce. Photo: Public domain via Wikimedia Commons

https://commons.wikimedia.org/wiki/File:Olga_Bozna%C5%84ska_-_Portret_W%C5%82odzimiery_Lipo%C5%84skiej.jpg

p161

Photo of Olga Boznańska in her studio, c. 1930–31. National Digital Archive, Poland. Photo: Narodowe Archiwum Cyfrowe, Public domain via Wikimedia Commons

https://commons.wikimedia.org/wiki/File:Olga_Bozna%C5%84ska_(1-K-2307).jpg

p162

Olga Boznańska. *Yearning (Tęsknota),* 1900. Private collection. Photo: Artepics/Alamy Stock Photo

p163

Olga Boznańska. *A Japanese Woman (Japonka)*, 1889. Oil on oak panel. National Museum, Warsaw. Photo: Public domain via Wikimedia Commons

https://commons.wikimedia.org/wiki/File:Olga_Bozna%C5%84ska_1889_Japonka.jpg

p165

Olga Boznańska. *Japanese Self-Portrait*, 1892. Oil on cardboard. Collection of the National Museum, Wrocław. Photo: Arkadiusz Podstawka/National Museum, Wrocław

p167

Hilma af Klint. *Self-Portrait*, date unknown. Oil on canvas. Hilma af Klint Foundation. Photo: Public domain via Wikimedia Commons

https://commons.wikimedia.org/wiki/File:Hilma_af_Klint_-_Self-portrait.jpg

p168

Wassily Kandinsky. *Landscape with Two Poplars*, 1912. Oil on canvas. Art Institute of Chicago. Photo: Public domain via Wikimedia Commons

https://commons.wikimedia.org/wiki/File:Vasily_Kandinsky_-_Landscape_with_Two_Poplars_-_1931.508_-_Art_Institute_of_Chicago.jpg

p169 (top)

Hilma af Klint. *Late Summer*, 1903. Oil on canvas. Hilma af Klint Foundation. Photo: Public domain via Wikimedia Commons

https://commons.wikimedia.org/wiki/File:Eftersommar_Hilma_af_Klint_1903.jpeg

p169 (bottom)
Hilma af Klint. *Primordial Chaos, No. 16 from The WU/ROSEN Series Group 1*, 1906–07. Oil on canvas. Hilma af Klint Foundation. Photo: Public domain via Wikimedia Commons
https://commons.wikimedia.org/wiki/File:Hilma_af_Klint,_1906-07,_Primordial_Chaos_-_No_16.jpg

p170
Hilma af Klint. *Group IX SUW, The Swan No. 9*, 1915. Oil on canvas. Hilma af Klint Foundation. Photo: Public domain/Rhododendrites CC BY-SA 4.0 <https://creativecommons.org/licenses/by-sa/4.0>, via Wikimedia Commons
https://commons.wikimedia.org/wiki/File:Group_IX_SUW,_The_Swan_No._9_by_Hilma_af_Klint_(13939).jpg

p171
Hilma af Klint. *The Swan*, 1914. Oil on canvas. Hilma af Klint Foundation. Photo: Public domain via Wikimedia Commons
https://commons.wikimedia.org/wiki/File:Hilma_af_Klint_-_1914_-_Svanen.jpg

p172
Hilma af Klint. *The Swan No. 18*, 1915. Oil on canvas. Hilma af Klint Foundation. Photo: Public domain via Wikimedia Commons
https://commons.wikimedia.org/wiki/File:Hilma_Af_Klint_-_1915_-_The_Swan,_No._18.jpg

p173
Hilma af Klint. *The Dove, No. 3, Group IX/UW, The SUW/UW Series*, 1915. Oil on canvas. Hilma af Klint Foundation. Photo: Public domain via Wikimedia Commons
https://commons.wikimedia.org/wiki/File:Hilma_af_Klint_-_1915_-_The_Dove_-_No_2_-_Group_IX-UW_-_The_SUW-UW_Series.jpg

p174
Hilma af Klint. *The Ten Largest No. 3 – Youth*, 1907. Tempera on paper, mounted on canvas. Hilma af Klint Foundation. Photo: Public domain via Wikimedia Commons
https://commons.wikimedia.org/wiki/File:Hilma_af_Klint_-_The_Ten_Largest_No._3_-_Youth_-_1907.jpg

p175
Hilma af Klint. *The Ten Largest No. 2 – Childhood*, 1907. Tempera on paper, mounted on canvas. Hilma af Klint Foundation. Photo: Public domain via Wikimedia Commons
https://commons.wikimedia.org/wiki/File:Hilma_af_Klint_-_The_Ten_Largest_No._2_-_Childhood_-_1907.jpg

p177
Hilma af Klint. *The Large Figure Paintings, No. 5, The Key to All Works to Date, Group III, The WU/Rosen Series*, 1907. Tempera on paper, mounted on canvas. Hilma af Klint Foundation. Photo: Public domain via Wikimedia Commons/Albin Dahlström/Moderna Museet
https://commons.wikimedia.org/wiki/File:Hilma_af_Klint_-_1907_-_The_Large_Figure_Paintings_-_nr_5_-_The_Key_to_All_Works_to_Date_-_Group_III_-_The_WU-Rosen_Series.jpg

p179
Barbara Hepworth with *The Unknown Political Prisoner*, 1953. Wood. Barbara Hepworth © Bowness. Photo: Alamy Stock Photo/Mirrorpix/Trinity Mirror.

p180
Barbara Hepworth. *Two forms*, 1933. Alabaster on limestone base. Tate T07123. Barbara Hepworth © Bowness. Photo: © Tate

p181
Barbara Hepworth. *Mother and Child*, 1934. Cumberland alabaster on marble base. Tate T06676. Barbara Hepworth © Bowness. Photo: © Tate

p182

Barbara Hepworth examining her artwork 'Oval Sculpture, 1943', 1958. © The Estate of Tom Picton. Artwork Barbara Hepworth © Bowness. Photo: © Tate

p183

Barbara Hepworth. *Tides I*, 1946. Holly wood. Tate T02008. Barbara Hepworth © Bowness. Photo: © Tate

p184

Interior of plaster workshop at Trewyn Studio, Barbara Hepworth Museum and Sculpture Garden, St Ives. Artwork Barbara Hepworth © Bowness. Photo © Tate (Marcus Leith & Andrew Dunkley) 2011

p185

Barbara Hepworth. *Corinthos*, 1954–55. Guarea wood, paint, wooden base. Tate T00531. Barbara Hepworth © Bowness. Photo: © Tate

p186

Barbara Hepworth. *Winged Figure,* 1963. Aluminum and steel rods. John Lewis building, London. Barbara Hepworth © Bowness. Photo: Wikimedia Commons/Justinc

https://commons.wikimedia.org/wiki/File:Barbara_Hepworth_Winged_Figure_1963.jpg

p187

Barbara Hepworth. Three of the nine figures from *The Family of Man*, 1970. Bronze. Fitzwilliam Museum, Cambridge on loan to Britten Pears Arts, permanently sited at Snape Maltings, UK. Barbara Hepworth © Bowness. Photo: Alan Stanton, CC BY-SA 2.0 <https://creativecommons.org/licenses/by-sa/2.0>, via Wikimedia Commons

https://commons.wikimedia.org/wiki/File:Barbara_Hepworth_-_The_Family_of_Man_(5806213928).jpg

p190

Robert Henri. *Gertrude Vanderbilt Whitney,* 1916. Oil on canvas, 49 15/16 × 72 in. (126.8 × 182.9 cm). Whitney Museum of American Art, New York; gift of Flora Whitney Miller 86.70.3. Photo: Public domain via Wikimedia Commons

https://commons.wikimedia.org/wiki/File:Gertrude_Vanderbilt_Whitney,_Henri.jpg

p192

Photo of Gertrude Whitney from September 1921 edition of *Tatler*. Photo: Public domain via Wikimedia Commons/Alfred Cheney Johnston

https://commons.wikimedia.org/wiki/File:Gertrude_Vanderbilt_Whitney_-_Sep_1921_Tatler.jpg

p193

Gertrude Whitney. *El Dorado Fountain*—photo detail of the sculpture at the Pan-Pacific Exposition, San Francisco, 1915. Marble. Photo: Bain News Service/United States Library of Congress Prints and Photographs Division, Washington, D.C. Public domain.

http://loc.gov/pictures/resource/ggbain.21096/

p194

Gertrude Whitney. *Titanic Memorial*, 1931. Granite. Washington D.C. Photo: APK, CC BY-SA 4.0 <https://creativecommons.org/licenses/by-sa/4.0>, via Wikimedia Commons

https://commons.wikimedia.org/wiki/File:Titanic_Memorial_(Washington,_D.C.).jpg

p195

Gertrude Whitney standing with her statue of soldiers, 1920. Photographic print. Photo: United States Library of Congress Prints and Photographs Division, Washington, D.C. Public domain.

http://loc.gov/pictures/resource/cph.3c11853/

p196

George Benjamin Luks. *Armistice Night*, 1918. Oil on canvas. Whitney Museum of American Art, New York. Photo: Public domain via Wikimedia Commons

https://commons.wikimedia.org/wiki/File:George_Luks_-_Armistice_Night_-_Google_Art_Project.jpg

p197

Edward Hopper. *New York Interior*, 1921. Oil on canvas. Whitney Museum of American Art, New York. Photo: © Fine Art Images/Bridgeman Images. Artwork: © 2022 Heirs of Josephine N. Hopper/Licensed by Artists Rights Society (ARS), NY

p198

George Bellows. *Dempsey and Firpo*, 1924. Oil on canvas. Whitney Museum of American Art, New York. Photo: Public domain via Wikimedia Commons

https://commons.wikimedia.org/wiki/File:Bellows_George_Dempsey_and_Firpo_1924.jpg

p199

View of the Whitney Museum of American Art from Gansevoort Street. Photo: Ed Lederman, 2015. © Whitney Museum of American Art, New York.

p201

Andres Zorn. *Isabella Stewart Gardner in Venice*, 1894. Oil on canvas. Isabella Stewart Gardner Museum, Boston. Photo: Public domain via Wikimedia Commons

https://commons.wikimedia.org/wiki/File:Anders_Zorn_-_Isabella_Stewart_Gardner_in_Venice_-_P17e10_-_Isabella_Stewart_Gardner_Museum.jpg

p202

Rembrandt van Rijn. *The Storm on the Sea of Galilee*, 1633. Oil on canvas. Stolen from Isabella Stewart Gardner Museum, Boston in 1990. Photo: Public domain via Wikimedia Commons

https://commons.wikimedia.org/wiki/File:Rembrandt_Christ_in_the_Storm_on_the_Lake_of_Galilee.jpg

p203

James McNeill Whistler. *The Little Note in Yellow and Gold*, 1866. Chalk and pastel on cardboard. Isabella Stewart Gardner Museum, Boston. Photo: Public domain via Wikimedia Commons

https://commons.wikimedia.org/wiki/File:The_Little_Note_in_Yellow_and_Gold_(1886)_by_James_McNeill_Whistler.jpg

p204

Titian. *The Rape of Europa*, 1551. Oil on canvas. Isabella Stewart Gardner Museum, Boston. Photo: Public domain via Wikimedia Commons

https://commons.wikimedia.org/wiki/File:Titian_-_Rape_of_Europa_-_Google_Art_Project.jpg

p206

John Singer Sargent. *Portrait of Isabella Stewart Gardner,* 1888. Oil on canvas. Isabella Stewart Gardner Museum, Boston. Photo: Public domain via Wikimedia Commons

https://commons.wikimedia.org/wiki/File:Isabella_Stewart_Gardner_(John_Singer_Sargent).jpg

p207

John Singer Sargent. *Mrs. Fiske Warren (Gretchen Osgood) and Her Daughter Rachel*, 1903. Oil on canvas. Museum of Fine Arts, Boston. Photo: Public domain via Wikimedia Commons

https://commons.wikimedia.org/wiki/File:John_Singer_Sargent_-_Mrs._Fiske_Warren_(Gretchen_Osgood)_and_Her_Daughter_Rachel_-_Google_Art_Project.jpg

p208

John Singer Sargent. *Mrs. Gardner in White*, 1922. Watercolor on paper. Isabella Stewart Gardner Museum, Boston. Photo: Public domain via Wikimedia Commons
https://commons.wikimedia.org/wiki/File:Mrs._Gardner_in_White_(1922)_by_John_Singer_Sargent.jpg

p209

Francesco Guardi. *View of the Riva degli Schiavoni and the Piazzetta from the Bacino di San Marco,* 1760s. Oil on canvas. Isabella Stewart Gardner Museum, Boston. Photo: Public domain via Wikimedia Commons
https://commons.wikimedia.org/wiki/File:Guardi_-_View_of_the_Riva_degli_Schiavoni_and_the_Piazzetta_from_the_Bacino_di_San_Marco,_1760s,_P25w47.jpg

p210

Johannes Vermeer. *The Concert*, 1663–66. Oil on canvas. Stolen from Isabella Stewart Gardner Museum, Boston in 1990. Photo: Public domain via Wikimedia Commons
https://commons.wikimedia.org/wiki/File:Vermeer_The_Concert.jpg

p211

Sandro Botticelli. *The Story of Lucretia*, 1496–1504. Tempera and oil on wood. Isabella Stewart Gardner Museum, Boston. Photo: Public domain via Wikimedia Commons
https://commons.wikimedia.org/wiki/File:Sandro_Botticelli_078.jpg

p212

View of the courtyard of the Isabella Stewart Gardner Museum, Boston. Photo: © Isabella Stewart Gardner Museum/Photo © Sean Dungan/Bridgeman Images

p213

John Singer Sargent. *El Jaleo*, 1882. Oil on canvas. Isabella Stewart Gardner Museum, Boston. Photo: Public domain via Wikimedia Commons
https://commons.wikimedia.org/wiki/File:EL_JALEO-SINGER.jpg

p214

John Singer Sargent's *El Jaleo* in the Spanish Cloister, Isabella Stewart Gardner Museum, Boston. Photo: © Isabella Stewart Gardner Museum/Photo © Sean Dungan/Bridgeman Images

p215

A picture acquired by Gardner through Bernard Berenson in 1907. (Attr.) Piero della Pollaiuolo. *A Woman in Green and Crimson*, c. 1490–99. Oil on panel. Isabella Stewart Gardner Museum, Boston. Photo: Public domain via Wikimedia Commons
https://commons.wikimedia.org/wiki/File:Piero_del_Pollaiuolo_-_A_Woman_in_Green_and_Crimson_-_P16w7_-_Isabella_Stewart_Gardner_Museum.jpg

p217

Johanna Bonger in April 1899. Studio photo by Woodbury & Page. Photo: Woodbury & Page/National Library of The Netherlands/Public domain via Wikimedia Commons
https://commons.wikimedia.org/wiki/File:Jo_van_Gogh-Bonger,_by_Woodbury_and_Page-2.jpg

p218

Vincent van Gogh. *Red Vineyards at Arles,* 1888. Oil on canvas. Ivan Morozov Collection, Pushkin Museum of Fine Art, Moscow. Photo: Public domain via Wikimedia Commons
https://commons.wikimedia.org/wiki/File:Red_vineyards.jpg

p219

Vincent van Gogh. *The Langlois Bridge at Arles with Women Washing*, 1888. Oil on canvas. Kröller-Müller Museum, Otterlo. Photo: Public domain via Wikimedia Commons
https://commons.wikimedia.org/wiki/File:Vincent_Willem_van_Gogh_-_Pont_de_Langlois_-_Kr%C3%B6ller-M%C3%BCller.jpg

p220

Johan Cohen Gosschalk. *Portrait of Johanna Bonger*, 1905. Chalk and watercolor on paper. Drents Museum, Assen. Photo: The History Collection/Alamy Stock Photo

p221

Vincent van Gogh. *Roses,* 1890. Oil on canvas. National Gallery of Art, Washington, D.C./Gift of Pamela Harriman in memory of W. Averell Harriman. Photo: Courtesy National Gallery of Art/Public Domain Open Access CC0
https://www.nga.gov/collection/art-object-page.72328.html

p222

Vincent van Gogh. *Wheatfield with Crows*, 1890. Oil on canvas. Van Gogh Museum, Amsterdam. Photo: Public domain via Wikimedia Commons
https://commons.wikimedia.org/wiki/File:Vincent_van_Gogh_-_Wheatfield_with_crows_-_Google_Art_Project.jpg

p223

Vincent van Gogh. *Painter on His Way to Work*, 1888. Oil on canvas. Destroyed during WWII. Photo: Public domain via Wikimedia Commons
https://commons.wikimedia.org/wiki/File:Van_Gogh_-_Der_Maler_auf_dem_Weg_zur_Arbeit.jpeg

p224

Bernard Eilers. Vincent Willem van Gogh, Jo Cohen Gosschalk-Bonger and Johan Cohen Gosschalk (from left to right) in the Dining Room of the House at Koninginneweg 77, Amsterdam, 1910–1911. Print on paper. Photo credit: Van Gogh Museum, Amsterdam (Vincent van Gogh Foundation)

p225

Vincent van Gogh. *Self-Portrait*, 1889. Oil on canvas. National Gallery of Art, Washington, D.C./Collection of Mr. and Mrs. John Hay Whitney. Photo: Courtesy National Gallery of Art/Public Domain Open Access CC0
https://www.nga.gov/collection/art-object-page.106382.html

p226

Mary Cassatt. *Young Girl at a Window*, c. 1883–84. Oil on canvas. National Gallery of Art, Washington, D.C./Corcoran Collection (Museum Purchase, Gallery Fund). Photo: Courtesy National Gallery of Art/Public Domain Open Access CC0
https://www.nga.gov/collection/art-object-page.97663.html

INDEX

L

M

N

O

P

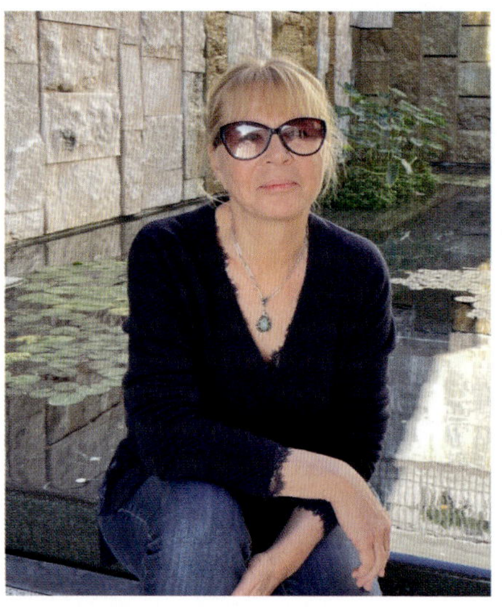

ABOUT THE AUTHOR

As the acclaimed author of the "Food for the Soul" art and entertainment column at the Solari Report (**food4thesoul.solari.com**), Nina Heyn visits galleries and museums all over the world, reporting on art ranging from established masterpieces to the up-and-coming. Drawing on her previous careers as a Hollywood publicist, entertainment journalist, and corporate executive, Nina's distinctive voice as an art storyteller is user-friendly while at the same time anchored in a stunning breadth and depth of knowledge about art from antiquity to the present day. Raised in Europe by her Chinese mother, and influenced by her father, who was an academician and a painter, Nina has spent most of her adult life in California. Her multicultural and multilingual upbringing—marking her as a European, Asian, and American all in one—helped instill her deep love and understanding of fine art, as expressed in this book.